ドラゴン騎士団.9

DRAGON KNIGHTS 9

押上美猫

Mineko Ohkami

ALSO AVAILABLE FROM 🔵 TOKYOPOP®

MANGA

HACK//LEGEND OF THE TWILIGHT (September 2003)
@LARGE (COMING SOON)
ANGELIC LAYER*
BABY BIRTH* (September 2003)
BATTLE ROYALE*
BRAIN POWERED*
BRIGADOON* (August 2003)
CARDCAPTOR SAKURA
CARDCAPTOR SAKURA: MASTER OF THE CLOW*
CHOBITS*
CHRONICLES OF THE CURSED SWORD
CLAMP SCHOOL DETECTIVES*
CLOVER
CONFIDENTIAL CONFESSIONS*
CORRECTOR YUI
COWBOY BEBOP*
COWBOY BEBOP: SHOOTING STAR*
DEMON DIARY
DIGIMON*
DRAGON HUNTER
DRAGON KNIGHTS*
DUKLYON: CLAMP SCHOOL DEFENDERS*
ERICA SAKURAZAWA*
FAKE*
FLCL* (September 2003)
FORBIDDEN DANCE* (August 2003)
GATE KEEPERS*
G GUNDAM*
GRAVITATION*
GTO*
GUNDAM WING
GUNDAM WING: BATTLEFIELD OF PACIFISTS
GUNDAM WING: ENDLESS WALTZ*
GUNDAM WING: THE LAST OUTPOST*
HAPPY MANIA*
HARLEM BEAT
I.N.V.U.
INITIAL D*
ISLAND
JING: KING OF BANDITS*
JULINE
KARE KANO*
KINDAICHI CASE FILES, THE*
KING OF HELL
KODOCHA: SANA'S STAGE*
LOVE HINA*
LUPIN III*
MAGIC KNIGHT RAYEARTH* (August 2003)
MAGIC KNIGHT RAYEARTH II* (COMING SOON)

MAN OF MANY FACES*
MARMALADE BOY*
MARS*
MIRACLE GIRLS
MIYUKI-CHAN IN WONDERLAND* (October 2003)
MONSTERS, INC.
PARADISE KISS*
PARASYTE
PEACH GIRL
PEACH GIRL: CHANGE OF HEART*
PET SHOP OF HORRORS*
PLANET LADDER*
PLANETES* (October 2003)
PRIEST
RAGNAROK
RAVE MASTER*
REALITY CHECK
REBIRTH
REBOUND*
RISING STARS OF MANGA
SABER MARIONETTE J*
SAILOR MOON
SAINT TAIL
SAMURAI DEEPER KYO*
SAMURAI GIRL: REAL BOUT HIGH SCHOOL*
SCRYED*
SHAOLIN SISTERS*
SHIRAHIME-SYO: SNOW GODDESS TALES* (Dec. 2003)
SHUTTERBOX (November 2003)
SORCERER HUNTERS
THE SKULL MAN*
THE VISION OF ESCAFLOWNE
TOKYO MEW MEW*
UNDER THE GLASS MOON
VAMPIRE GAME*
WILD ACT*
WISH*
WORLD OF HARTZ (COMING SOON)
X-DAY* (August 2003)
ZODIAC P.I. *

For more information visit www.TOKYOPOP.com

*INDICATES 100% AUTHENTIC MANGA (RIGHT-TO-LEFT FORMAT)

CINE-MANGA™

CARDCAPTORS
JACKIE CHAN ADVENTURES (COMING SOON)
JIMMY NEUTRON (September 2003)
KIM POSSIBLE
LIZZIE MCGUIRE
POWER RANGERS: NINJA STORM (August 2003)
SPONGEBOB SQUAREPANTS (September 2003)
SPY KIDS 2

NOVELS

KARMA CLUB (April 2004)
SAILOR MOON

TOKYOPOP KIDS

STRAY SHEEP (September 2003)

ART BOOKS

CARDCAPTOR SAKURA*
MAGIC KNIGHT RAYEARTH*

ANIME GUIDES

COWBOY BEBOP ANIME GUIDES
GUNDAM TECHNICAL MANUALS
SAILOR MOON SCOUT GUIDES

6-5-03

Dragon Knights

Written and Illustrated by
Mineko Ohkami

Volume 9

TOKYOPOP®

Los Angeles • Tokyo • London

Translator - Agnes Yoshida
English Adaptation - Stephanie Sheh
Contributing Editors - Tim Beedle
Retouch and Lettering - Olaf Malachowski
Cover Layout - Anna Kernbaum

Editor - Luis Reyes
Managing Editor - Jill Freshney
Production Coordinator - Antonio DePietro
Production Manager - Jennifer Miller
Art Director - Matt Alford
Editorial Director - Jeremy Ross
VP of Production - Ron Klamert
President & C.O.O. - John Parker
Publisher & C.E.O. - Stuart Levy

Email: editor@TOKYOPOP.com
Come visit us online at www.TOKYOPOP.com

A **TOKYOPOP** Manga

TOKYOPOP Inc.
5900 Wilshire Blvd. Suite 2000
Los Angeles, CA 90036

ISBN: 1-59182-113-4

First TOKYOPOP printing: August 2003

10 9 8 7 6 5 4 3 2 1
Printed in the USA

From the Chronicles of Dusis, the West Continent...

The Beginnings: Nadil and Lord Lykouleon

When the Yokai Nadil, the leader of the Demon Forces, kidnapped the Dragon Queen Raseleane, the Dragon Lord Lykouleon ventured to the Demon Realm to rescue her. He defeated Nadil by cutting off his head, but not before the demon leader rendered Raseleane barren, unable to give Lykouleon a child...and the Dragon Kingdom an heir. Now the Demon and Yokai forces, under the command of Shydeman and Shyrendora, plot to attack Draqueen, the Dragon Kingdom, and retrieve their leader's head in the hopes of reviving him. But other shady characters such as Master Kharl the Alchemist, the evil sorcerer Kirukulus, and the rogue Yokai Bierrez have also entered the contest for control of Dusis. The Dragon Officers and Lord Lykouleon desperately try to ready the Dragon Palace to repel an assault by the Demon Forces.

The Dragon Knights: A Motley Trio

The Dragon Knights are three specially chosen warriors granted the power of the various elemental dragons for the protection of the Dragon Realm. Dispatched on three separate missions, the human thief Thatz, the Dragon Knight of Earth, as well as the Elfin prince Rune, the Dragon Knight of Water, have returned to Draqueen. Only the Yokai Rath, the Dragon Knight of Fire, has yet to finish his quest of finding the mysterious power at Mt. Emphaza capable of reviving Crewger, the fallen Dragon Dog.

A Crucial Quest

Rath and the fortuneteller Cesia, also a Yokai, have reached Mt. Emphaza, only to find their attempts to resurrect Crewger thwarted by a vicious demon that is guarding the entrance to Emphaza. They have been told of the demon by Dragon Officer Kai-Stern, who has also come to Emphaza searching for the power, and met with near disastrous results. Undeterred, Rath vows to kill the demon and unlock the secrets of the mysterious power within the mountain, which he believes might actually be the missing Wind Dragon.

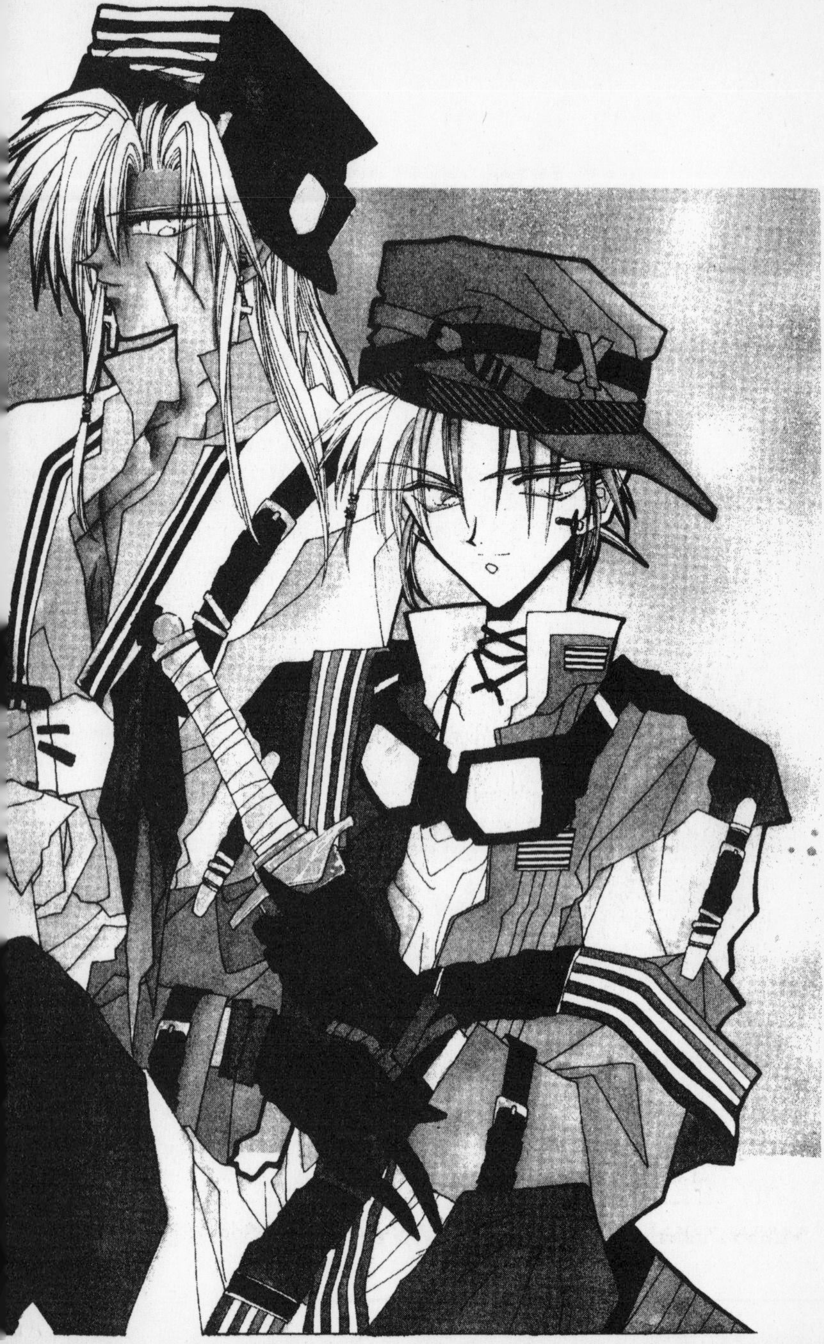

YGN
F
SHE

b16100311

CONTENTS

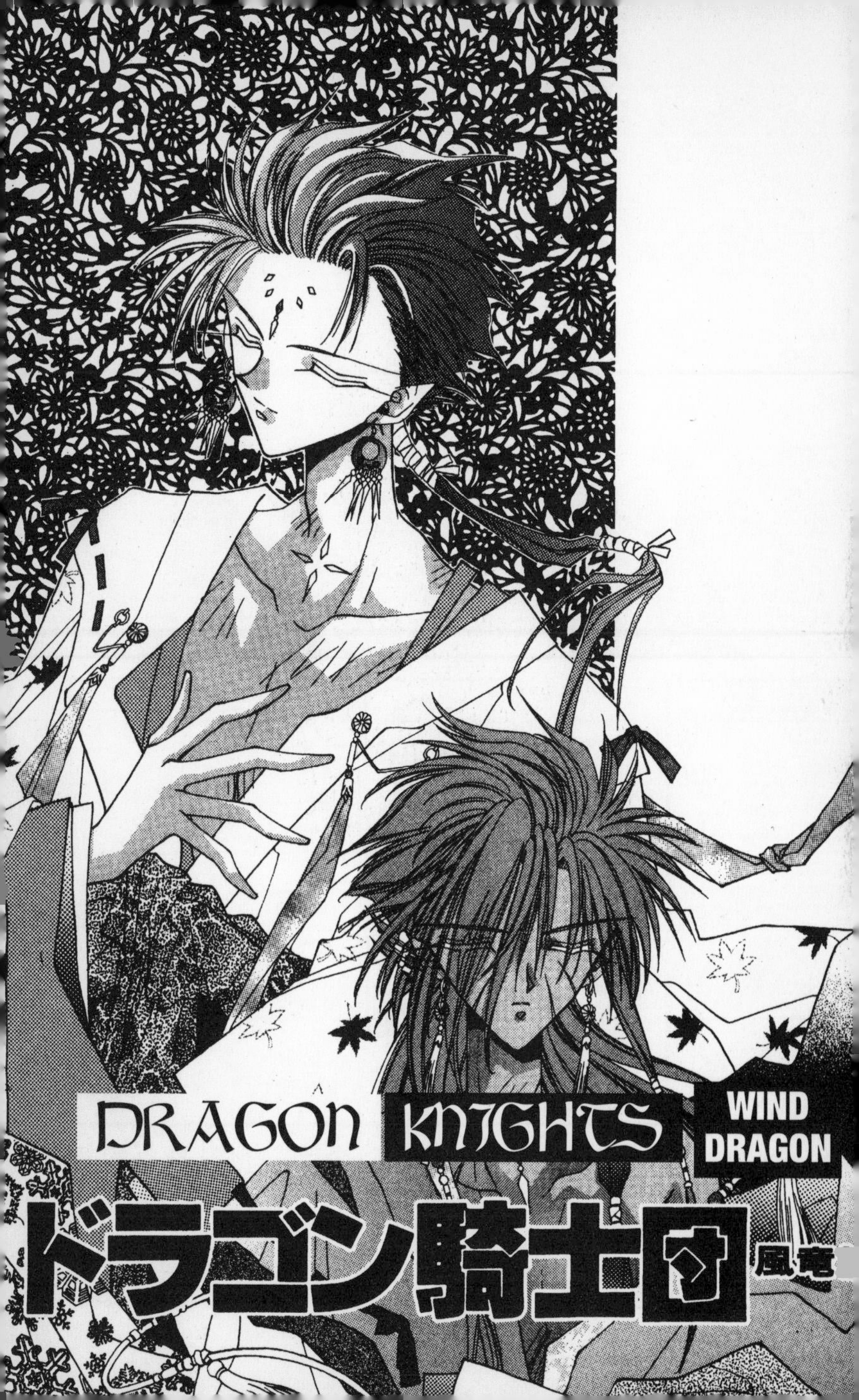
DRAGON KNIGHTS
WIND DRAGON
ドラゴン騎士団
風竜

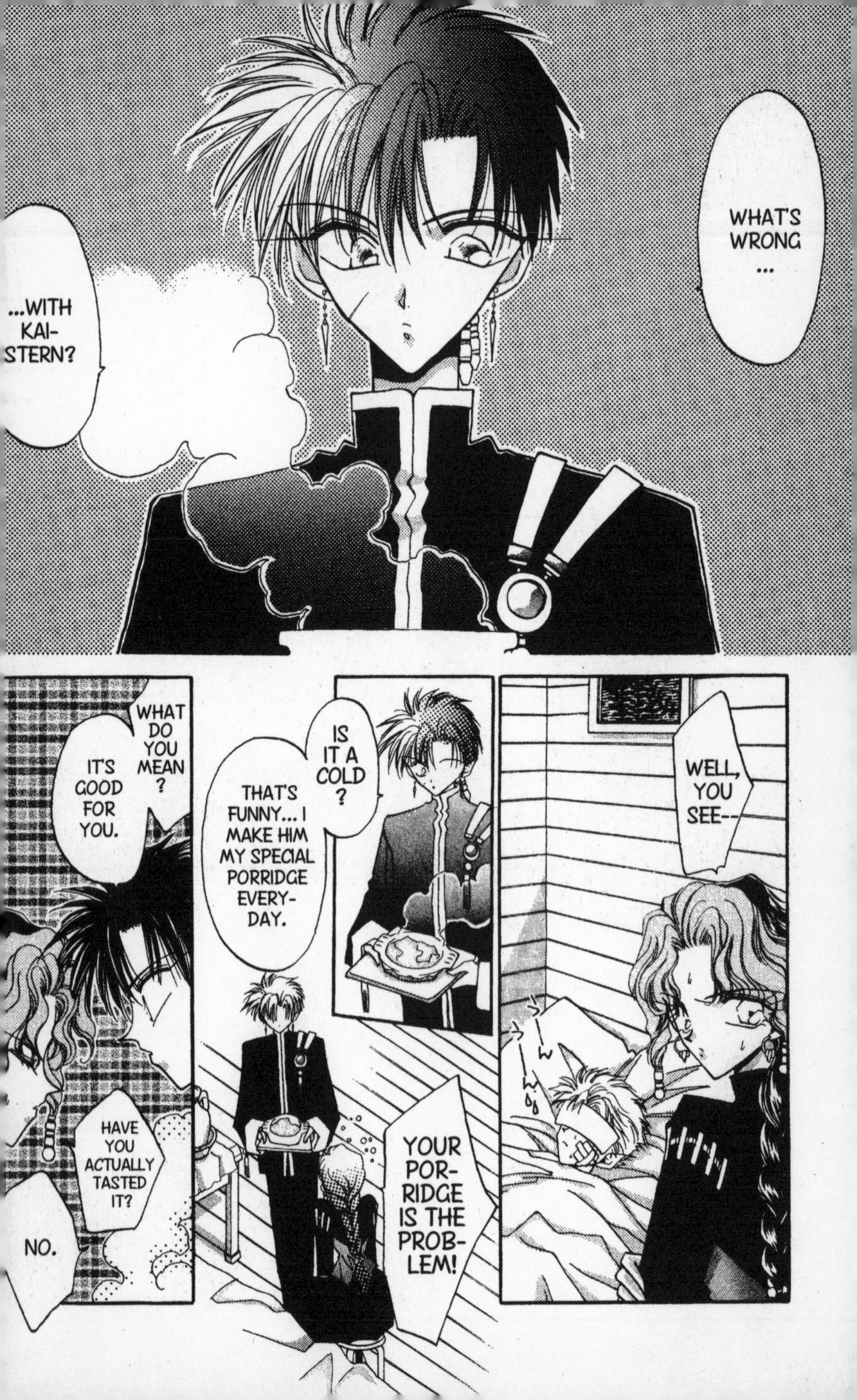
WHAT'S WRONG ...
...WITH KAI-STERN?
WELL, YOU SEE--
IS IT A COLD?
THAT'S FUNNY... I MAKE HIM MY SPECIAL PORRIDGE EVERY-DAY.
YOUR POR-RIDGE IS THE PROB-LEM!
WHAT DO YOU MEAN?
IT'S GOOD FOR YOU.
HAVE YOU ACTUALLY TASTED IT?
NO.

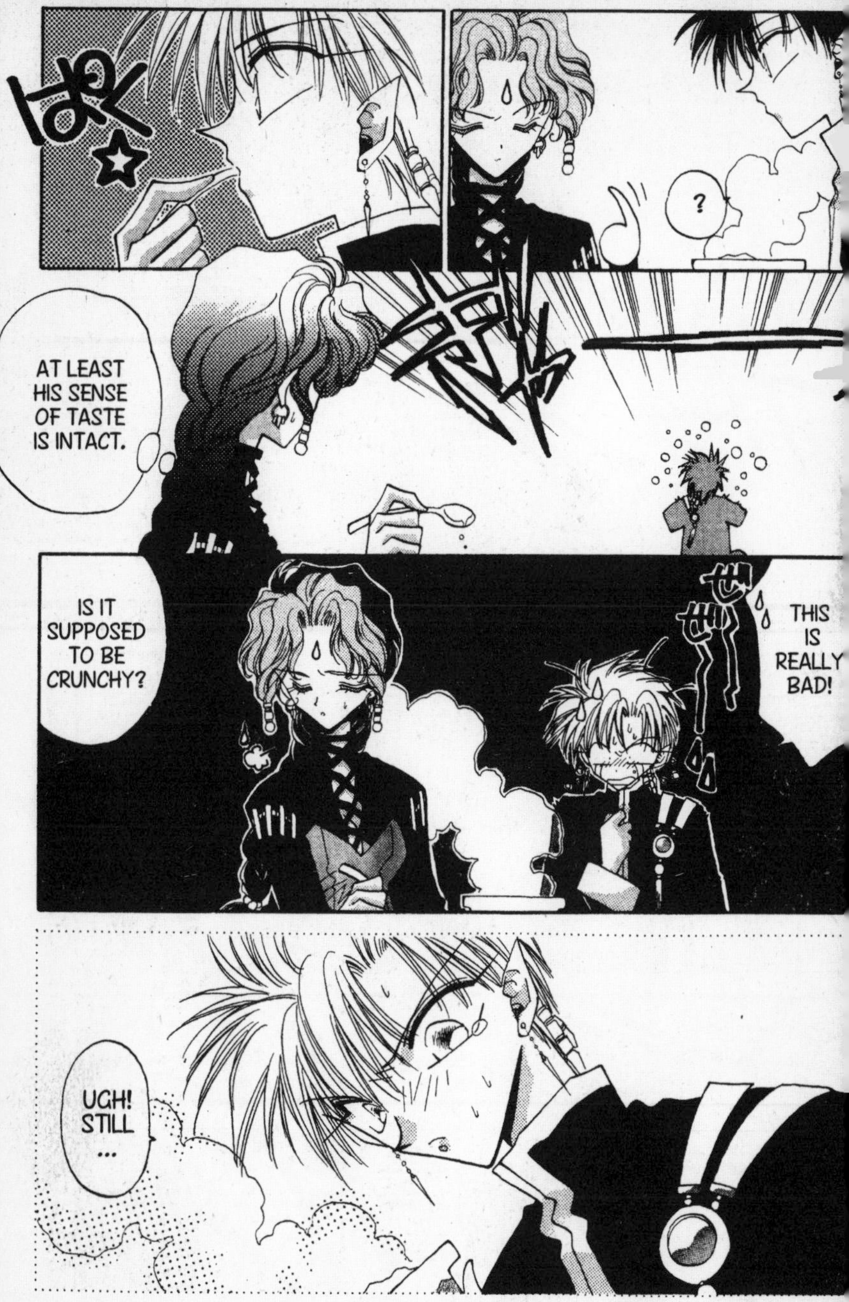

?
ぱく☆
AT LEAST HIS SENSE OF TASTE IS INTACT.
THIS IS REALLY BAD!
IS IT SUPPOSED TO BE CRUNCHY?
UGH! STILL ...

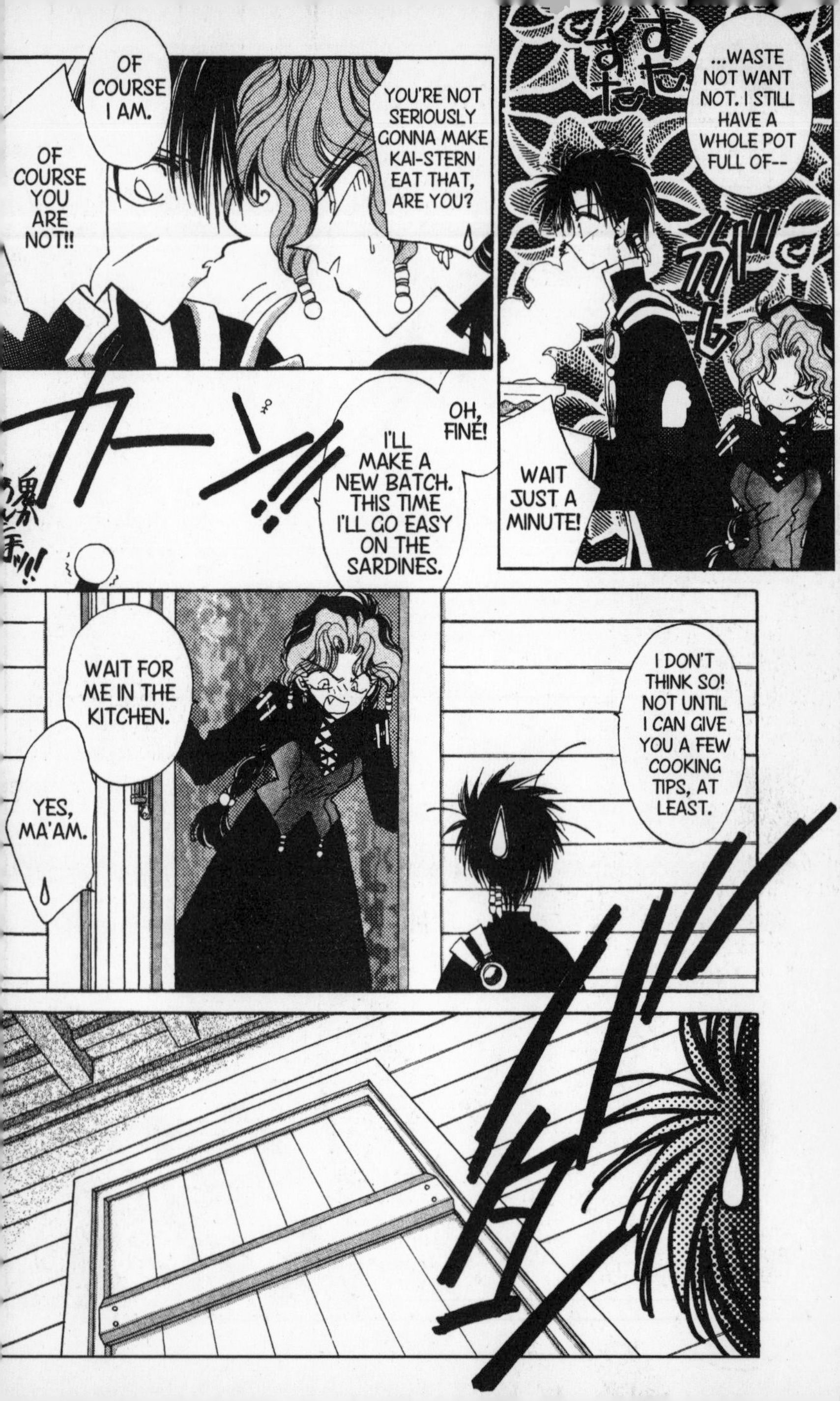
...WASTE NOT WANT NOT. I STILL HAVE A WHOLE POT FULL OF--
WAIT JUST A MINUTE!
YOU'RE NOT SERIOUSLY GONNA MAKE KAI-STERN EAT THAT, ARE YOU?
OF COURSE I AM.
OF COURSE YOU ARE NOT!!
OH, FINE! I'LL MAKE A NEW BATCH. THIS TIME I'LL GO EASY ON THE SARDINES.
I DON'T THINK SO! NOT UNTIL I CAN GIVE YOU A FEW COOKING TIPS, AT LEAST.
WAIT FOR ME IN THE KITCHEN.
YES, MA'AM.

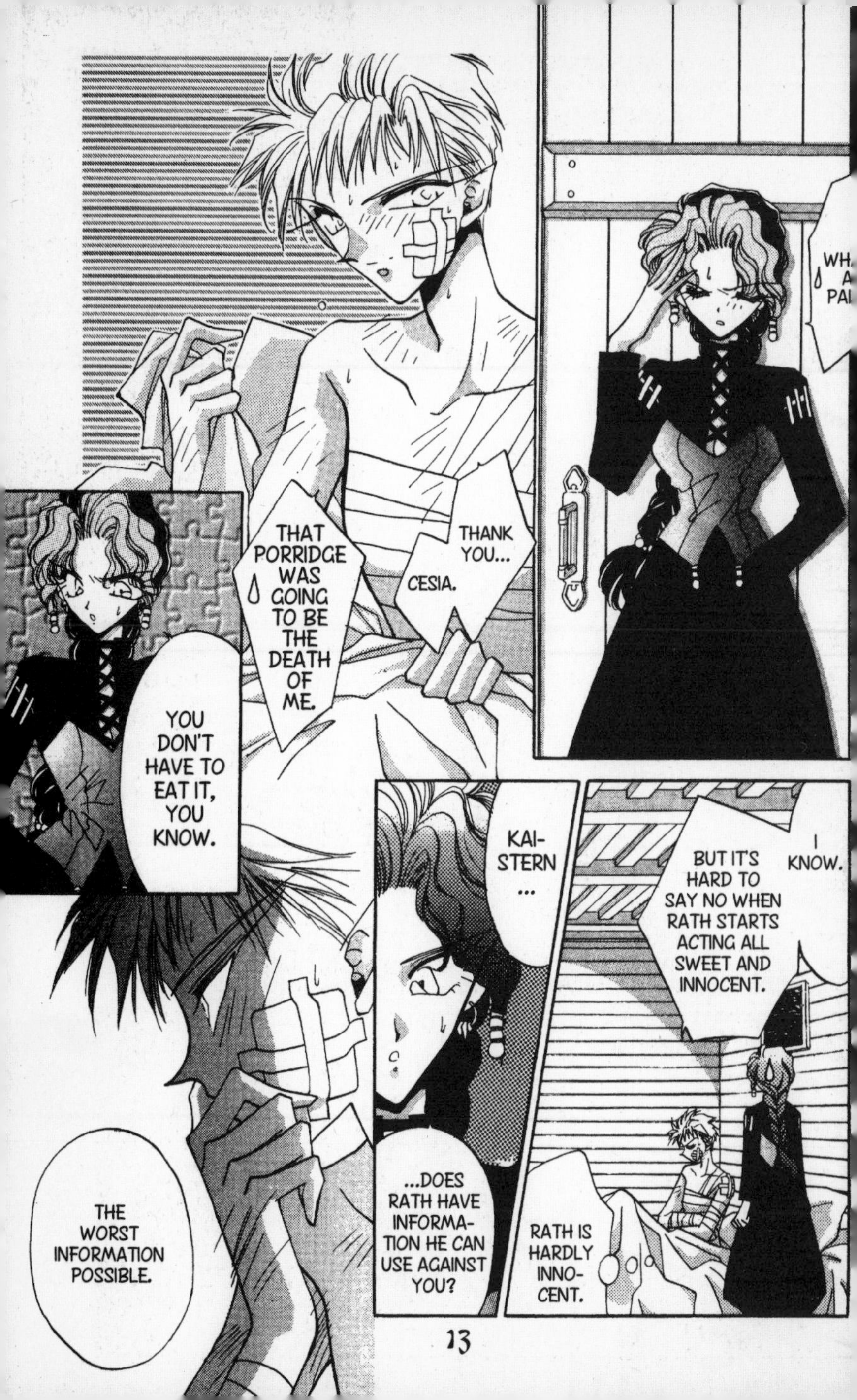
WHA A PAI
THANK YOU...
CESIA.
THAT PORRIDGE WAS GOING TO BE THE DEATH OF ME.
YOU DON'T HAVE TO EAT IT, YOU KNOW.
I KNOW.
BUT IT'S HARD TO SAY NO WHEN RATH STARTS ACTING ALL SWEET AND INNOCENT.
RATH IS HARDLY INNO-CENT.
KAI-STERN ...
...DOES RATH HAVE INFORMA-TION HE CAN USE AGAINST YOU?
THE WORST INFORMATION POSSIBLE.

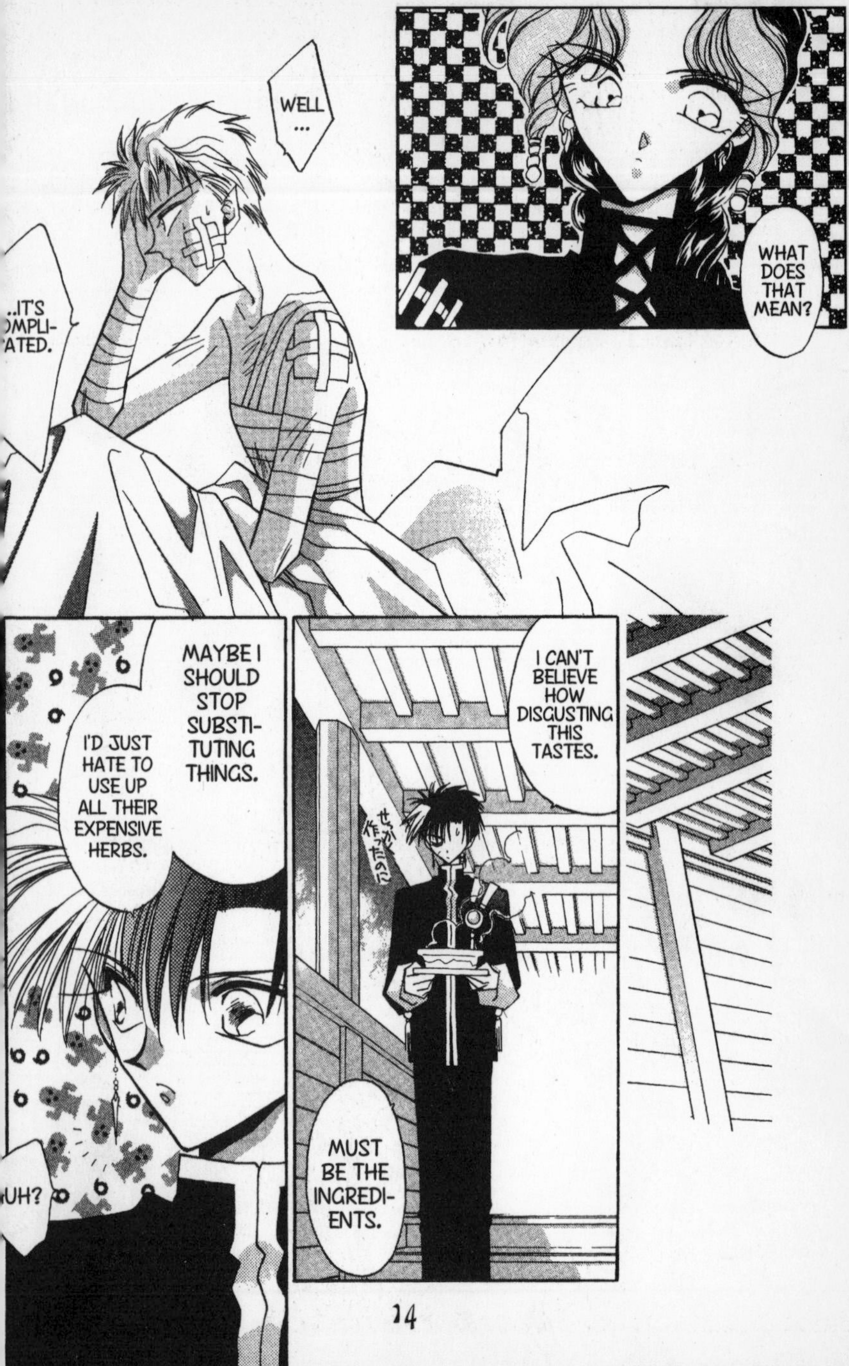
WHAT DOES THAT MEAN?
WELL ...
..IT'S OMPLI- ATED.
I CAN'T BELIEVE HOW DISGUSTING THIS TASTES.
せっかく作ったのに
MUST BE THE INGREDI- ENTS.
MAYBE I SHOULD STOP SUBSTI- TUTING THINGS.
I'D JUST HATE TO USE UP ALL THEIR EXPENSIVE HERBS.
UH?

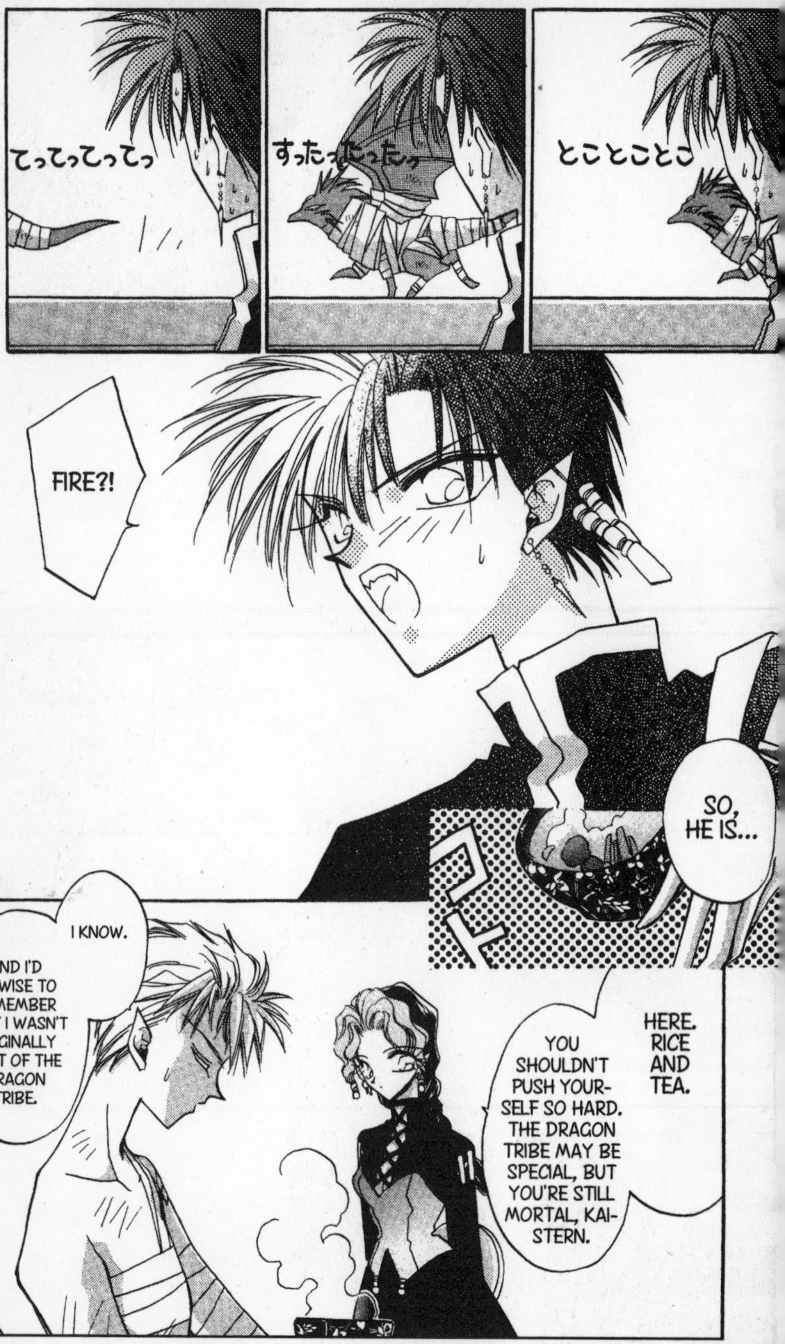
とことことこ
すったったったっ
てってってっ
FIRE?!
SO, HE IS...
HERE. RICE AND TEA.
YOU SHOULDN'T PUSH YOUR-SELF SO HARD. THE DRAGON TRIBE MAY BE SPECIAL, BUT YOU'RE STILL MORTAL, KAI-STERN.
I KNOW.
AND I'D BE WISE TO REMEMBER THAT I WASN'T ORIGINALLY PART OF THE DRAGON TRIBE.

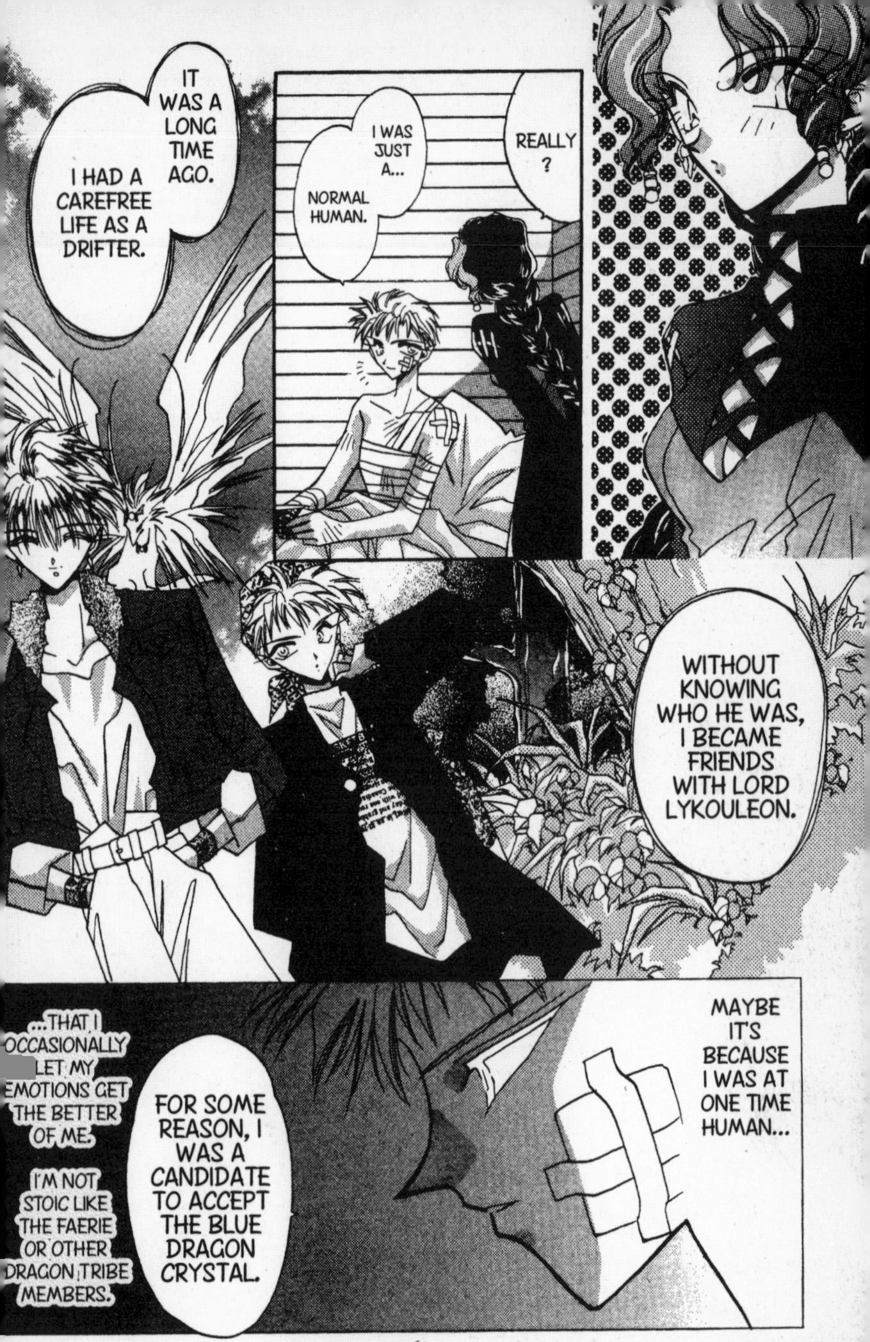
REALLY?
I WAS JUST A...
NORMAL HUMAN.
IT WAS A LONG TIME AGO.
I HAD A CAREFREE LIFE AS A DRIFTER.
WITHOUT KNOWING WHO HE WAS, I BECAME FRIENDS WITH LORD LYKOULEON.
MAYBE IT'S BECAUSE I WAS AT ONE TIME HUMAN...
FOR SOME REASON, I WAS A CANDIDATE TO ACCEPT THE BLUE DRAGON CRYSTAL.
...THAT I OCCASIONALLY LET MY EMOTIONS GET THE BETTER OF ME.
I'M NOT STOIC LIKE THE FAERIE OR OTHER DRAGON TRIBE MEMBERS.

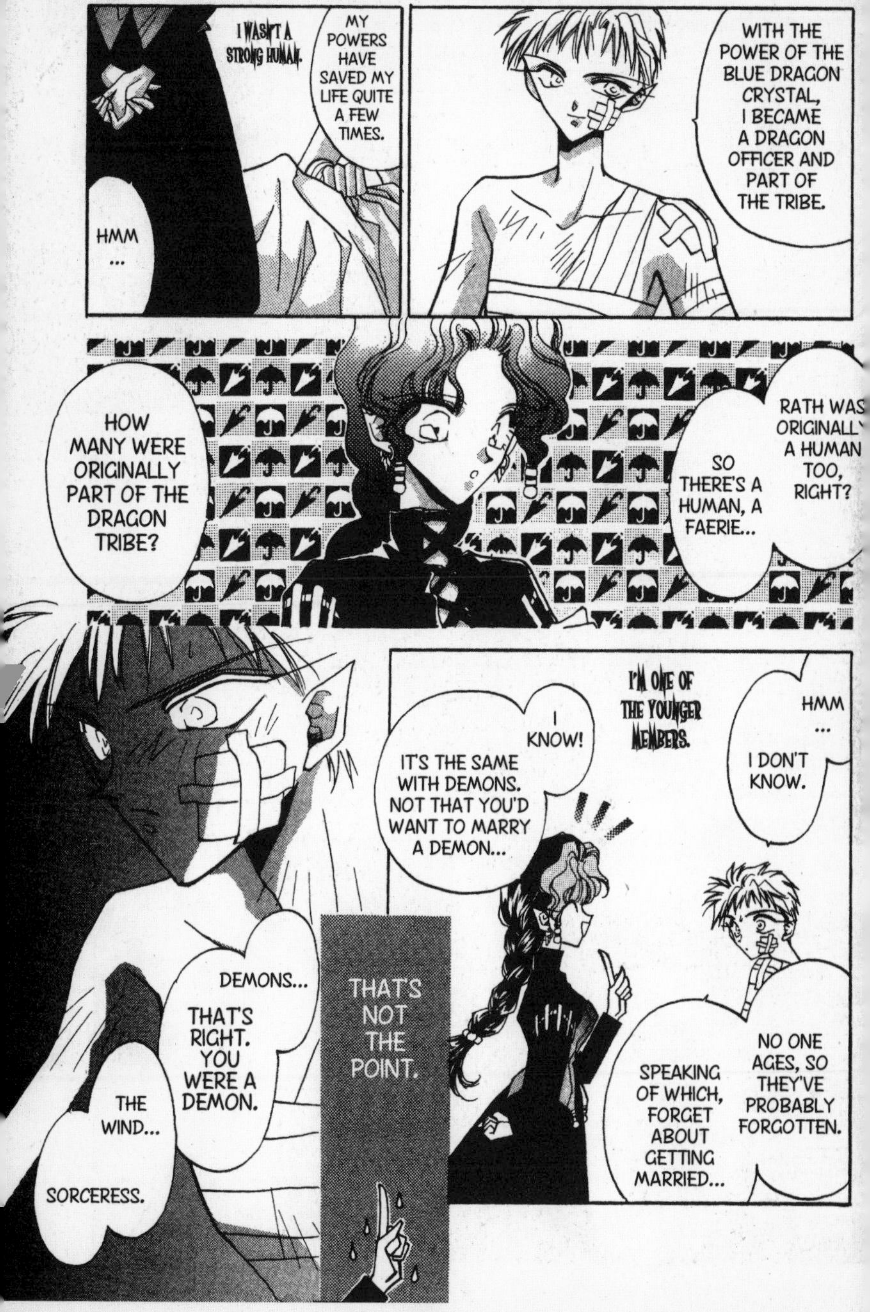

WITH THE POWER OF THE BLUE DRAGON CRYSTAL, I BECAME A DRAGON OFFICER AND PART OF THE TRIBE.
MY POWERS HAVE SAVED MY LIFE QUITE A FEW TIMES.
I WASN'T A STRONG HUMAN.
HMM ...
RATH WAS ORIGINALLY A HUMAN TOO, RIGHT?
SO THERE'S A HUMAN, A FAERIE...
HOW MANY WERE ORIGINALLY PART OF THE DRAGON TRIBE?
HMM ... I DON'T KNOW.
I'M ONE OF THE YOUNGER MEMBERS.
NO ONE AGES, SO THEY'VE PROBABLY FORGOTTEN.
SPEAKING OF WHICH, FORGET ABOUT GETTING MARRIED...
I KNOW!
IT'S THE SAME WITH DEMONS. NOT THAT YOU'D WANT TO MARRY A DEMON...
THAT'S NOT THE POINT.
DEMONS...
THAT'S RIGHT. YOU WERE A DEMON.
THE WIND...
SORCERESS.

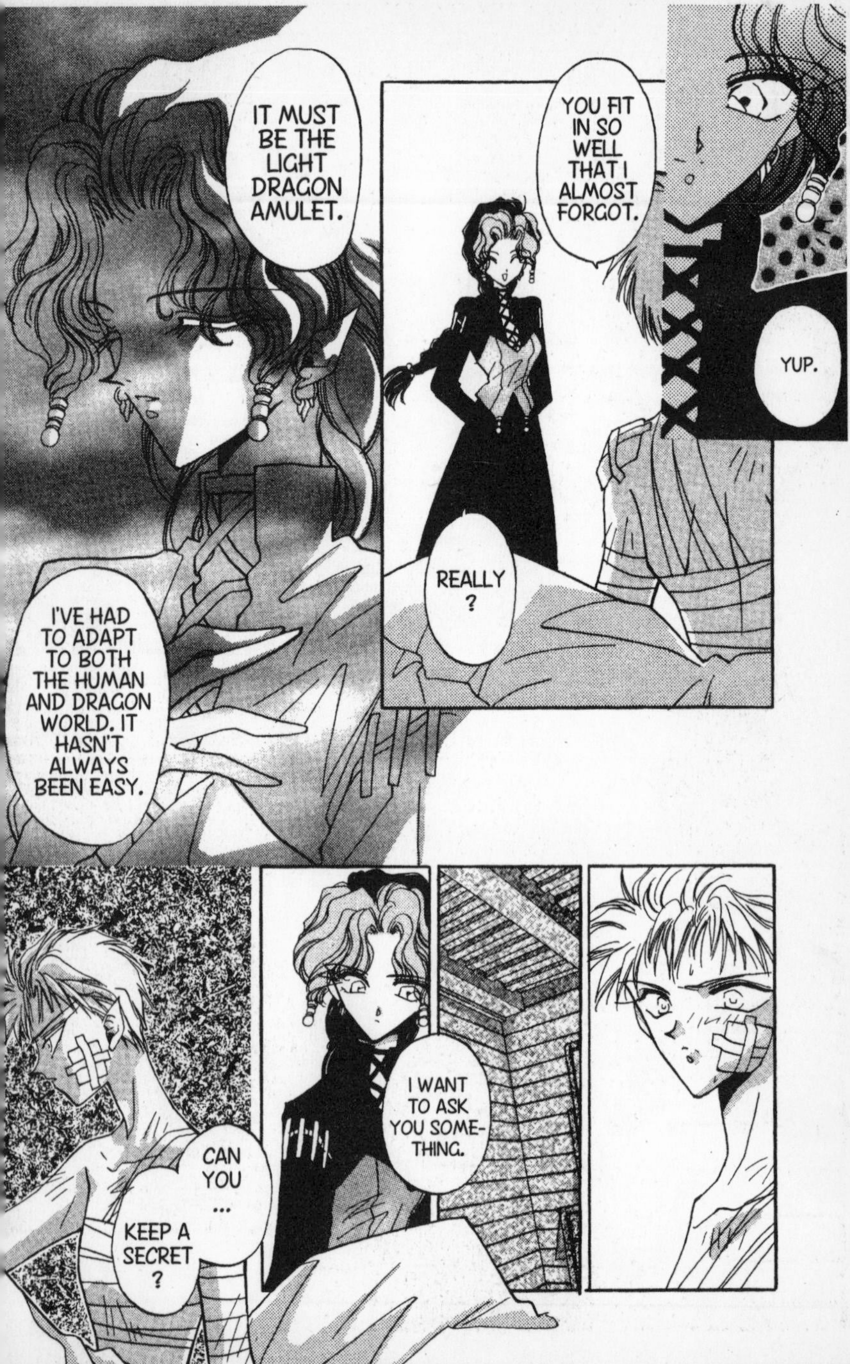

YOU FIT IN SO WELL THAT I ALMOST FORGOT.
YUP.
REALLY?
IT MUST BE THE LIGHT DRAGON AMULET.
I'VE HAD TO ADAPT TO BOTH THE HUMAN AND DRAGON WORLD. IT HASN'T ALWAYS BEEN EASY.
I WANT TO ASK YOU SOME-THING.
CAN YOU ... KEEP A SECRET?

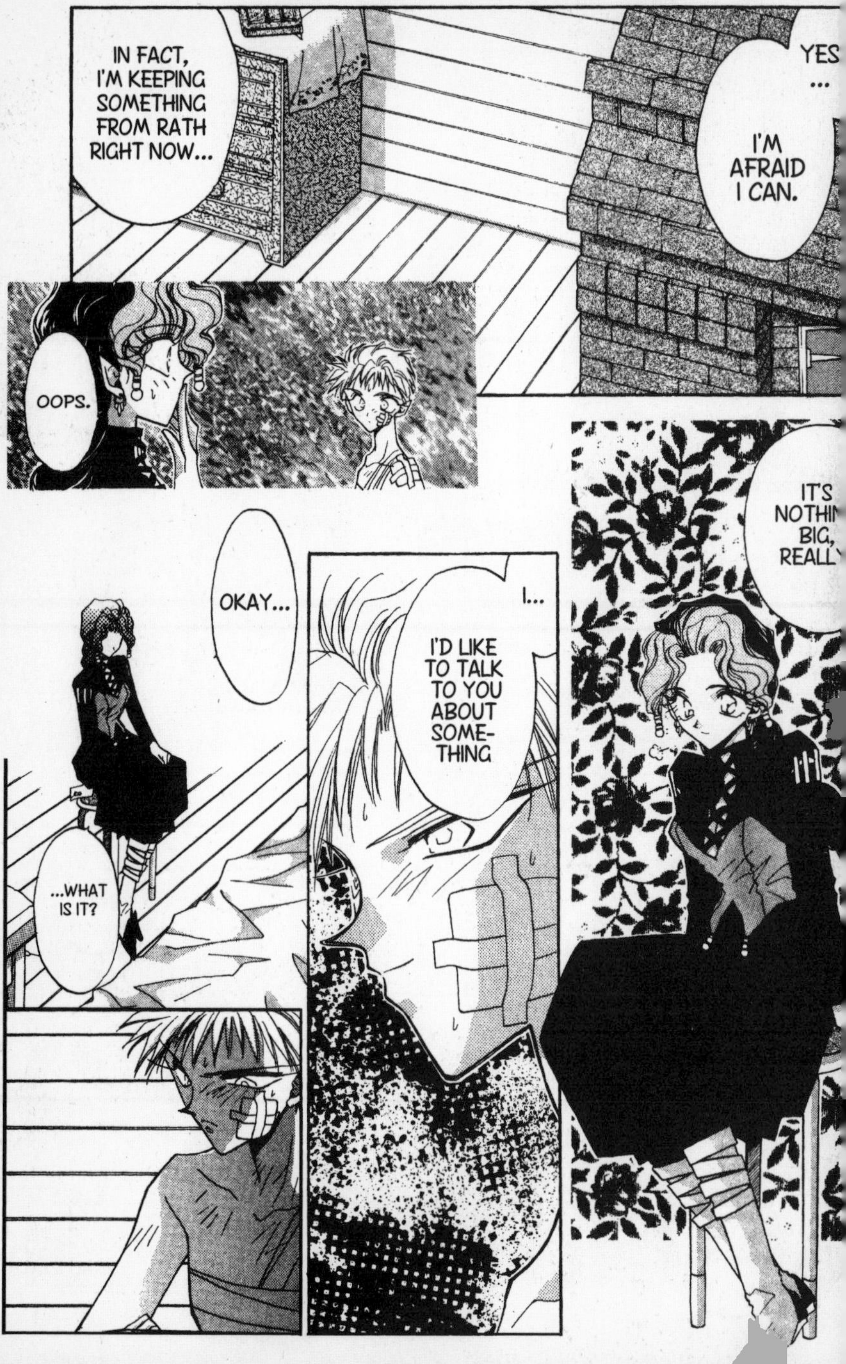
YES ... I'M AFRAID I CAN.
IN FACT, I'M KEEPING SOMETHING FROM RATH RIGHT NOW...
OOPS.
IT'S NOTHIN BIG, REALL
I...
I'D LIKE TO TALK TO YOU ABOUT SOME-THING
OKAY...
...WHAT IS IT?

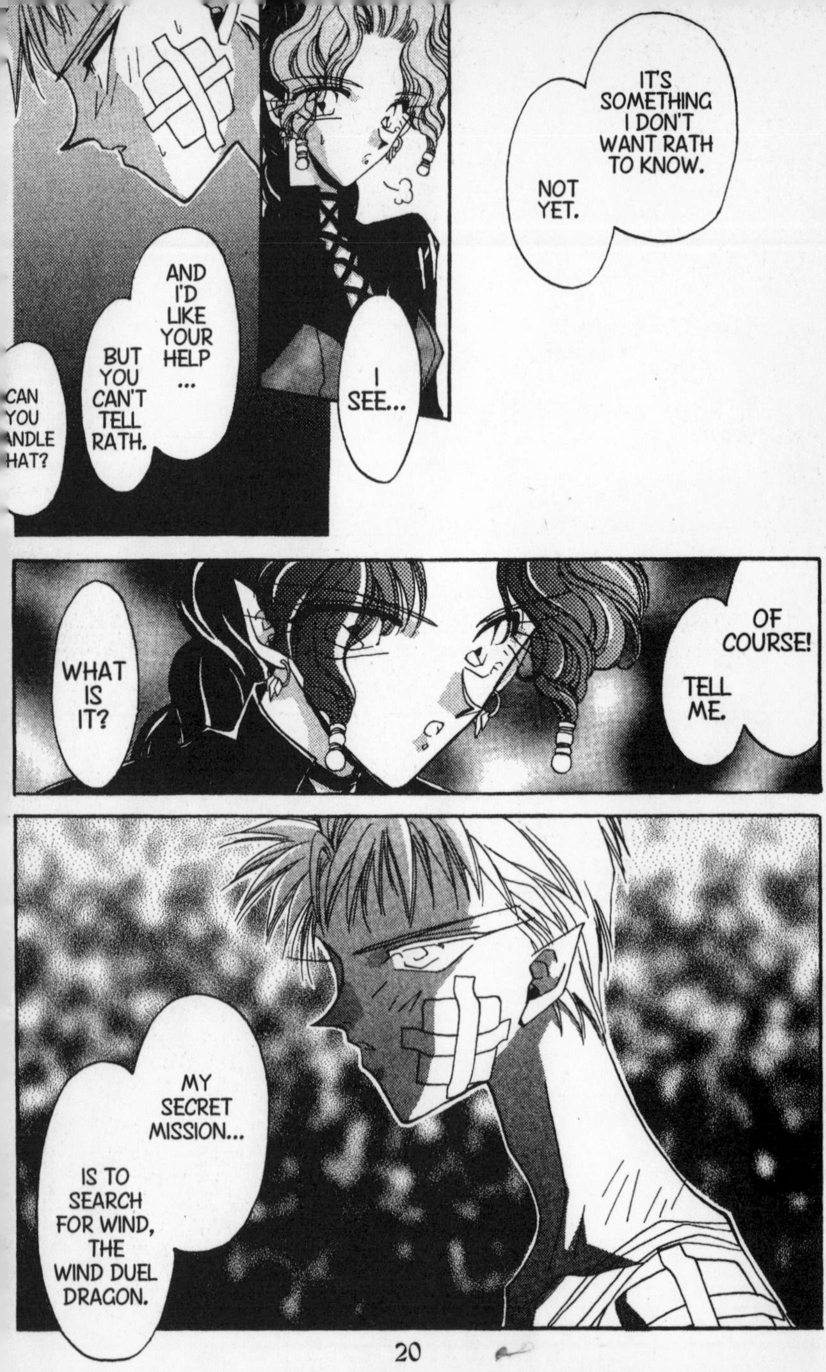
IT'S SOMETHING I DON'T WANT RATH TO KNOW.
NOT YET.
I SEE...
AND I'D LIKE YOUR HELP ...
BUT YOU CAN'T TELL RATH.
CAN YOU ANDLE HAT?
OF COURSE!
TELL ME.
WHAT IS IT?
MY SECRET MISSION...
IS TO SEARCH FOR WIND, THE WIND DUEL DRAGON.

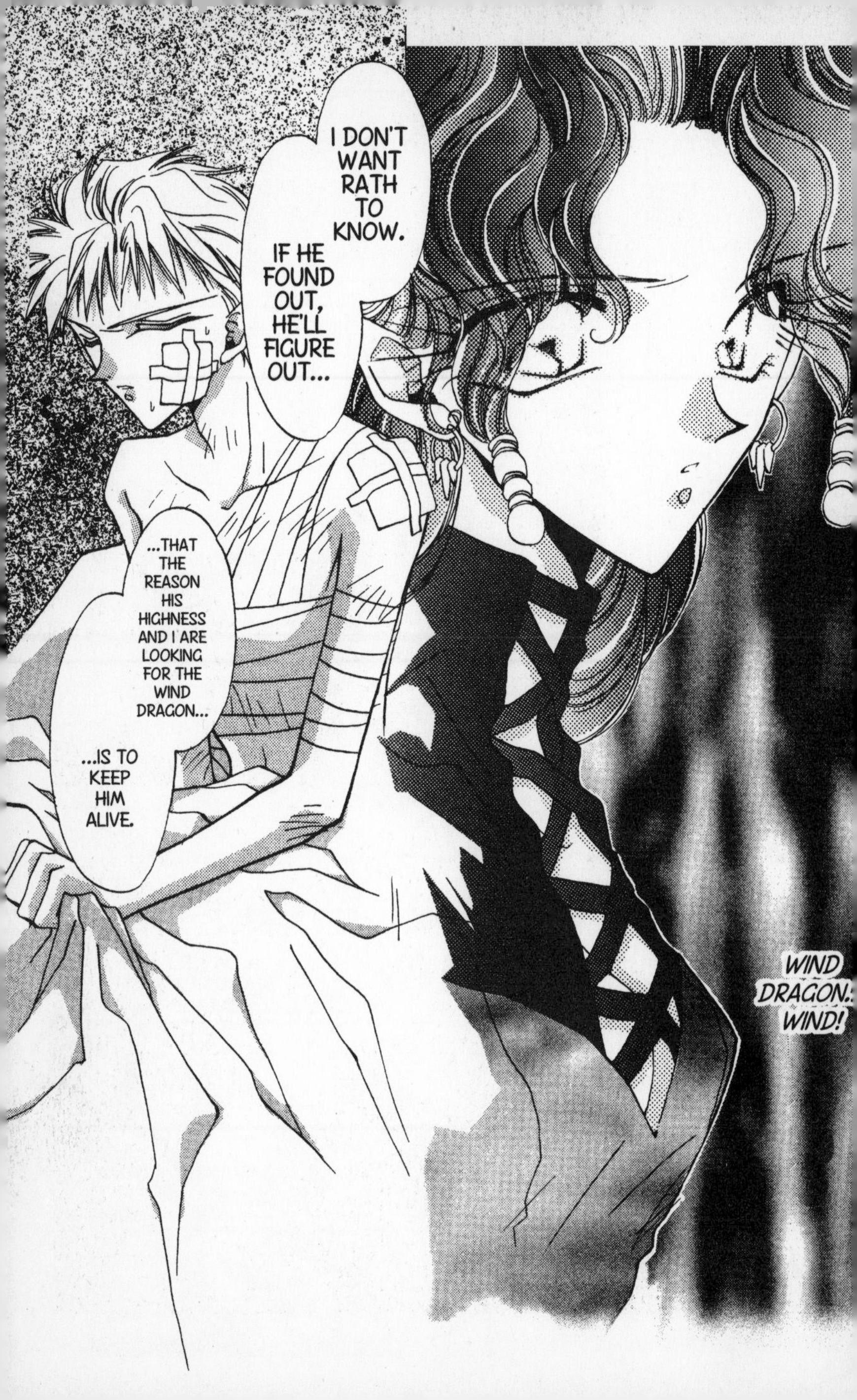
I DON'T WANT RATH TO KNOW.
IF HE FOUND OUT, HE'LL FIGURE OUT...
...THAT THE REASON HIS HIGHNESS AND I ARE LOOKING FOR THE WIND DRAGON...
...IS TO KEEP HIM ALIVE.
WIND DRAGON... WIND!

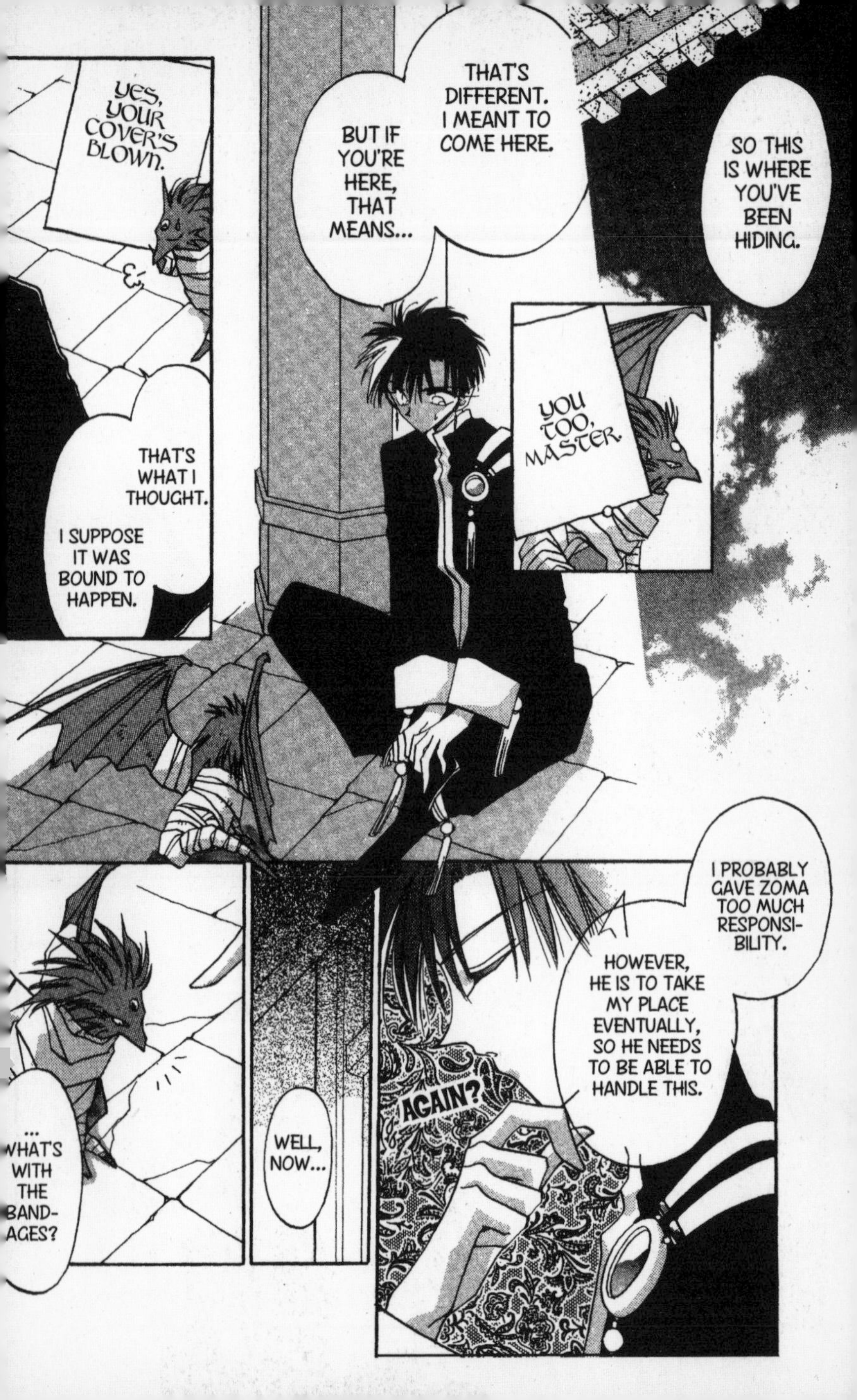
SO THIS IS WHERE YOU'VE BEEN HIDING.
THAT'S DIFFERENT. I MEANT TO COME HERE.
BUT IF YOU'RE HERE, THAT MEANS...
YOU TOO, MASTER.
YES, YOUR COVER'S BLOWN.
THAT'S WHAT I THOUGHT.
I SUPPOSE IT WAS BOUND TO HAPPEN.
I PROBABLY GAVE ZOMA TOO MUCH RESPONSIBILITY.
HOWEVER, HE IS TO TAKE MY PLACE EVENTUALLY, SO HE NEEDS TO BE ABLE TO HANDLE THIS.
AGAIN?
WELL, NOW...
...WHAT'S WITH THE BAND-AGES?

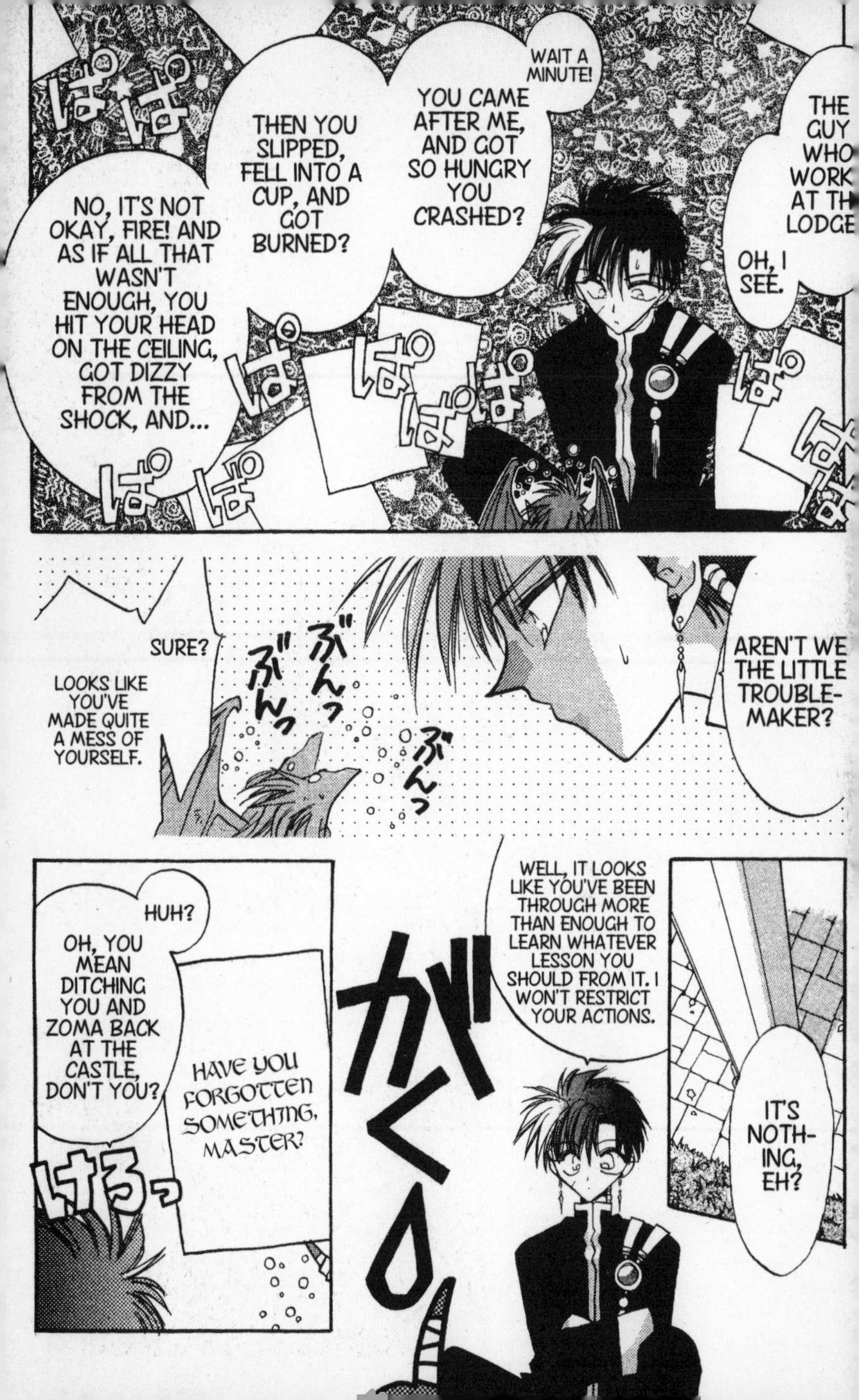
THE GUY WHO WORK AT TH LODGE
OH, I SEE.
WAIT A MINUTE!
YOU CAME AFTER ME, AND GOT SO HUNGRY YOU CRASHED?
THEN YOU SLIPPED, FELL INTO A CUP, AND GOT BURNED?
NO, IT'S NOT OKAY, FIRE! AND AS IF ALL THAT WASN'T ENOUGH, YOU HIT YOUR HEAD ON THE CEILING, GOT DIZZY FROM THE SHOCK, AND...
ぱ ぱ ぱ ぱ ぱ ぱ ぱ ぱ ぱ
AREN'T WE THE LITTLE TROUBLE-MAKER?
ぶんっ ぶんっ ぶんっ
SURE?
LOOKS LIKE YOU'VE MADE QUITE A MESS OF YOURSELF.
IT'S NOTH-ING, EH?
WELL, IT LOOKS LIKE YOU'VE BEEN THROUGH MORE THAN ENOUGH TO LEARN WHATEVER LESSON YOU SHOULD FROM IT. I WON'T RESTRICT YOUR ACTIONS.
がくっ
HAVE YOU FORGOTTEN SOMETHING, MASTER?
HUH?
OH, YOU MEAN DITCHING YOU AND ZOMA BACK AT THE CASTLE, DON'T YOU?
けろっ

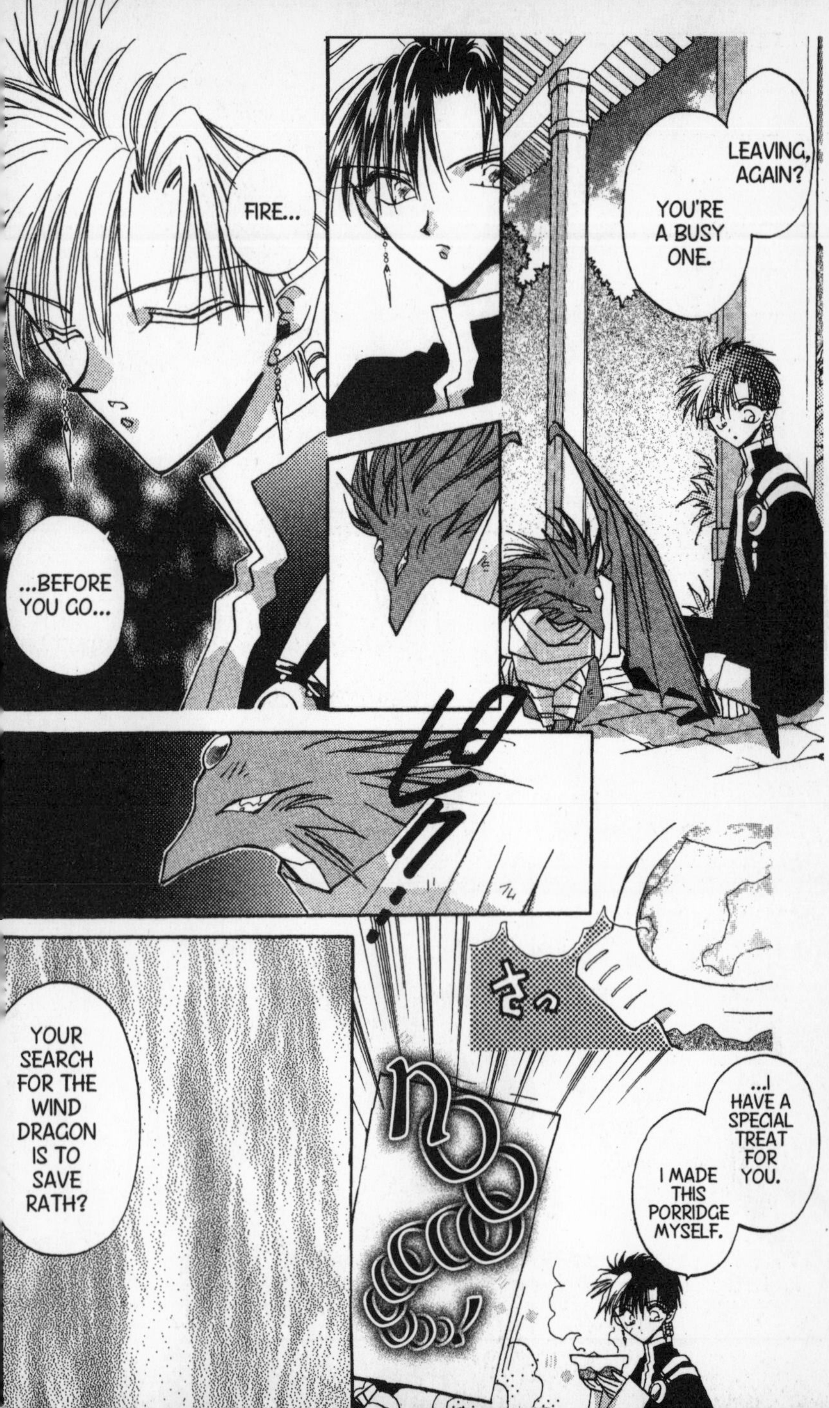
LEAVING, AGAIN?
YOU'RE A BUSY ONE.
FIRE...
...BEFORE YOU GO...
さっ
...I HAVE A SPECIAL TREAT FOR YOU.
I MADE THIS PORRIDGE MYSELF.
YOUR SEARCH FOR THE WIND DRAGON IS TO SAVE RATH?

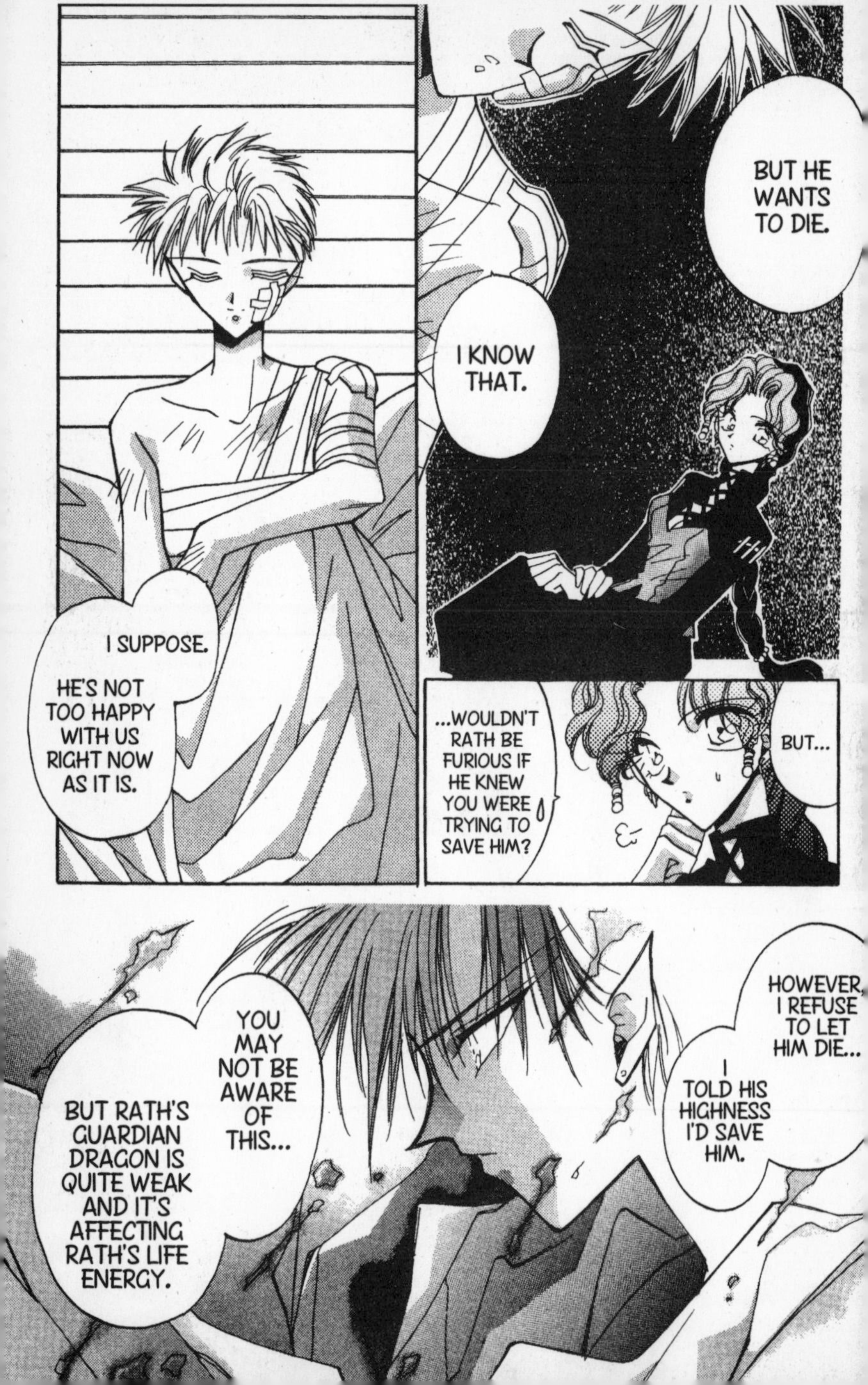
BUT HE WANTS TO DIE.
I KNOW THAT.
BUT...
...WOULDN'T RATH BE FURIOUS IF HE KNEW YOU WERE TRYING TO SAVE HIM?
I SUPPOSE.
HE'S NOT TOO HAPPY WITH US RIGHT NOW AS IT IS.
HOWEVER, I REFUSE TO LET HIM DIE...
I TOLD HIS HIGHNESS I'D SAVE HIM.
YOU MAY NOT BE AWARE OF THIS...
BUT RATH'S GUARDIAN DRAGON IS QUITE WEAK AND IT'S AFFECTING RATH'S LIFE ENERGY.

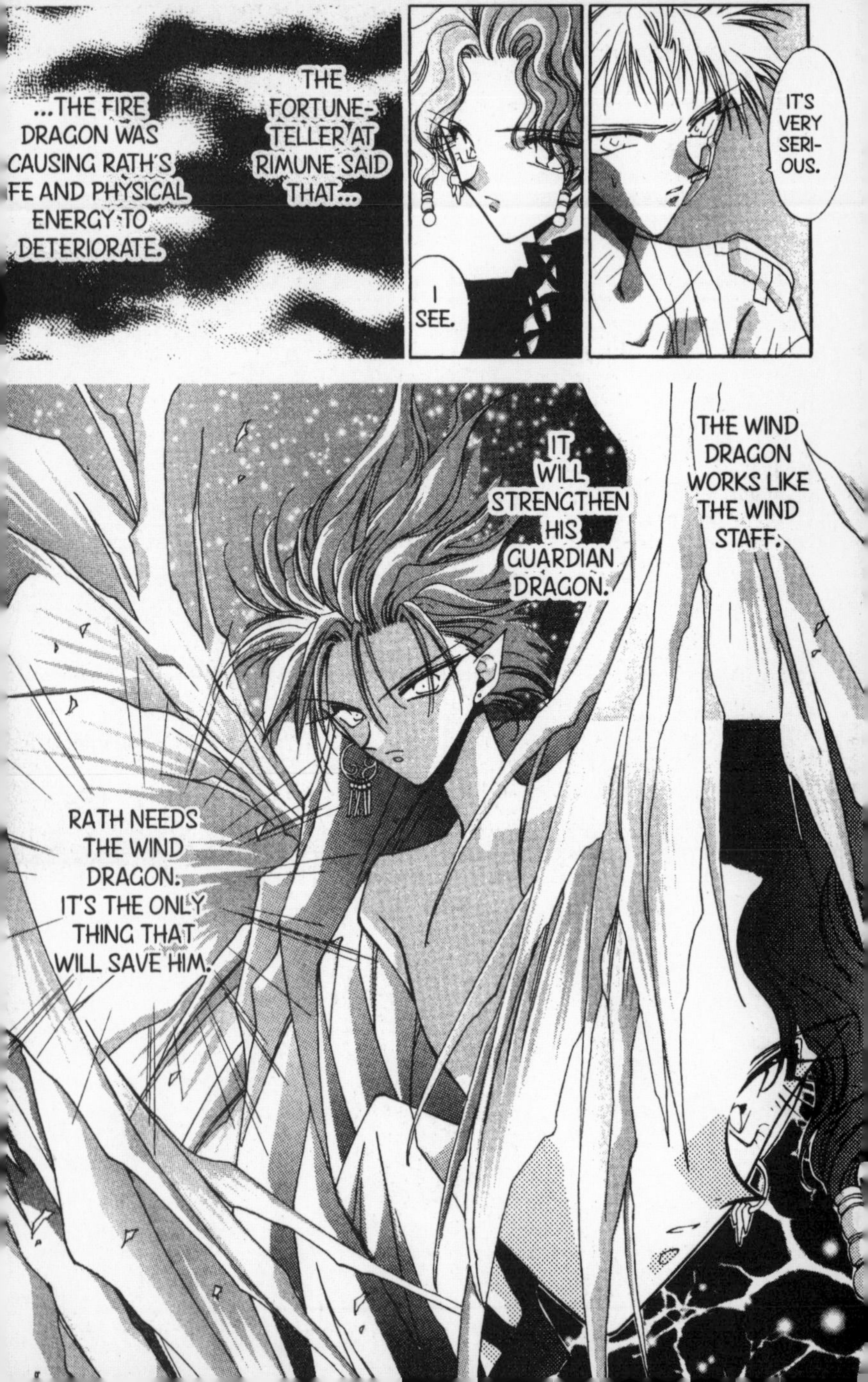
IT'S VERY SERI-OUS.
I SEE.
THE FORTUNE-TELLER AT RIMUNE SAID THAT...
...THE FIRE DRAGON WAS CAUSING RATH'S FE AND PHYSICAL ENERGY TO DETERIORATE.
THE WIND DRAGON WORKS LIKE THE WIND STAFF.
IT WILL STRENGTHEN HIS GUARDIAN DRAGON.
RATH NEEDS THE WIND DRAGON. IT'S THE ONLY THING THAT WILL SAVE HIM.

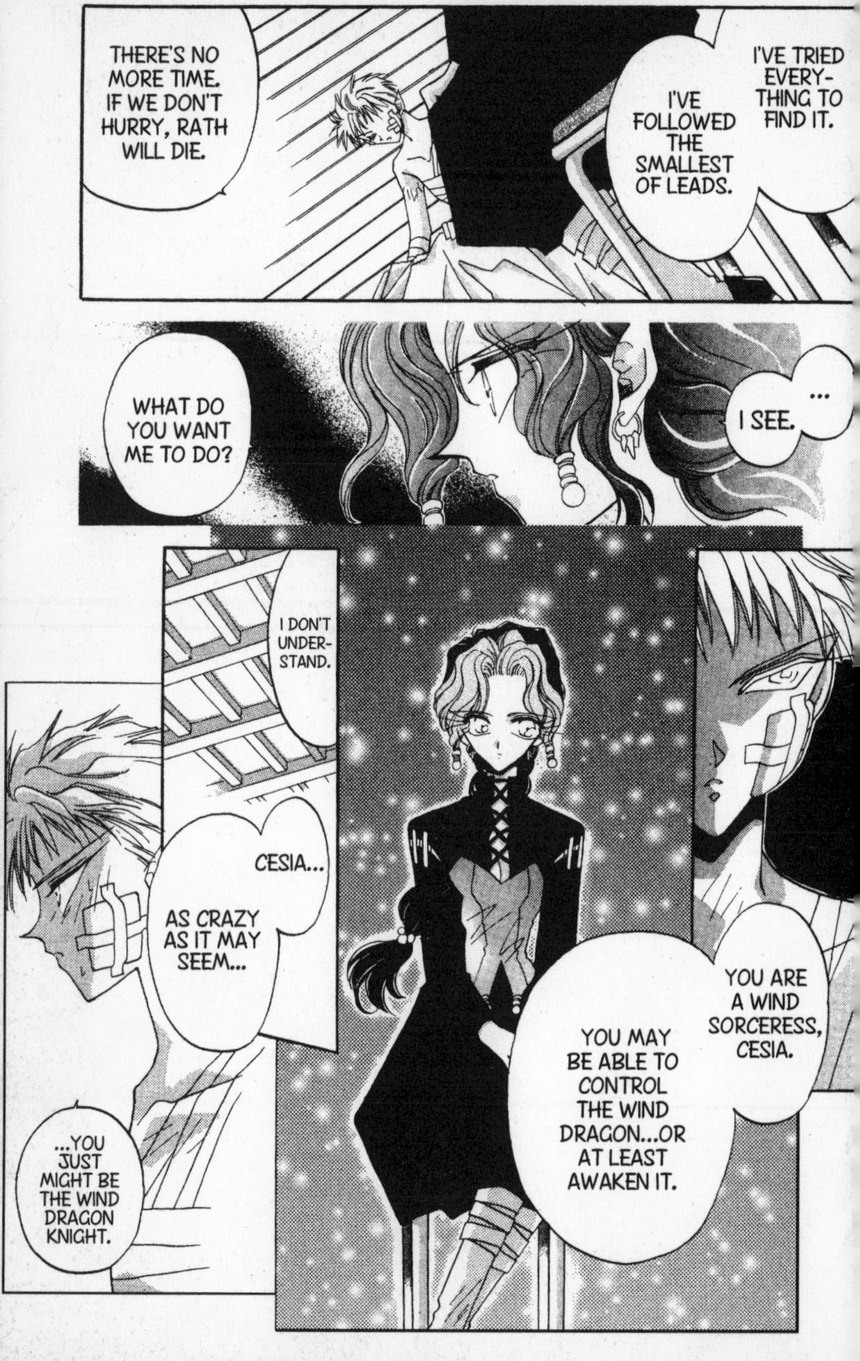
I'VE TRIED EVERYTHING TO FIND IT.
I'VE FOLLOWED THE SMALLEST OF LEADS.
THERE'S NO MORE TIME. IF WE DON'T HURRY, RATH WILL DIE.
... I SEE.
WHAT DO YOU WANT ME TO DO?
YOU ARE A WIND SORCERESS, CESIA.
YOU MAY BE ABLE TO CONTROL THE WIND DRAGON...OR AT LEAST AWAKEN IT.
I DON'T UNDERSTAND.
CESIA...
AS CRAZY AS IT MAY SEEM...
...YOU JUST MIGHT BE THE WIND DRAGON KNIGHT.

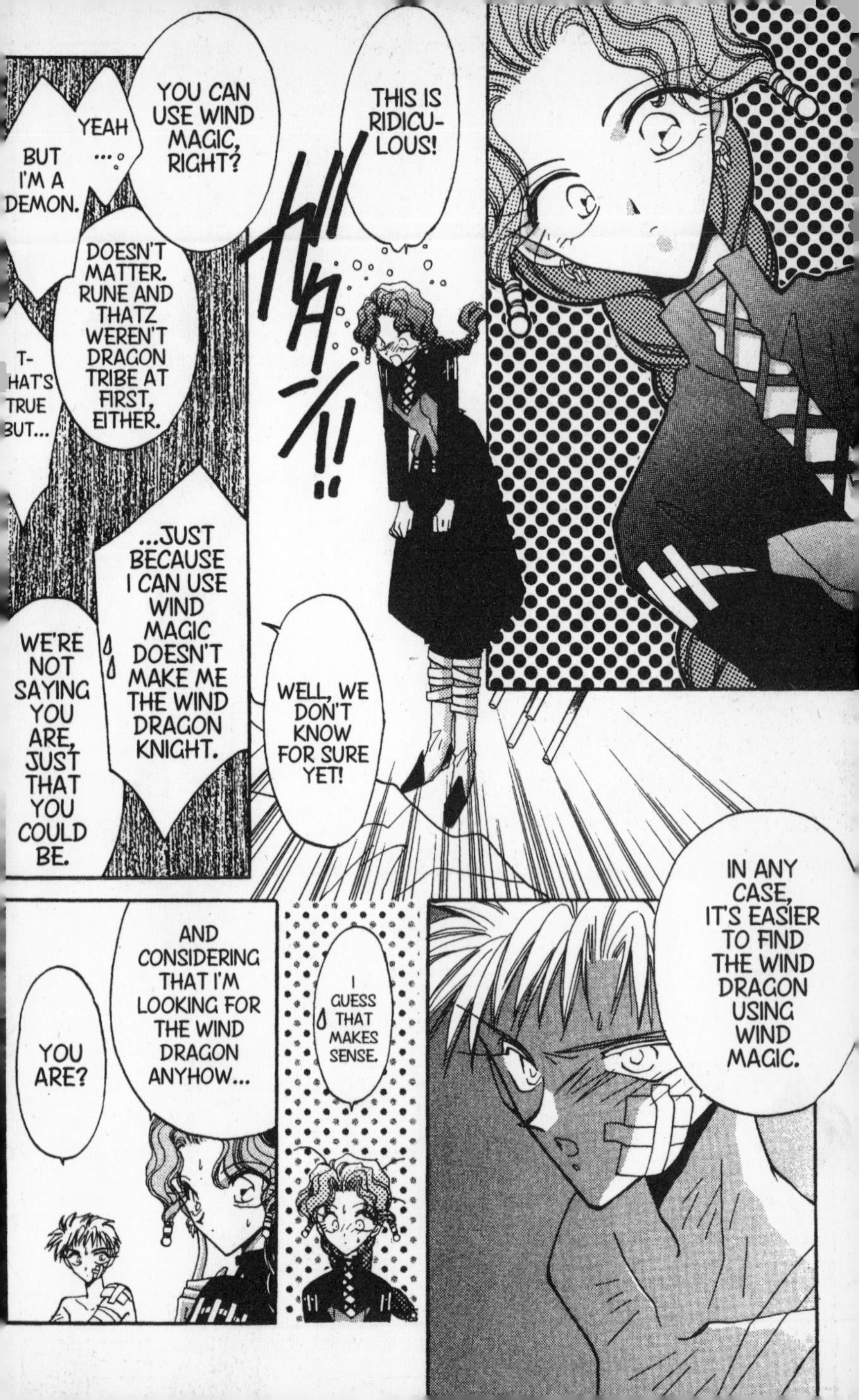
THIS IS RIDICULOUS!
YOU CAN USE WIND MAGIC, RIGHT?
YEAH ...
BUT I'M A DEMON.
DOESN'T MATTER. RUNE AND THATZ WEREN'T DRAGON TRIBE AT FIRST, EITHER.
T-HAT'S TRUE BUT...
WELL, WE DON'T KNOW FOR SURE YET!
...JUST BECAUSE I CAN USE WIND MAGIC DOESN'T MAKE ME THE WIND DRAGON KNIGHT.
WE'RE NOT SAYING YOU ARE, JUST THAT YOU COULD BE.
IN ANY CASE, IT'S EASIER TO FIND THE WIND DRAGON USING WIND MAGIC.
I GUESS THAT MAKES SENSE.
AND CONSIDERING THAT I'M LOOKING FOR THE WIND DRAGON ANYHOW...
YOU ARE?

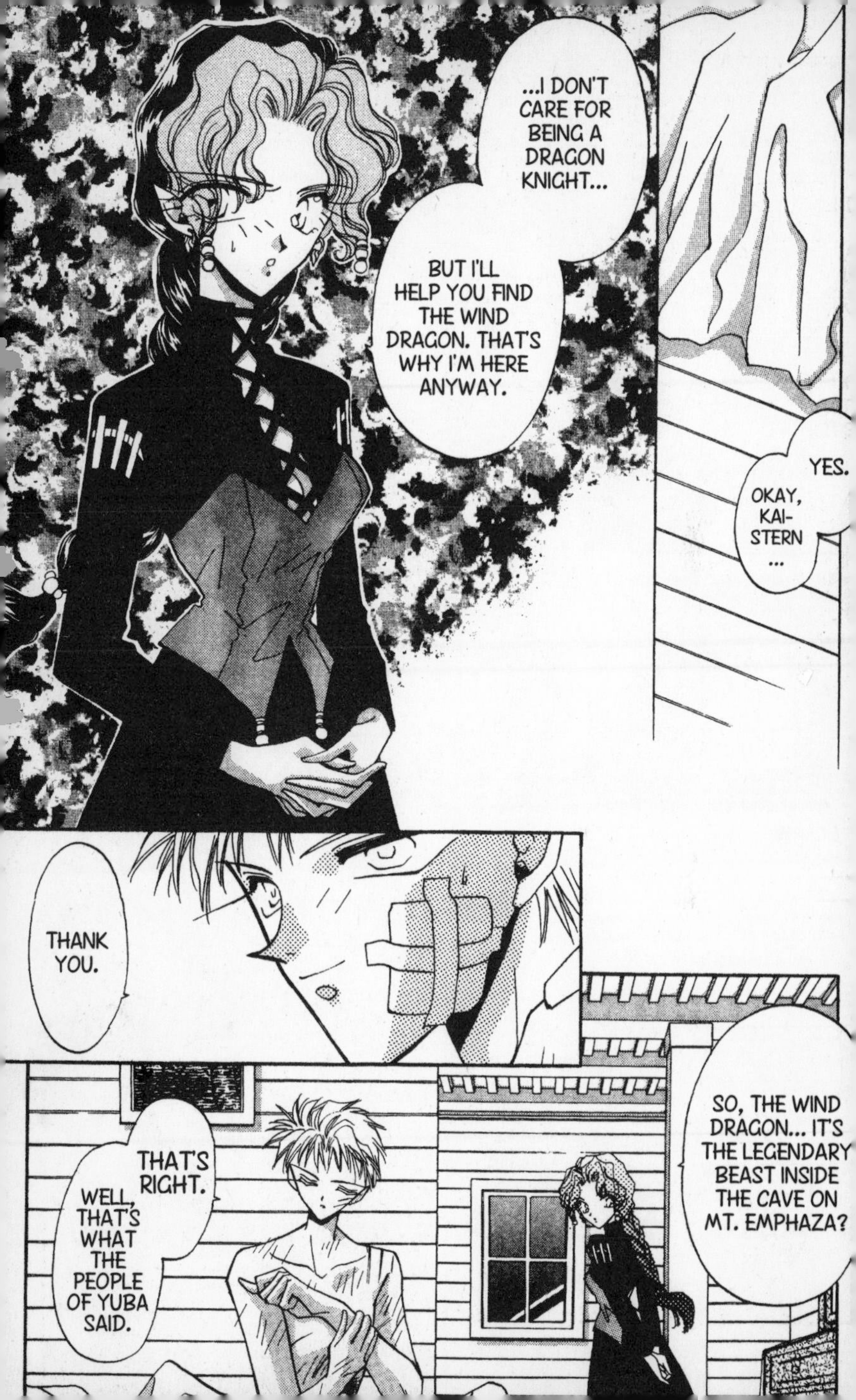
YES.
OKAY, KAI-STERN ...
...I DON'T CARE FOR BEING A DRAGON KNIGHT...
BUT I'LL HELP YOU FIND THE WIND DRAGON. THAT'S WHY I'M HERE ANYWAY.
THANK YOU.
SO, THE WIND DRAGON... IT'S THE LEGENDARY BEAST INSIDE THE CAVE ON MT. EMPHAZA?
THAT'S RIGHT.
WELL, THAT'S WHAT THE PEOPLE OF YUBA SAID.

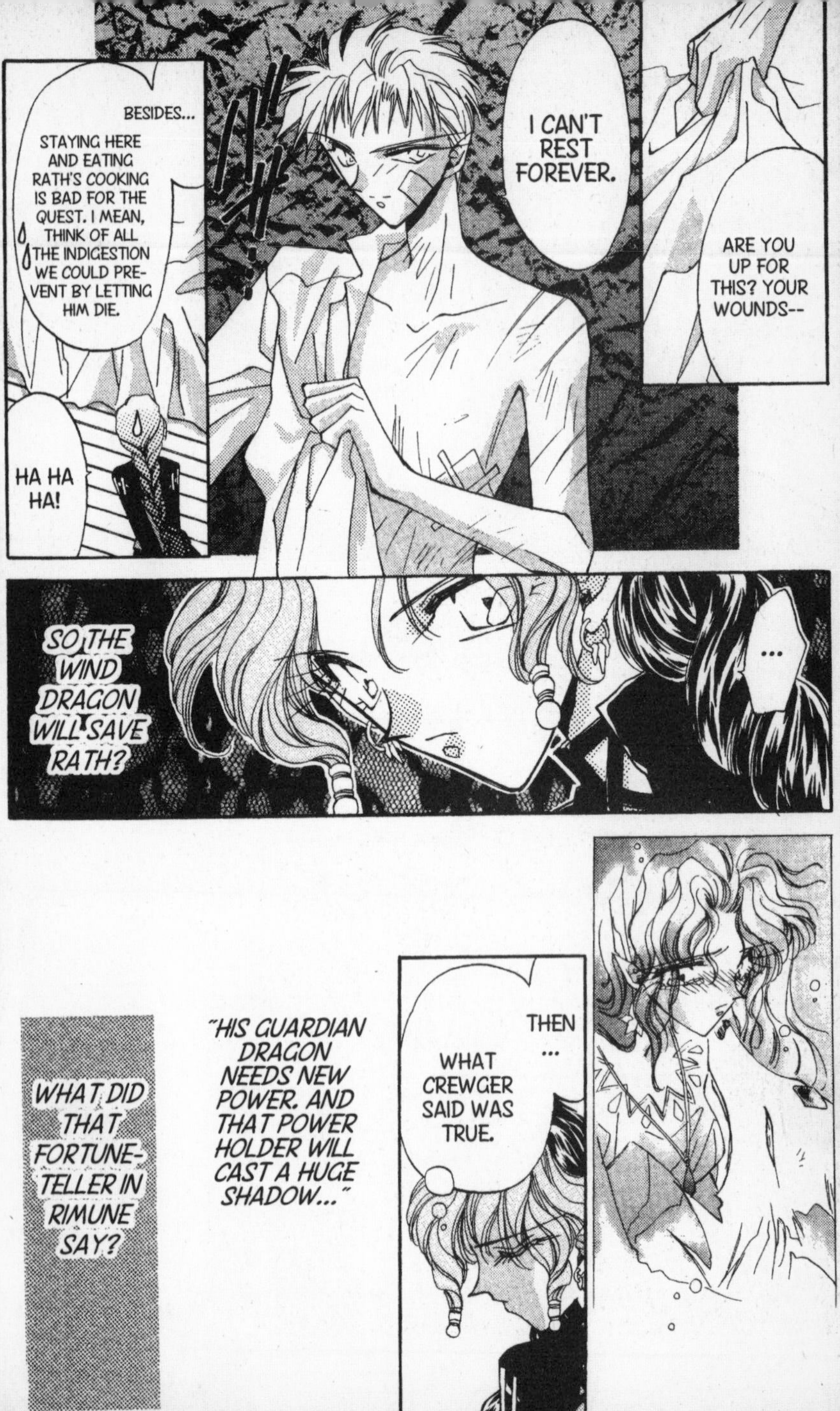
ARE YOU UP FOR THIS? YOUR WOUNDS--
I CAN'T REST FOREVER.
BESIDES...
STAYING HERE AND EATING RATH'S COOKING IS BAD FOR THE QUEST. I MEAN, THINK OF ALL THE INDIGESTION WE COULD PREVENT BY LETTING HIM DIE.
HA HA HA!
...
SO THE WIND DRAGON WILL SAVE RATH?
THEN...
WHAT CREWGER SAID WAS TRUE.
"HIS GUARDIAN DRAGON NEEDS NEW POWER. AND THAT POWER HOLDER WILL CAST A HUGE SHADOW..."
WHAT DID THAT FORTUNE-TELLER IN RIMUNE SAY?

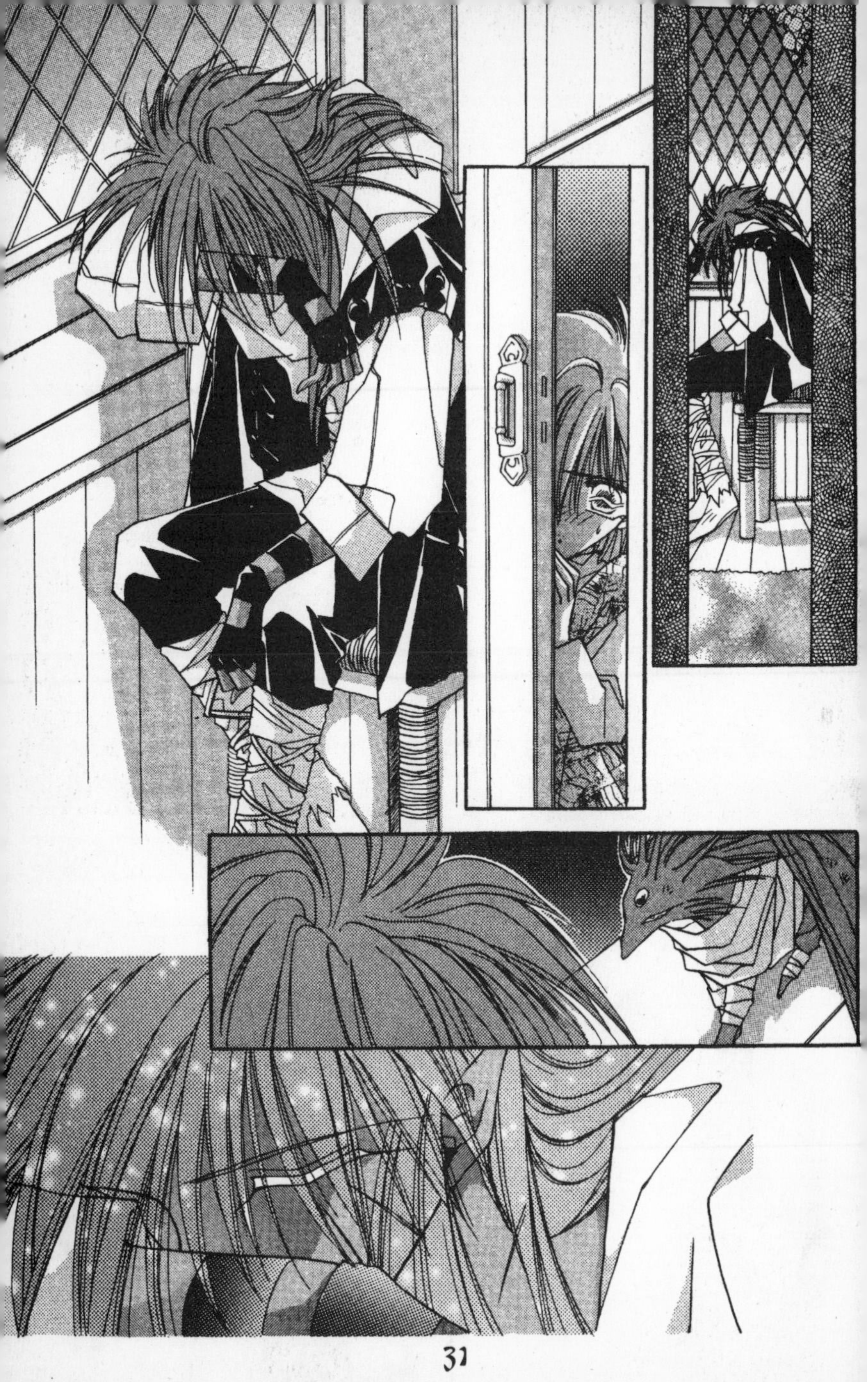

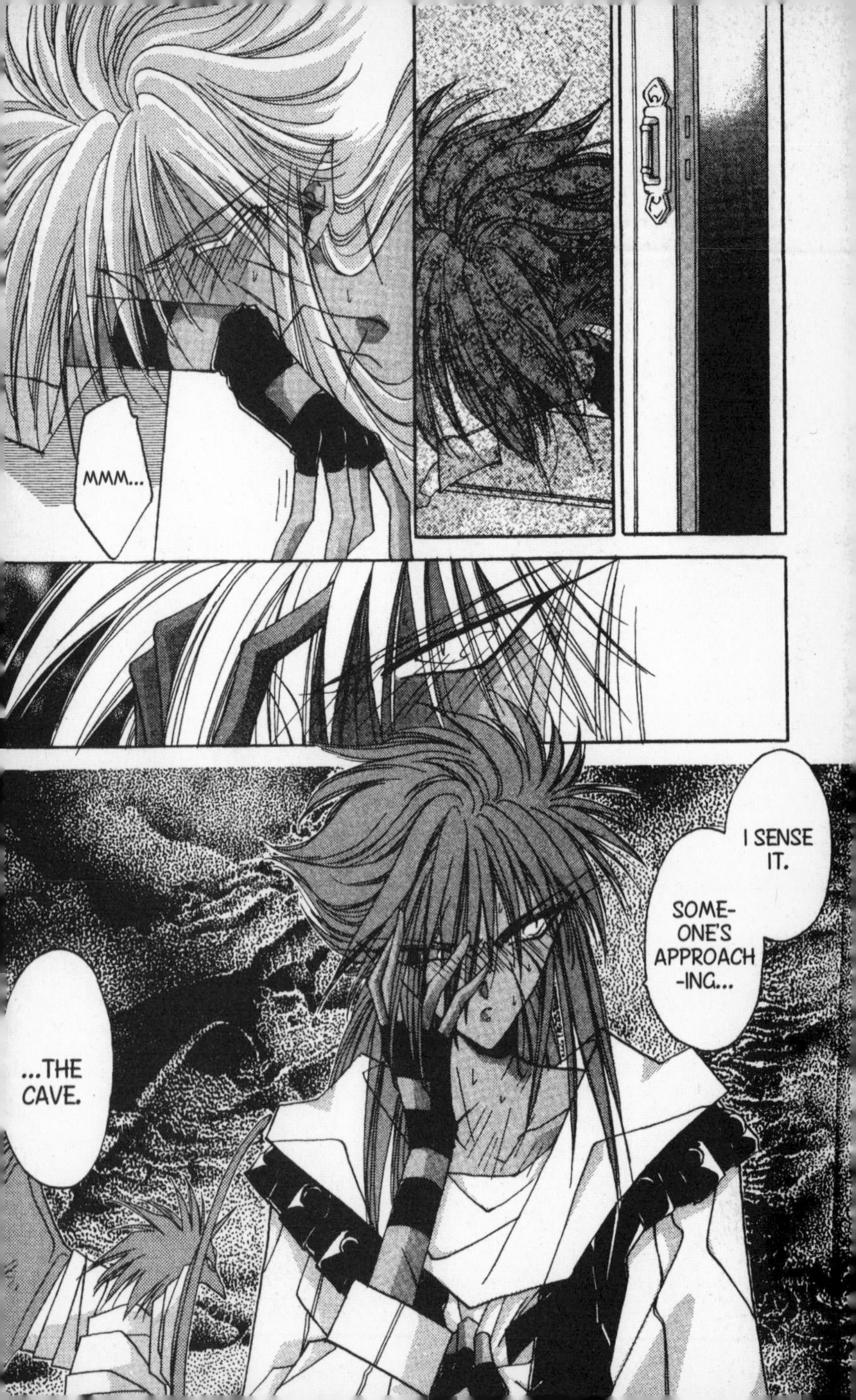
MMM...
I SENSE IT.
SOME-ONE'S APPROACH-ING...
...THE CAVE.

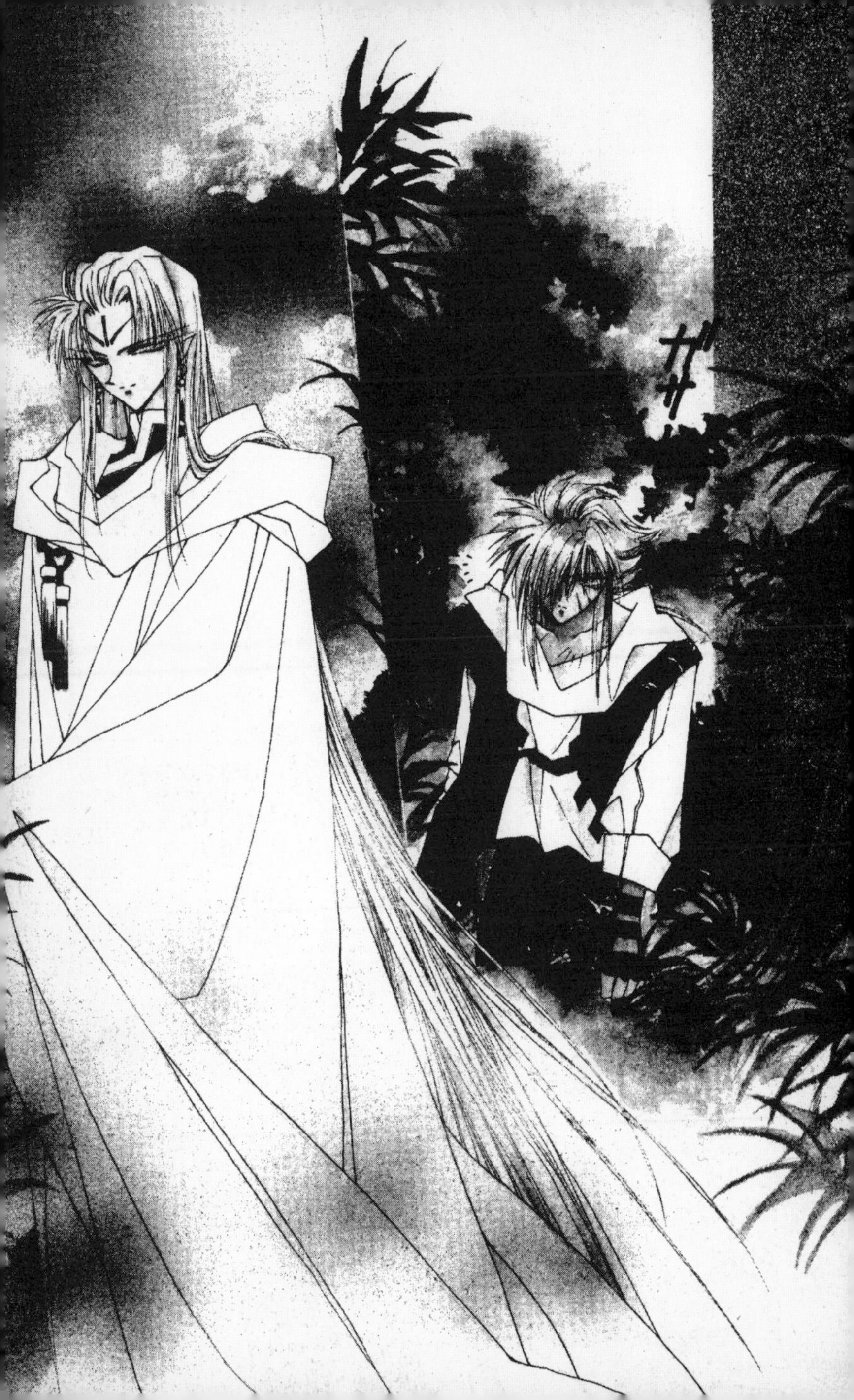
ガサ

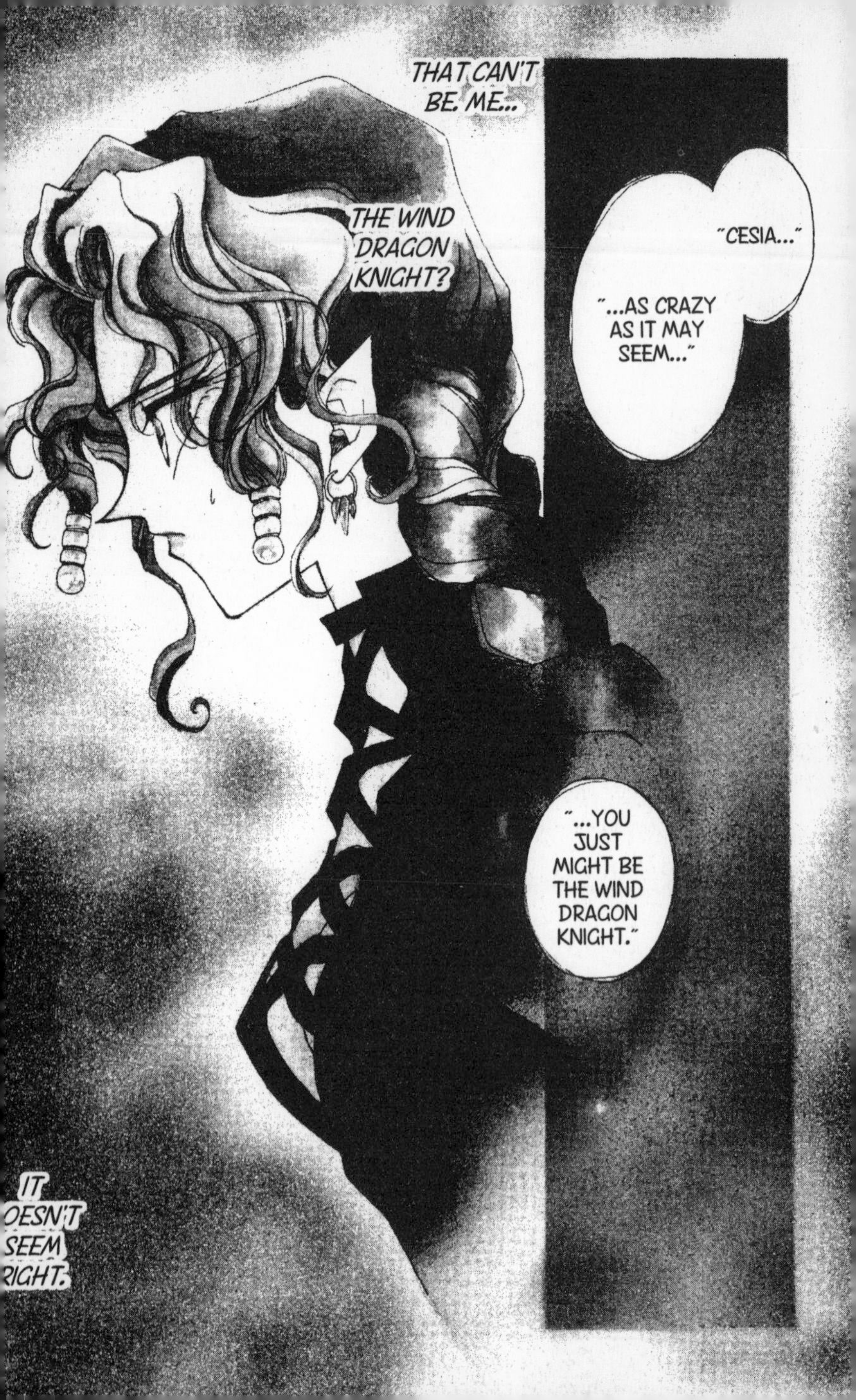
"CESIA..."
"...AS CRAZY AS IT MAY SEEM..."
"...YOU JUST MIGHT BE THE WIND DRAGON KNIGHT."
THAT CAN'T BE. ME...
THE WIND DRAGON KNIGHT?
IT OESN'T SEEM IGHT.

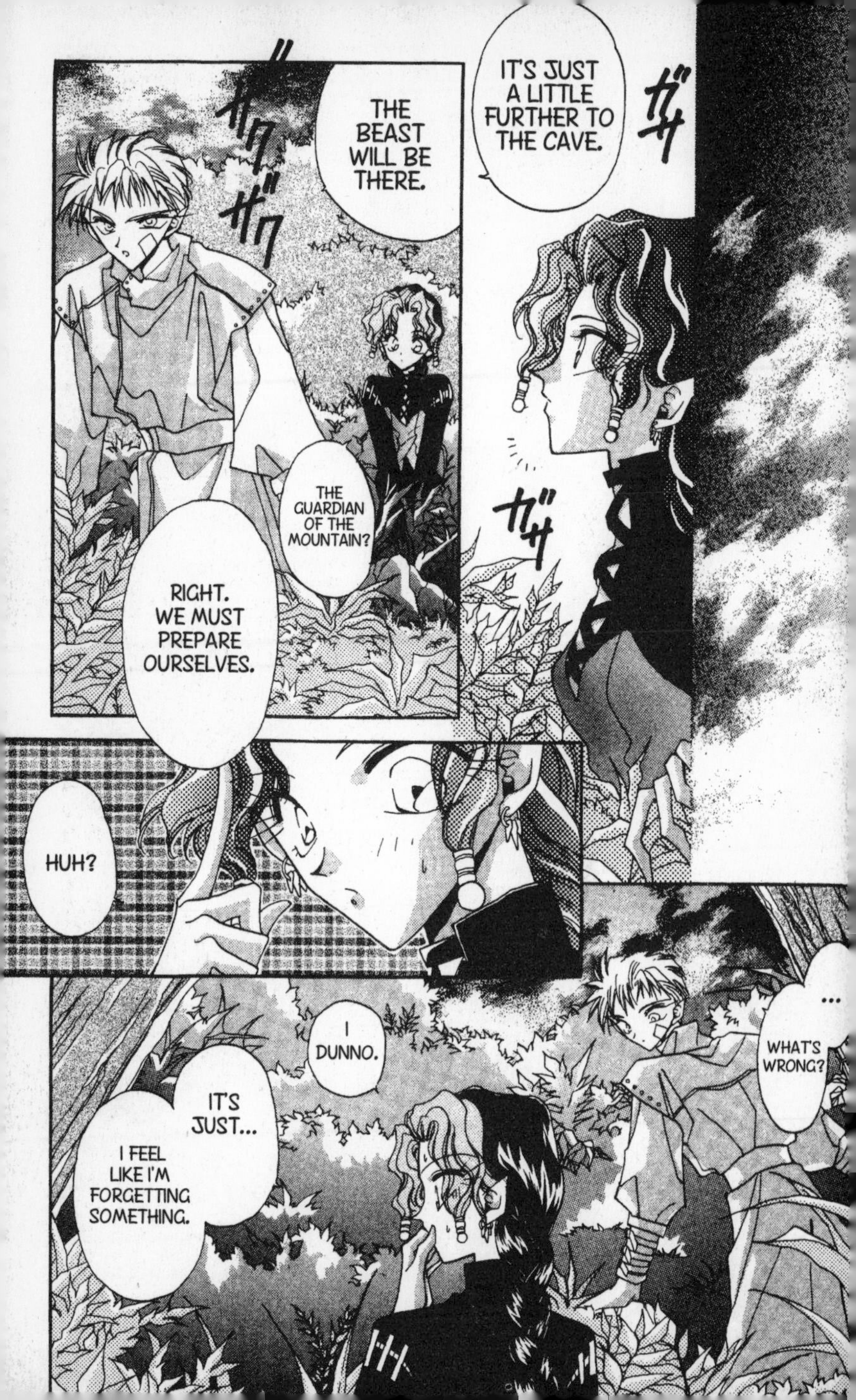
IT'S JUST A LITTLE FURTHER TO THE CAVE.
ガサ
ガサ
ザクザク
THE BEAST WILL BE THERE.
THE GUARDIAN OF THE MOUNTAIN?
RIGHT. WE MUST PREPARE OURSELVES.
HUH?
...
WHAT'S WRONG?
I DUNNO.
IT'S JUST...
I FEEL LIKE I'M FORGETTING SOMETHING.

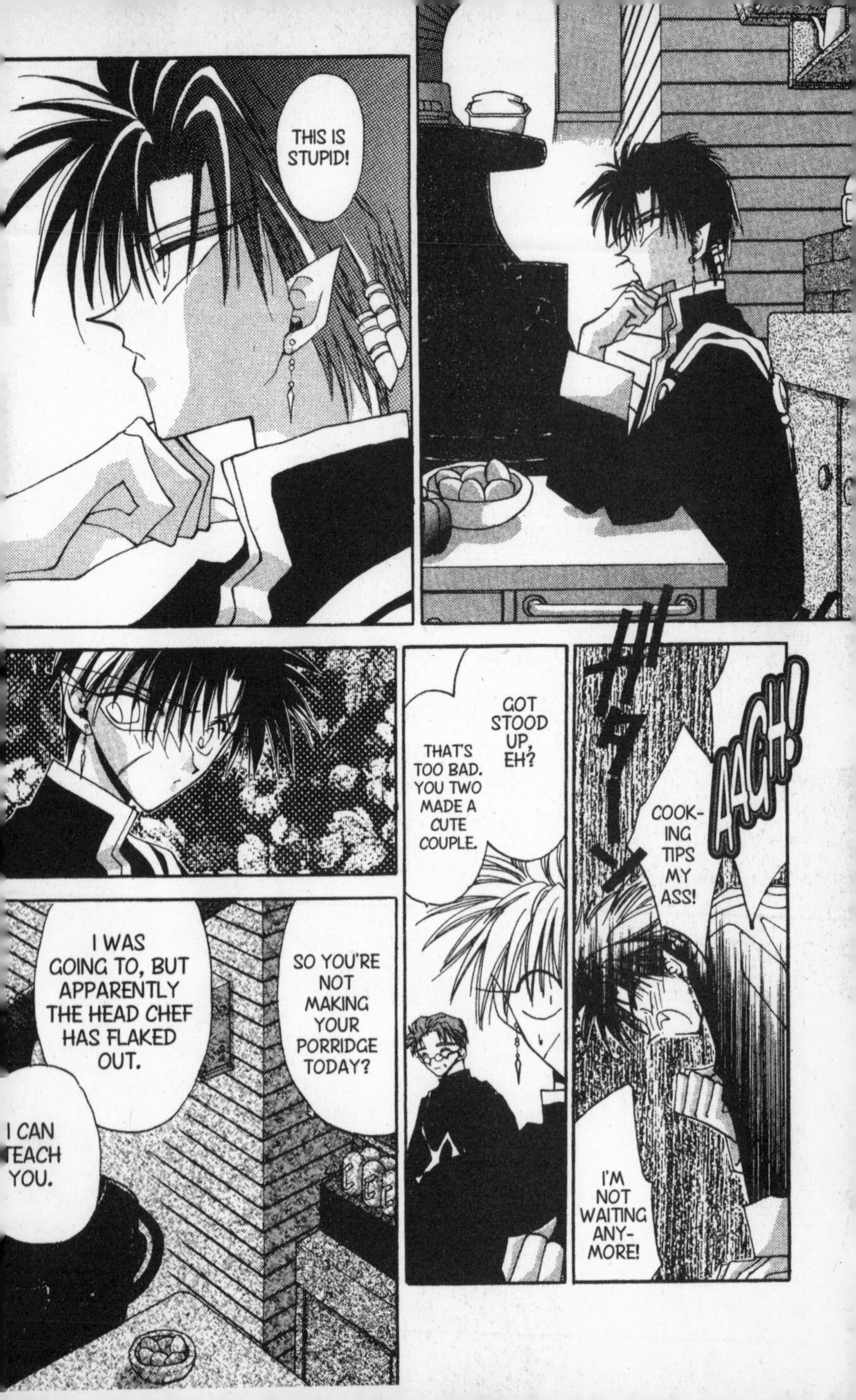
THIS IS STUPID!
AACH!
COOK-ING TIPS MY ASS!
I'M NOT WAITING ANY-MORE!
GOT STOOD UP, EH?
THAT'S TOO BAD. YOU TWO MADE A CUTE COUPLE.
SO YOU'RE NOT MAKING YOUR PORRIDGE TODAY?
I WAS GOING TO, BUT APPARENTLY THE HEAD CHEF HAS FLAKED OUT.
I CAN TEACH YOU.

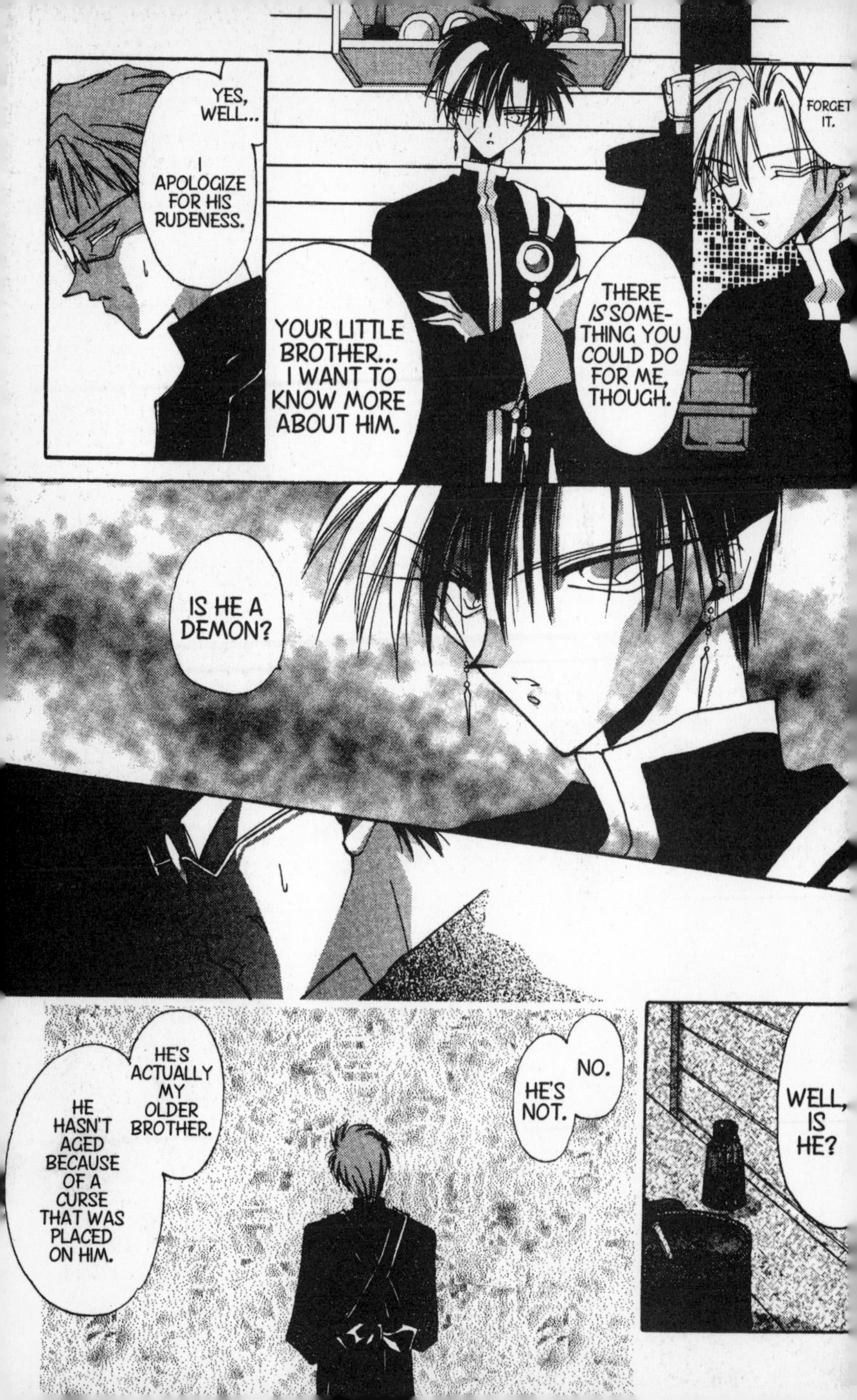
FORGET IT.
THERE *IS* SOMETHING YOU COULD DO FOR ME, THOUGH.
YOUR LITTLE BROTHER... I WANT TO KNOW MORE ABOUT HIM.
YES, WELL...
I APOLOGIZE FOR HIS RUDENESS.
IS HE A DEMON?
WELL, IS HE?
NO.
HE'S NOT.
HE'S ACTUALLY MY OLDER BROTHER.
HE HASN'T AGED BECAUSE OF A CURSE THAT WAS PLACED ON HIM.

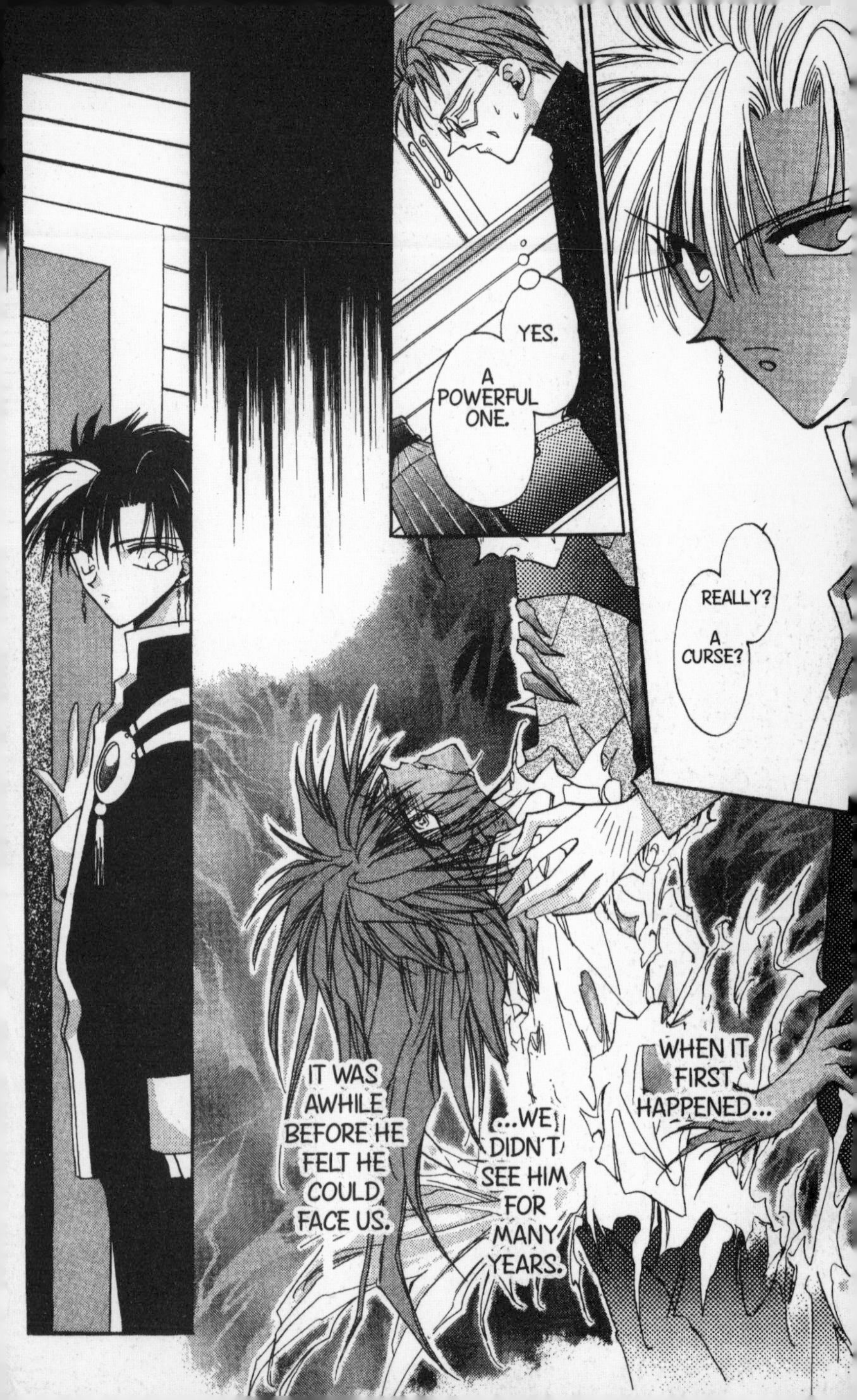
YES.
A POWERFUL ONE.
REALLY?
A CURSE?
WHEN IT FIRST HAPPENED...
...WE DIDN'T SEE HIM FOR MANY YEARS.
IT WAS AWHILE BEFORE HE FELT HE COULD FACE US.

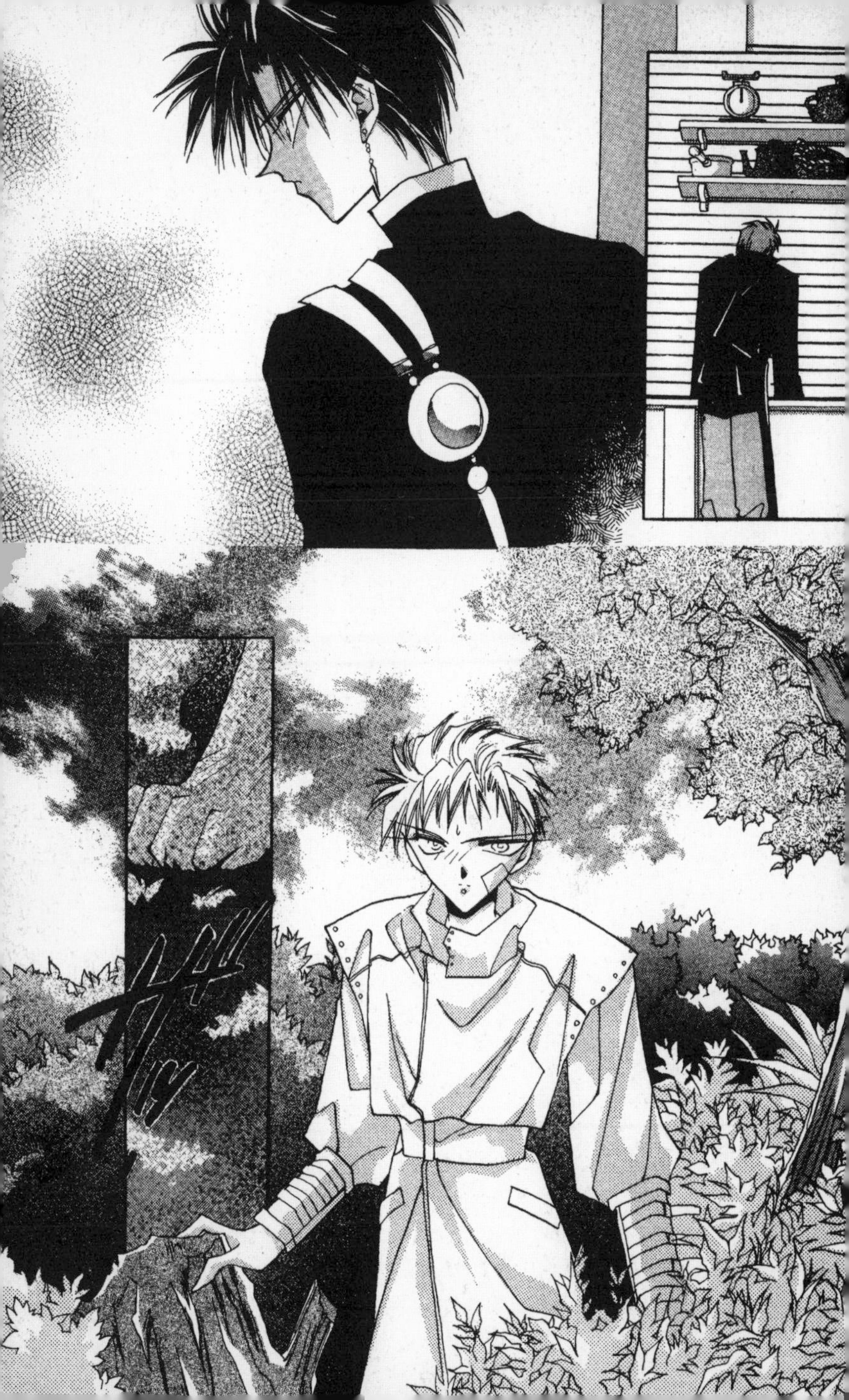

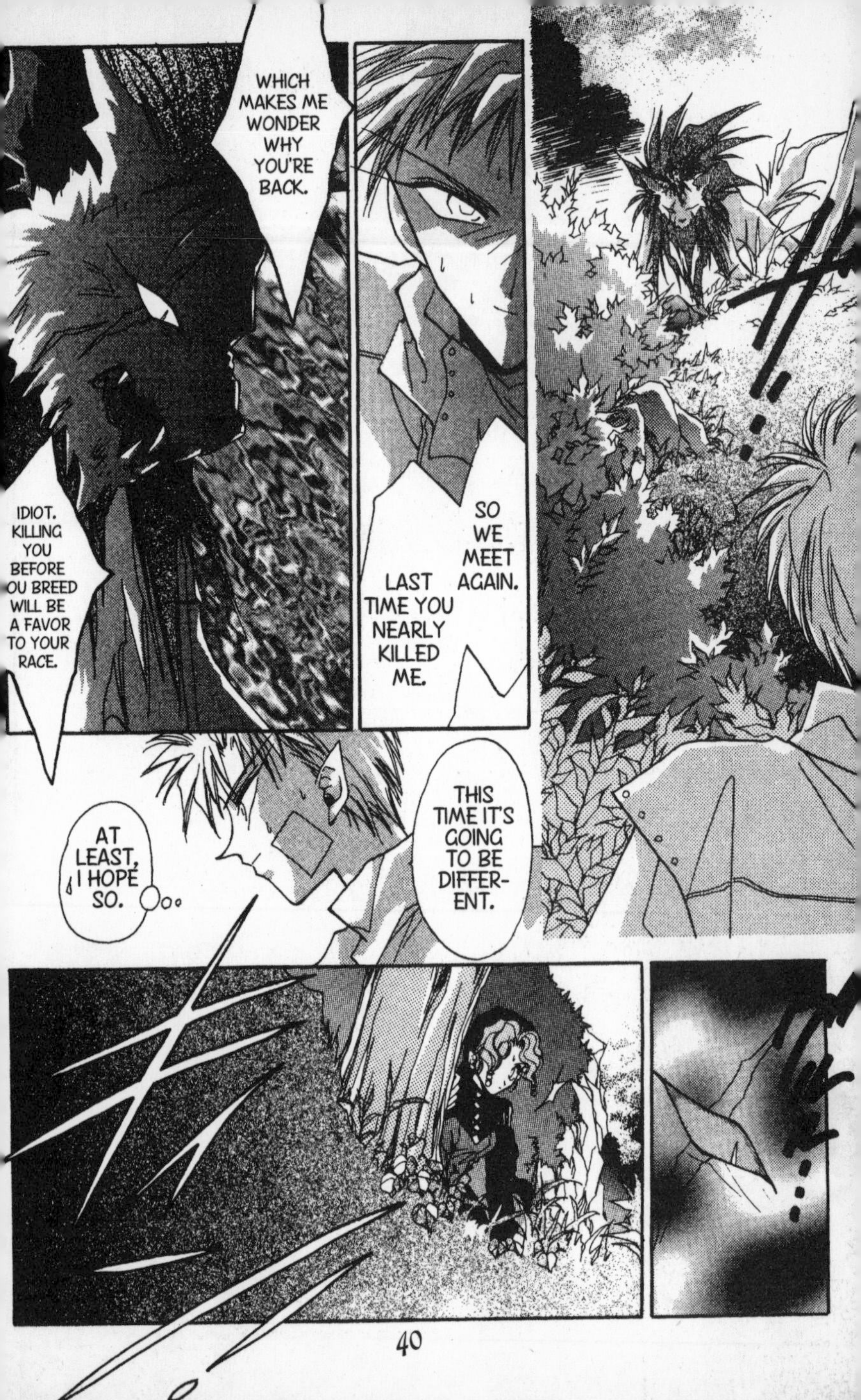
SO WE MEET AGAIN.
LAST TIME YOU NEARLY KILLED ME.
WHICH MAKES ME WONDER WHY YOU'RE BACK.
IDIOT. KILLING YOU BEFORE OU BREED WILL BE A FAVOR TO YOUR RACE.
THIS TIME IT'S GOING TO BE DIFFER-ENT.
AT LEAST, I HOPE SO.

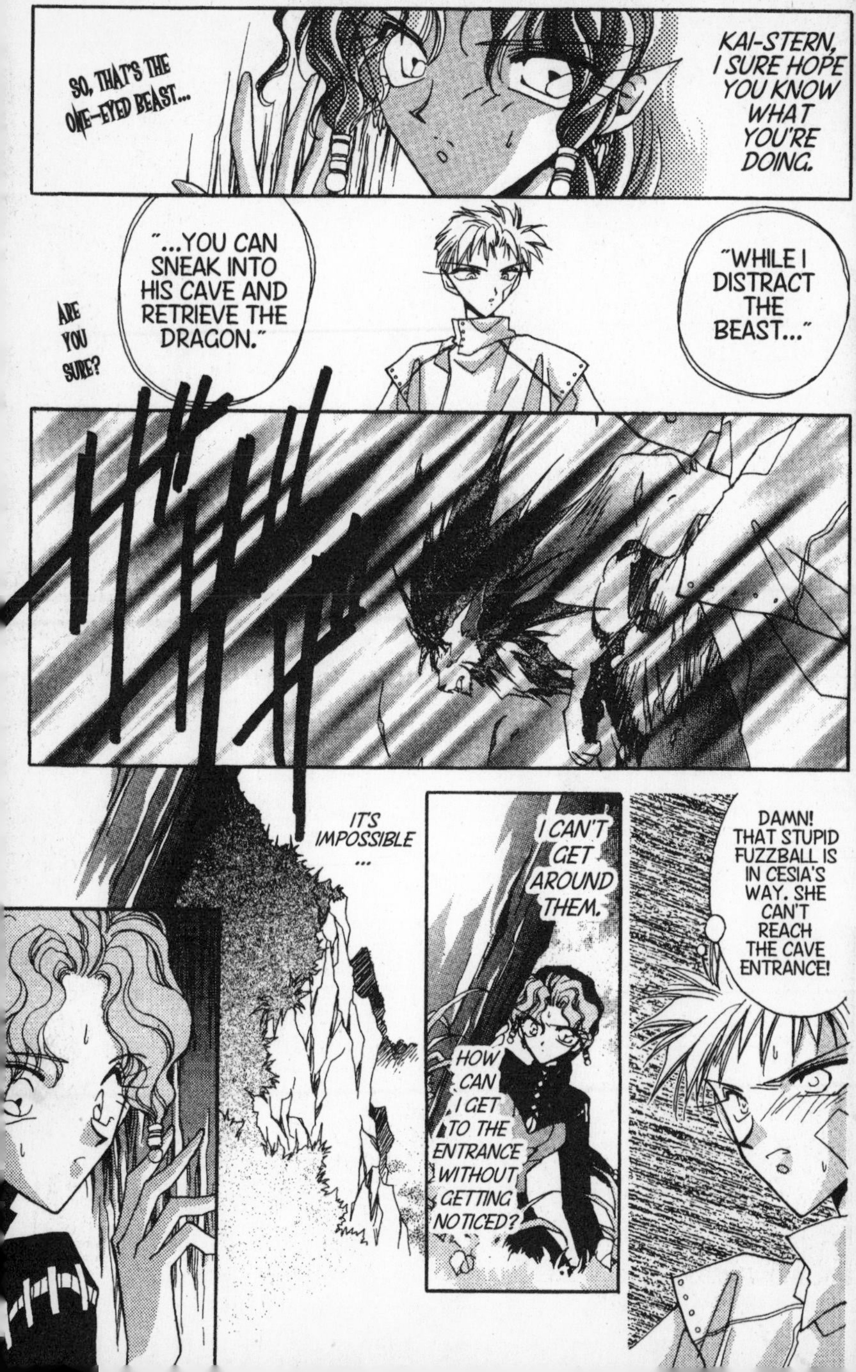
KAI-STERN, I SURE HOPE YOU KNOW WHAT YOU'RE DOING.
SO, THAT'S THE ONE-EYED BEAST...
"WHILE I DISTRACT THE BEAST..."
"...YOU CAN SNEAK INTO HIS CAVE AND RETRIEVE THE DRAGON."
ARE YOU SURE?
DAMN! THAT STUPID FUZZBALL IS IN CESIA'S WAY. SHE CAN'T REACH THE CAVE ENTRANCE!
I CAN'T GET AROUND THEM.
HOW CAN I GET TO THE ENTRANCE WITHOUT GETTING NOTICED?
IT'S IMPOSSIBLE ...

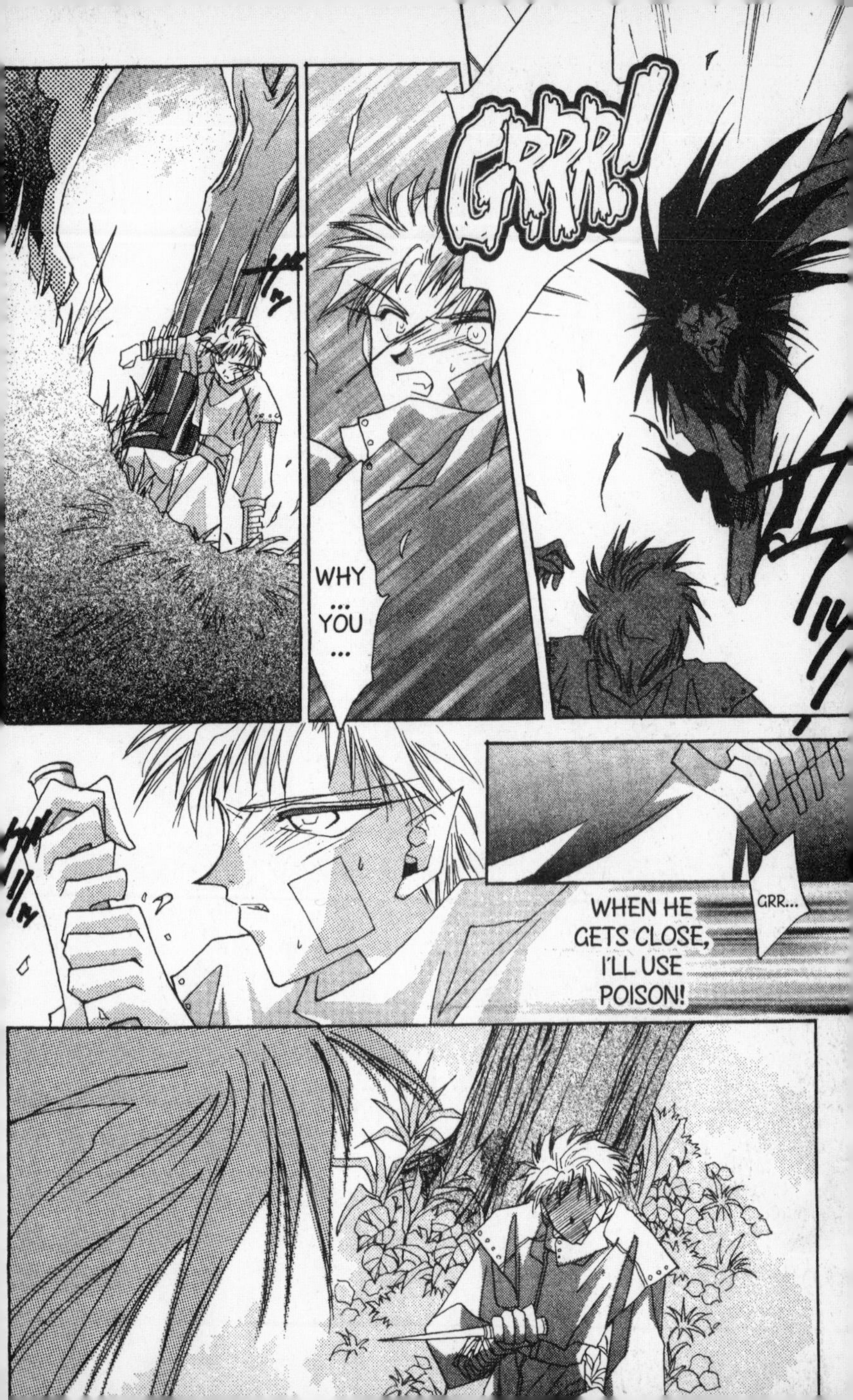
GRRR!
WHY ... YOU ...
GRR...
WHEN HE GETS CLOSE, I'LL USE POISON!

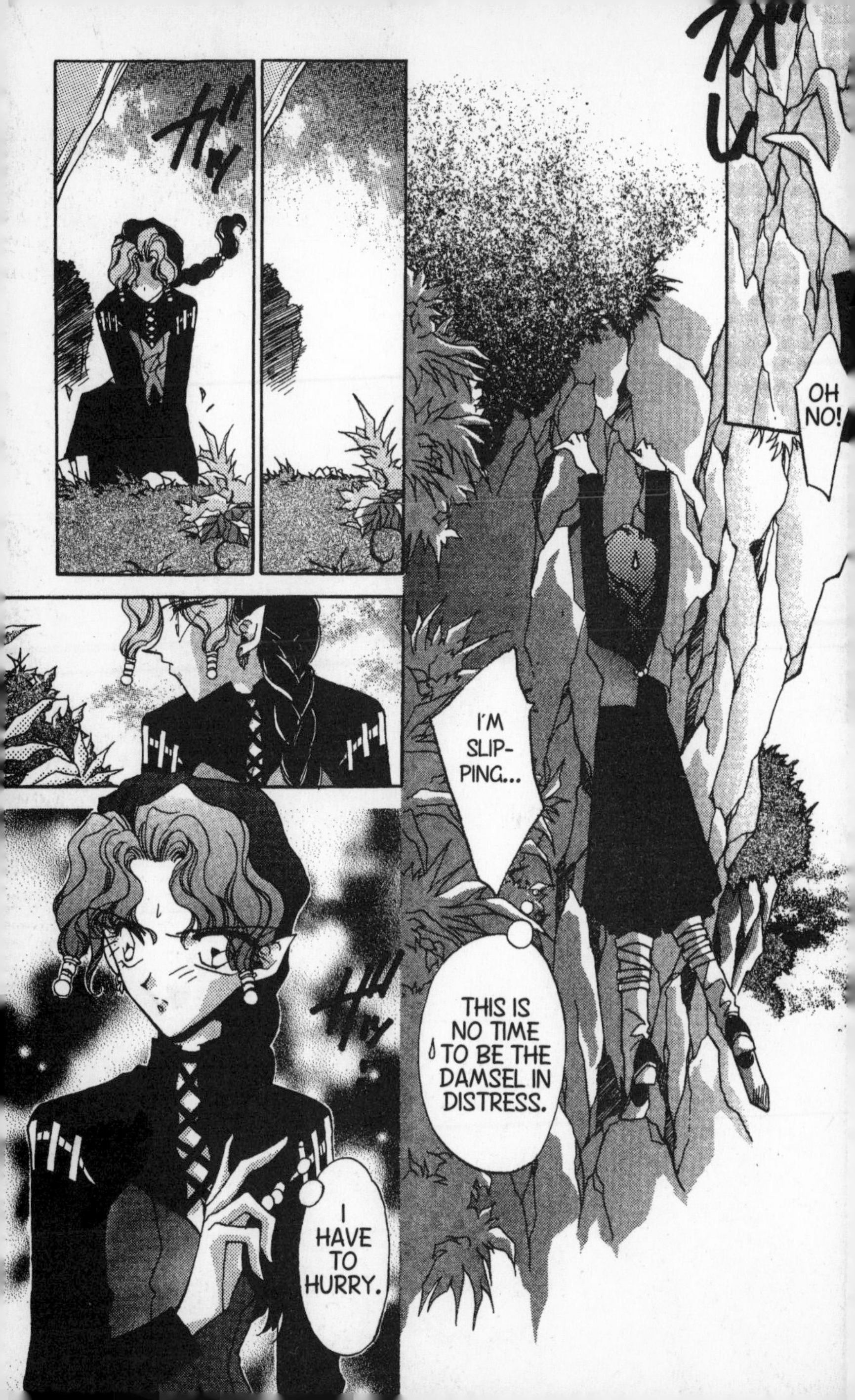
OH NO!
I'M SLIP-PING...
THIS IS NO TIME TO BE THE DAMSEL IN DISTRESS.
I HAVE TO HURRY.

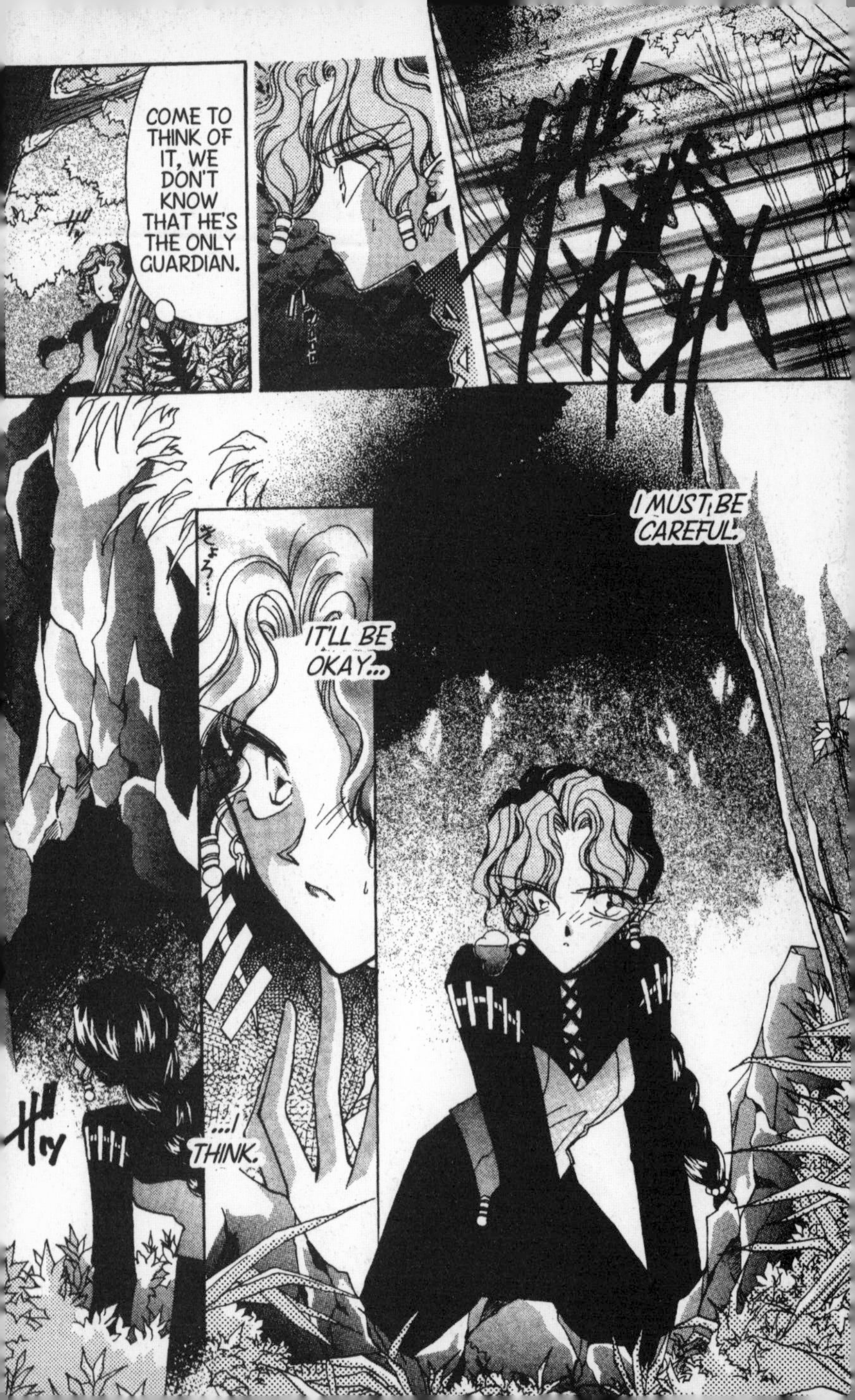
COME TO THINK OF IT, WE DON'T KNOW THAT HE'S THE ONLY GUARDIAN.
I MUST BE CAREFUL.
IT'LL BE OKAY...
...I THINK.

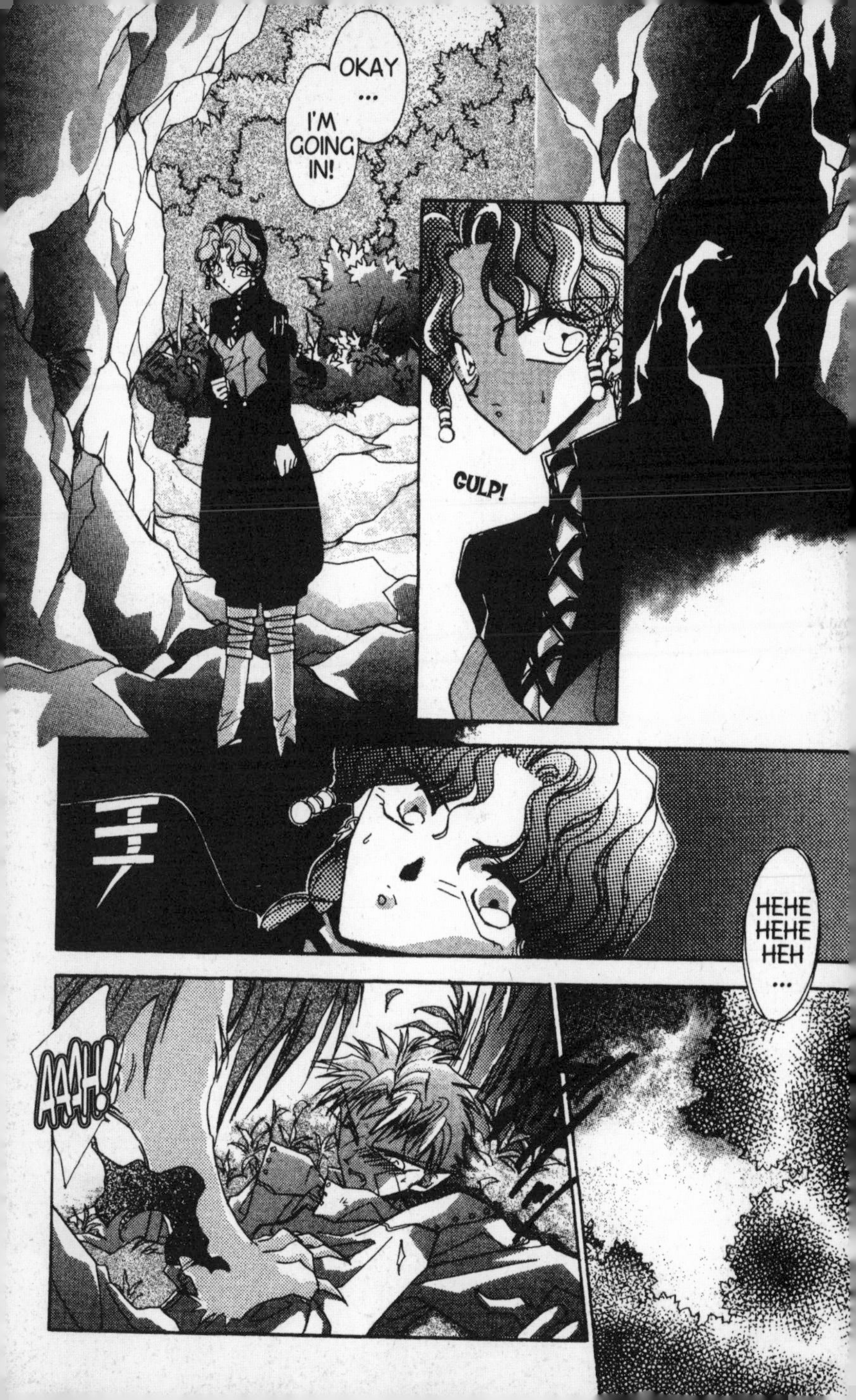
OKAY ... I'M GOING IN!
GULP!
HEHE HEHE HEH ...
AAAH!

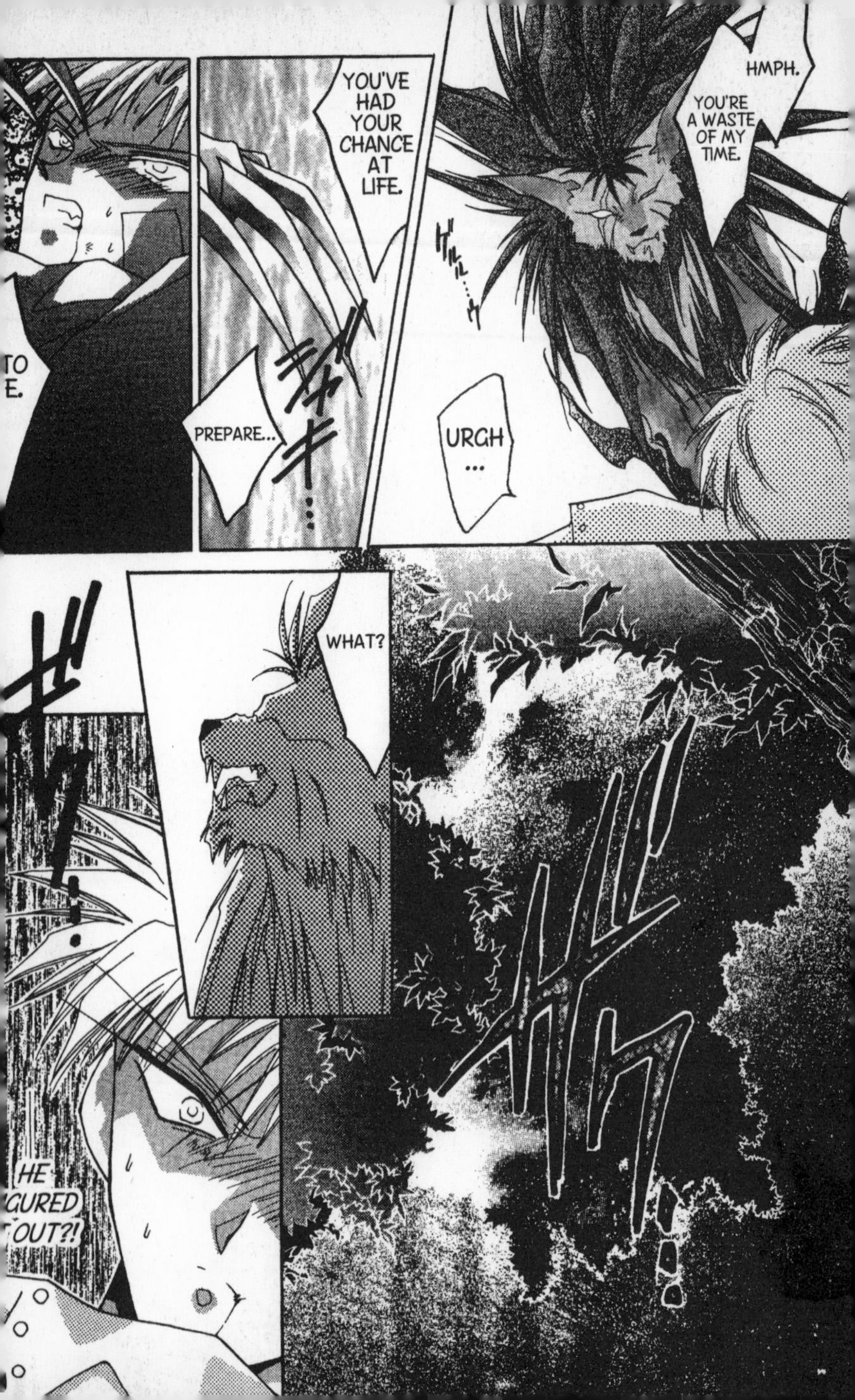
HMPH.
YOU'RE A WASTE OF MY TIME.
URGH ...
YOU'VE HAD YOUR CHANCE AT LIFE.
PREPARE...
TO
E.
WHAT?
HE
GURED
OUT?!

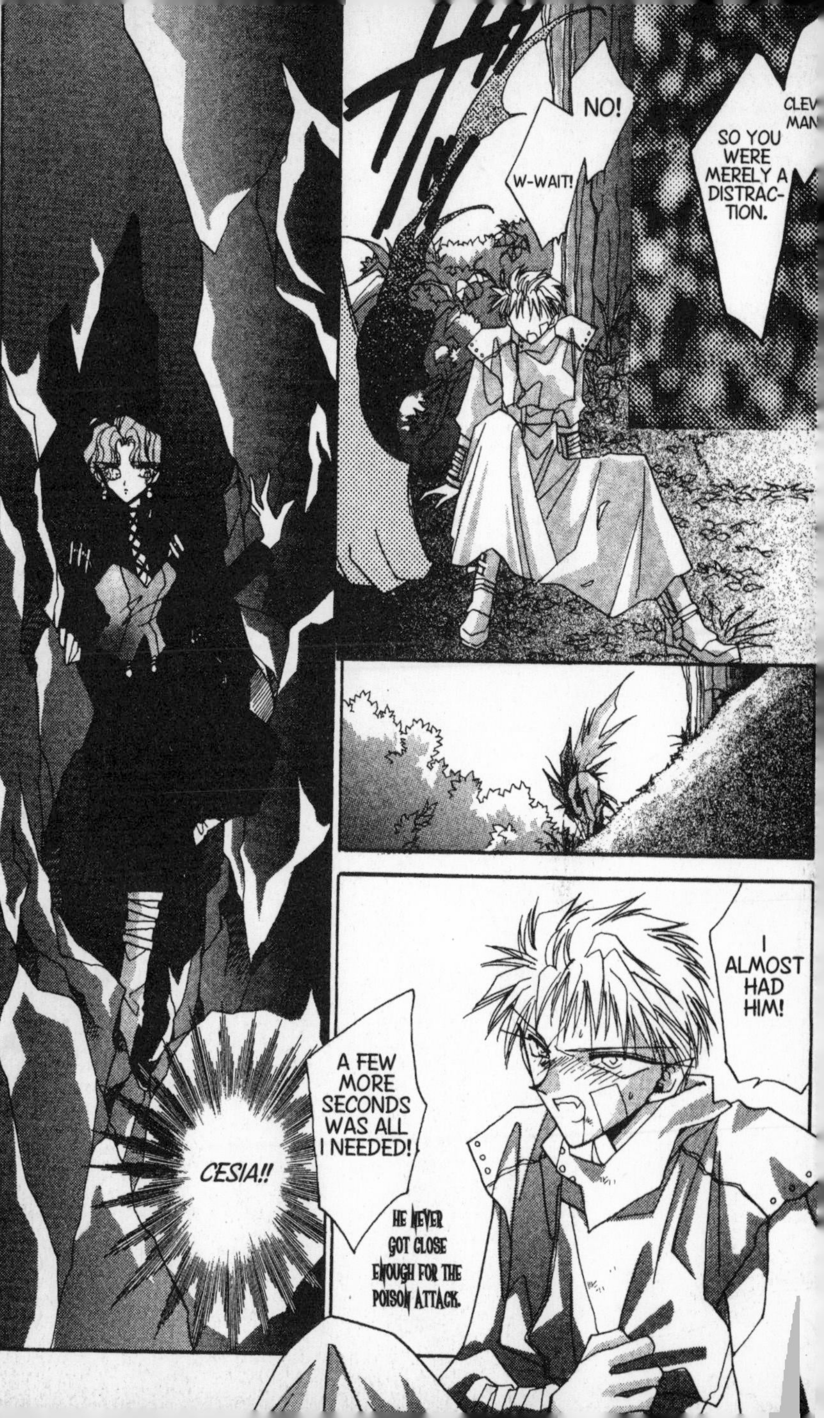
CLEV
MAN
SO YOU WERE MERELY A DISTRACTION.
NO!
W-WAIT!
I ALMOST HAD HIM!
A FEW MORE SECONDS WAS ALL I NEEDED!
HE NEVER GOT CLOSE ENOUGH FOR THE POISON ATTACK.
CESIA!!

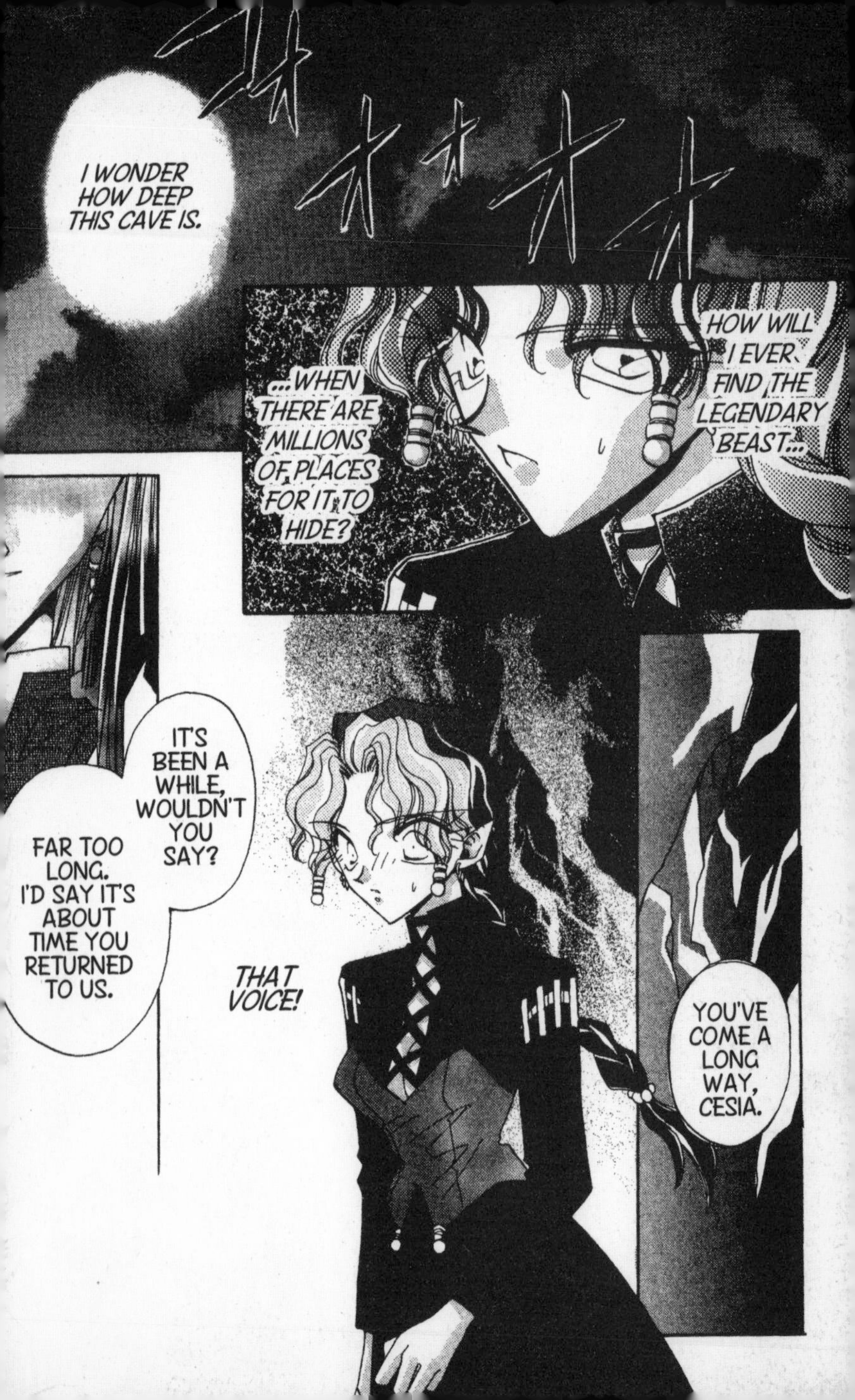
I WONDER HOW DEEP THIS CAVE IS.
HOW WILL I EVER FIND THE LEGENDARY BEAST...
...WHEN THERE ARE MILLIONS OF PLACES FOR IT TO HIDE?
YOU'VE COME A LONG WAY, CESIA.
THAT VOICE!
IT'S BEEN A WHILE, WOULDN'T YOU SAY?
FAR TOO LONG. I'D SAY IT'S ABOUT TIME YOU RETURNED TO US.

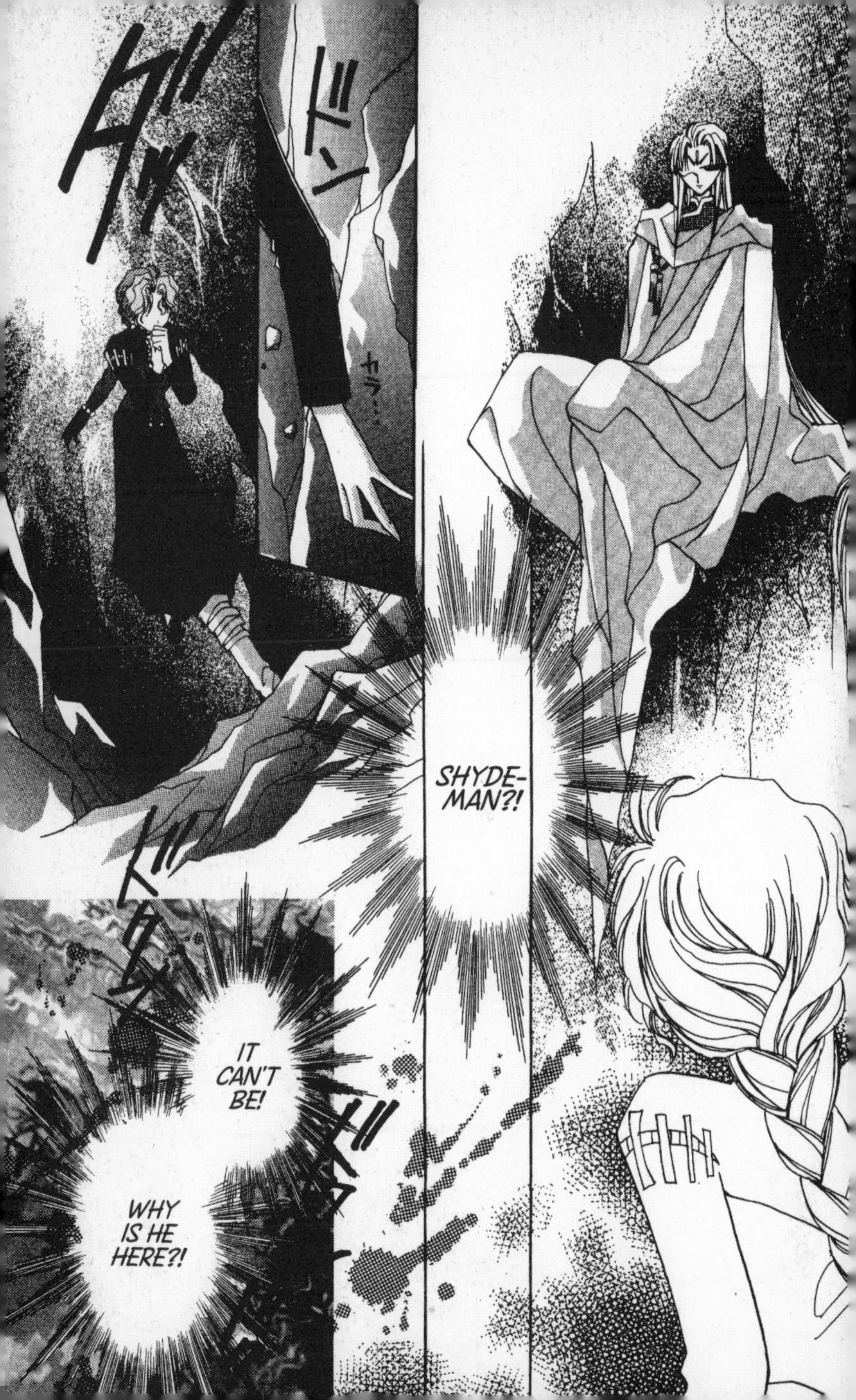
SHYDE-MAN?!
IT CAN'T BE!
WHY IS HE HERE?!

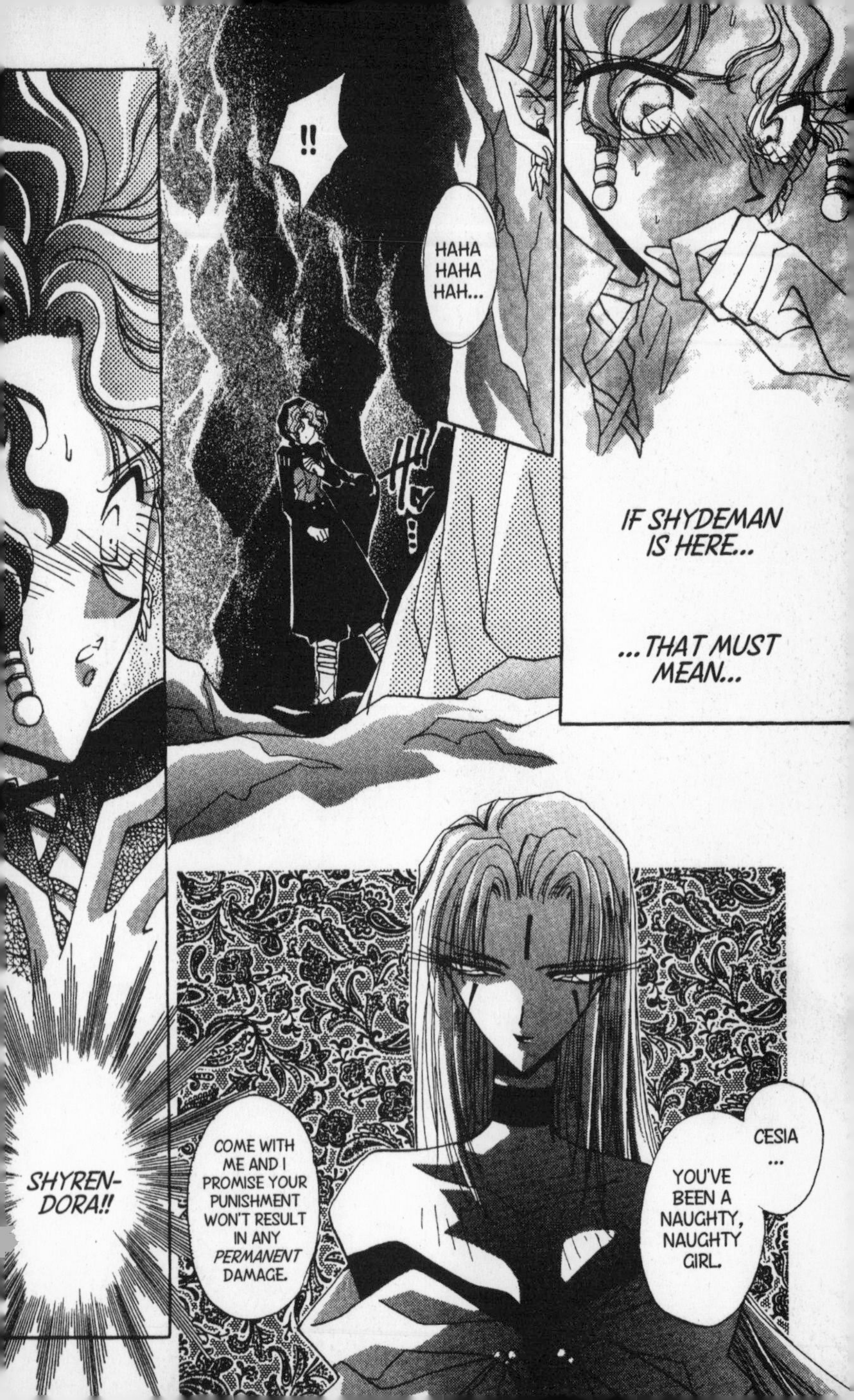
IF SHYDEMAN IS HERE...
...THAT MUST MEAN...
!!
HAHA HAHA HAH...
CESIA ...
YOU'VE BEEN A NAUGHTY, NAUGHTY GIRL.
COME WITH ME AND I PROMISE YOUR PUNISHMENT WON'T RESULT IN ANY *PERMANENT* DAMAGE.
SHYREN-DORA!!

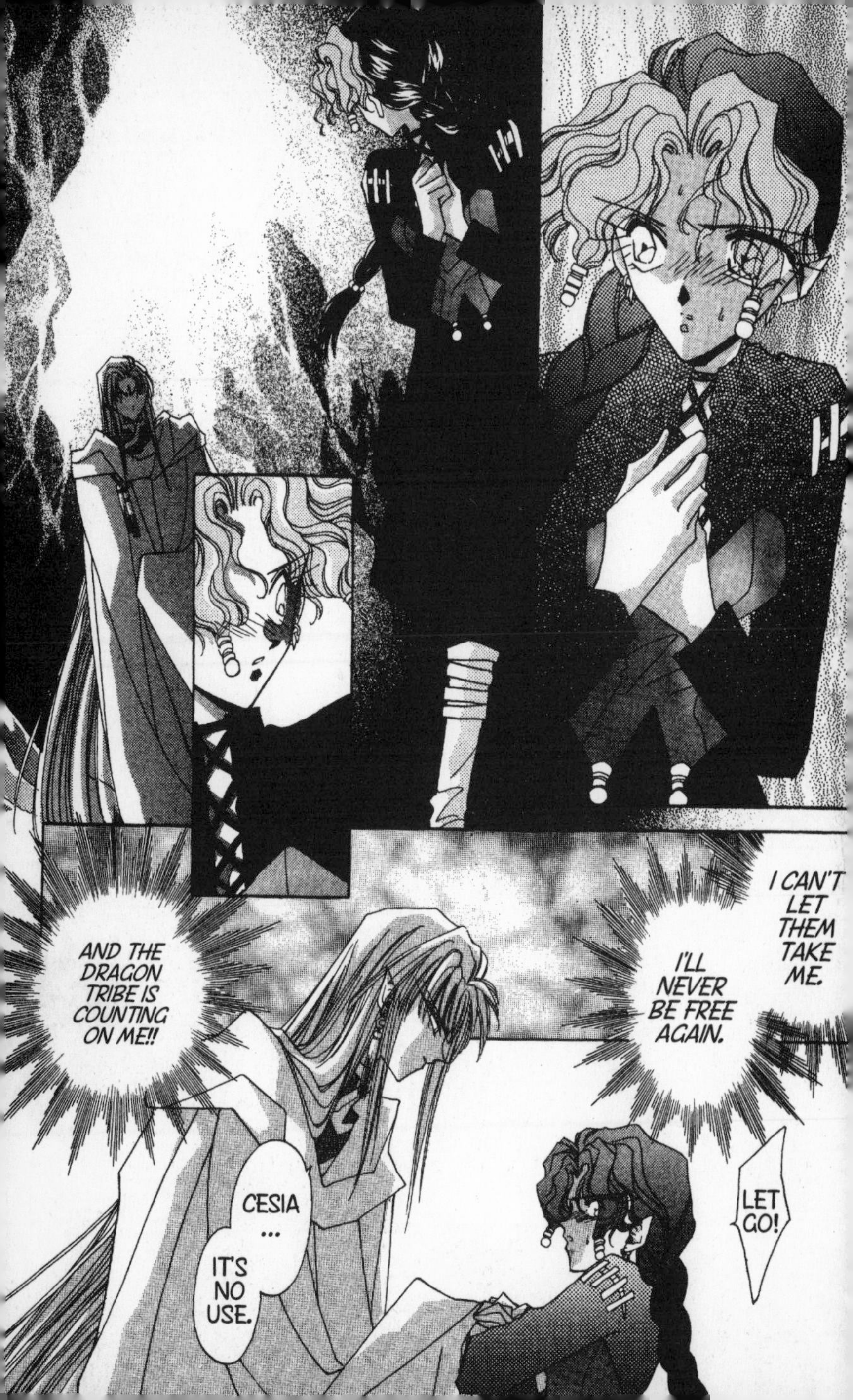
I CAN'T LET THEM TAKE ME.
I'LL NEVER BE FREE AGAIN.
AND THE DRAGON TRIBE IS COUNTING ON ME!!
LET GO!
CESIA ...
IT'S NO USE.

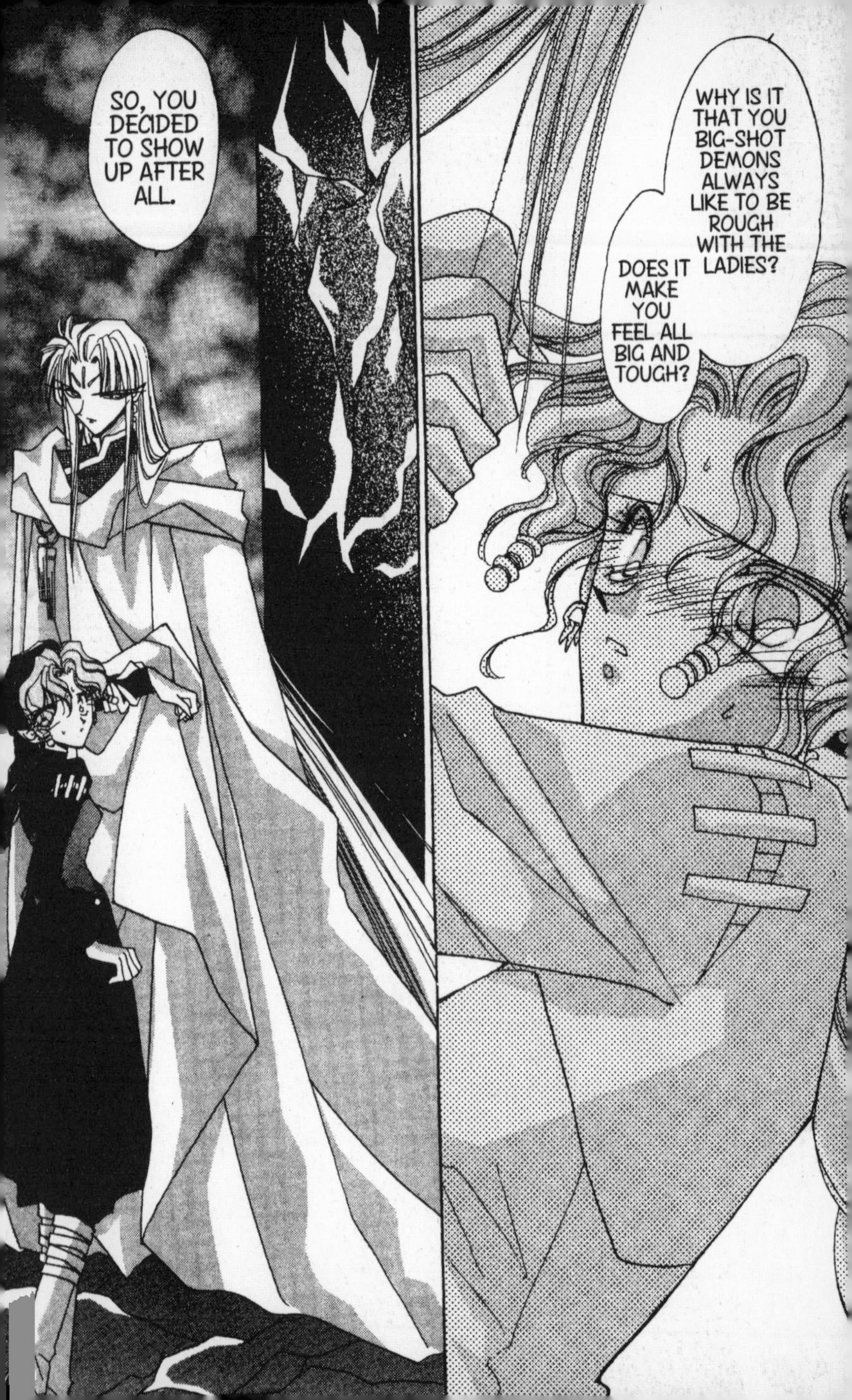
WHY IS IT THAT YOU BIG-SHOT DEMONS ALWAYS LIKE TO BE ROUGH WITH THE LADIES?
DOES IT MAKE YOU FEEL ALL BIG AND TOUGH?
SO, YOU DECIDED TO SHOW UP AFTER ALL.

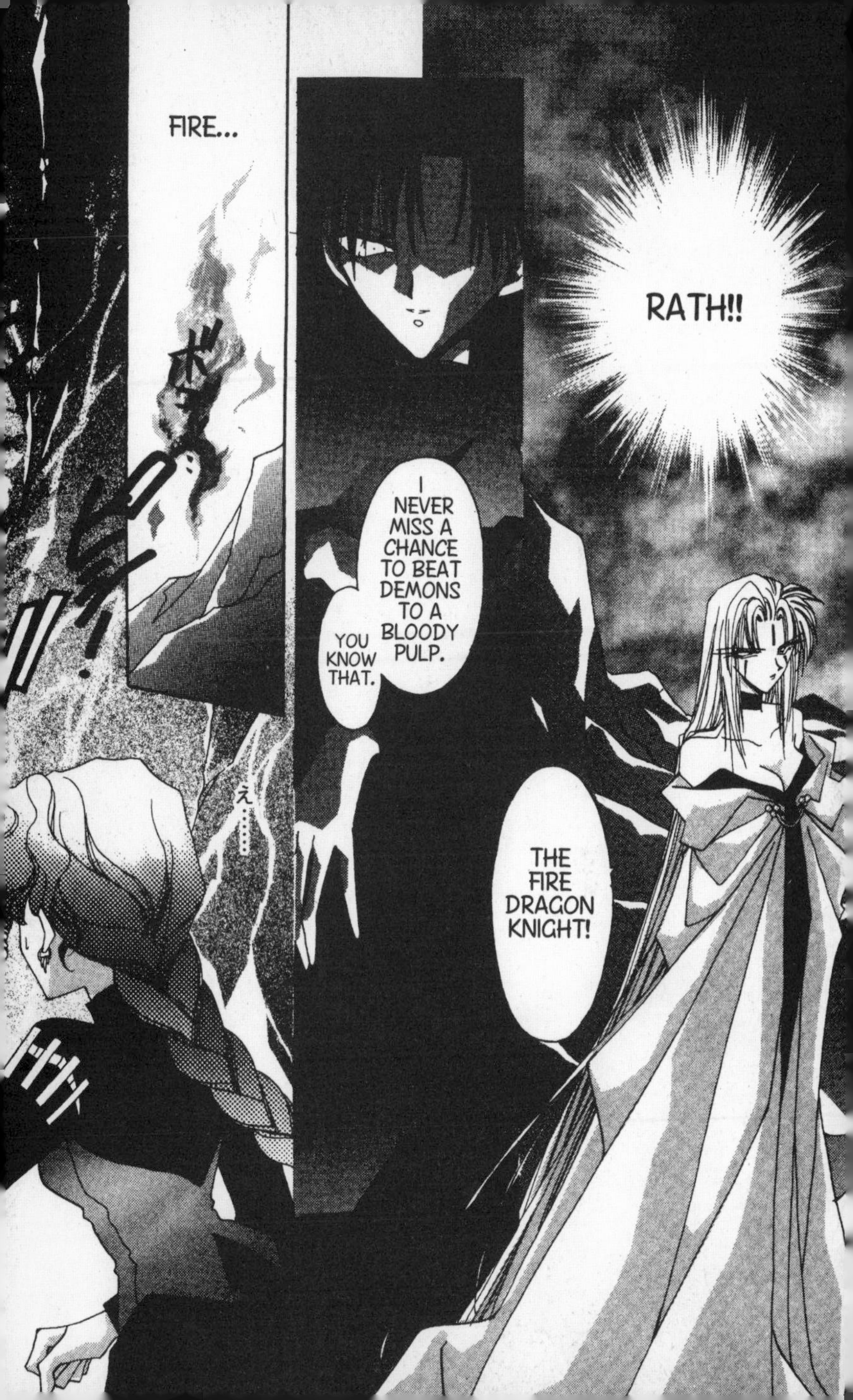
RATH!!
THE FIRE DRAGON KNIGHT!
I NEVER MISS A CHANCE TO BEAT DEMONS TO A BLOODY PULP.
YOU KNOW THAT.
FIRE...
え……

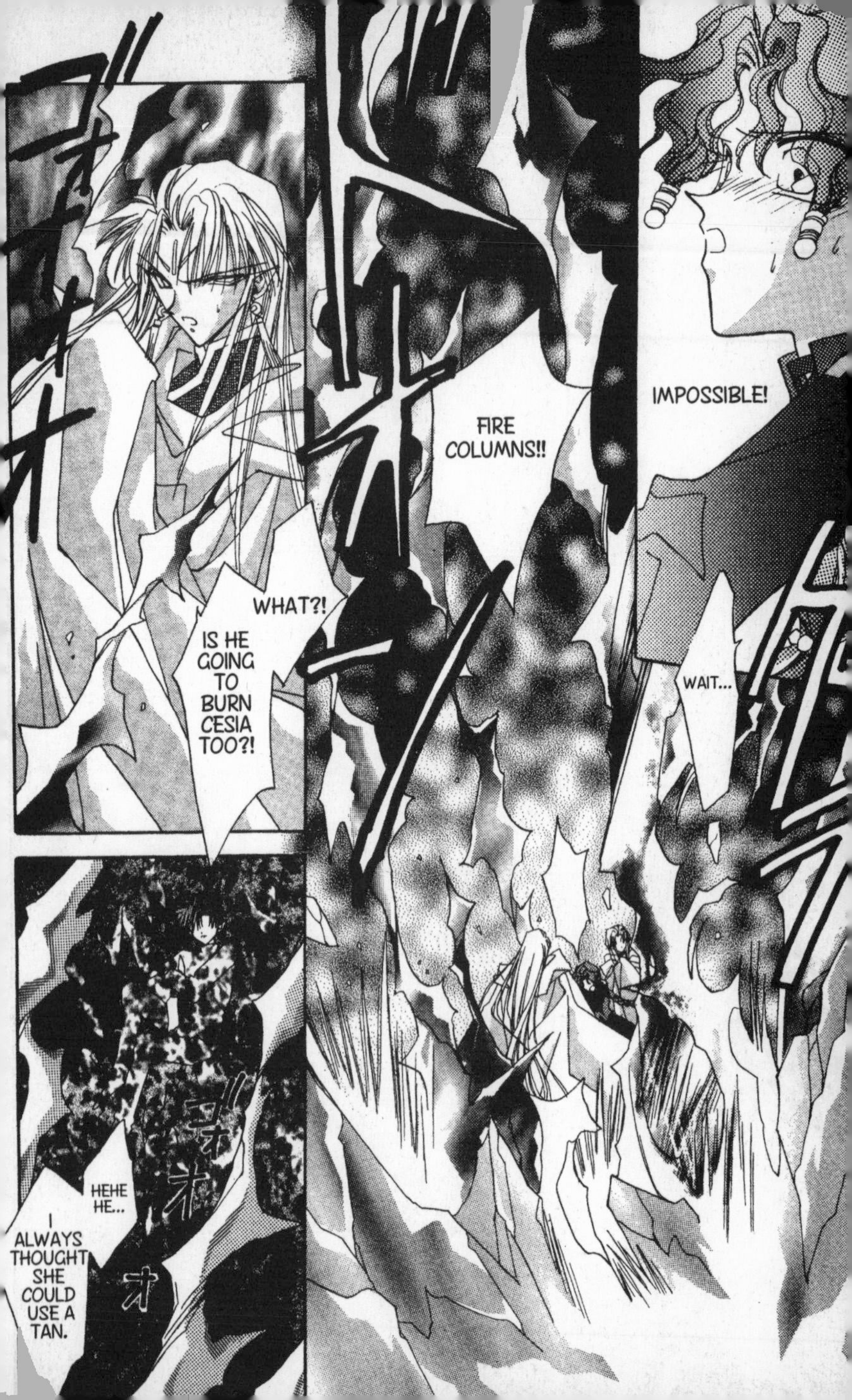
IMPOSSIBLE!
WAIT...
FIRE COLUMNS!!
WHAT?!
IS HE GOING TO BURN CESIA TOO?!
HEHE HE...
I ALWAYS THOUGHT SHE COULD USE A TAN.

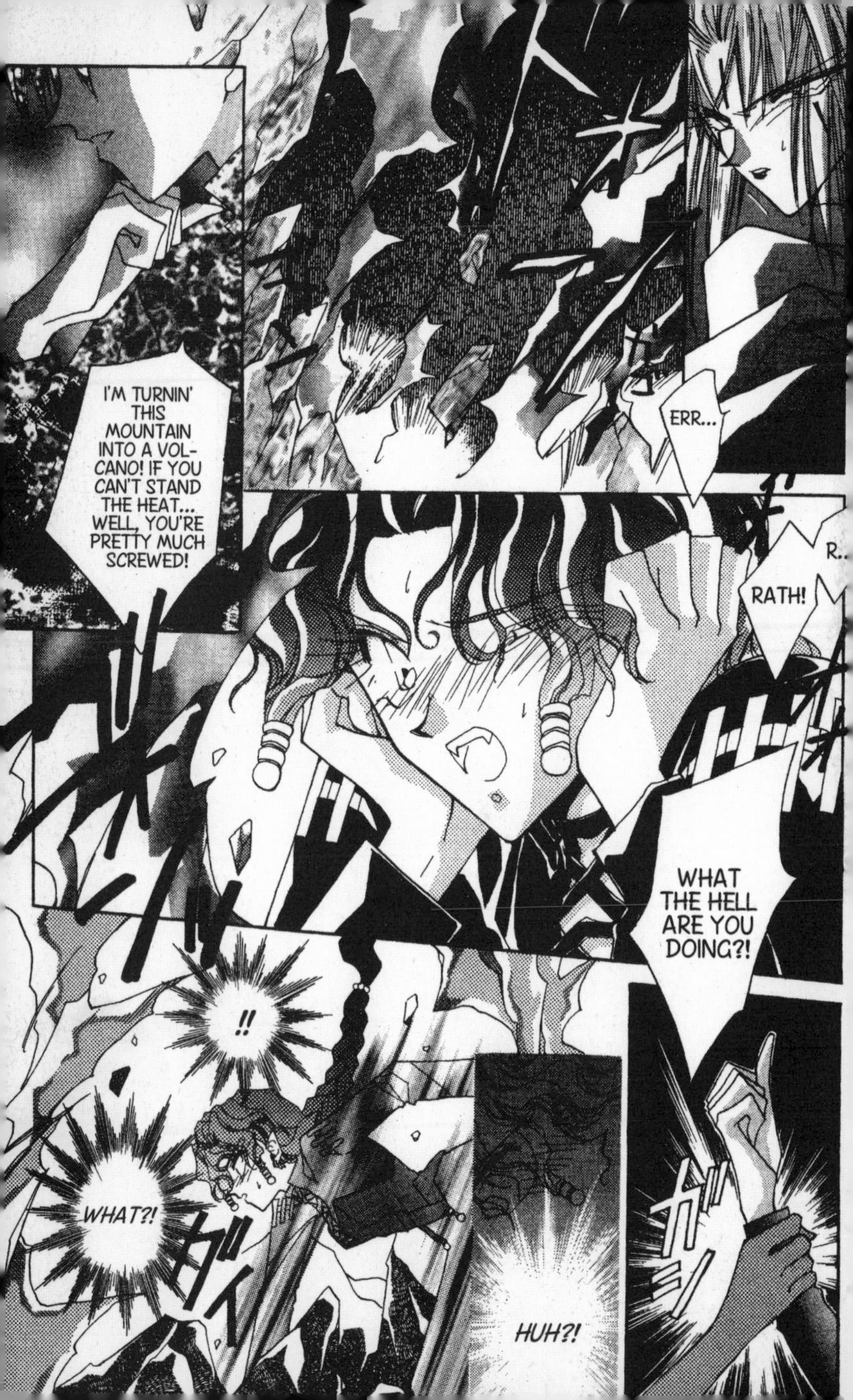
ERR...
I'M TURNIN' THIS MOUNTAIN INTO A VOLCANO! IF YOU CAN'T STAND THE HEAT... WELL, YOU'RE PRETTY MUCH SCREWED!
R...
RATH!
WHAT THE HELL ARE YOU DOING?!
HUH?!
!!
WHAT?!

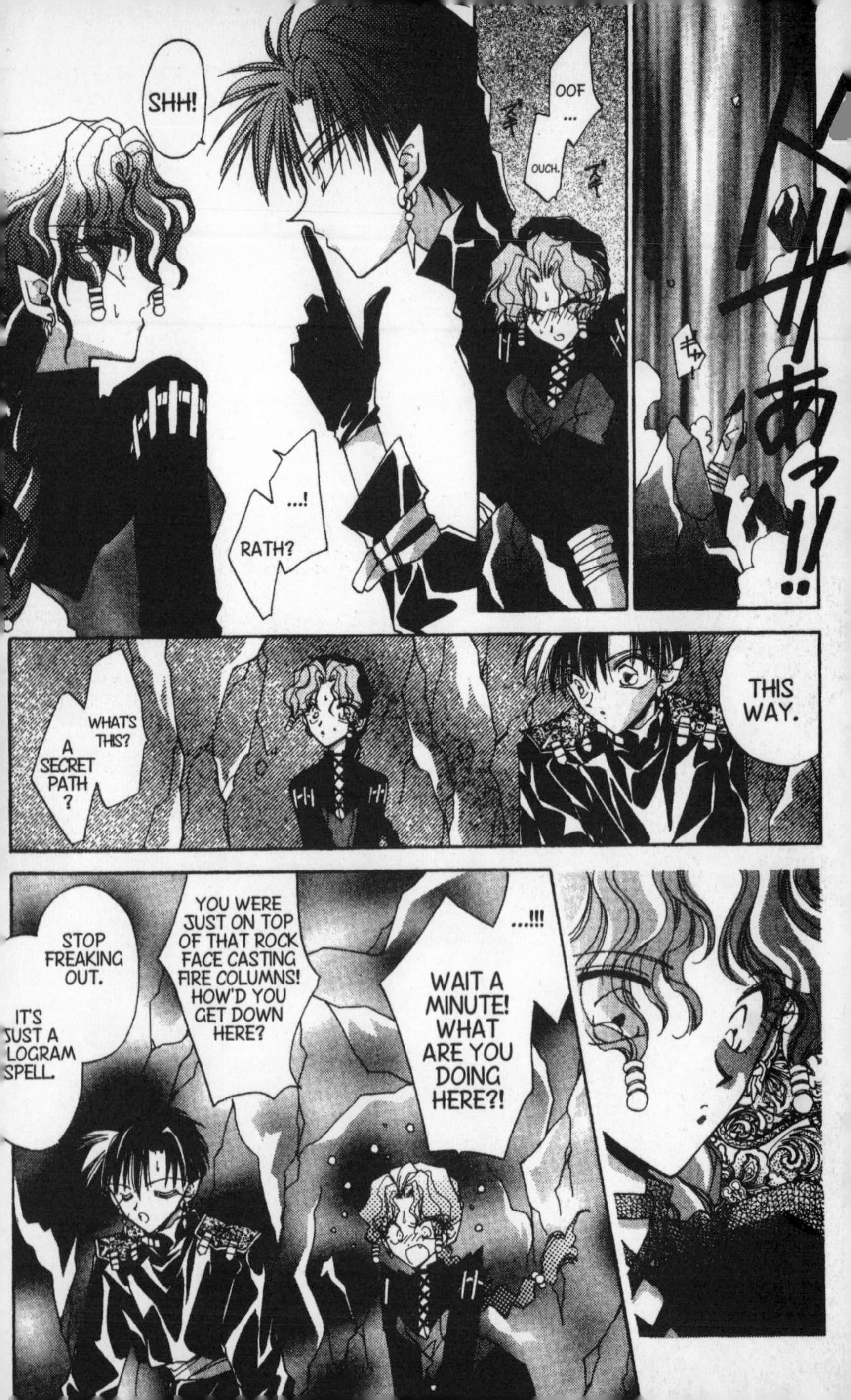
ドサあっ!!
OOF ... OUCH.
SHH!
...! RATH?
THIS WAY.
WHAT'S THIS? A SECRET PATH?
...!!!
WAIT A MINUTE! WHAT ARE YOU DOING HERE?!
YOU WERE JUST ON TOP OF THAT ROCK FACE CASTING FIRE COLUMNS! HOW'D YOU GET DOWN HERE?
STOP FREAKING OUT.
IT'S JUST A LOGRAM SPELL.

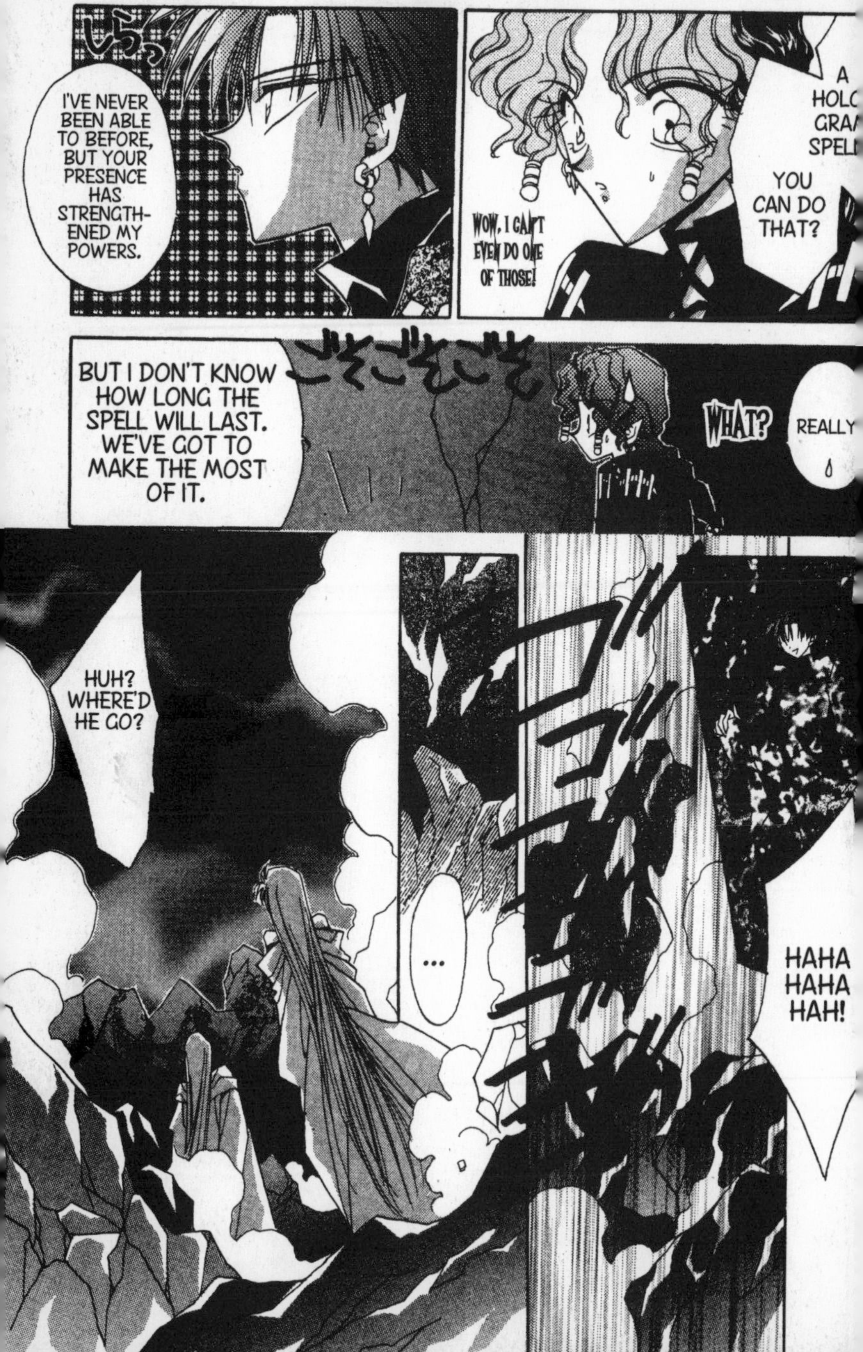
A HOLO GRA SPEL
YOU CAN DO THAT?
WOW, I CAN'T EVEN DO ONE OF THOSE!
しらっ
I'VE NEVER BEEN ABLE TO BEFORE, BUT YOUR PRESENCE HAS STRENGTH-ENED MY POWERS.
REALLY
WHAT?
ごそごそごそ
BUT I DON'T KNOW HOW LONG THE SPELL WILL LAST. WE'VE GOT TO MAKE THE MOST OF IT.
HAHA HAHA HAH!
...
HUH? WHERE'D HE GO?

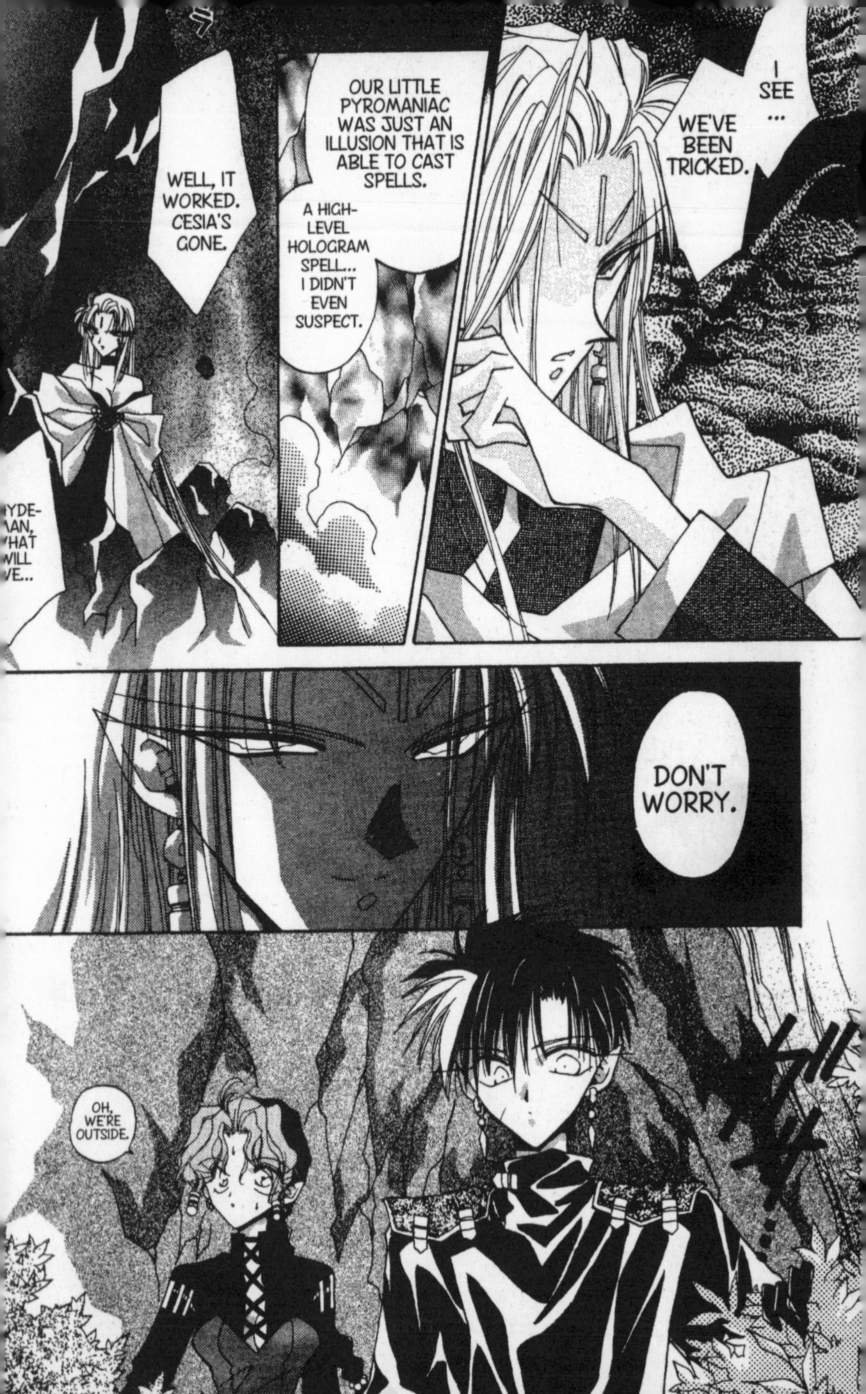
I SEE...
WE'VE BEEN TRICKED.
OUR LITTLE PYROMANIAC WAS JUST AN ILLUSION THAT IS ABLE TO CAST SPELLS.
A HIGH-LEVEL HOLOGRAM SPELL... I DIDN'T EVEN SUSPECT.
WELL, IT WORKED. CESIA'S GONE.
DON'T WORRY.
OH, WE'RE OUTSIDE.

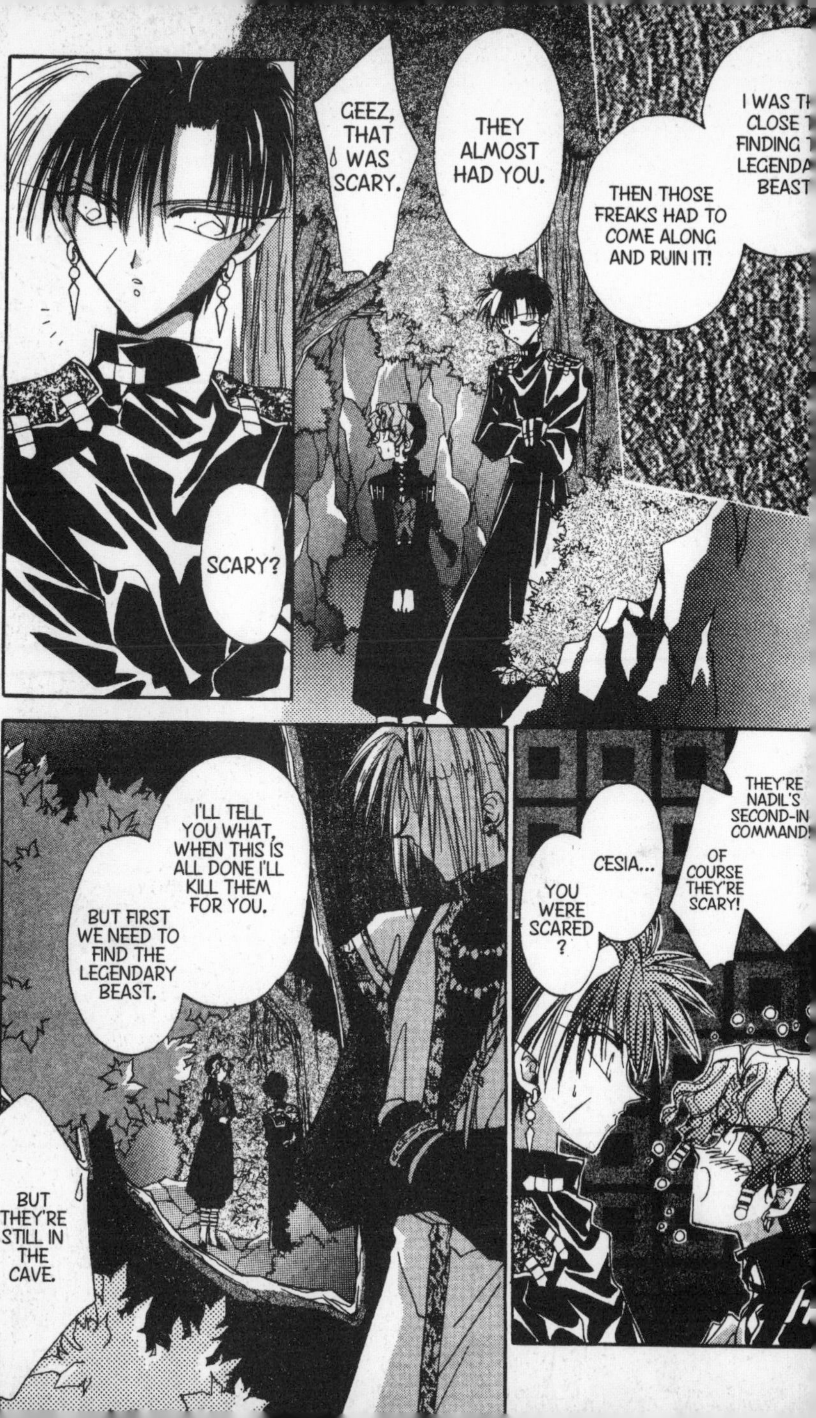
I WAS T CLOSE T FINDING T LEGENDA BEAST
THEN THOSE FREAKS HAD TO COME ALONG AND RUIN IT!
THEY ALMOST HAD YOU.
GEEZ, THAT WAS SCARY.
SCARY?
THEY'RE NADIL'S SECOND-IN COMMAND
OF COURSE THEY'RE SCARY!
CESIA...
YOU WERE SCARED?
I'LL TELL YOU WHAT, WHEN THIS IS ALL DONE I'LL KILL THEM FOR YOU.
BUT FIRST WE NEED TO FIND THE LEGENDARY BEAST.
BUT THEY'RE STILL IN THE CAVE.

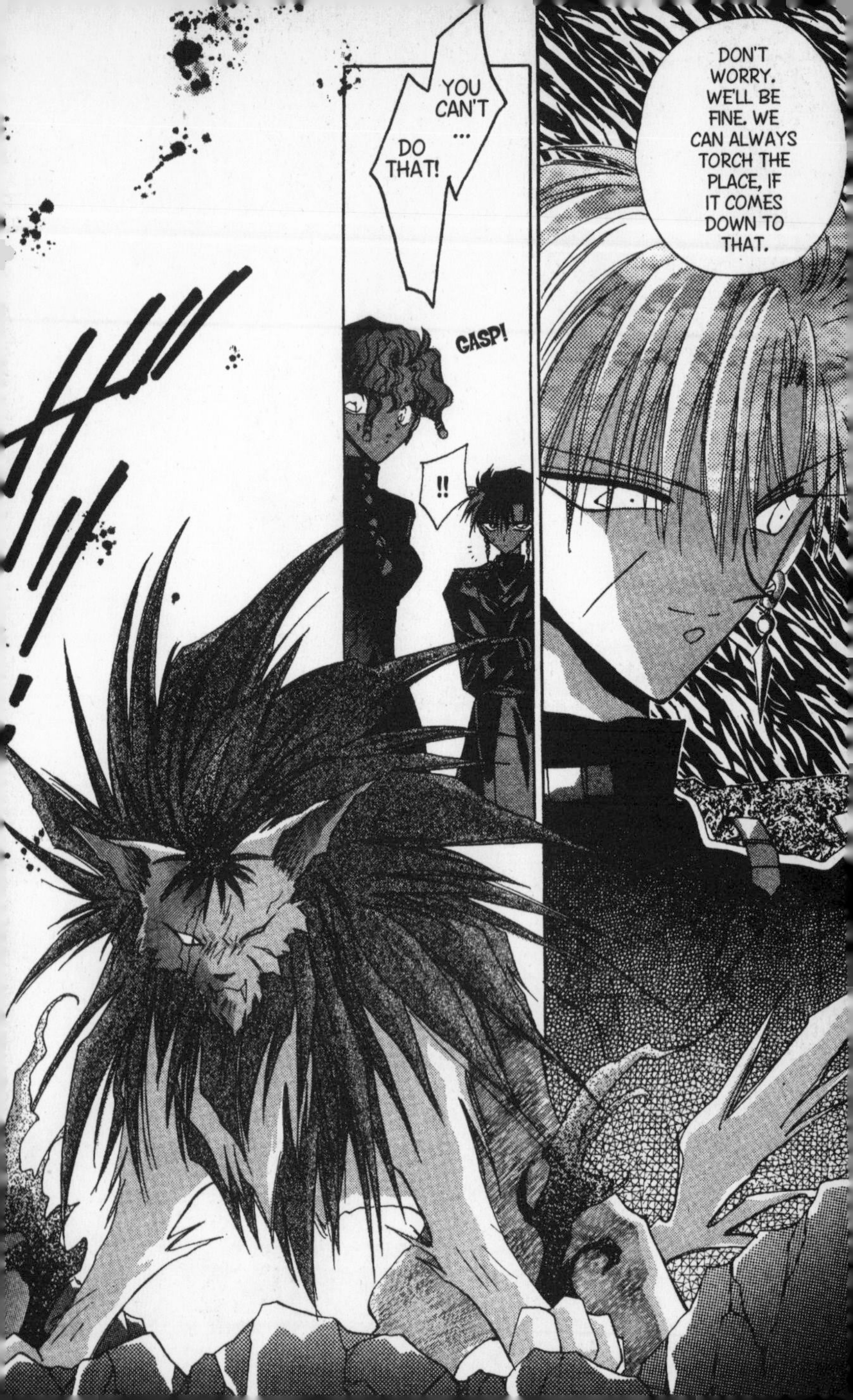
DON'T WORRY. WE'LL BE FINE. WE CAN ALWAYS TORCH THE PLACE, IF IT COMES DOWN TO THAT.
YOU CAN'T ... DO THAT!
GASP!
!!

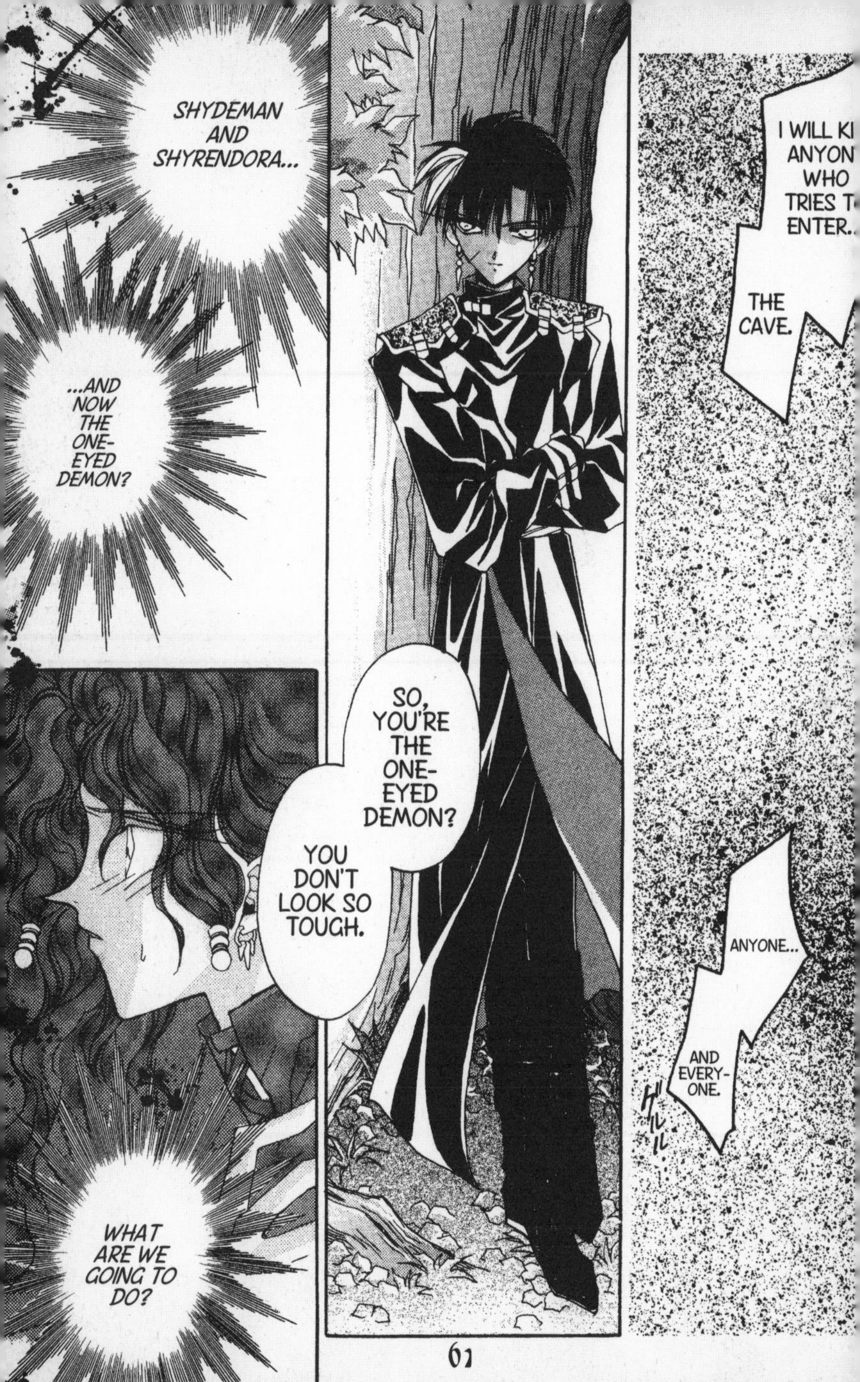
I WILL KI ANYON WHO TRIES T ENTER..
THE CAVE.
ANYONE...
AND EVERY-ONE.
SO, YOU'RE THE ONE-EYED DEMON?
YOU DON'T LOOK SO TOUGH.
SHYDEMAN AND SHYRENDORA...
...AND NOW THE ONE-EYED DEMON?
WHAT ARE WE GOING TO DO?

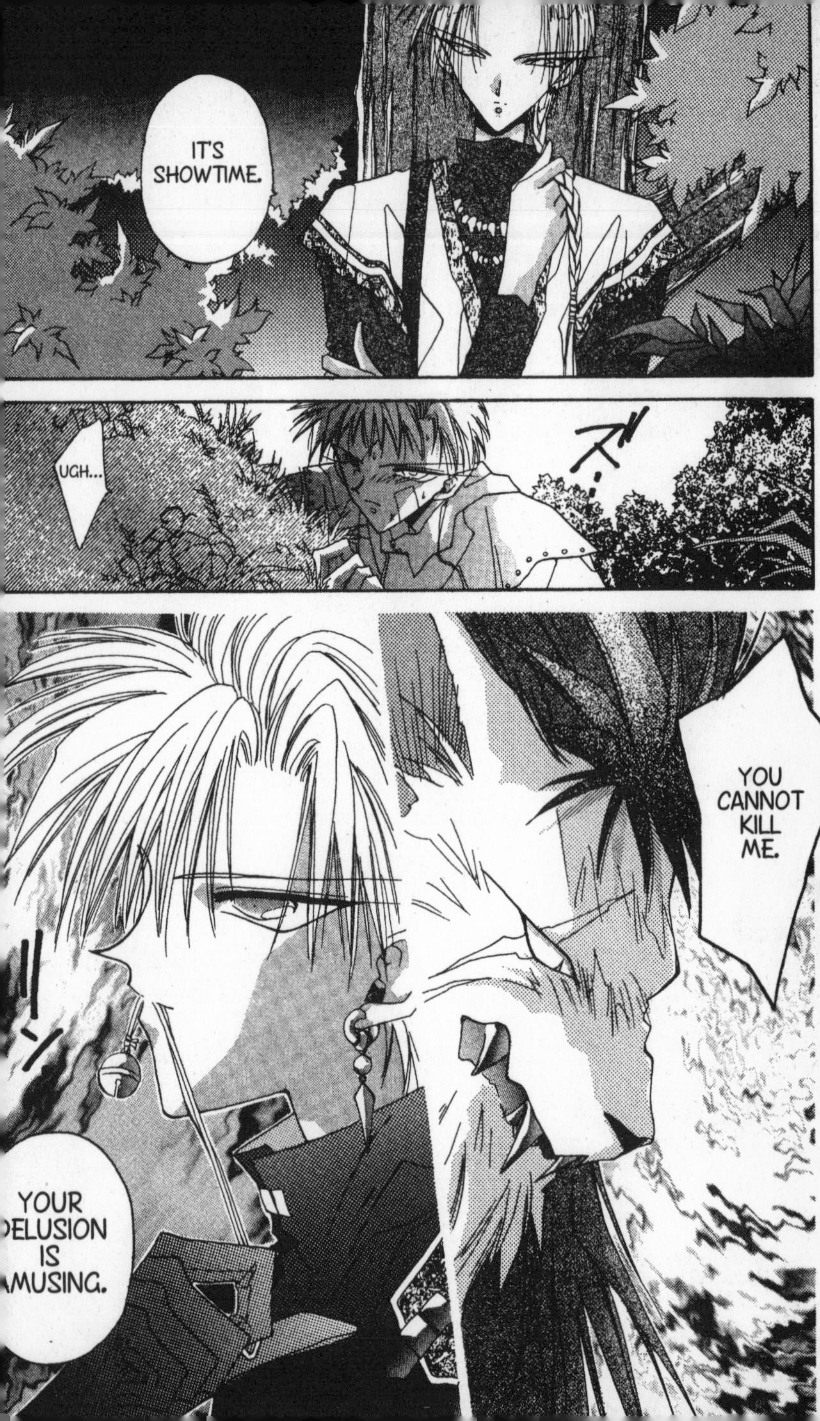
IT'S SHOWTIME.
UGH...
YOU CANNOT KILL ME.
YOUR ELUSION IS MUSING.

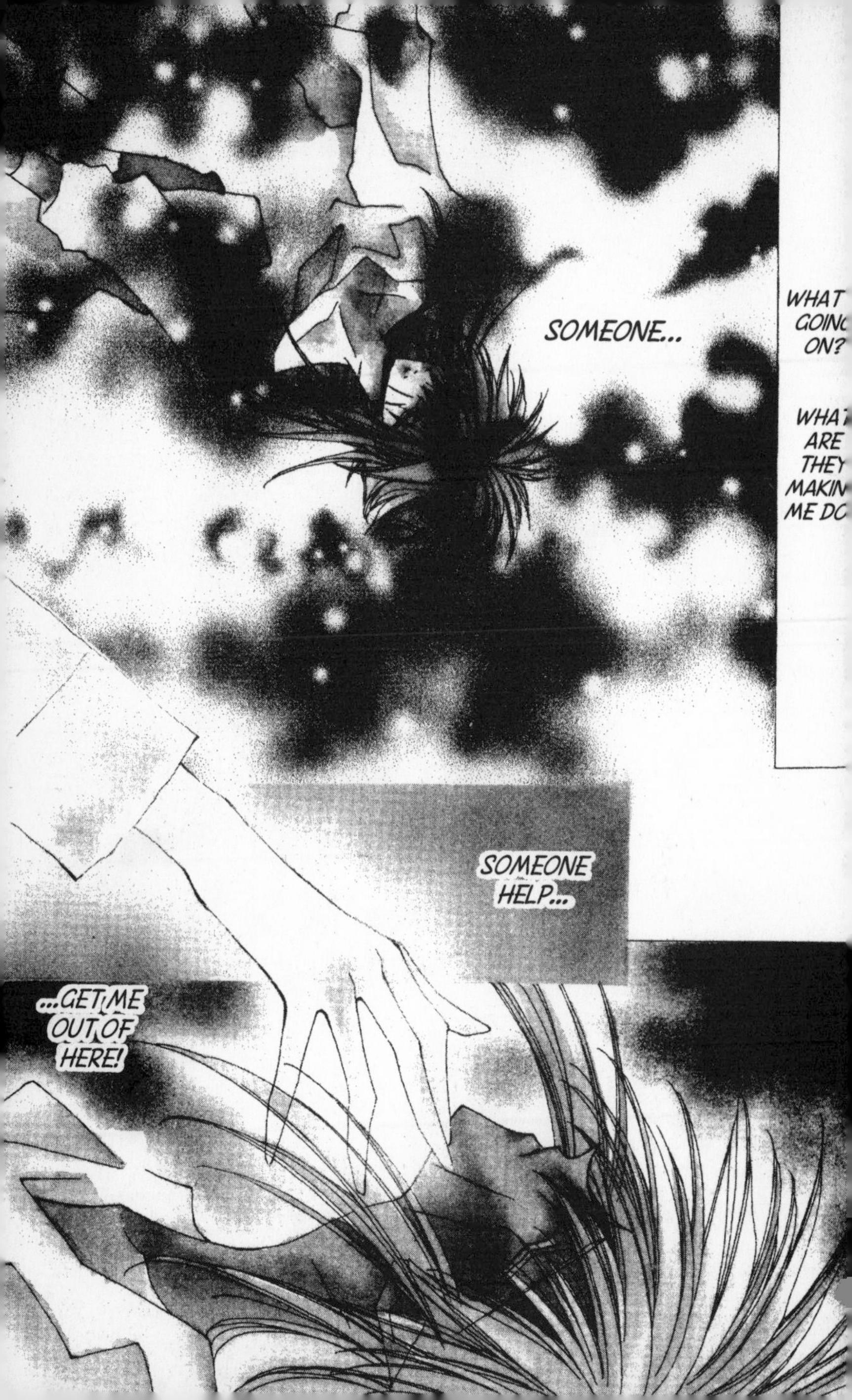
WHAT GOIN ON?
WHAT ARE THEY MAKIN ME DO
SOMEONE...
SOMEONE HELP...
...GET ME OUT OF HERE!

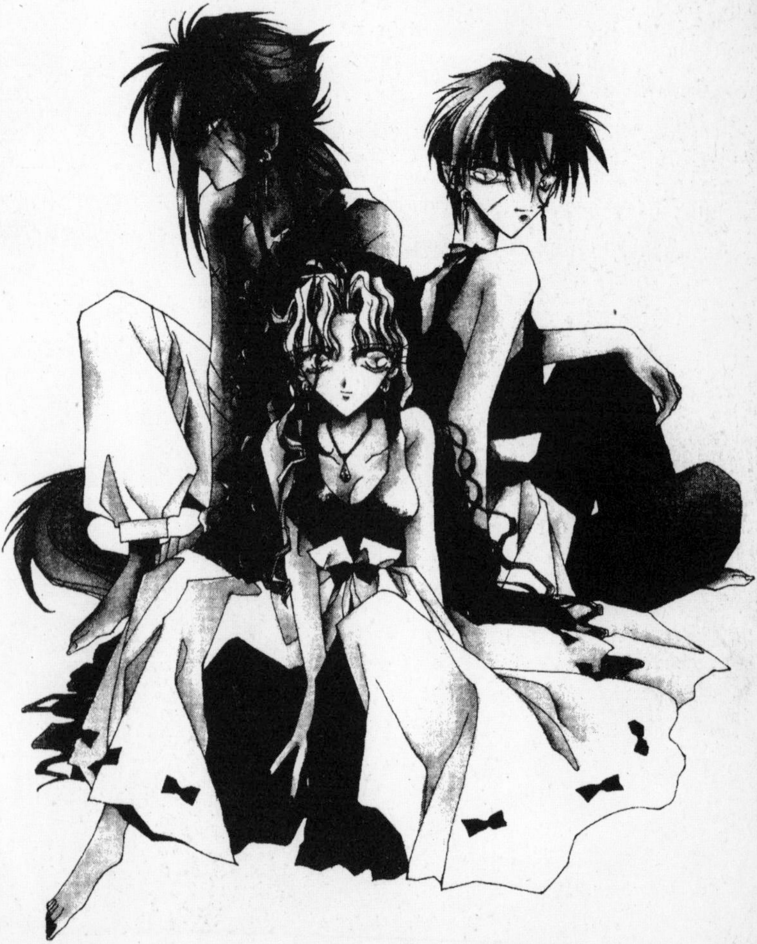

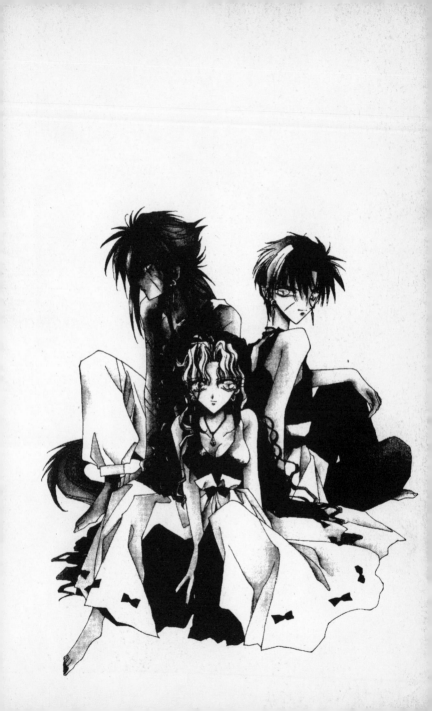

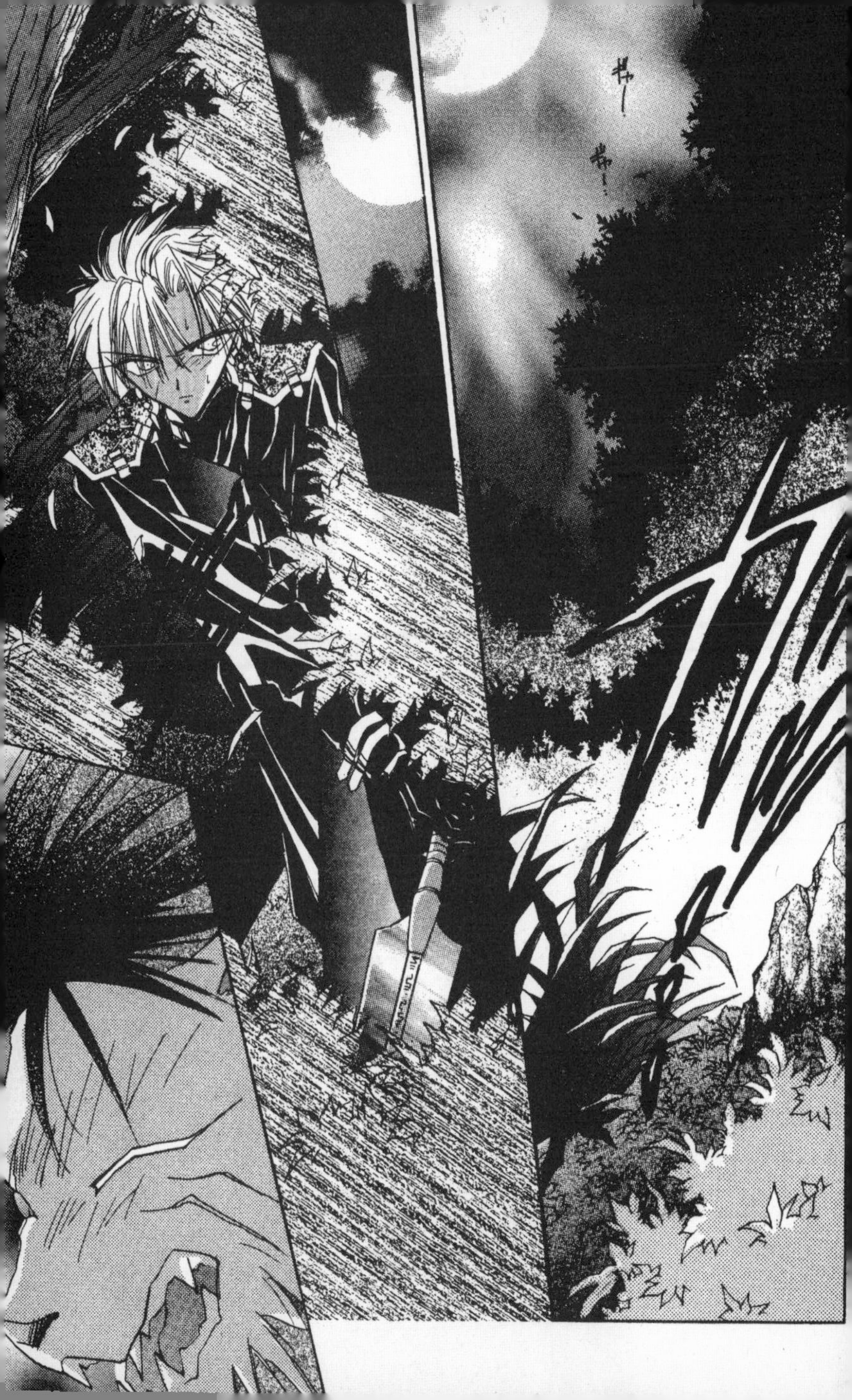
ギャー
ギャー…

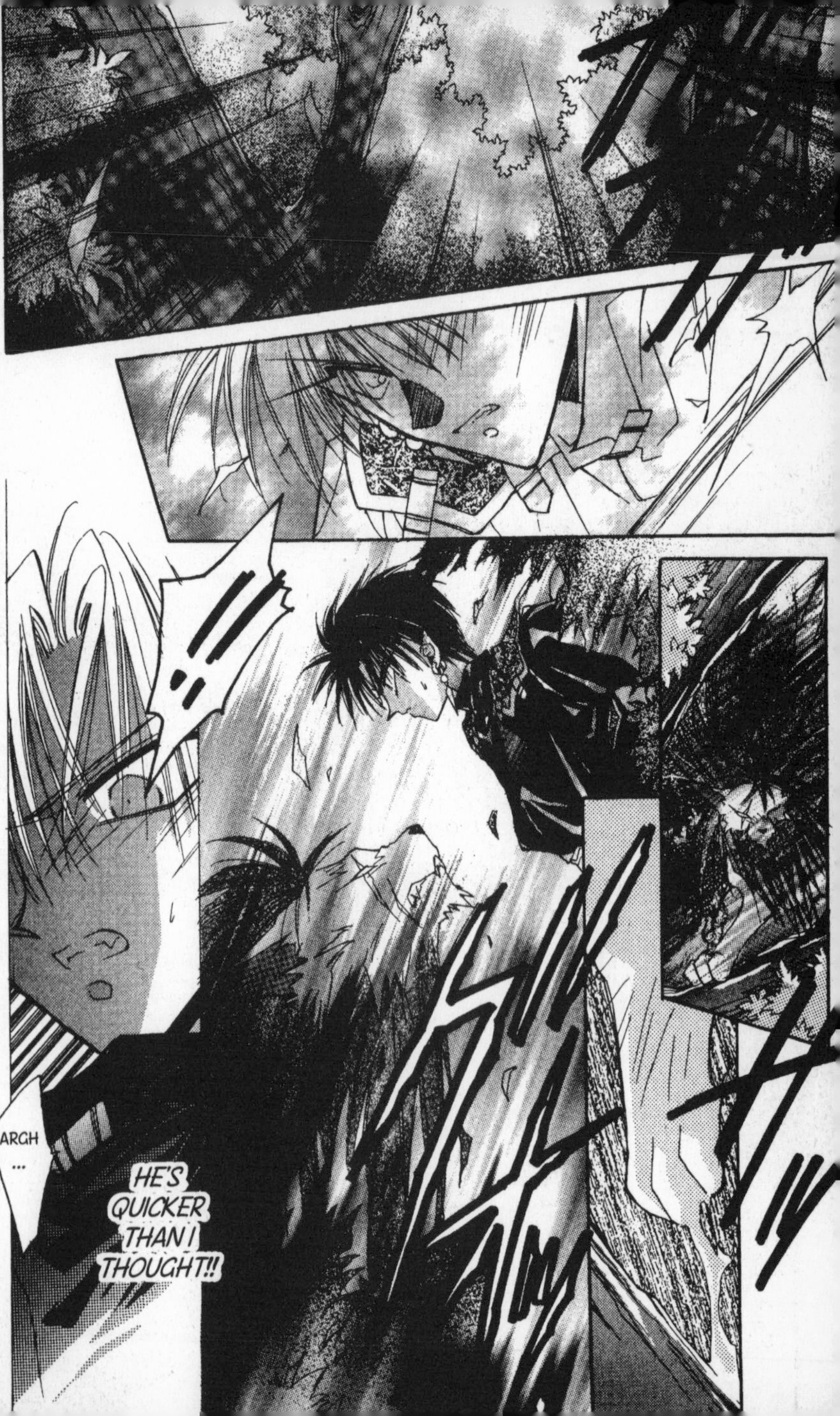
!!
ARGH
...
HE'S QUICKER THAN I THOUGHT!!

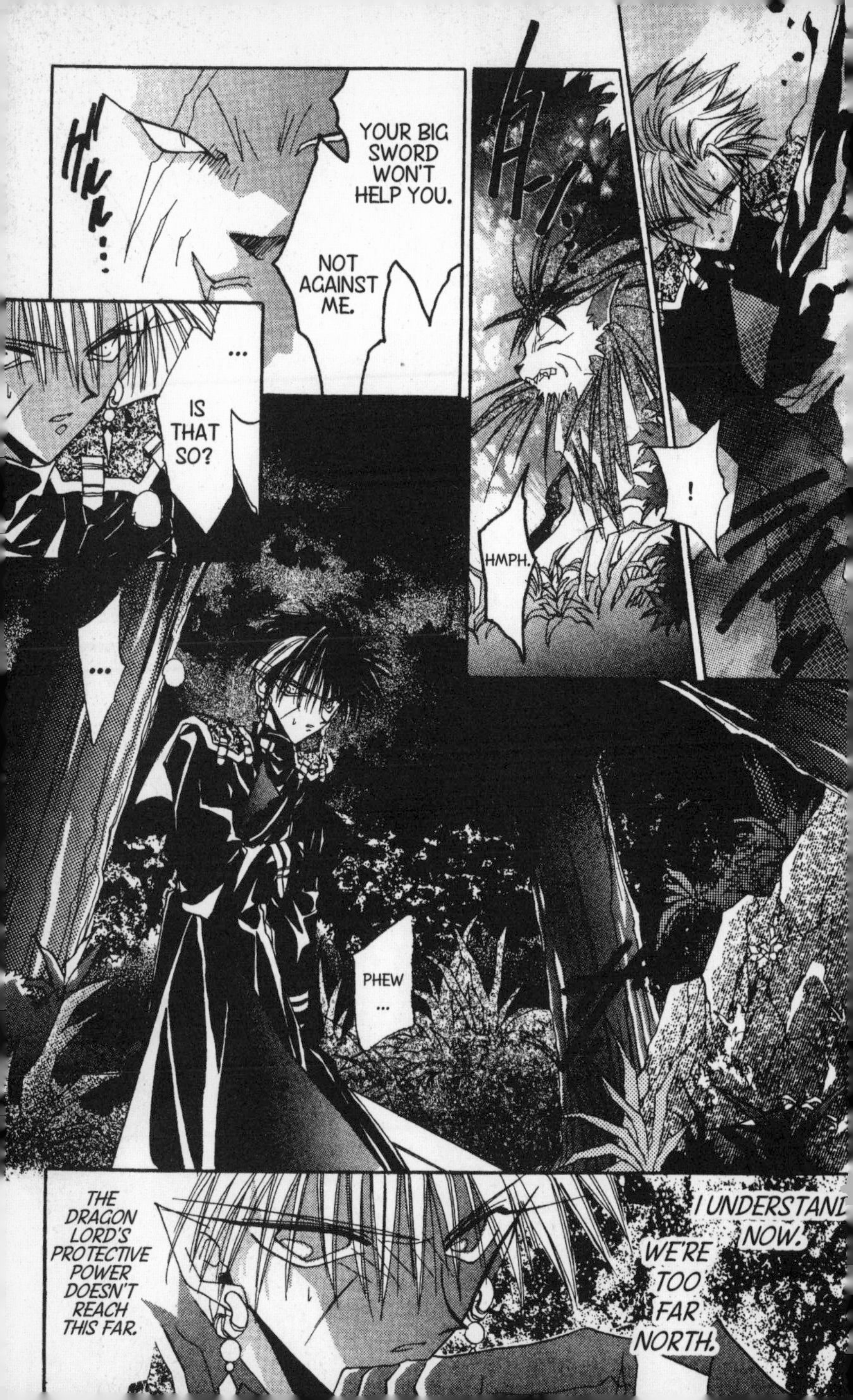
!
HMPH.
YOUR BIG SWORD WON'T HELP YOU.
NOT AGAINST ME.
...
IS THAT SO?
...
PHEW ...
I UNDERSTAND NOW.
WE'RE TOO FAR NORTH.
THE DRAGON LORD'S PROTECTIVE POWER DOESN'T REACH THIS FAR.

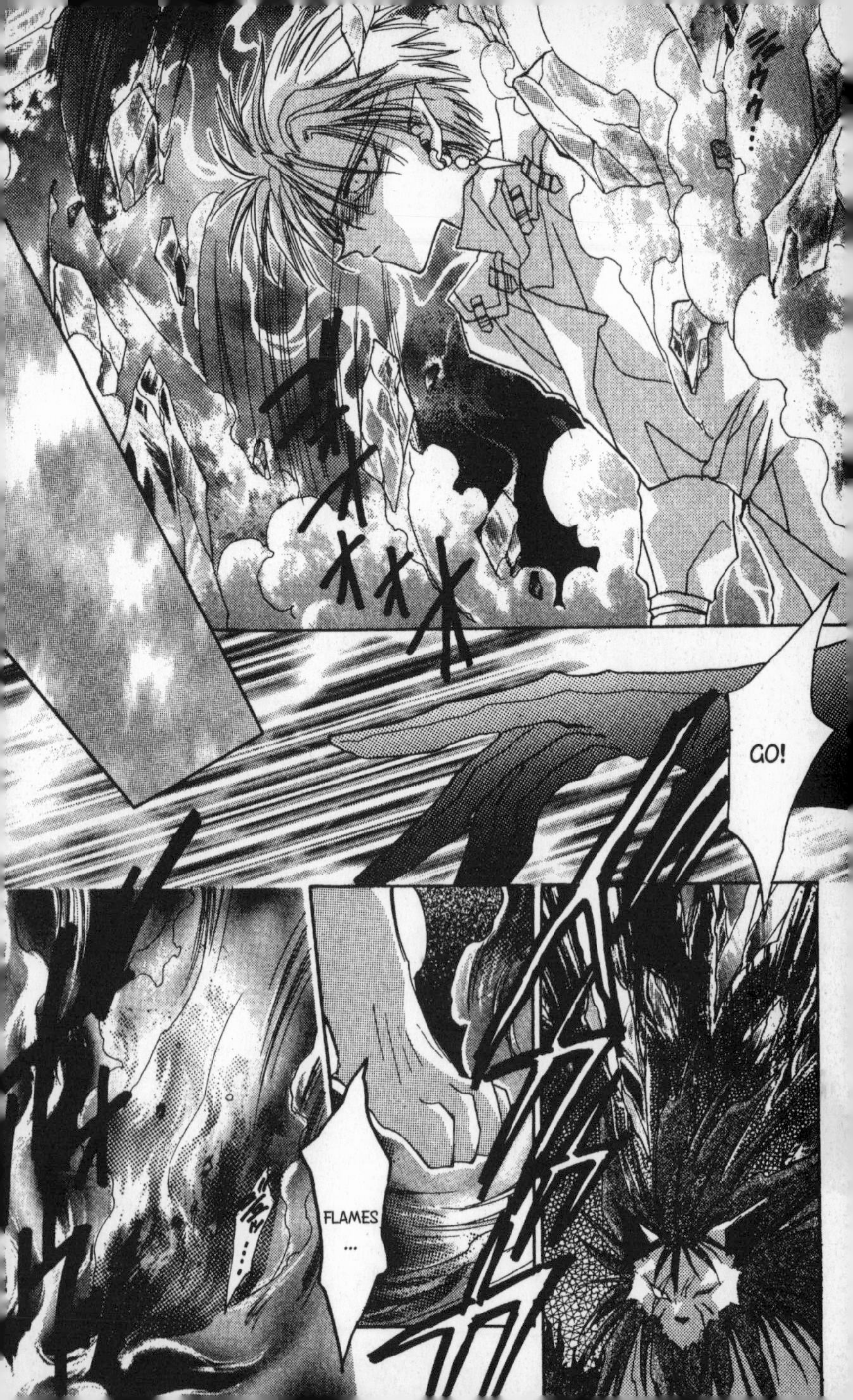
GO!
FLAMES ...

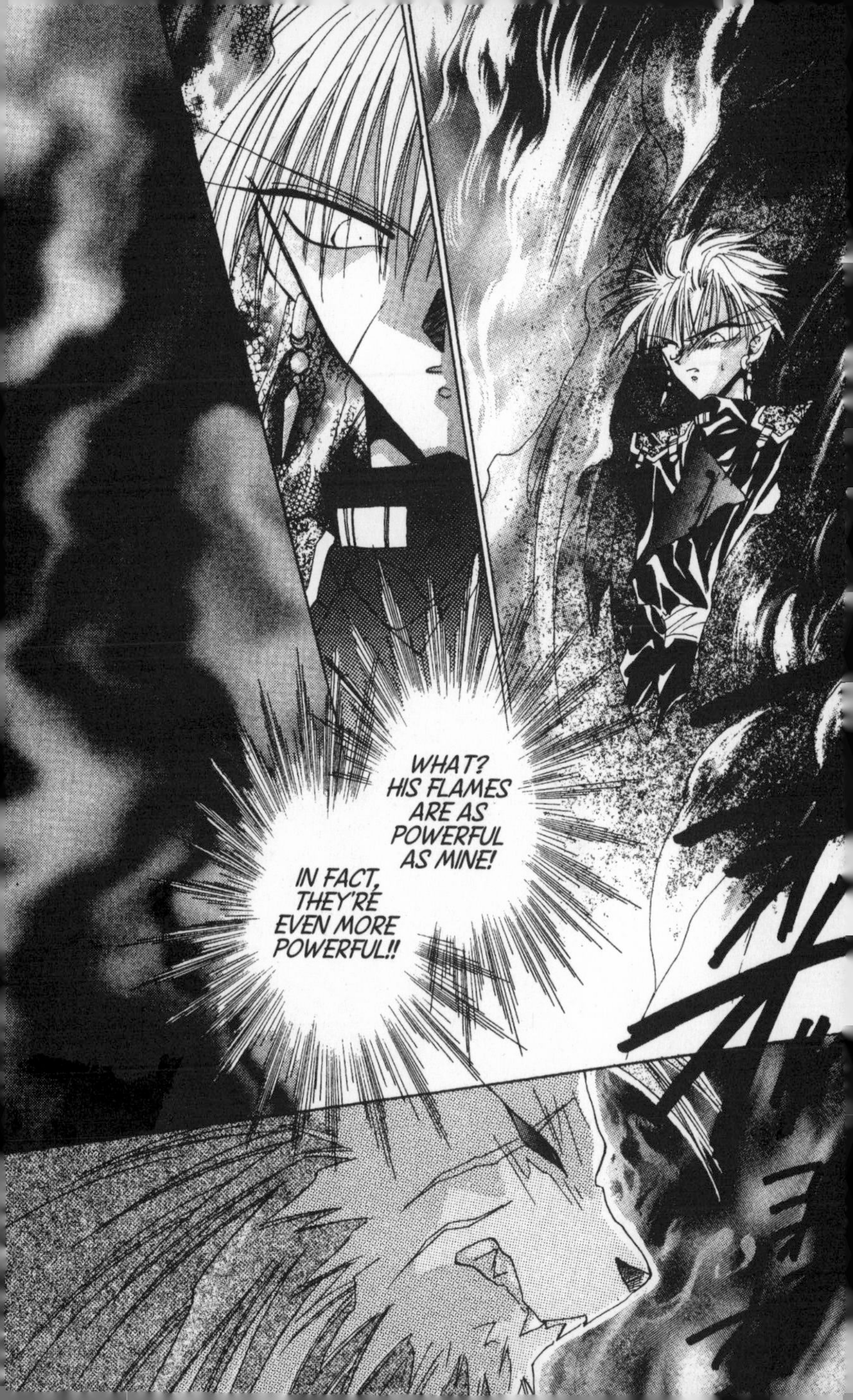
WHAT? HIS FLAMES ARE AS POWERFUL AS MINE!
IN FACT, THEY'RE EVEN MORE POWERFUL!!

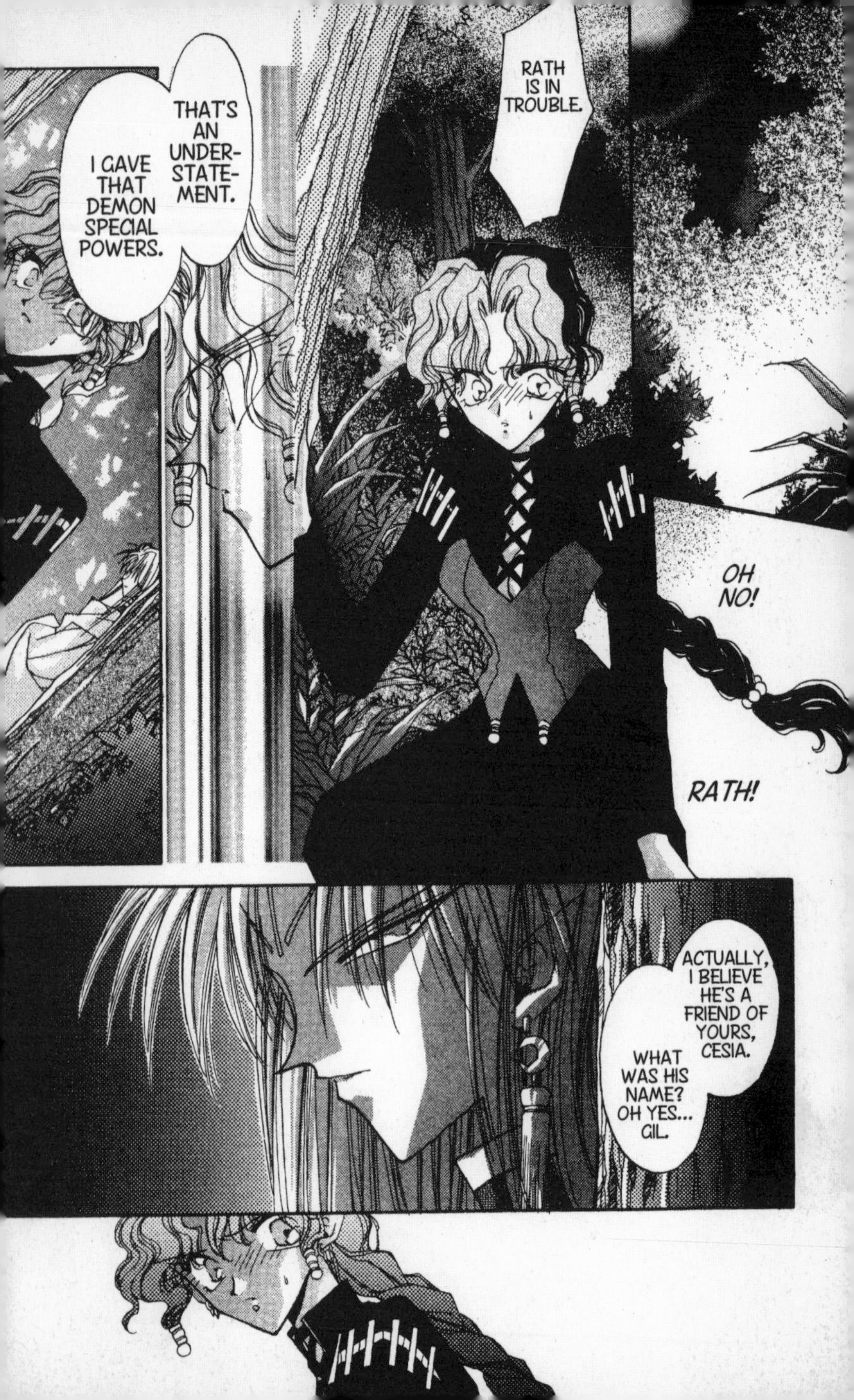
RATH IS IN TROUBLE.
OH NO!
RATH!
THAT'S AN UNDER-STATE-MENT.
I GAVE THAT DEMON SPECIAL POWERS.
ACTUALLY, I BELIEVE HE'S A FRIEND OF YOURS, CESIA.
WHAT WAS HIS NAME? OH YES... GIL.

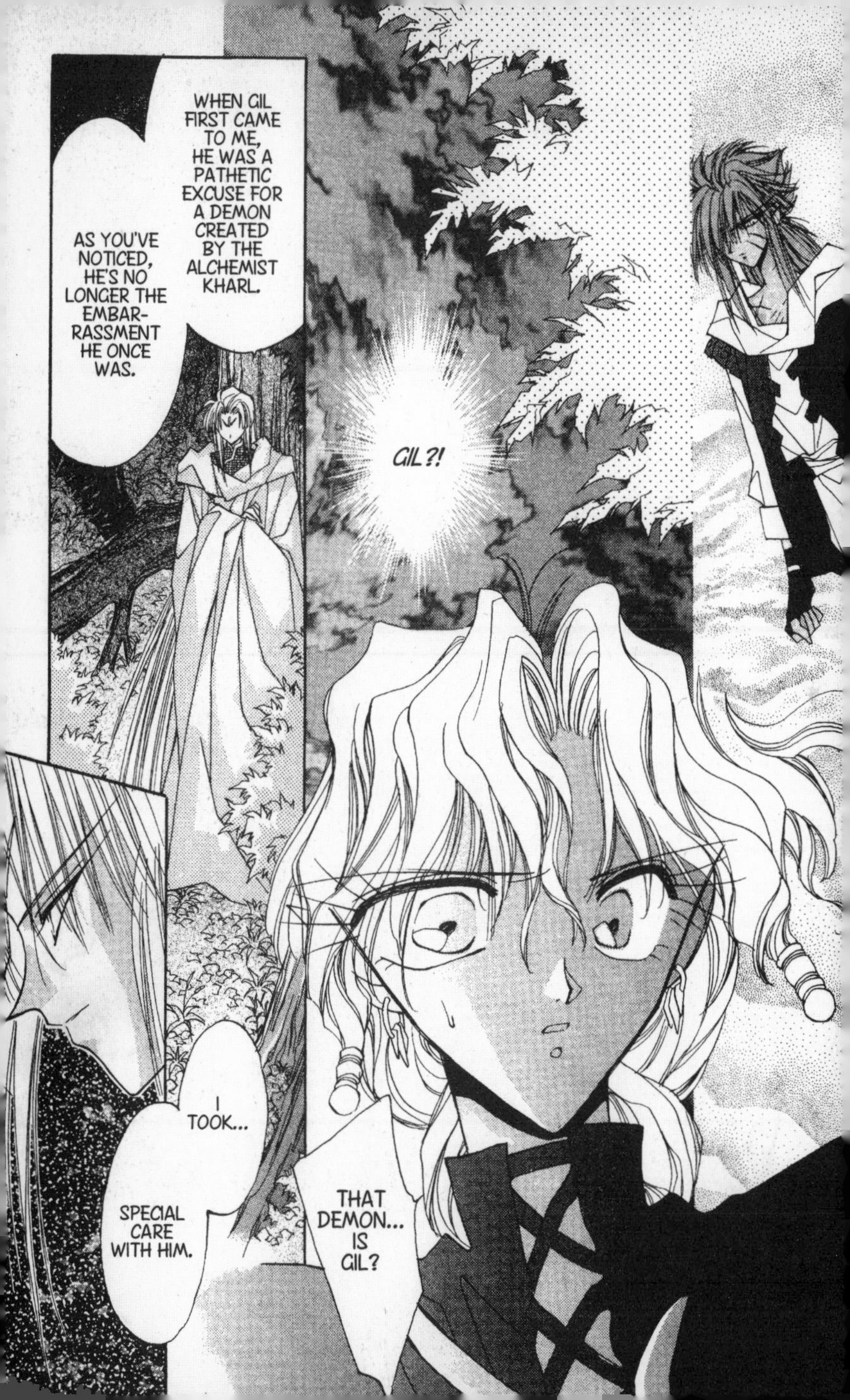
GIL?!
WHEN GIL FIRST CAME TO ME, HE WAS A PATHETIC EXCUSE FOR A DEMON CREATED BY THE ALCHEMIST KHARL.
AS YOU'VE NOTICED, HE'S NO LONGER THE EMBAR-RASSMENT HE ONCE WAS.
THAT DEMON... IS GIL?
I TOOK...
SPECIAL CARE WITH HIM.

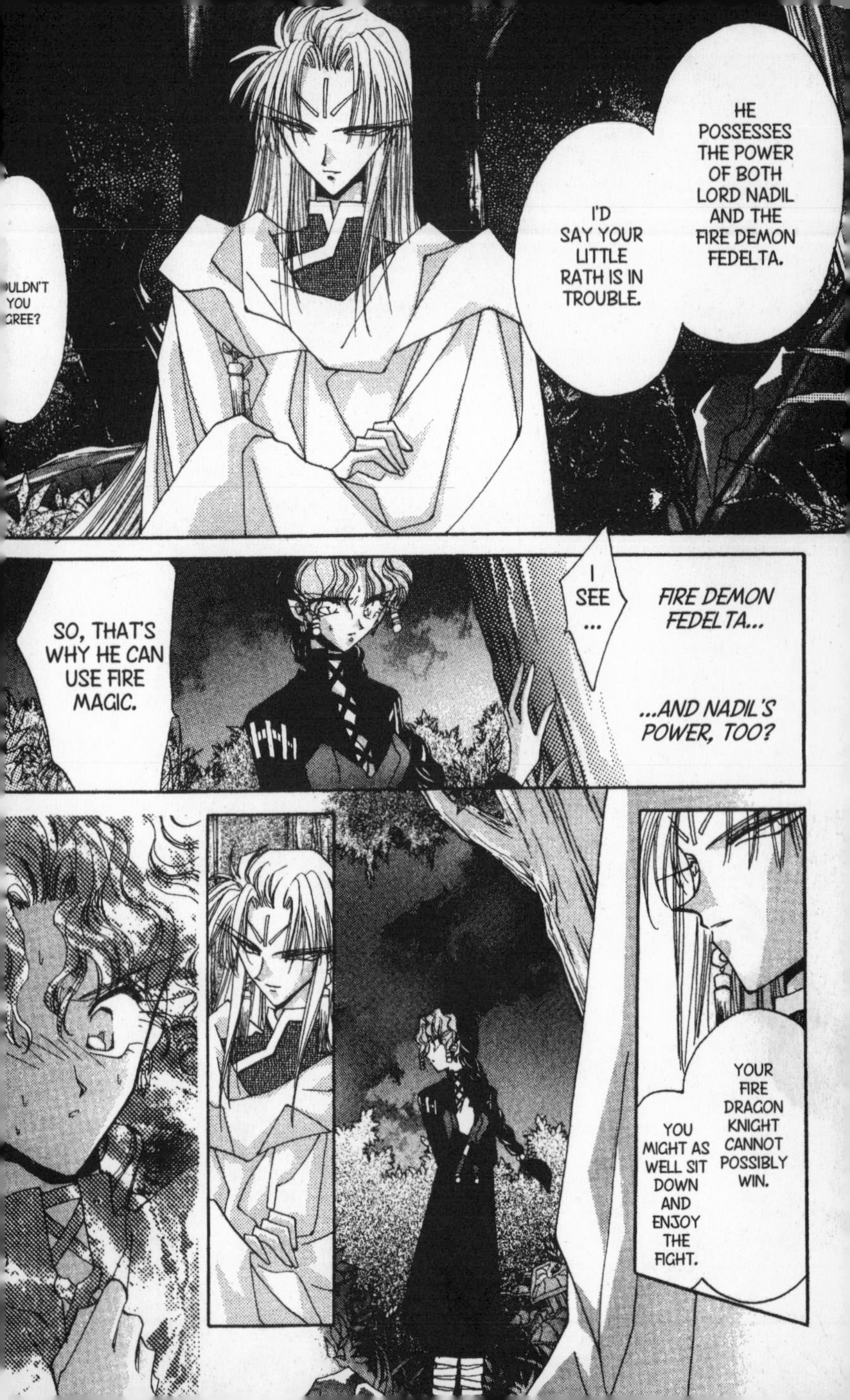
HE POSSESSES THE POWER OF BOTH LORD NADIL AND THE FIRE DEMON FEDELTA.
I'D SAY YOUR LITTLE RATH IS IN TROUBLE.
ULDN'T YOU GREE?
FIRE DEMON FEDELTA...
I SEE...
...AND NADIL'S POWER, TOO?
SO, THAT'S WHY HE CAN USE FIRE MAGIC.
YOUR FIRE DRAGON KNIGHT CANNOT POSSIBLY WIN.
YOU MIGHT AS WELL SIT DOWN AND ENJOY THE FIGHT.

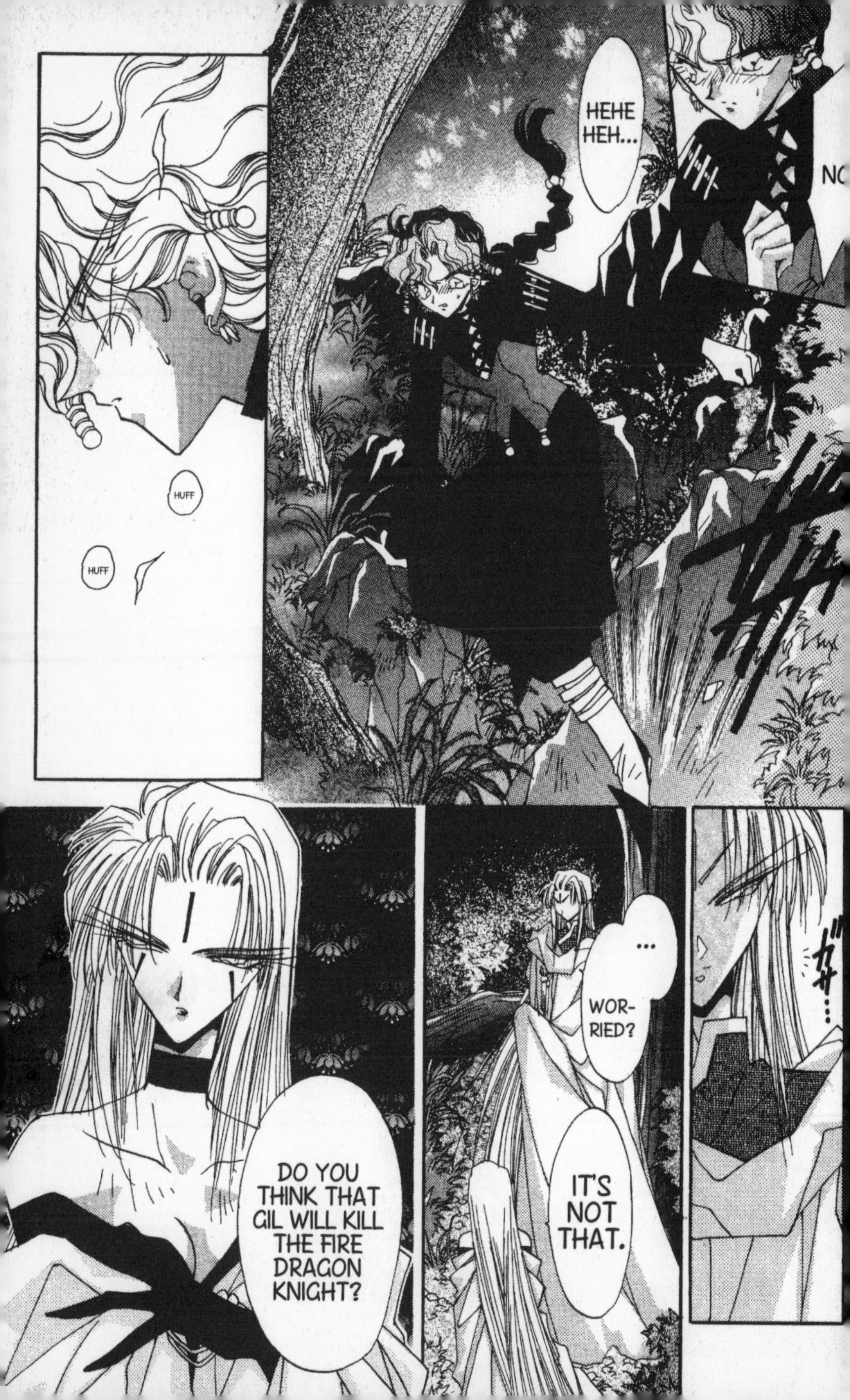
HEHE HEH...
HUFF
HUFF
...
WOR-RIED?
IT'S NOT THAT.
DO YOU THINK THAT GIL WILL KILL THE FIRE DRAGON KNIGHT?

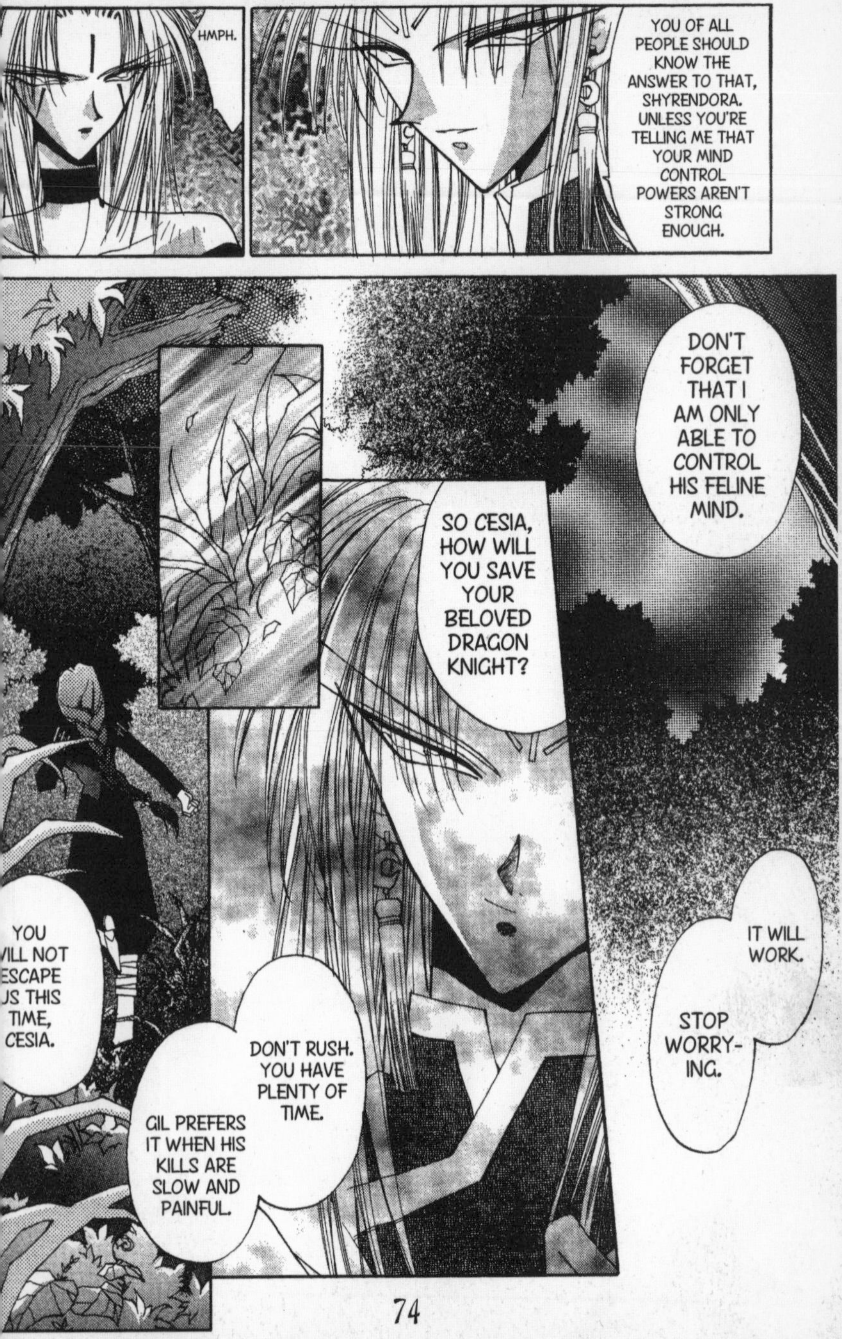
YOU OF ALL PEOPLE SHOULD KNOW THE ANSWER TO THAT, SHYRENDORA. UNLESS YOU'RE TELLING ME THAT YOUR MIND CONTROL POWERS AREN'T STRONG ENOUGH.
HMPH.
DON'T FORGET THAT I AM ONLY ABLE TO CONTROL HIS FELINE MIND.
SO CESIA, HOW WILL YOU SAVE YOUR BELOVED DRAGON KNIGHT?
IT WILL WORK.
STOP WORRY-ING.
DON'T RUSH. YOU HAVE PLENTY OF TIME.
GIL PREFERS IT WHEN HIS KILLS ARE SLOW AND PAINFUL.
YOU WILL NOT ESCAPE US THIS TIME, CESIA.

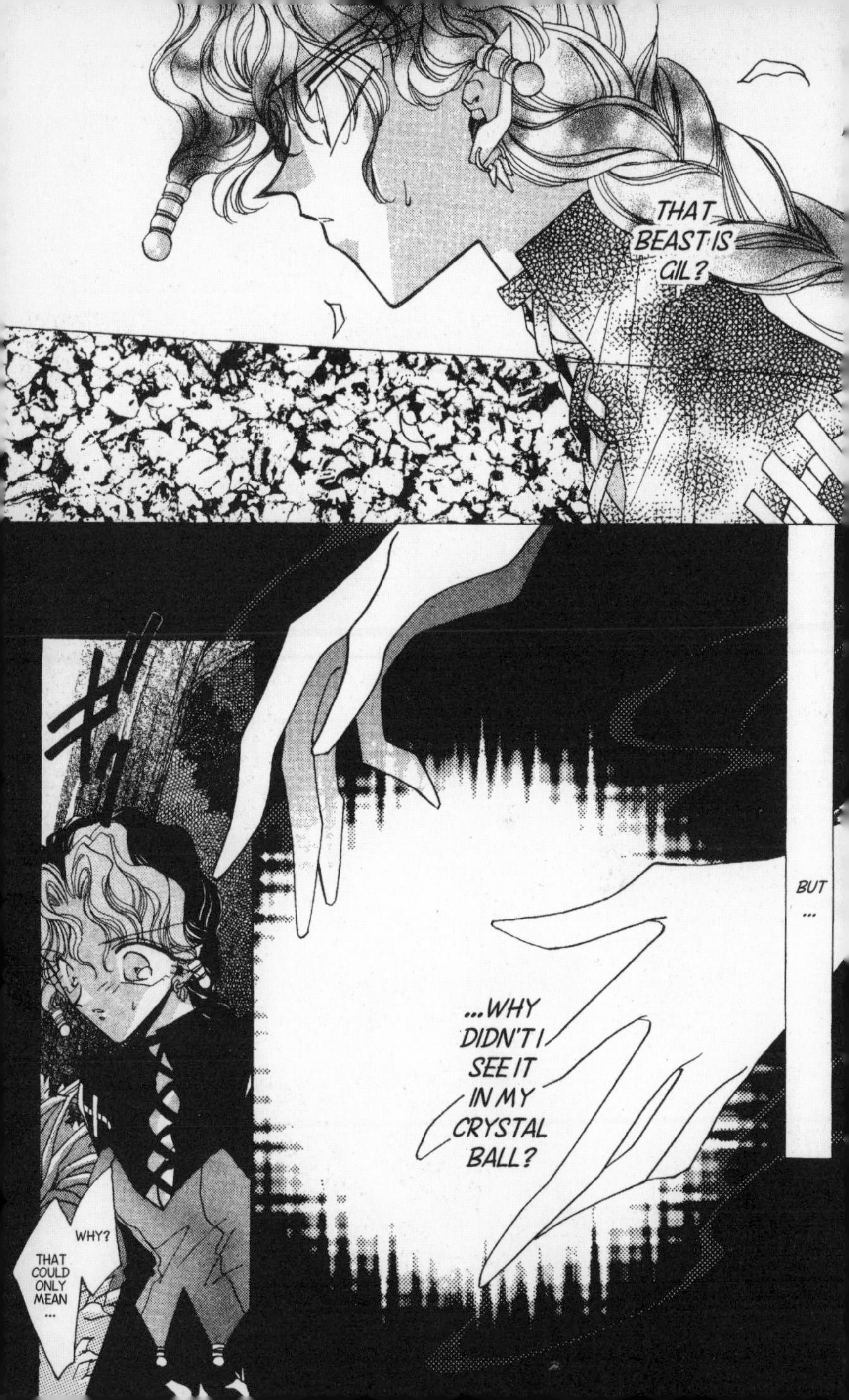
THAT BEAST IS GIL?
BUT ...
...WHY DIDN'T I SEE IT IN MY CRYSTAL BALL?
WHY?
THAT COULD ONLY MEAN ...

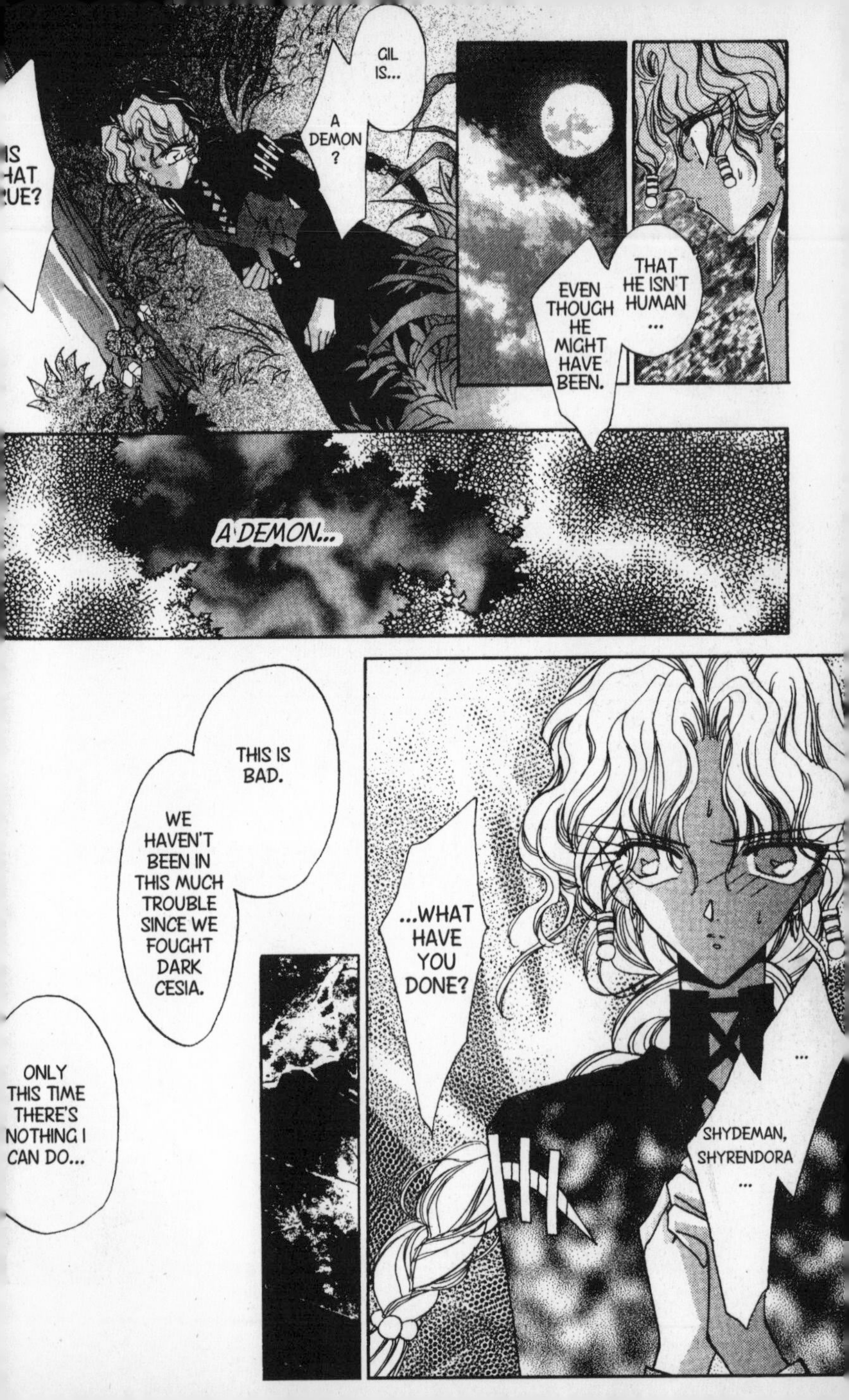
THAT HE ISN'T HUMAN ...
EVEN THOUGH HE MIGHT HAVE BEEN.
GIL IS...
A DEMON ?
IS HAT RUE?
A DEMON...
... SHYDEMAN, SHYRENDORA ...
...WHAT HAVE YOU DONE?
THIS IS BAD.
WE HAVEN'T BEEN IN THIS MUCH TROUBLE SINCE WE FOUGHT DARK CESIA.
ONLY THIS TIME THERE'S NOTHING I CAN DO...

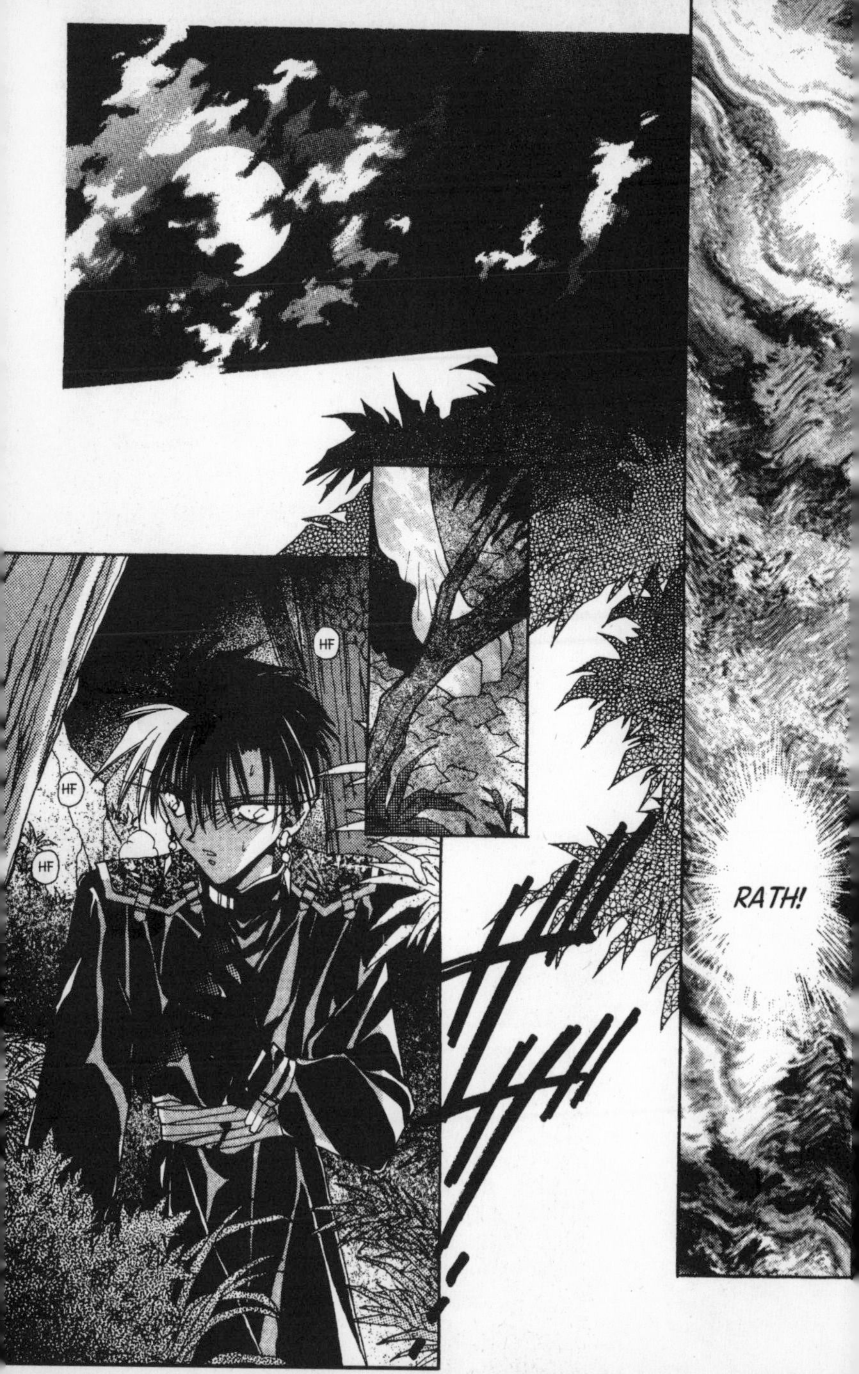
RATH!
HF
HF
HF

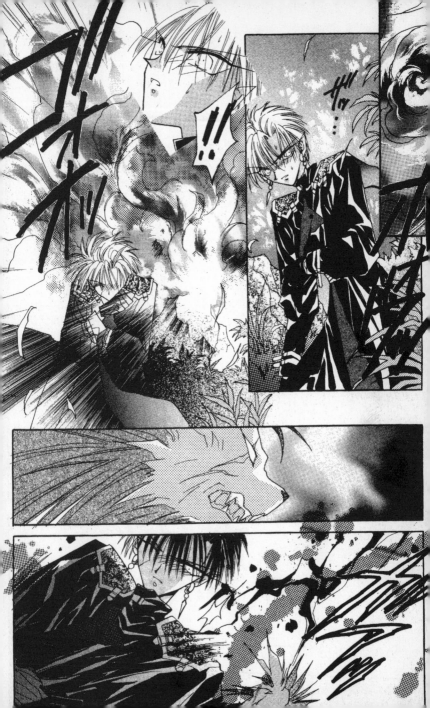

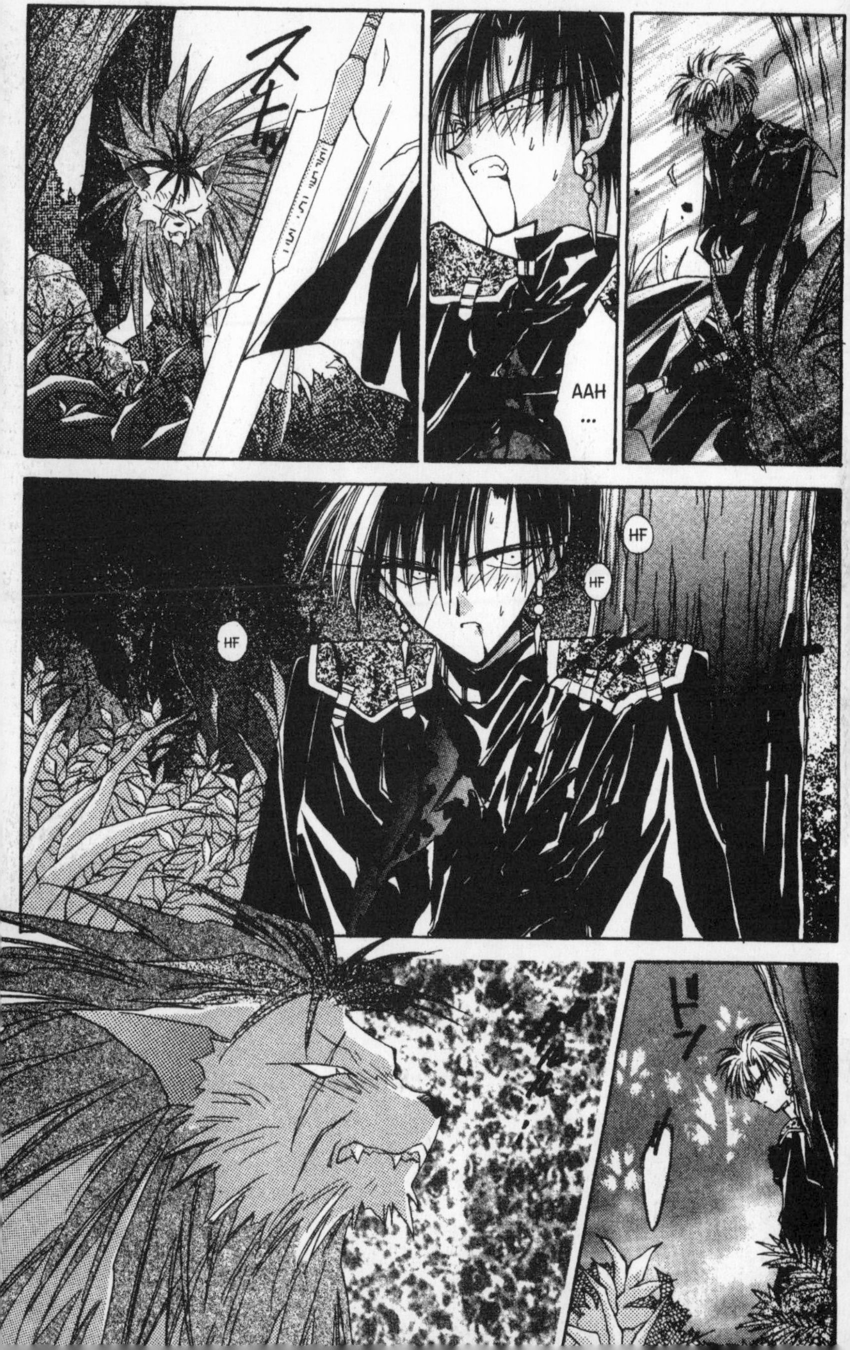
AAH
...
HF
HF
HF

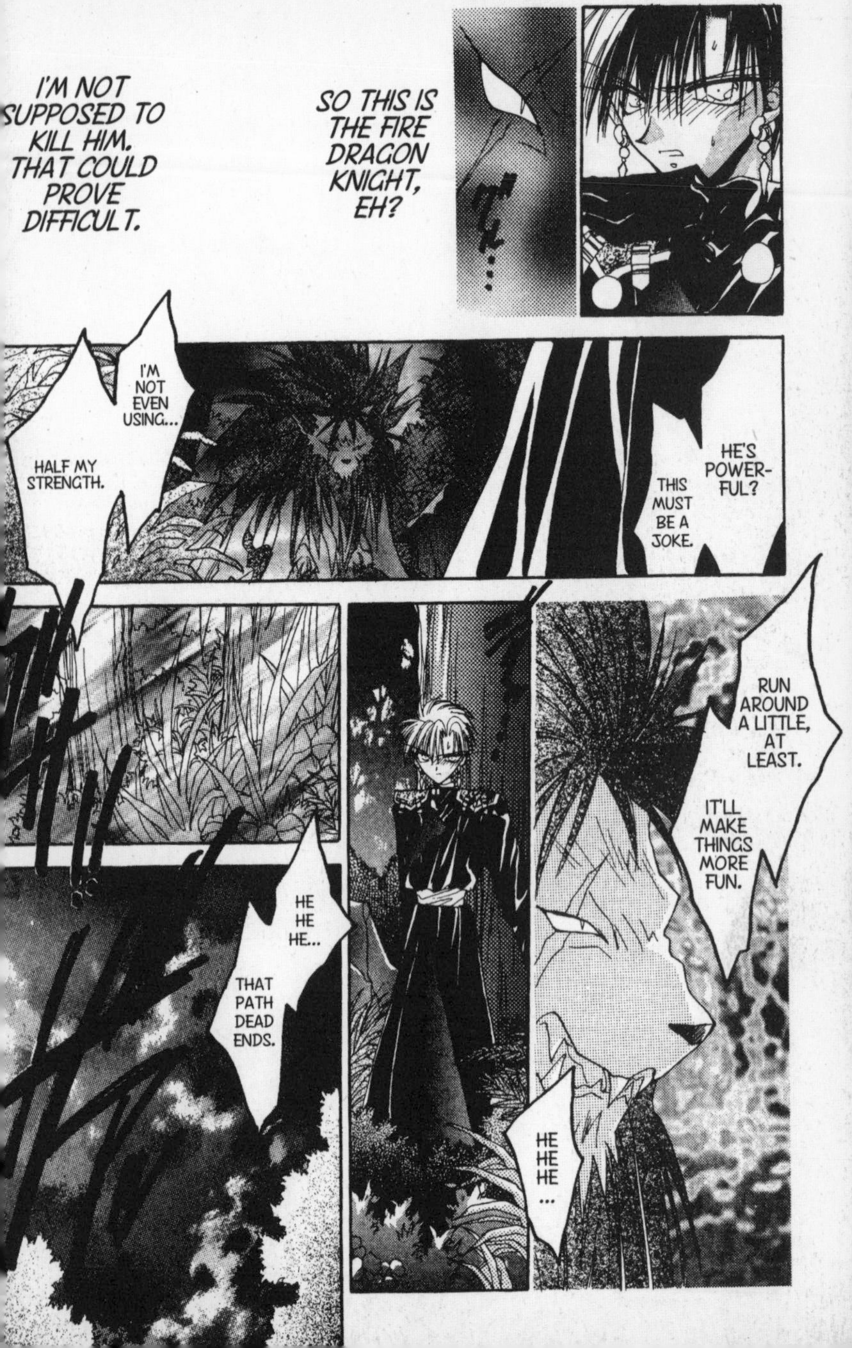
SO THIS IS THE FIRE DRAGON KNIGHT, EH?
I'M NOT SUPPOSED TO KILL HIM. THAT COULD PROVE DIFFICULT.
HE'S POWERFUL?
THIS MUST BE A JOKE.
I'M NOT EVEN USING...
HALF MY STRENGTH.
RUN AROUND A LITTLE, AT LEAST.
IT'LL MAKE THINGS MORE FUN.
HE HE HE ...
HE HE HE...
THAT PATH DEAD ENDS.

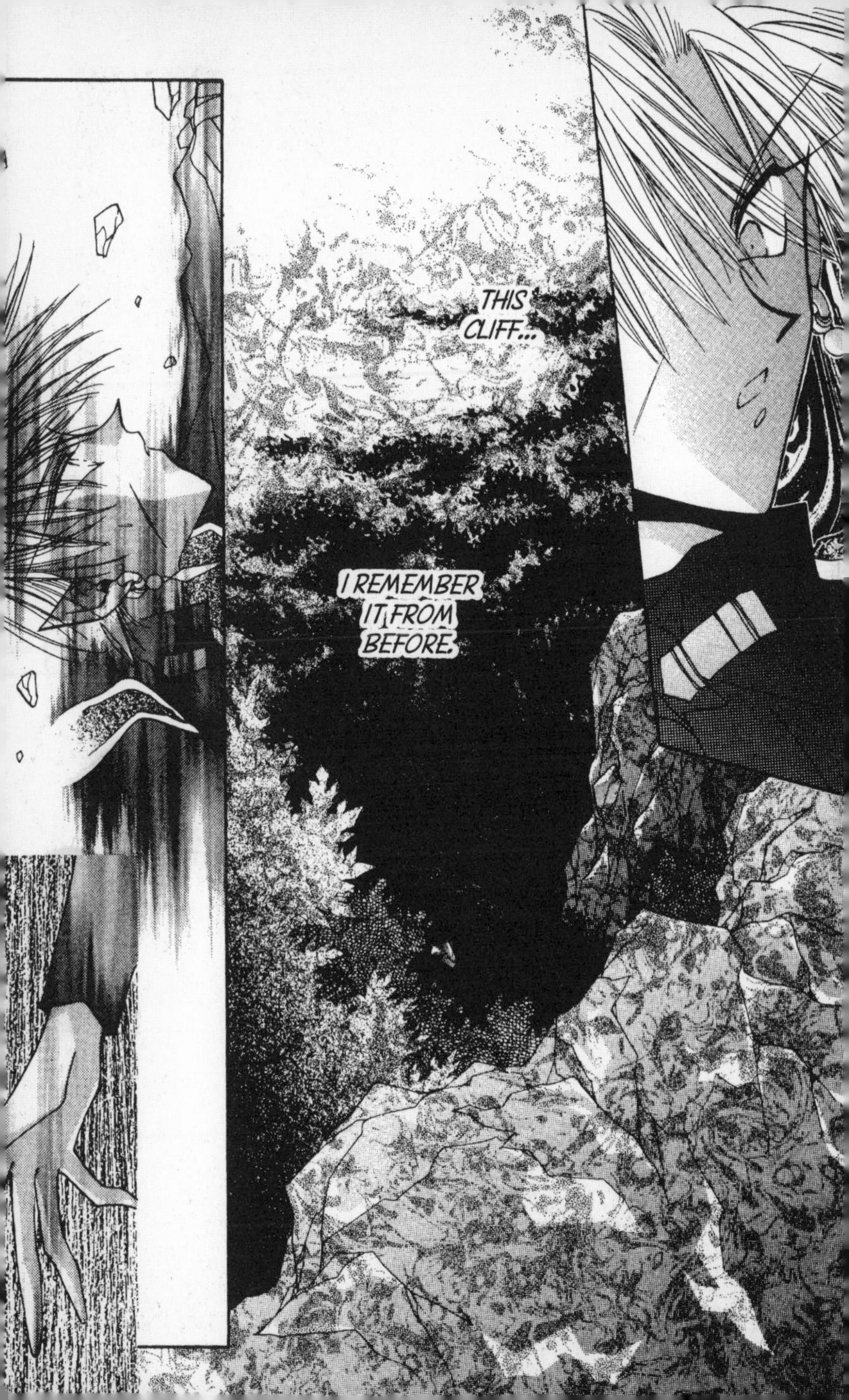
THIS CLIFF...
I REMEMBER IT FROM BEFORE.

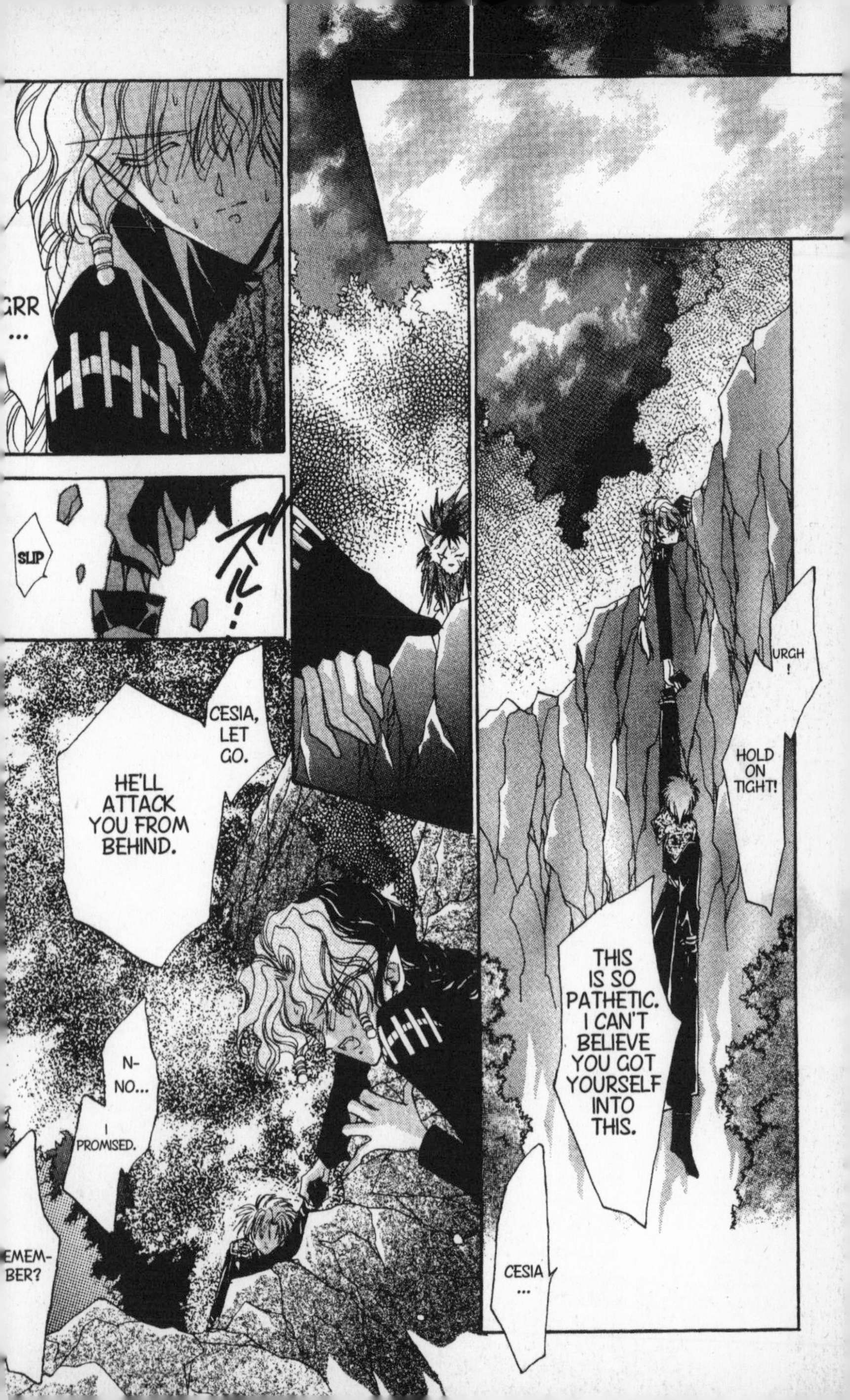
URGH!
HOLD ON TIGHT!
THIS IS SO PATHETIC. I CAN'T BELIEVE YOU GOT YOURSELF INTO THIS.
CESIA...
GRR...
SLIP
ズル…
CESIA, LET GO.
HE'LL ATTACK YOU FROM BEHIND.
N-NO...
I PROMISED.
EMEM-BER?

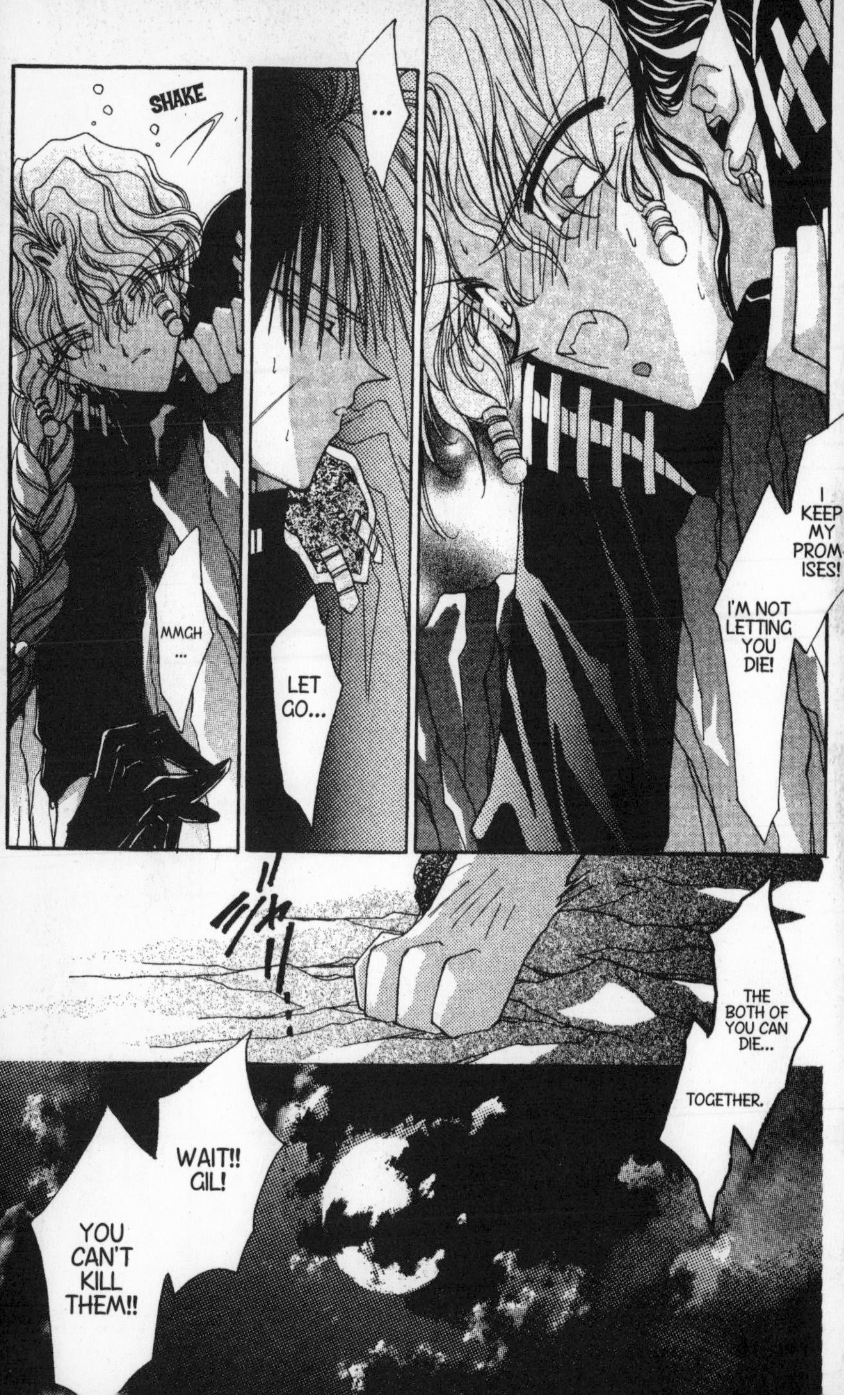
I KEEP MY PROMISES!
I'M NOT LETTING YOU DIE!
...
LET GO...
SHAKE
MMGH ...
THE BOTH OF YOU CAN DIE...
TOGETHER.
WAIT!! GIL!
YOU CAN'T KILL THEM!!

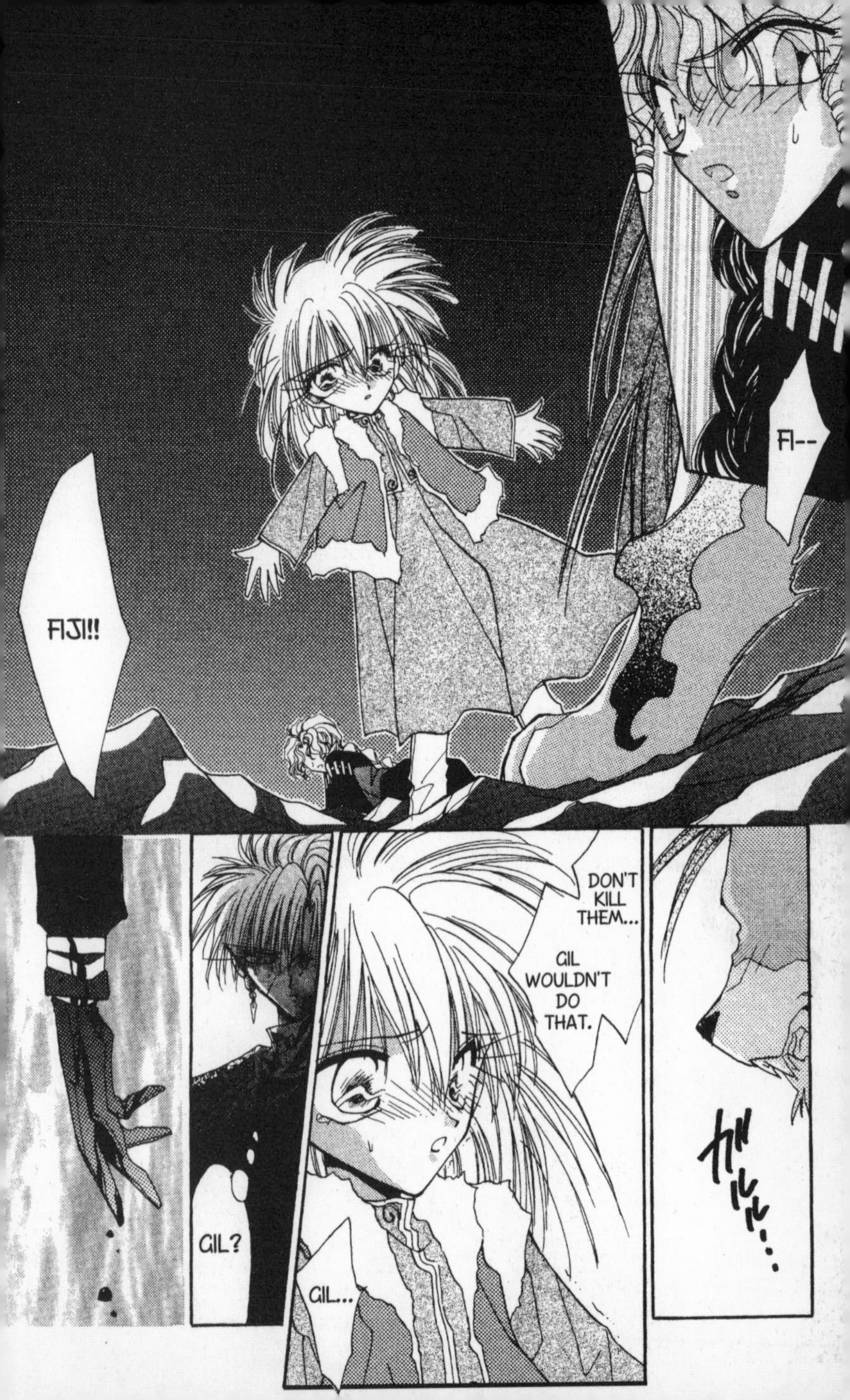
FI--
FIJI!!
ガルルル…
DON'T KILL THEM...
GIL WOULDN'T DO THAT.
GIL...
GIL?

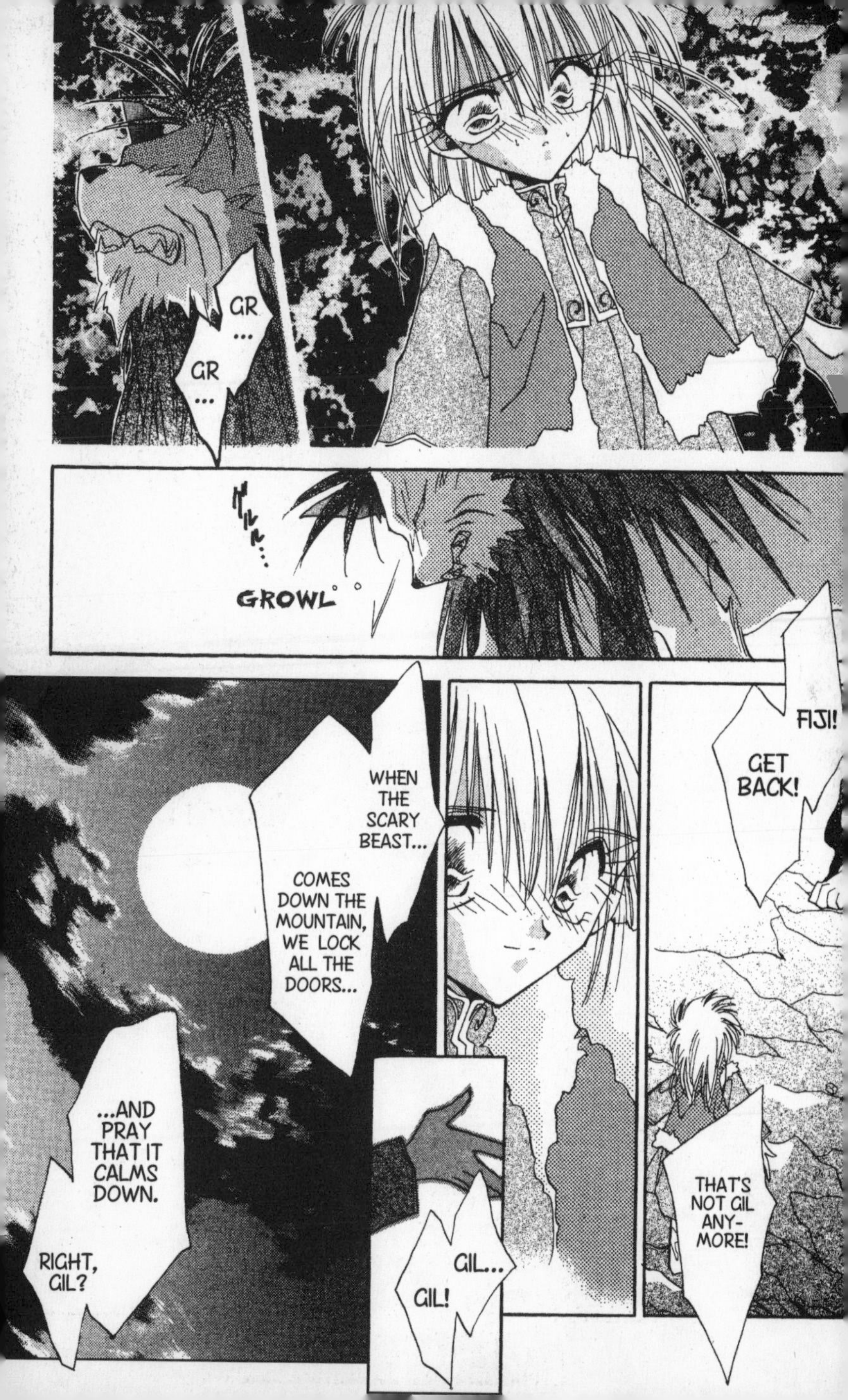
GR... GR...
GROWL
FIJI! GET BACK!
THAT'S NOT GIL ANYMORE!
GIL... GIL!
WHEN THE SCARY BEAST...
COMES DOWN THE MOUNTAIN, WE LOCK ALL THE DOORS...
...AND PRAY THAT IT CALMS DOWN.
RIGHT, GIL?

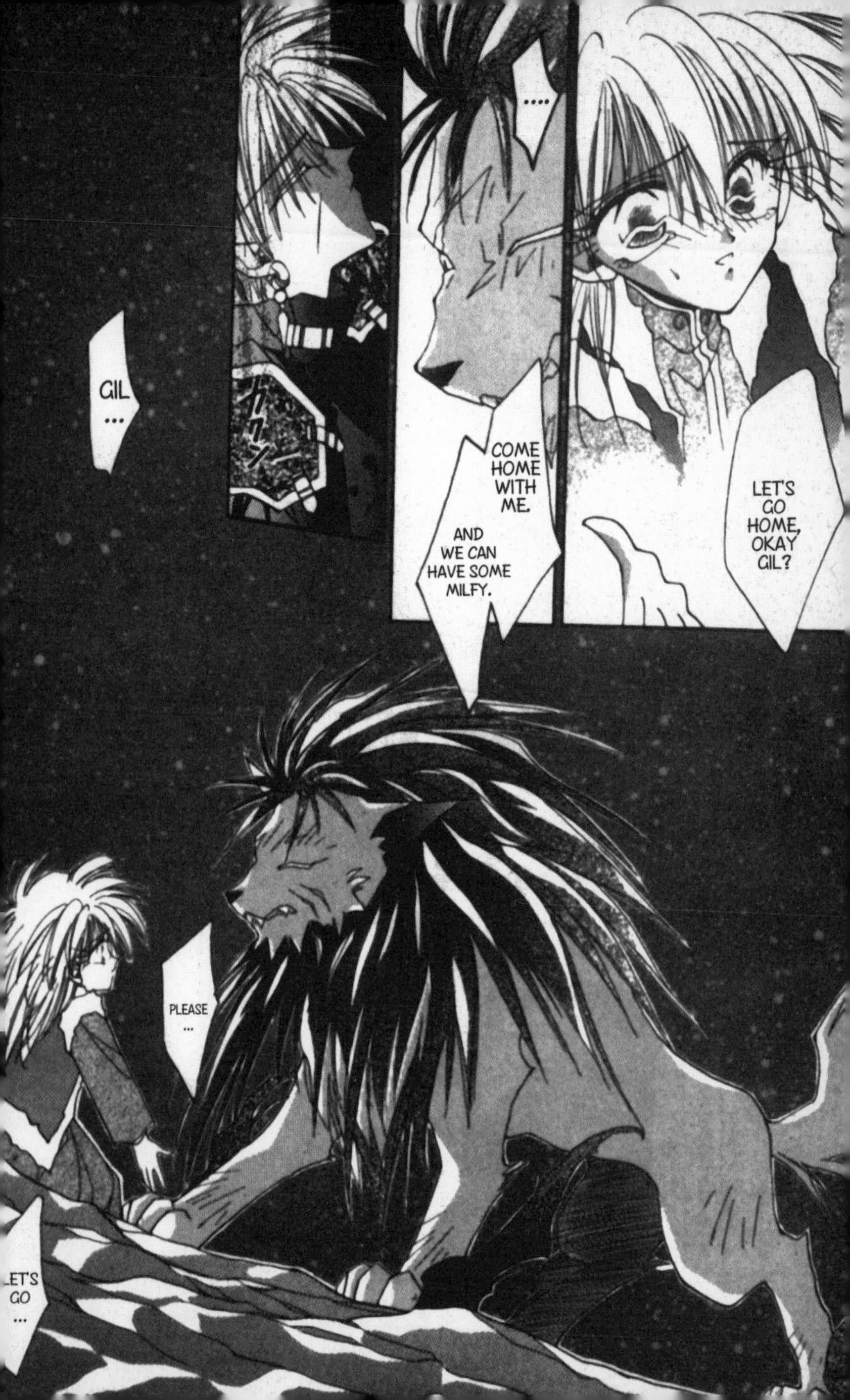
LET'S GO HOME, OKAY GIL?
....
COME HOME WITH ME.
AND WE CAN HAVE SOME MILFY.
GIL ...
PLEASE ...
LET'S GO ...

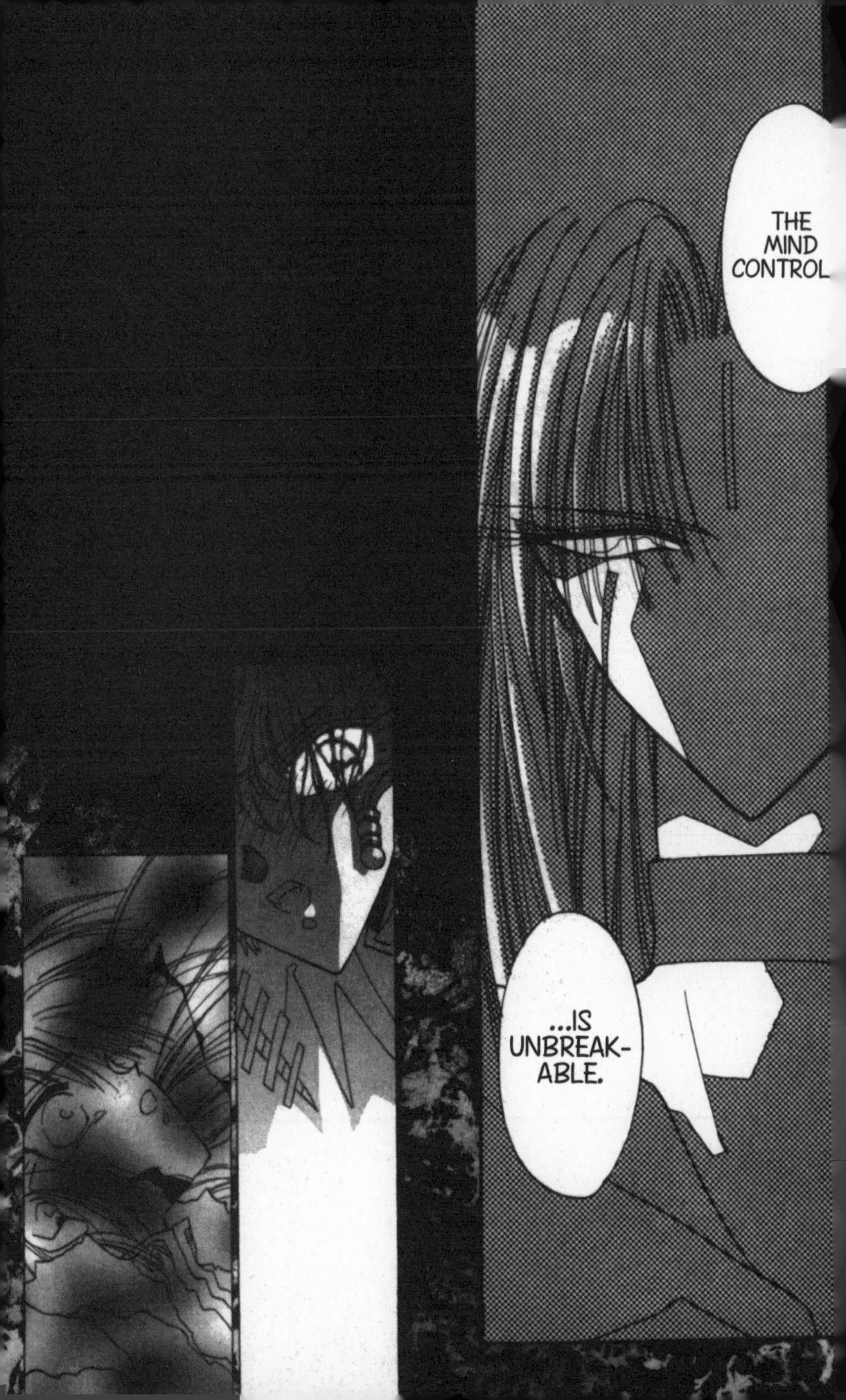
THE MIND CONTROL
...IS UNBREAKABLE.

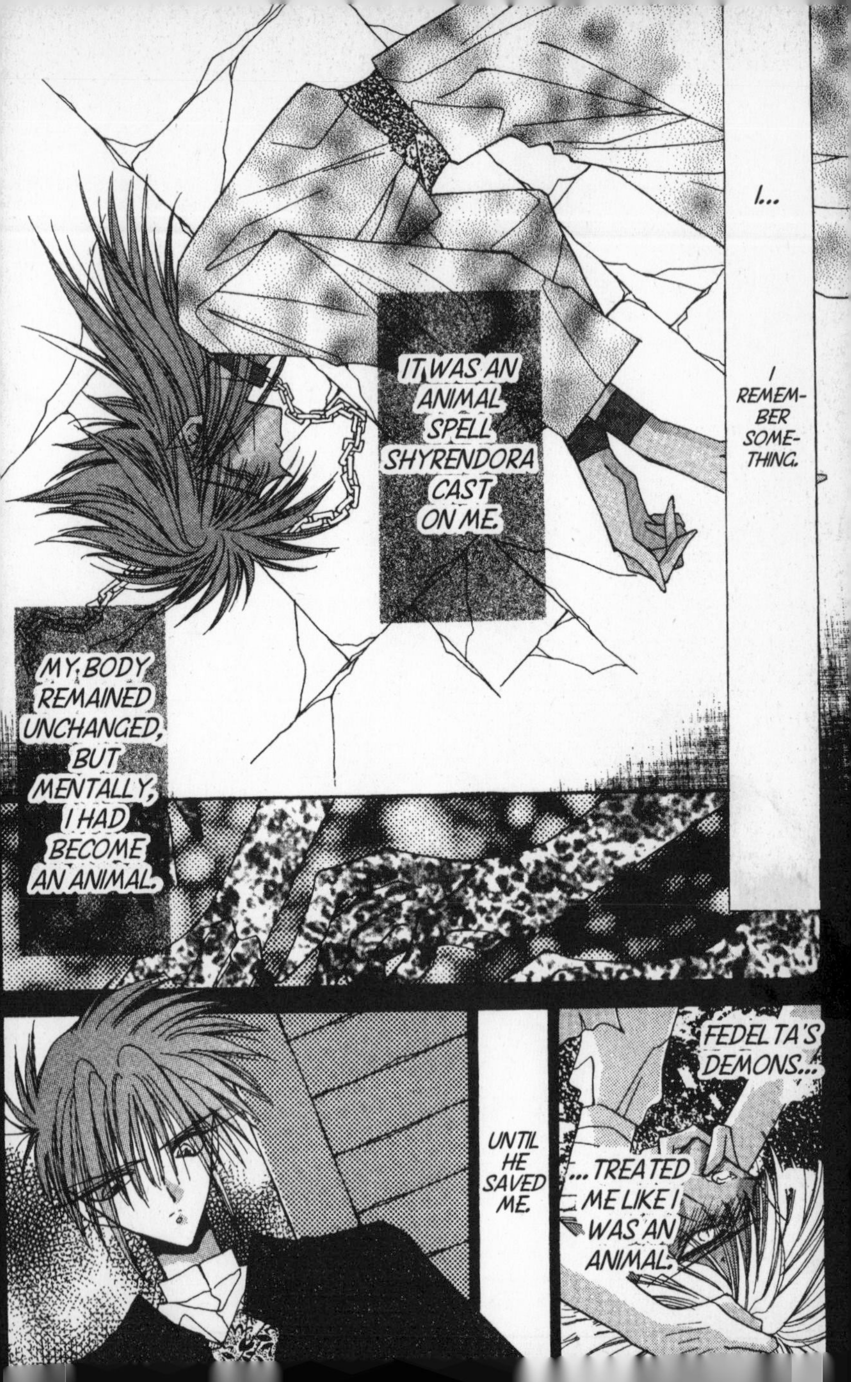
I...
I REMEMBER SOMETHING.
IT WAS AN ANIMAL SPELL SHYRENDORA CAST ON ME.
MY BODY REMAINED UNCHANGED, BUT MENTALLY, I HAD BECOME AN ANIMAL.
FEDELTA'S DEMONS...
...TREATED ME LIKE I WAS AN ANIMAL.
UNTIL HE SAVED ME.

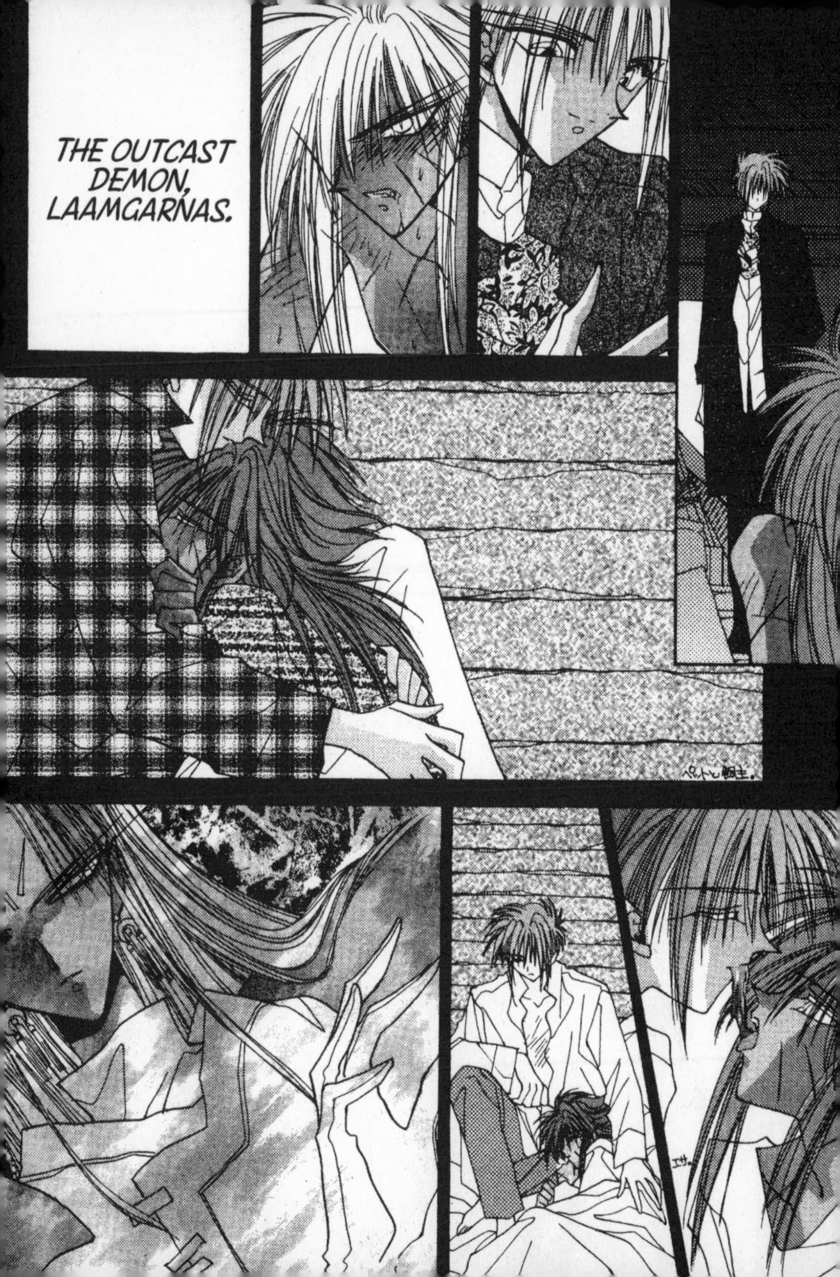
THE OUTCAST DEMON, LAAMGARNAS.
ペットと飼主。
エサ。

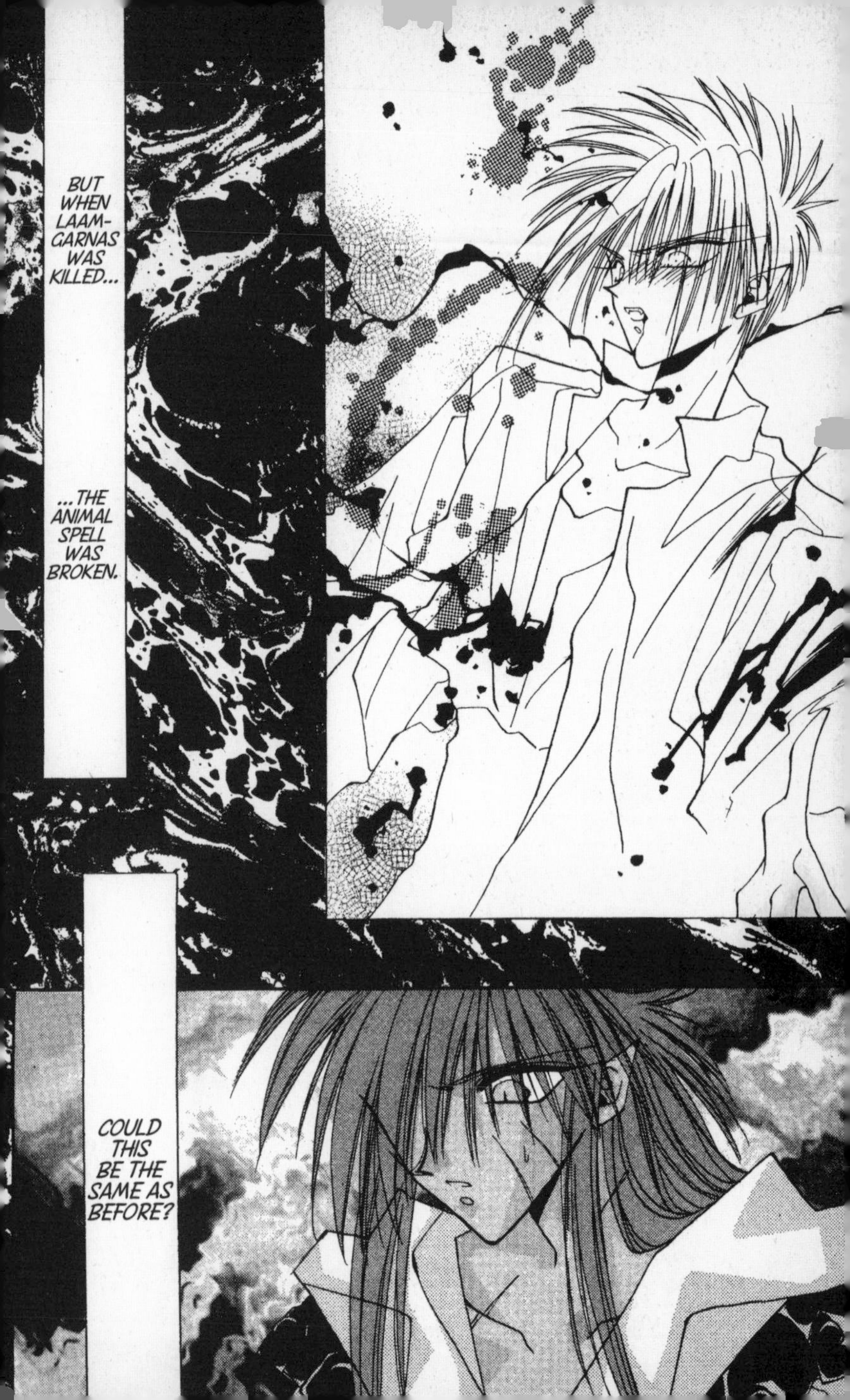
BUT WHEN LAAM-GARNAS WAS KILLED...
...THE ANIMAL SPELL WAS BROKEN.
COULD THIS BE THE SAME AS BEFORE?

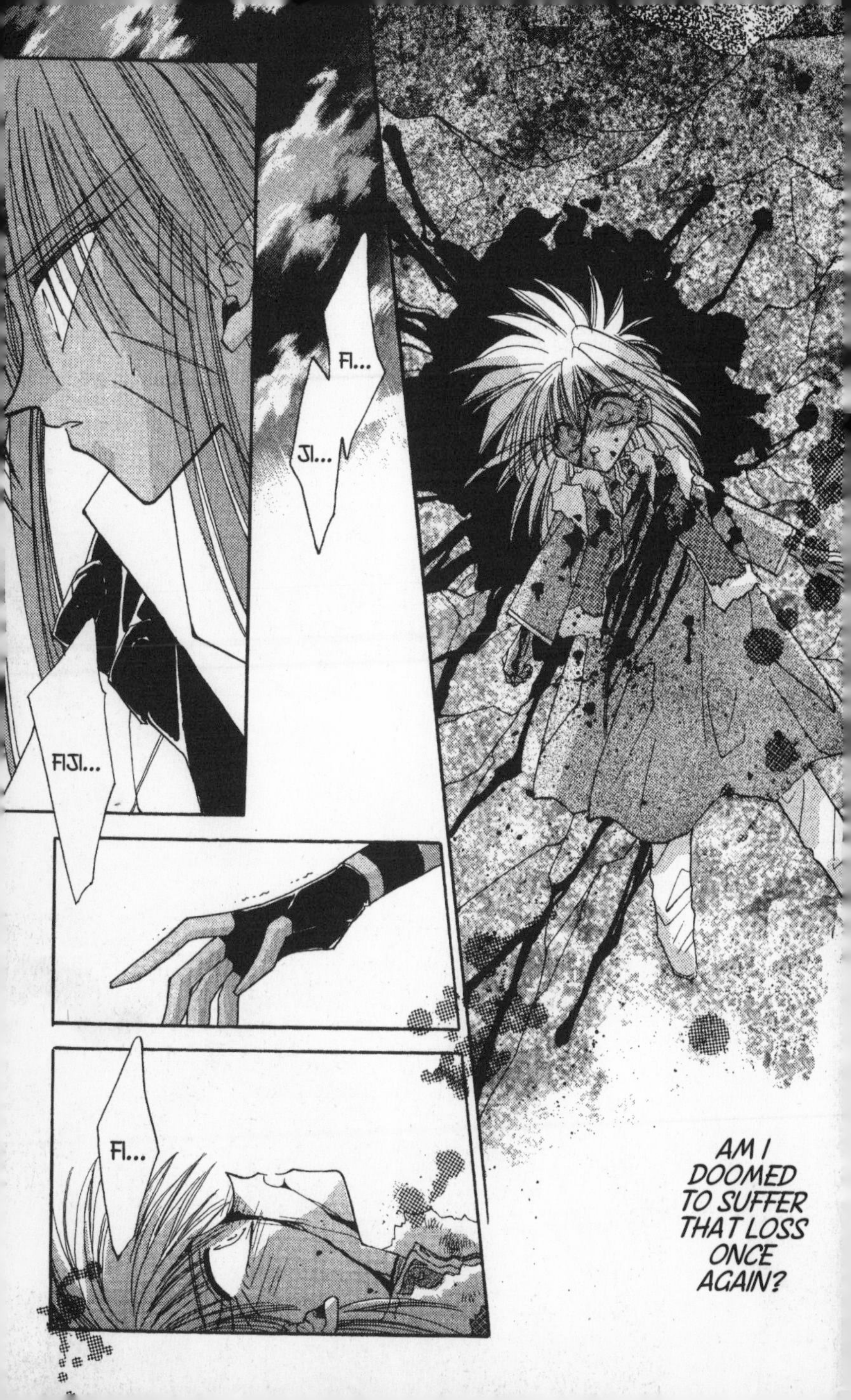
AM I DOOMED TO SUFFER THAT LOSS ONCE AGAIN?
FI...
JI...
FIJI...
FI...

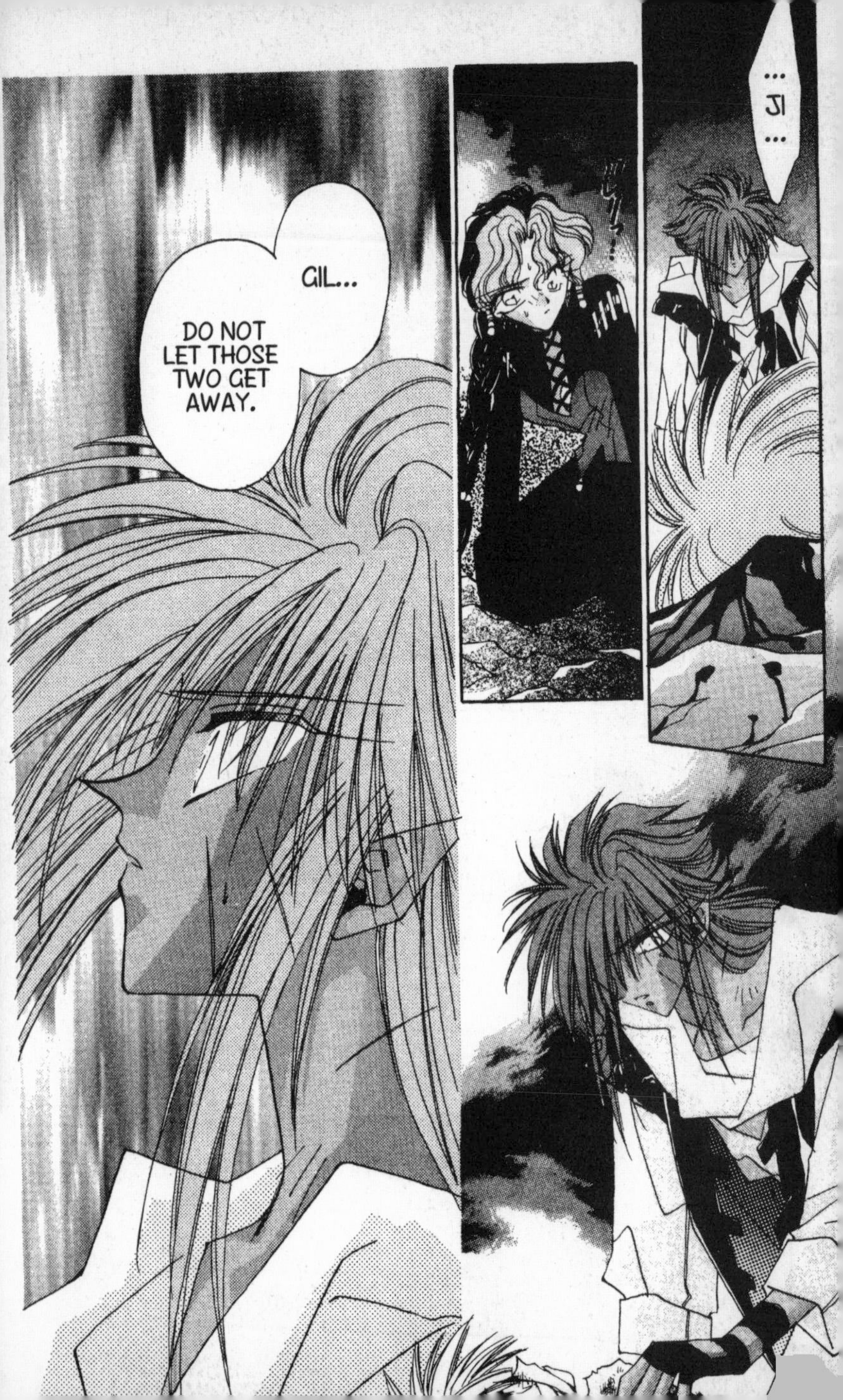
...JI...
GIL...
DO NOT LET THOSE TWO GET AWAY.

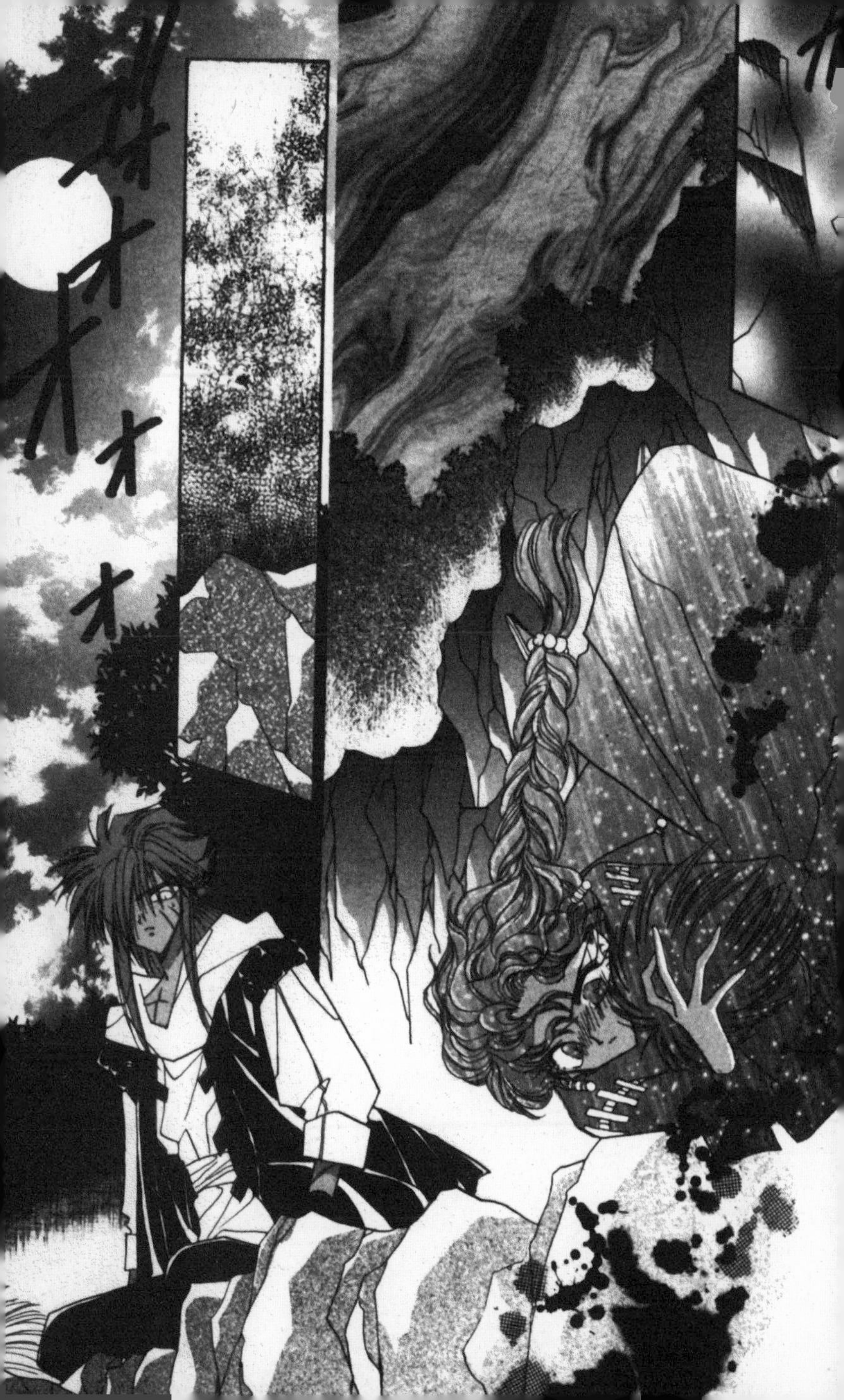
オオオオオ

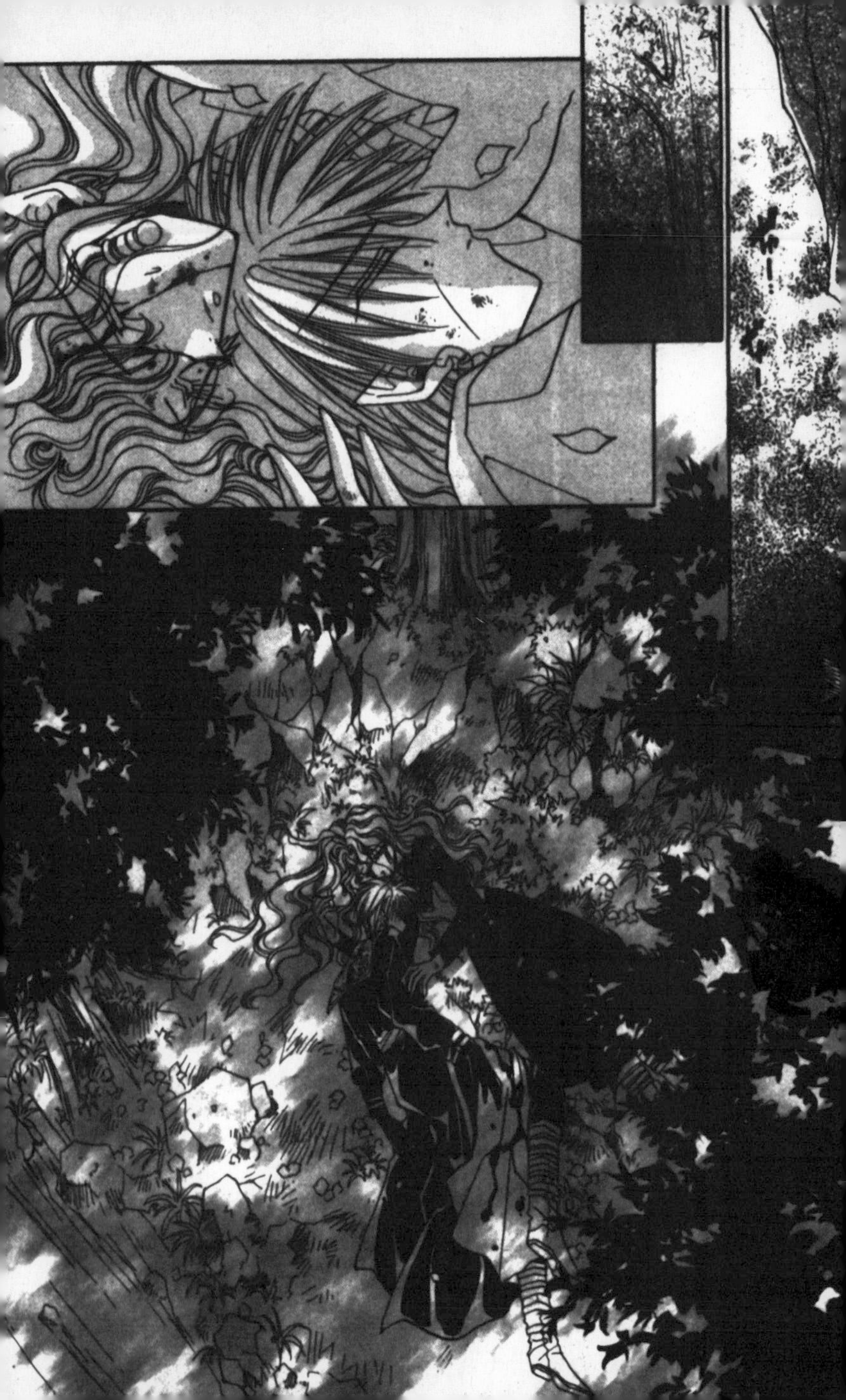
ザー…ザー

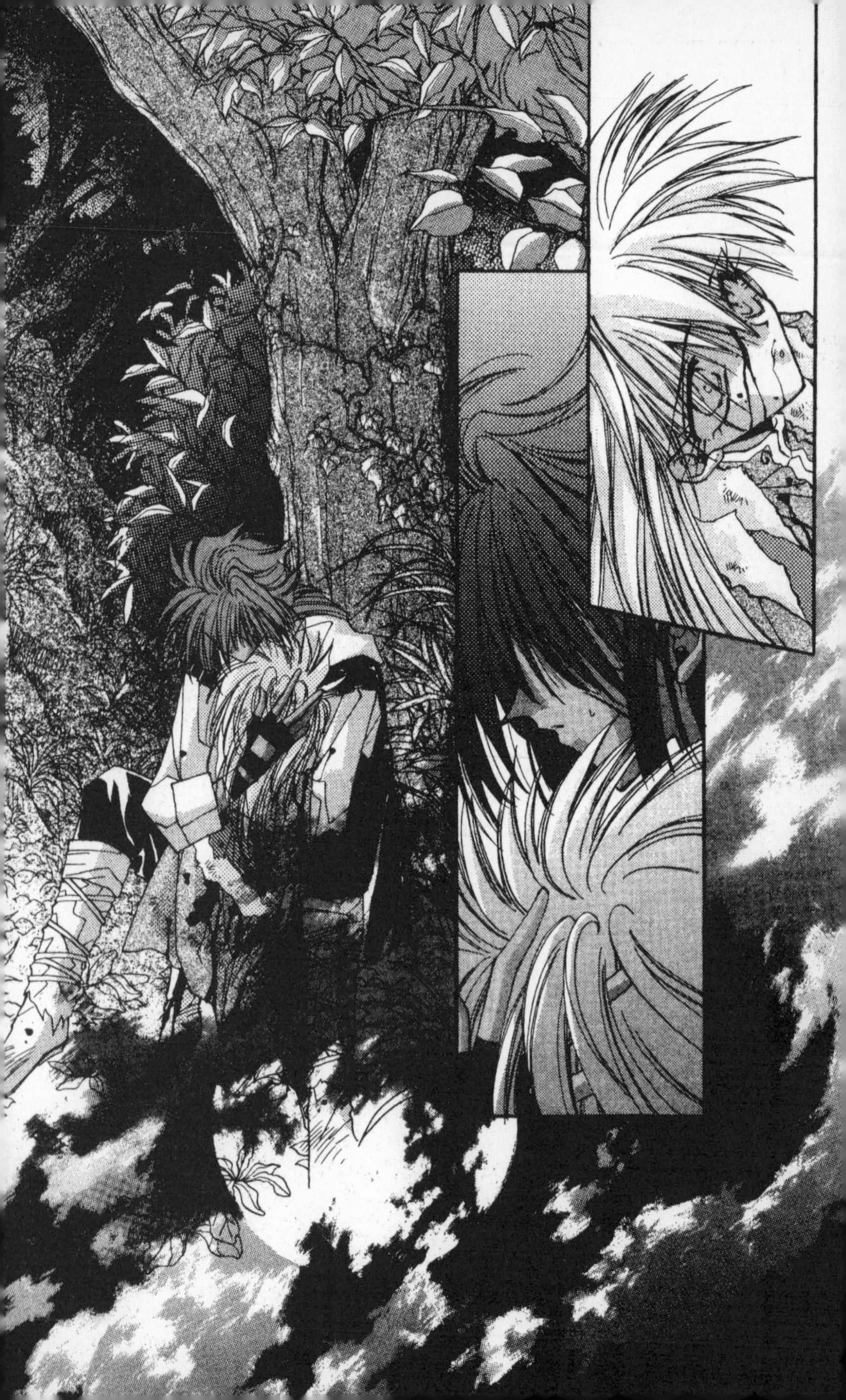

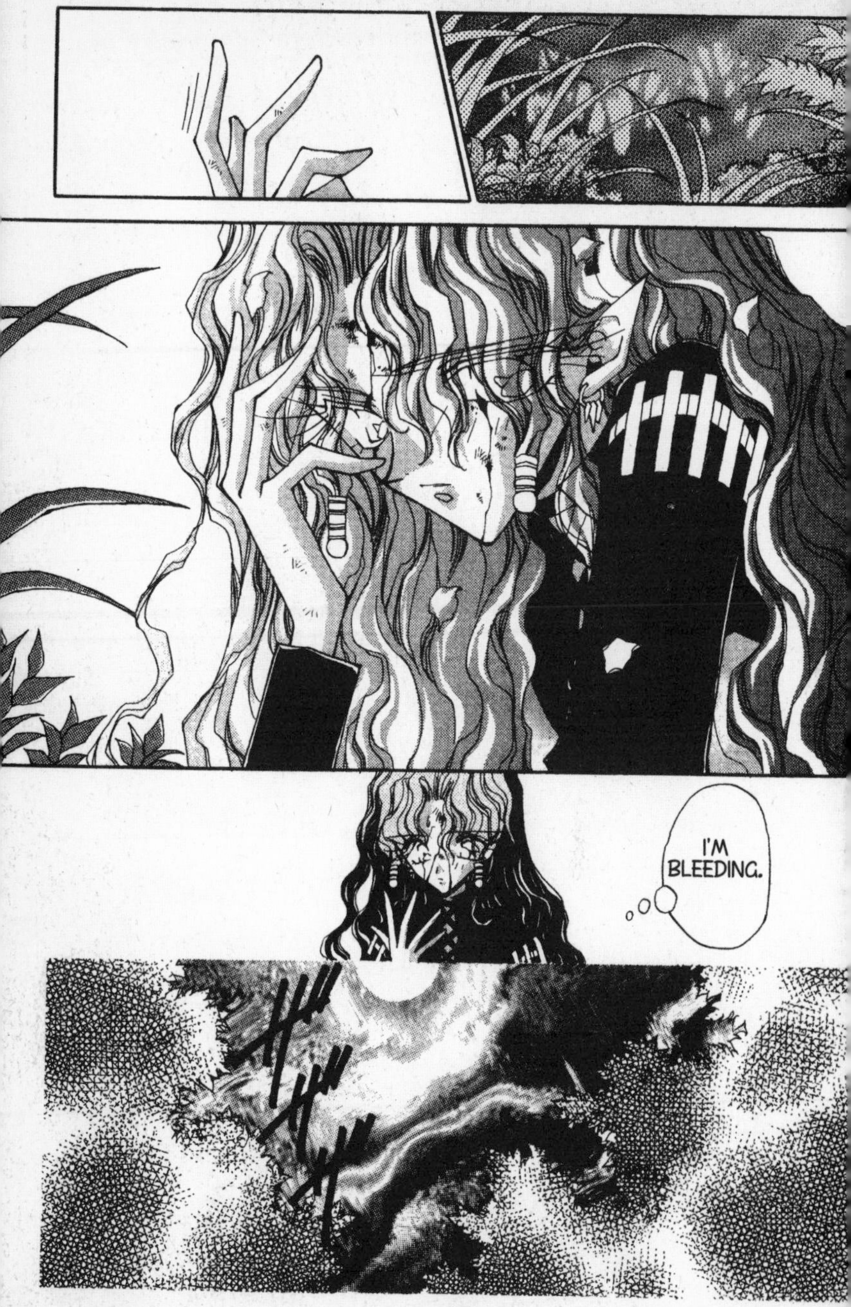
I'M BLEEDING.

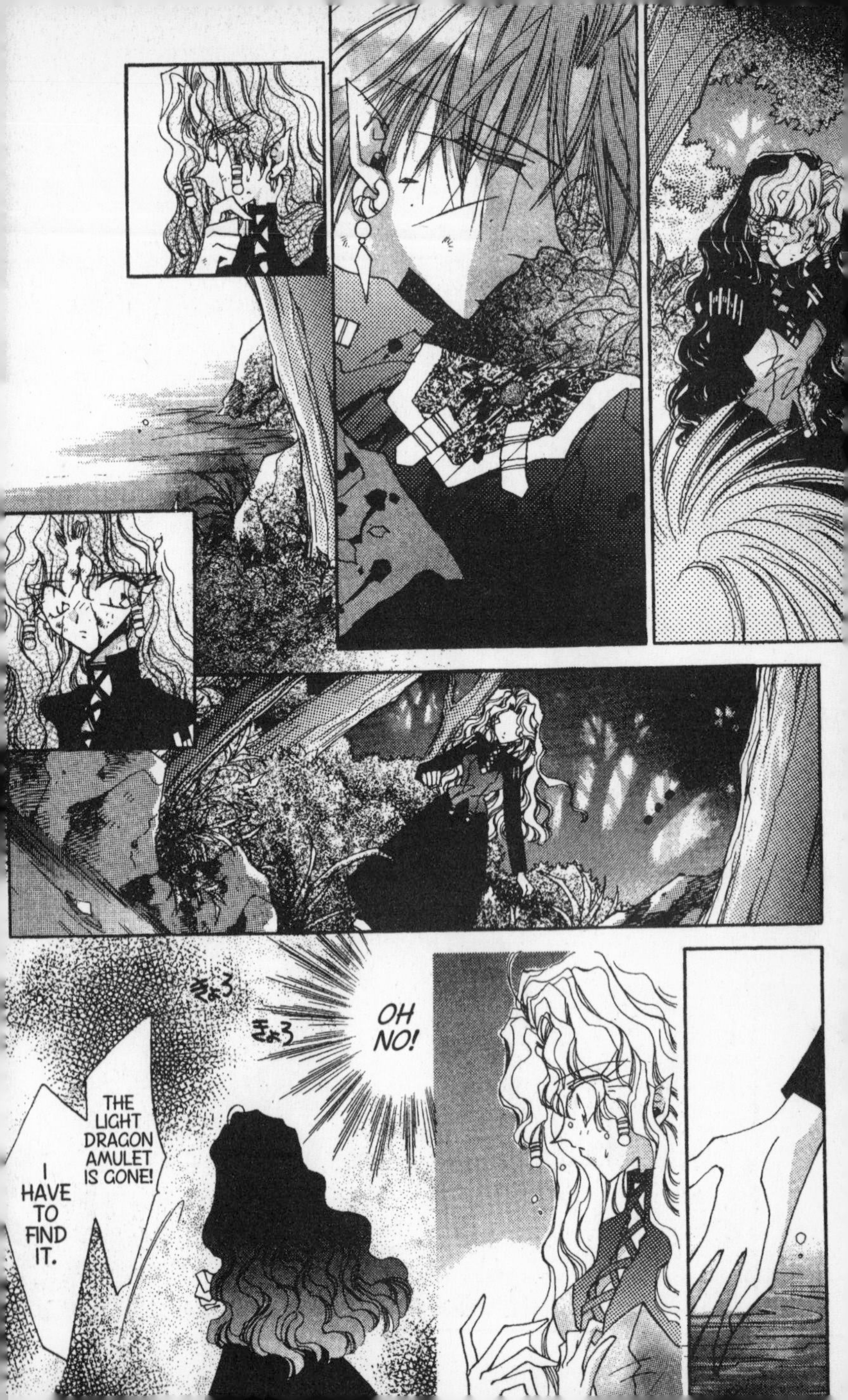
きょろ
きょろ
OH NO!
THE LIGHT DRAGON AMULET IS GONE!
I HAVE TO FIND IT.

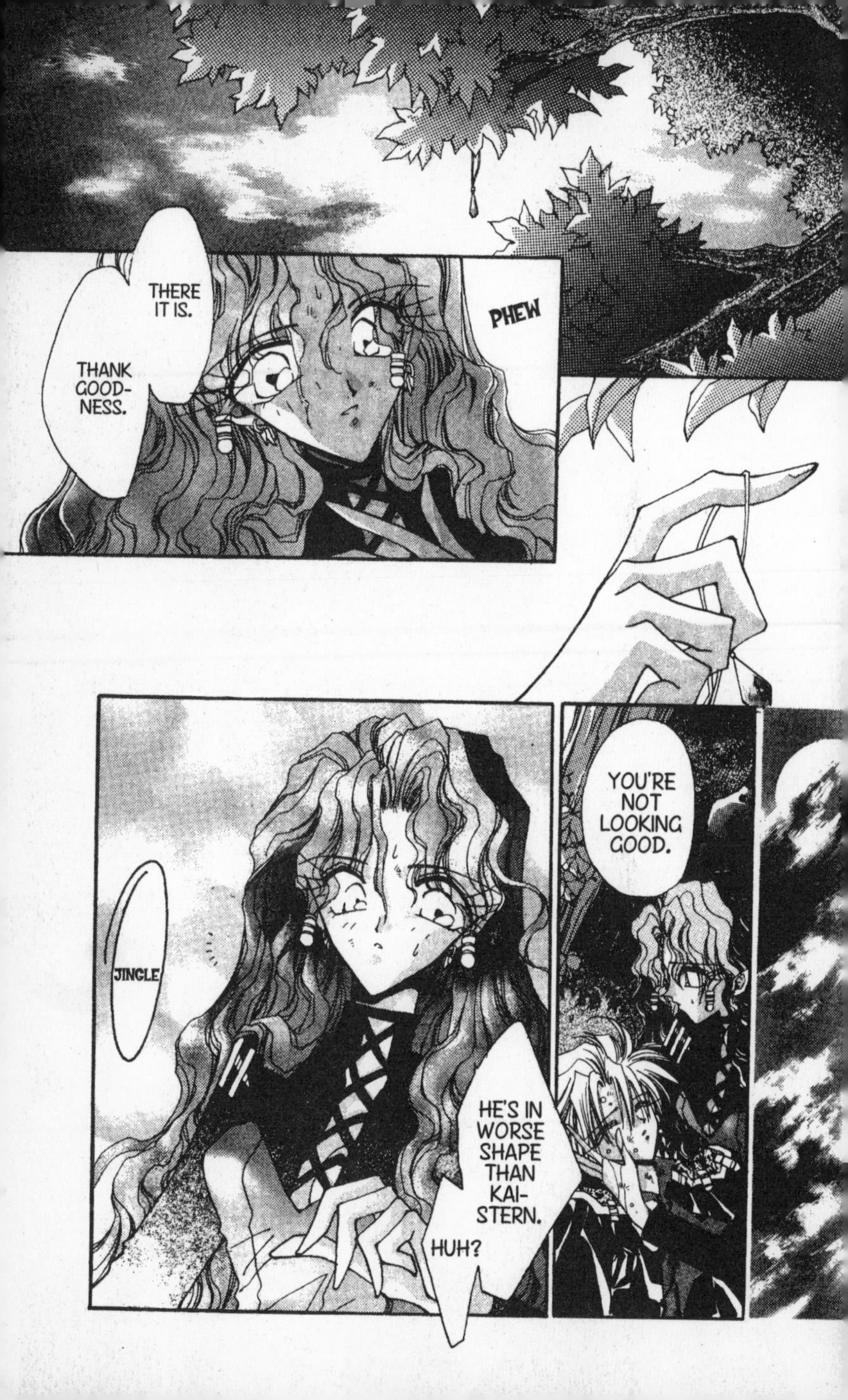
PHEW
THERE IT IS.
THANK GOOD-NESS.
YOU'RE NOT LOOKING GOOD.
HE'S IN WORSE SHAPE THAN KAI-STERN.
JINGLE
HUH?

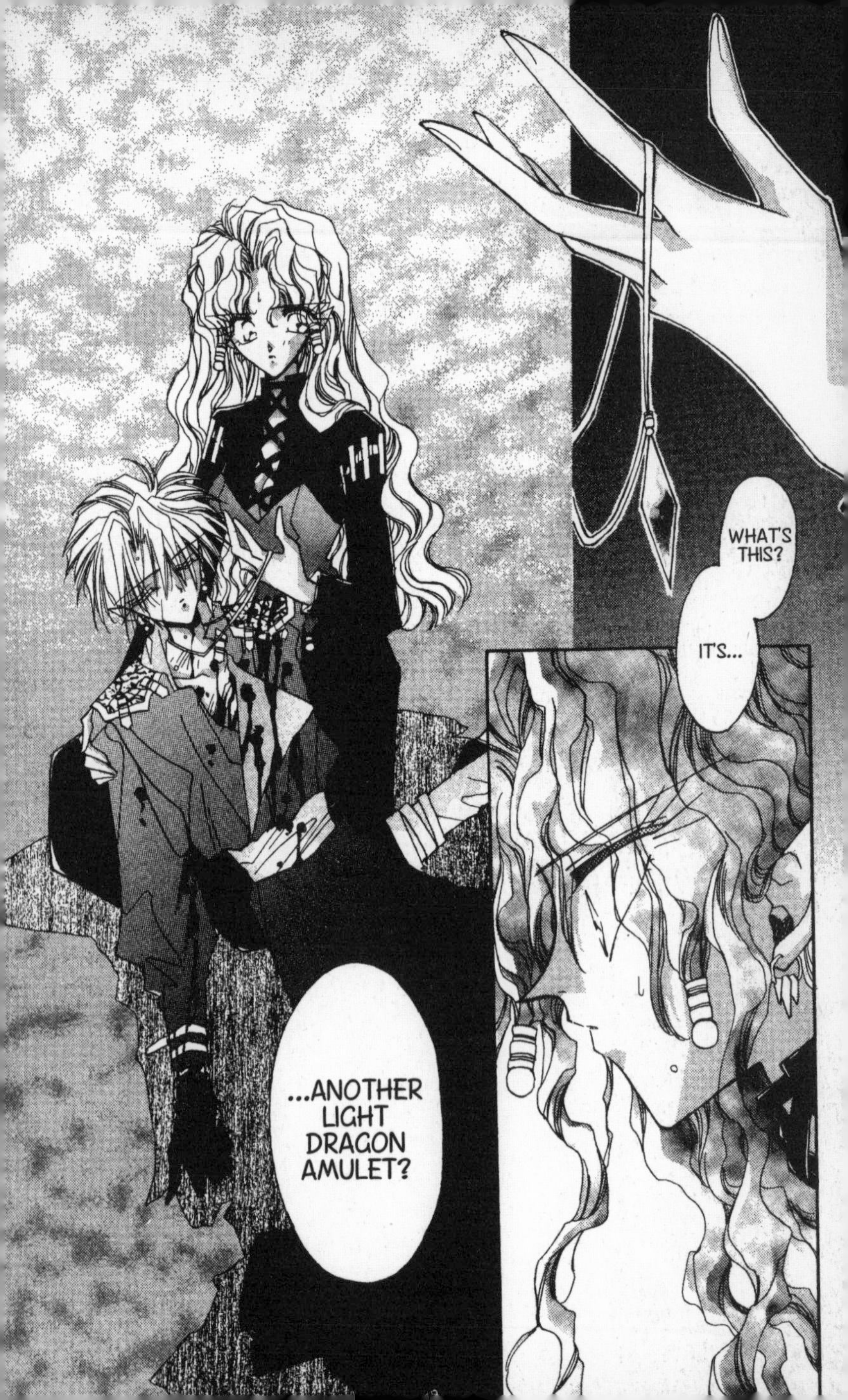
WHAT'S THIS?
IT'S...
...ANOTHER LIGHT DRAGON AMULET?

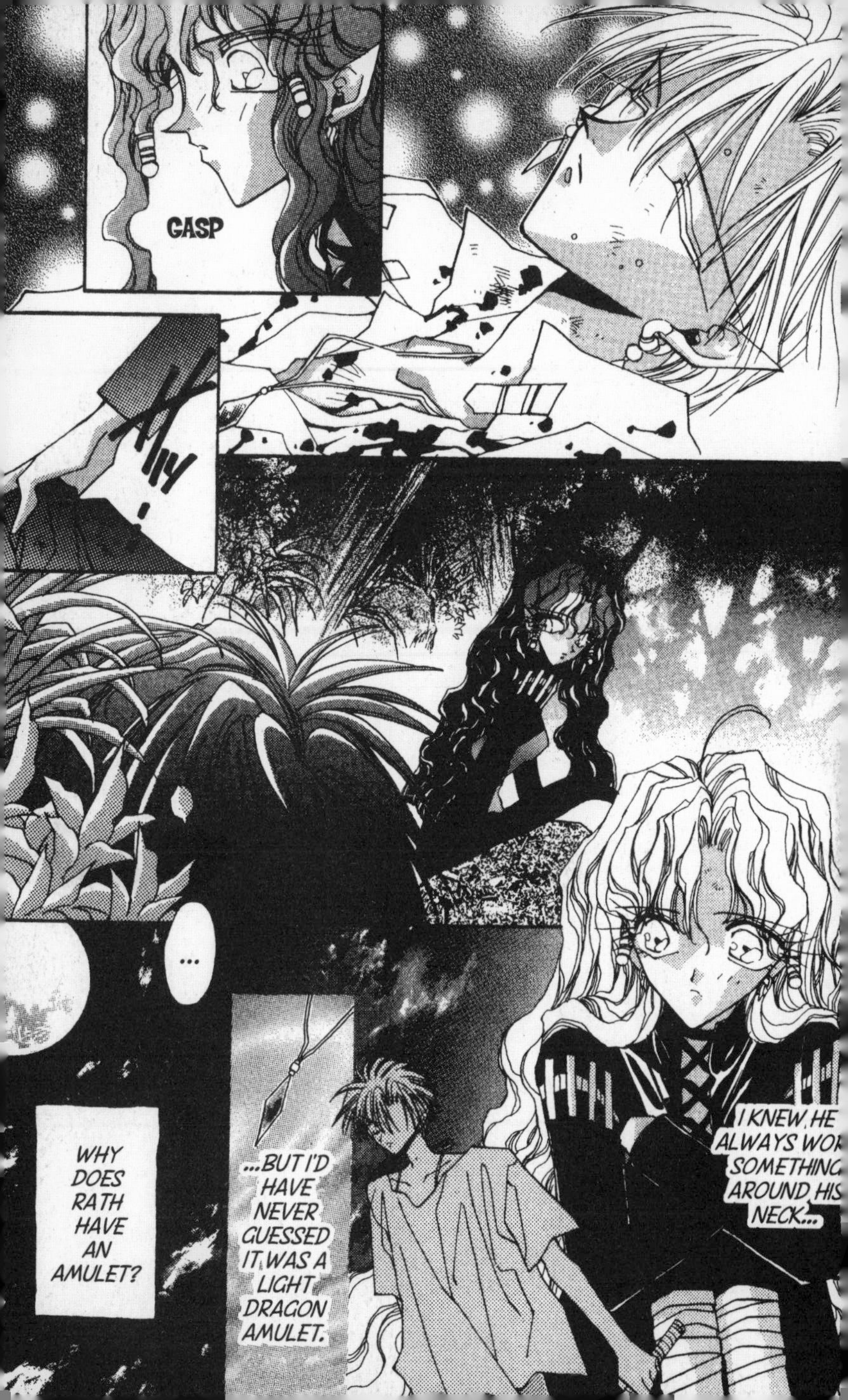
GASP
I KNEW HE ALWAYS WOR SOMETHING AROUND HIS NECK...
...BUT I'D HAVE NEVER GUESSED IT WAS A LIGHT DRAGON AMULET.
...
WHY DOES RATH HAVE AN AMULET?

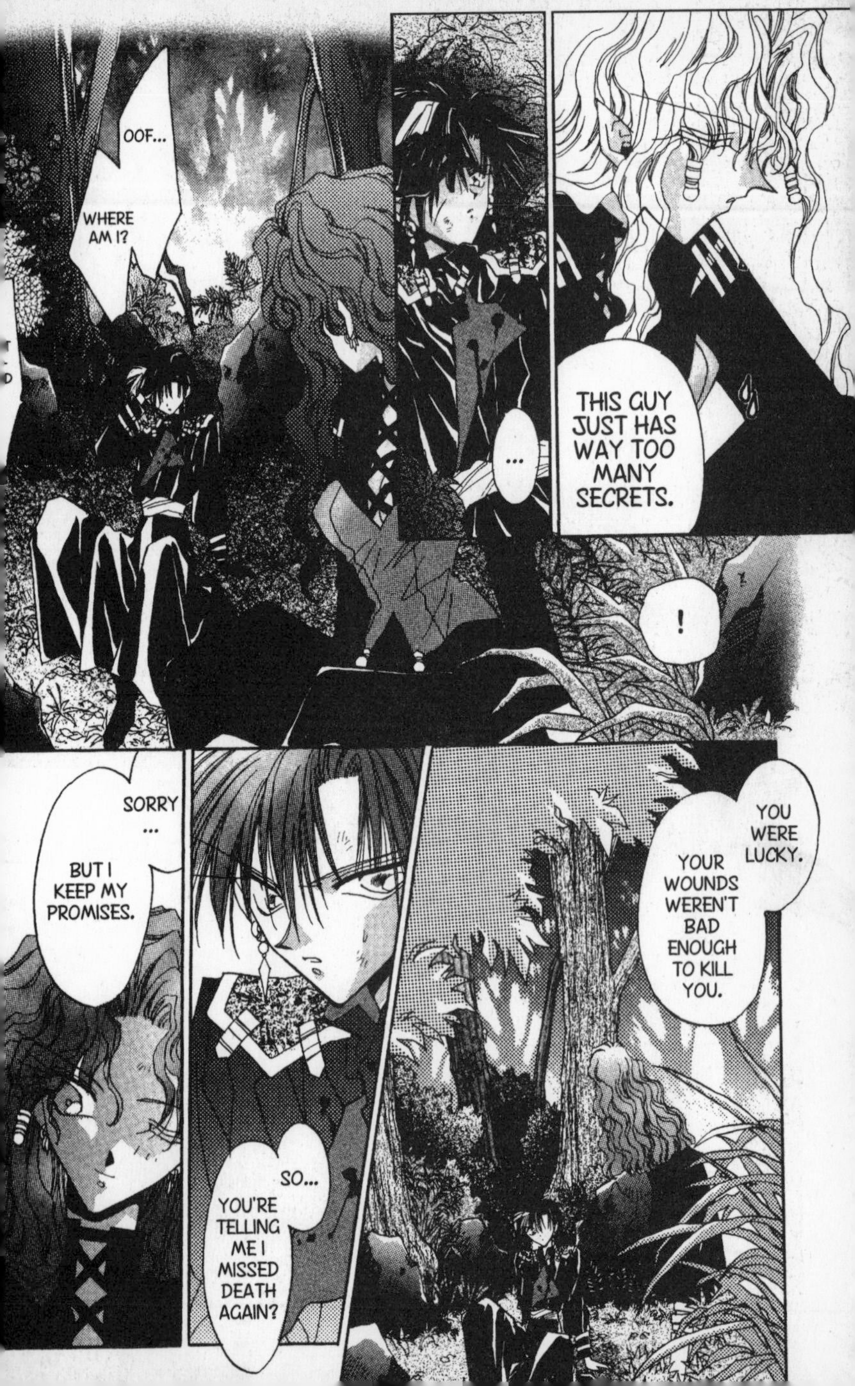
THIS GUY JUST HAS WAY TOO MANY SECRETS.
...
OOF...
WHERE AM I?
!
YOU WERE LUCKY.
YOUR WOUNDS WEREN'T BAD ENOUGH TO KILL YOU.
SO...
YOU'RE TELLING ME I MISSED DEATH AGAIN?
SORRY ...
BUT I KEEP MY PROMISES.

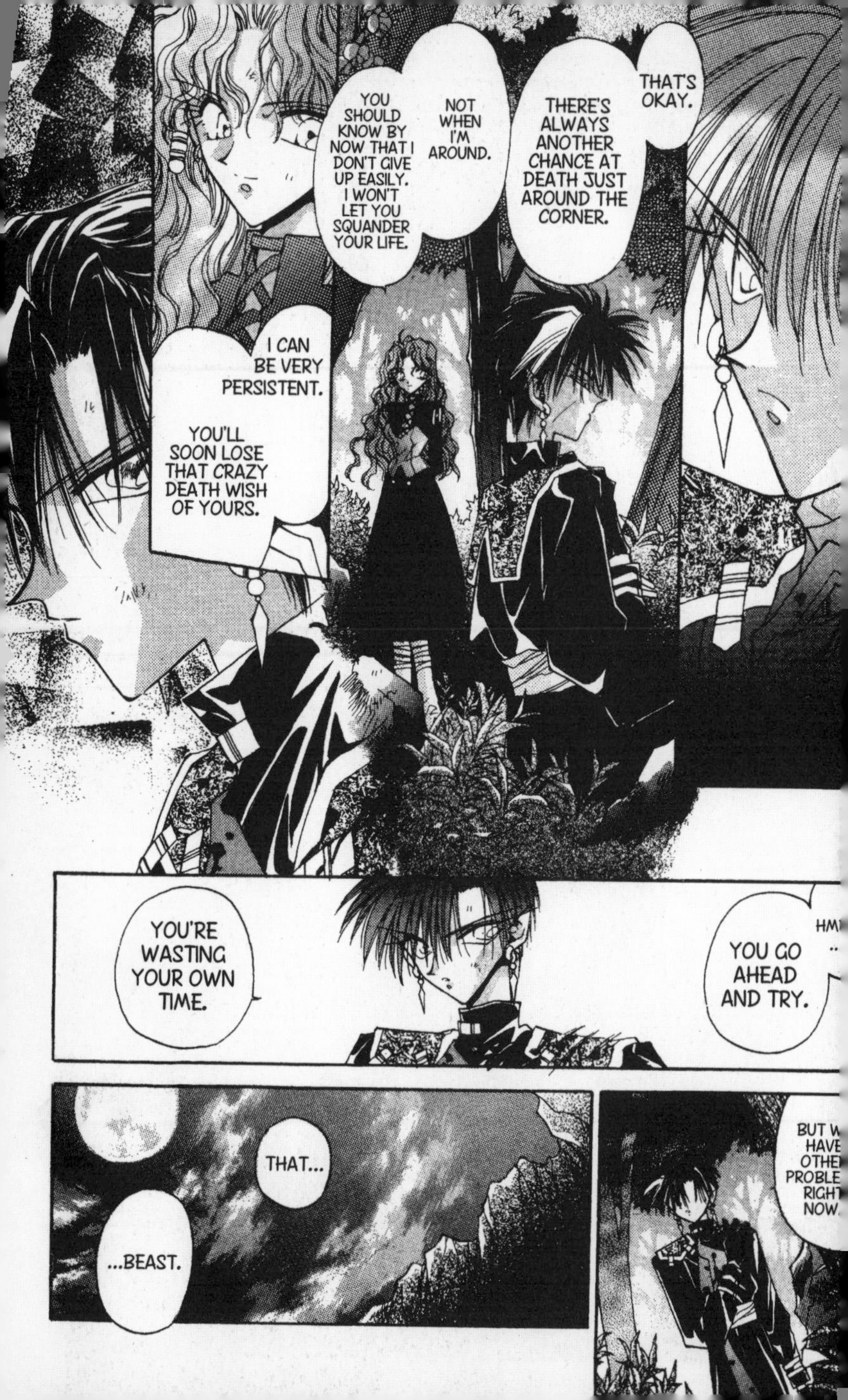
THAT'S OKAY.
THERE'S ALWAYS ANOTHER CHANCE AT DEATH JUST AROUND THE CORNER.
NOT WHEN I'M AROUND.
YOU SHOULD KNOW BY NOW THAT I DON'T GIVE UP EASILY. I WON'T LET YOU SQUANDER YOUR LIFE.
I CAN BE VERY PERSISTENT.
YOU'LL SOON LOSE THAT CRAZY DEATH WISH OF YOURS.
HM ..
YOU GO AHEAD AND TRY.
YOU'RE WASTING YOUR OWN TIME.
BUT W HAVE OTHE PROBLE RIGHT NOW.
THAT...
...BEAST.

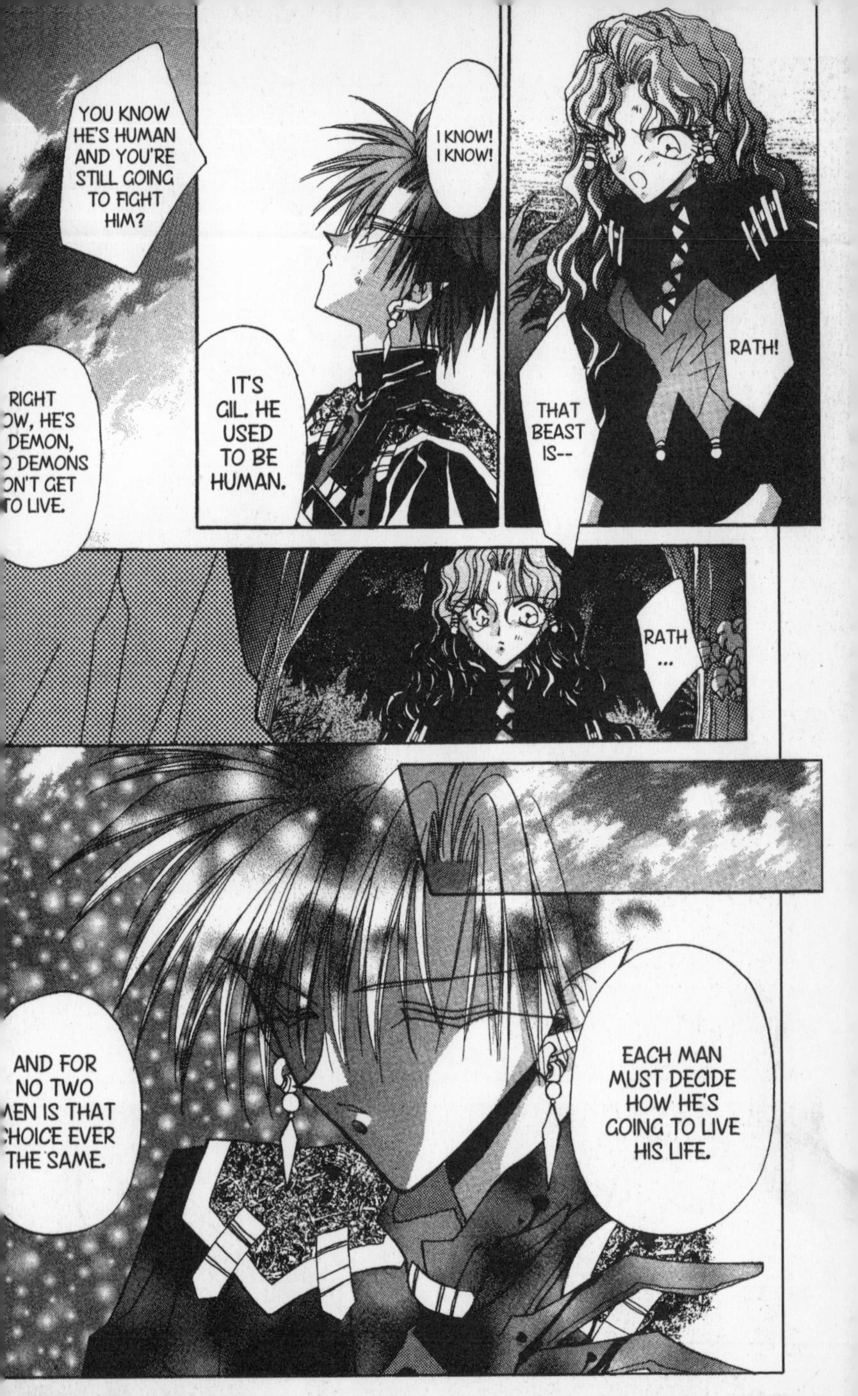
RATH!
THAT BEAST IS--
I KNOW! I KNOW!
IT'S GIL. HE USED TO BE HUMAN.
YOU KNOW HE'S HUMAN AND YOU'RE STILL GOING TO FIGHT HIM?
RIGHT OW, HE'S DEMON, DEMONS ON'T GET O LIVE.
RATH ...
EACH MAN MUST DECIDE HOW HE'S GOING TO LIVE HIS LIFE.
AND FOR NO TWO EN IS THAT HOICE EVER THE SAME.

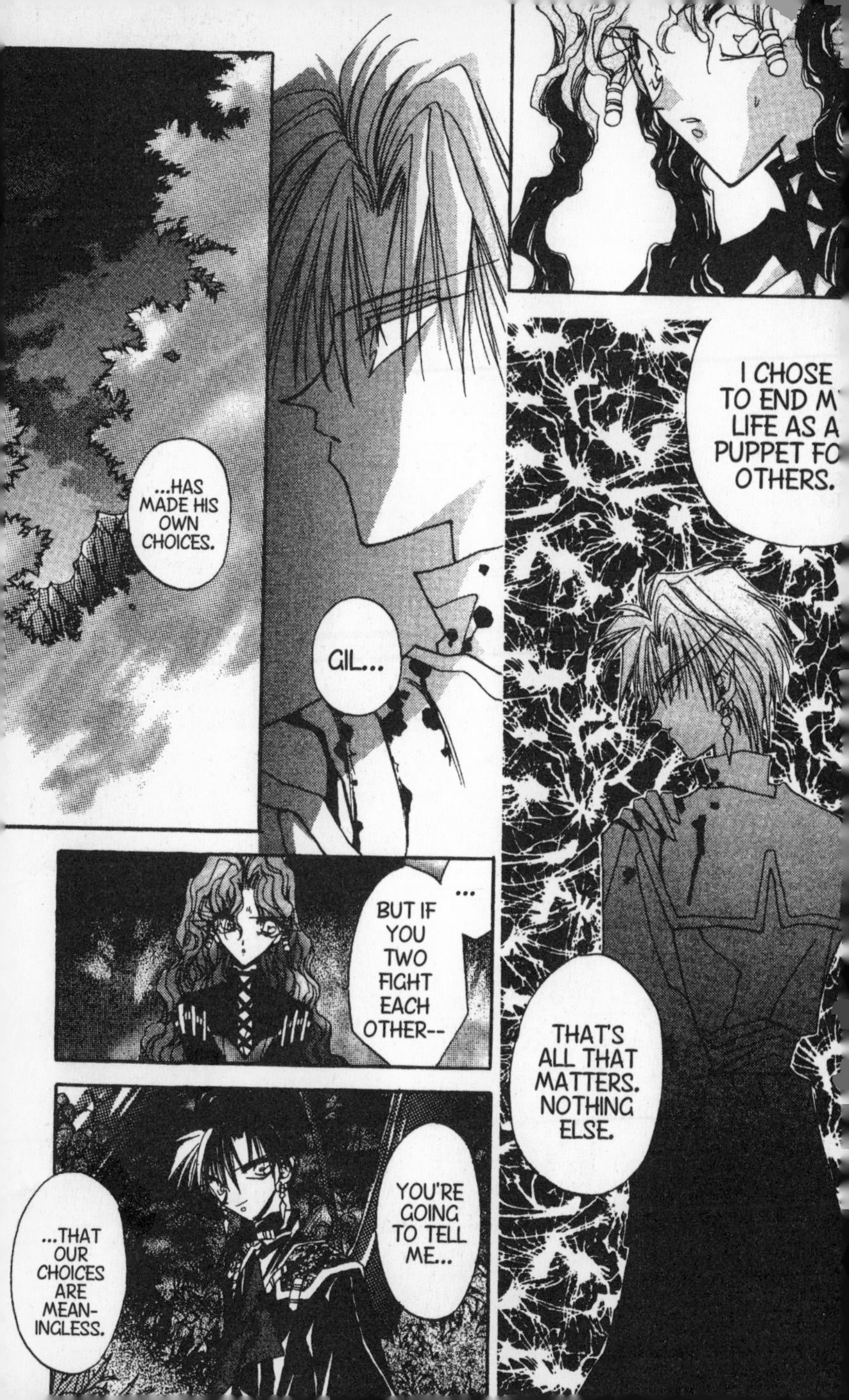
GIL...
...HAS MADE HIS OWN CHOICES.
I CHOSE TO END M LIFE AS A PUPPET FO OTHERS.
THAT'S ALL THAT MATTERS. NOTHING ELSE.
...
BUT IF YOU TWO FIGHT EACH OTHER--
YOU'RE GOING TO TELL ME...
...THAT OUR CHOICES ARE MEAN-INGLESS.

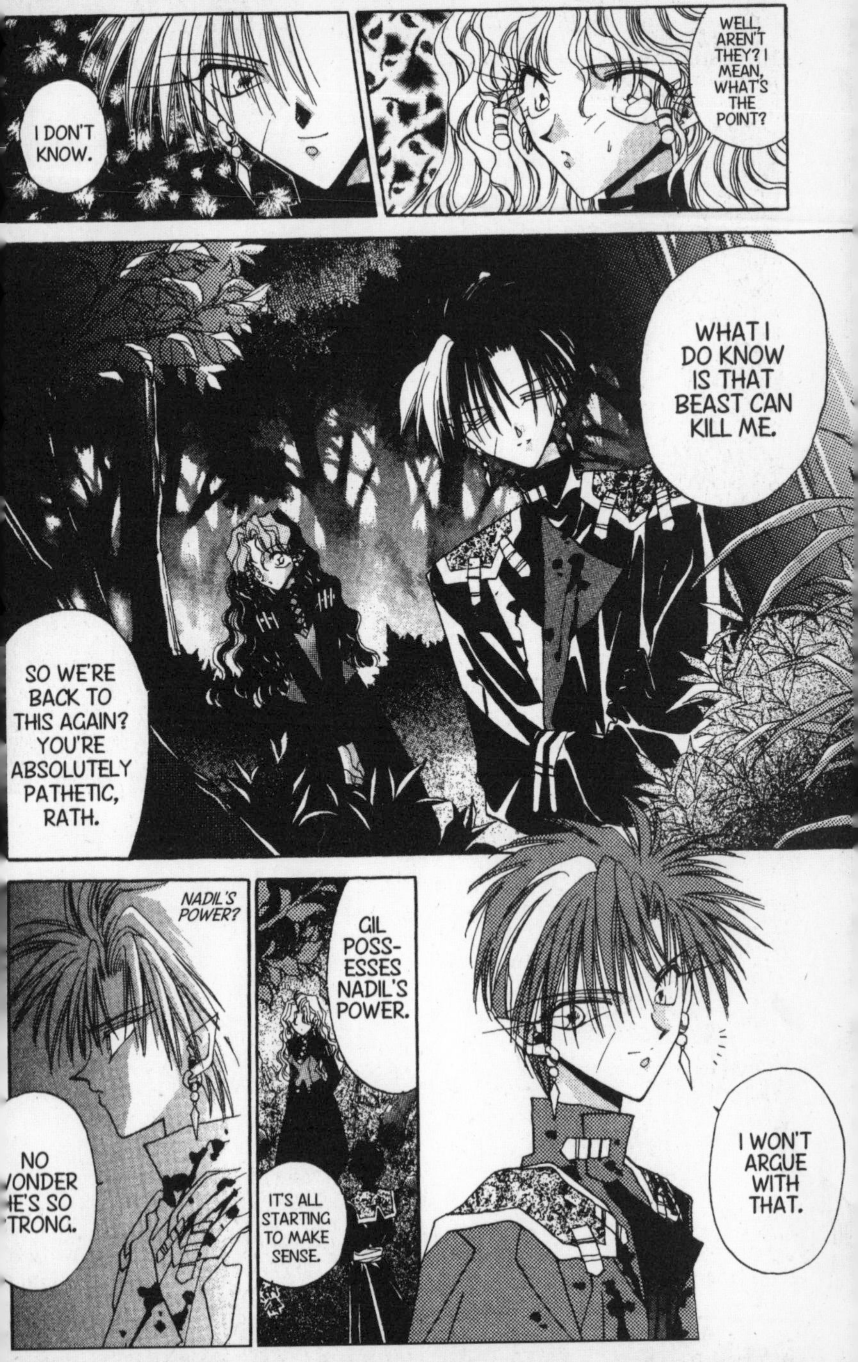

WELL, AREN'T THEY? I MEAN, WHAT'S THE POINT?
I DON'T KNOW.
WHAT I DO KNOW IS THAT BEAST CAN KILL ME.
SO WE'RE BACK TO THIS AGAIN? YOU'RE ABSOLUTELY PATHETIC, RATH.
I WON'T ARGUE WITH THAT.
GIL POSSESSES NADIL'S POWER.
IT'S ALL STARTING TO MAKE SENSE.
NADIL'S POWER?
NO WONDER HE'S SO TRONG.

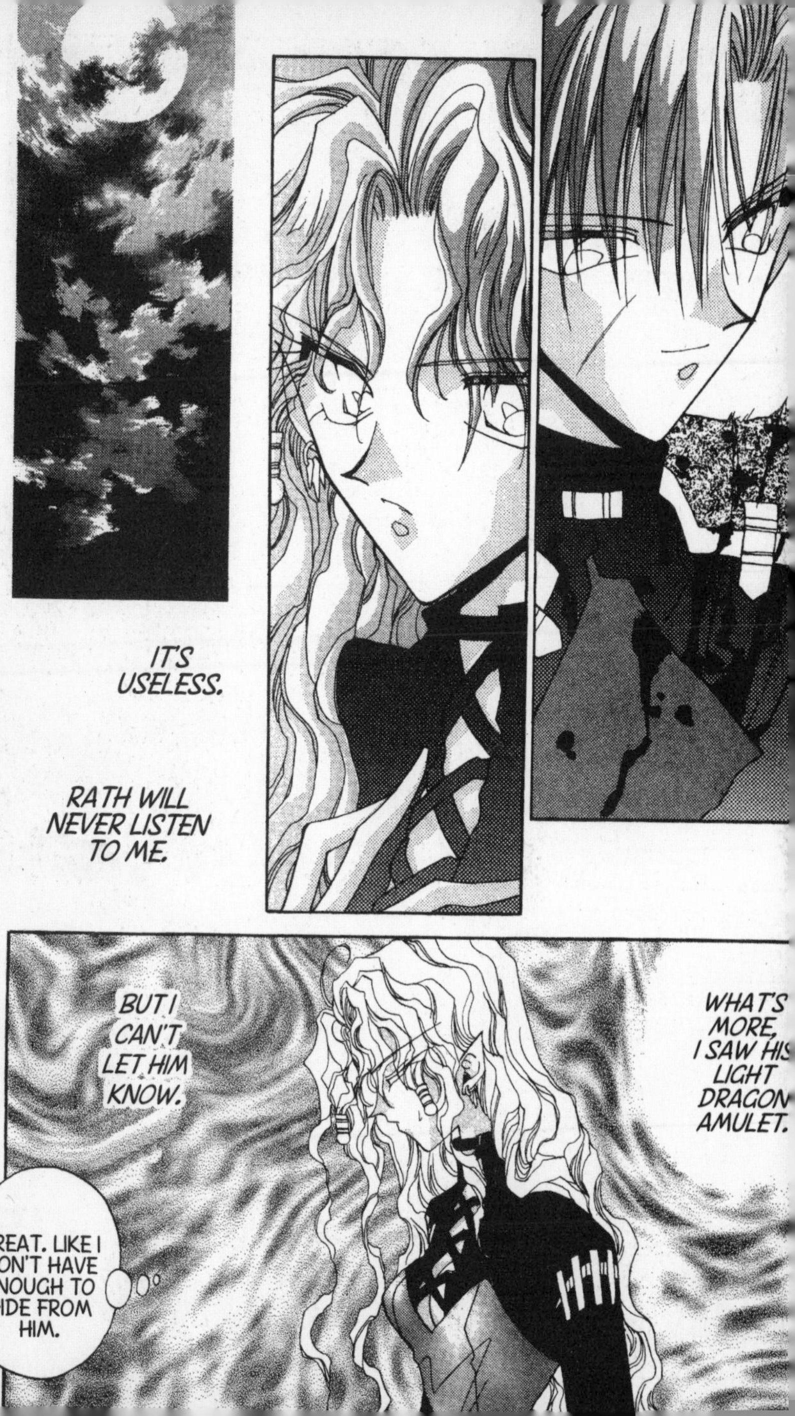
IT'S USELESS.
RATH WILL NEVER LISTEN TO ME.
WHAT'S MORE, I SAW HIS LIGHT DRAGON AMULET.
BUT I CAN'T LET HIM KNOW.
GREAT. LIKE I DON'T HAVE ENOUGH TO HIDE FROM HIM.

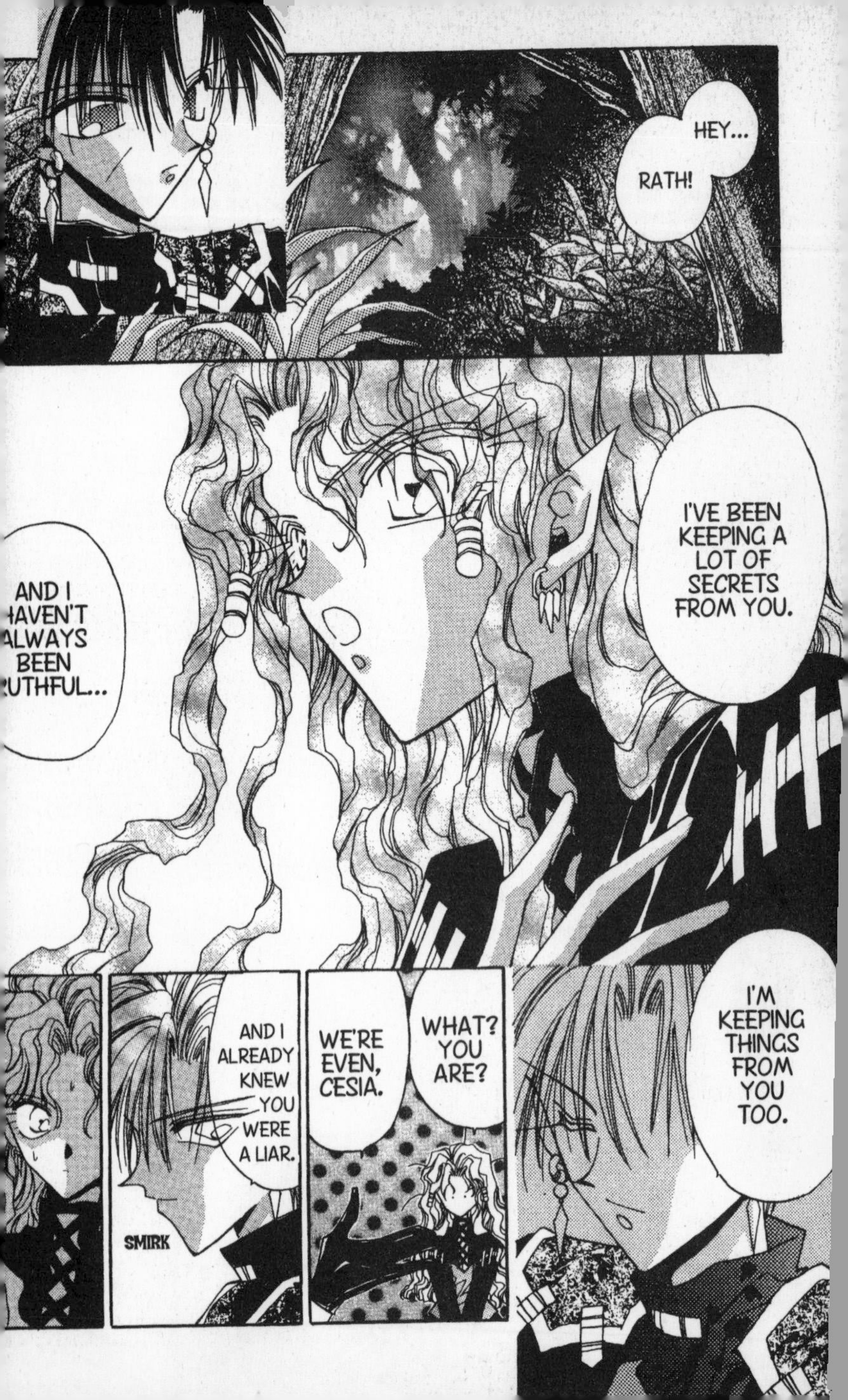
HEY... RATH!
I'VE BEEN KEEPING A LOT OF SECRETS FROM YOU.
AND I HAVEN'T ALWAYS BEEN TRUTHFUL...
I'M KEEPING THINGS FROM YOU TOO.
WHAT? YOU ARE?
WE'RE EVEN, CESIA.
AND I ALREADY KNEW YOU WERE A LIAR.
SMIRK

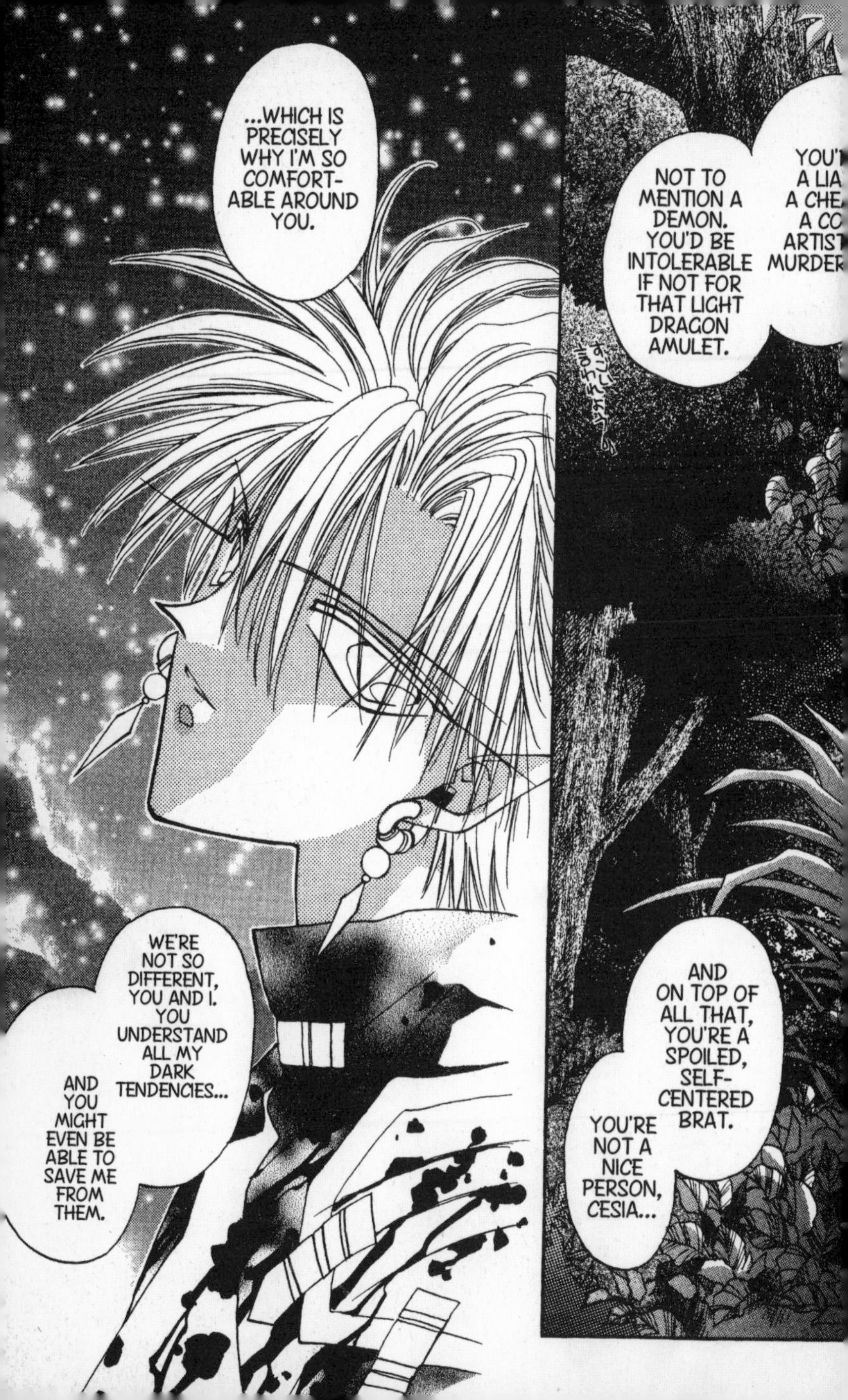
YOU' A LIA A CHE A CO ARTIST MURDER
NOT TO MENTION A DEMON. YOU'D BE INTOLERABLE IF NOT FOR THAT LIGHT DRAGON AMULET.
AND ON TOP OF ALL THAT, YOU'RE A SPOILED, SELF-CENTERED BRAT.
YOU'RE NOT A NICE PERSON, CESIA...
...WHICH IS PRECISELY WHY I'M SO COMFORT-ABLE AROUND YOU.
WE'RE NOT SO DIFFERENT, YOU AND I. YOU UNDERSTAND ALL MY DARK TENDENCIES...
AND YOU MIGHT EVEN BE ABLE TO SAVE ME FROM THEM.

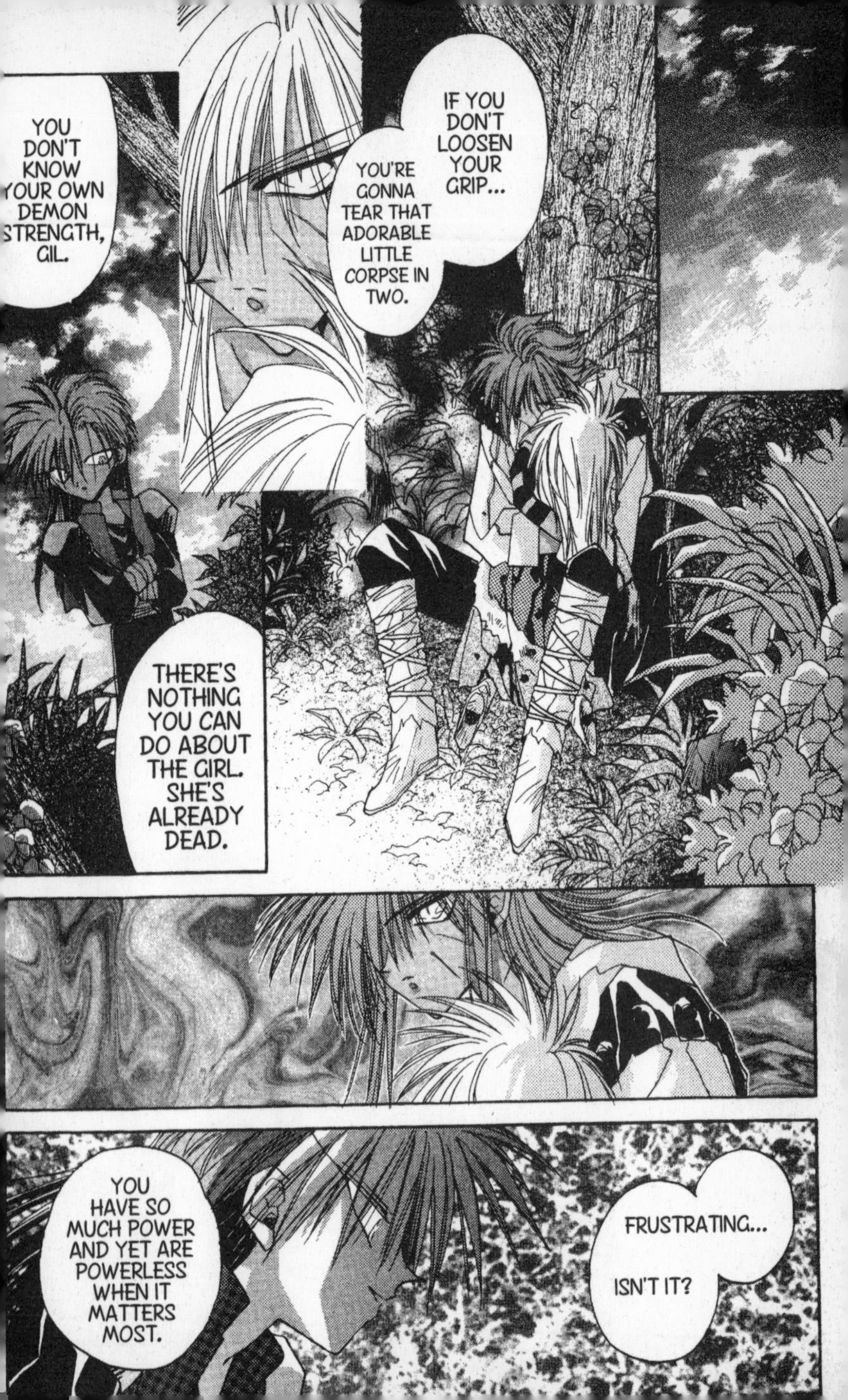

IF YOU DON'T LOOSEN YOUR GRIP...
YOU'RE GONNA TEAR THAT ADORABLE LITTLE CORPSE IN TWO.
YOU DON'T KNOW YOUR OWN DEMON STRENGTH, GIL.
THERE'S NOTHING YOU CAN DO ABOUT THE GIRL. SHE'S ALREADY DEAD.
FRUSTRATING...
ISN'T IT?
YOU HAVE SO MUCH POWER AND YET ARE POWERLESS WHEN IT MATTERS MOST.

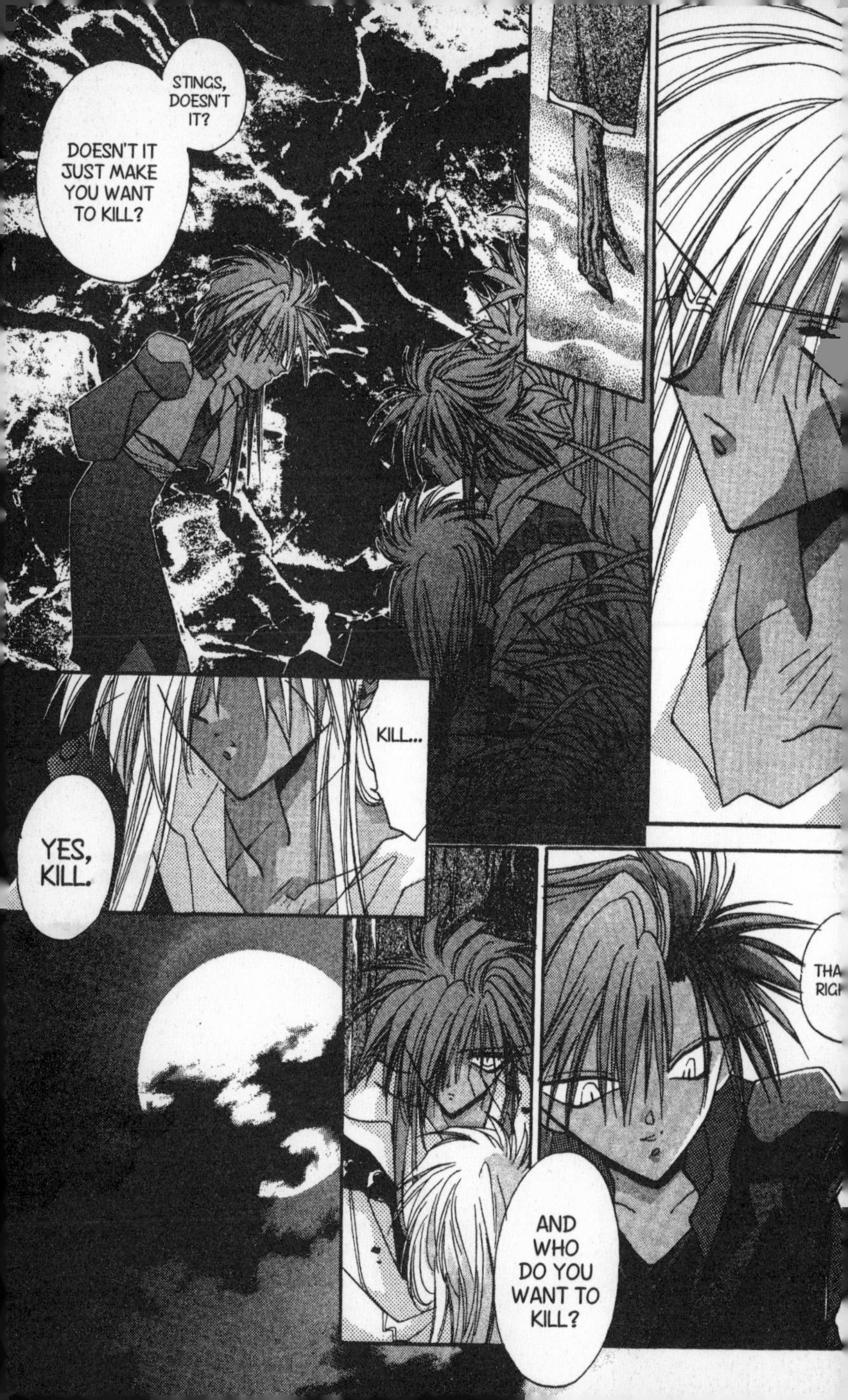
STINGS, DOESN'T IT?
DOESN'T IT JUST MAKE YOU WANT TO KILL?
KILL...
YES, KILL.
THA RIGH
AND WHO DO YOU WANT TO KILL?

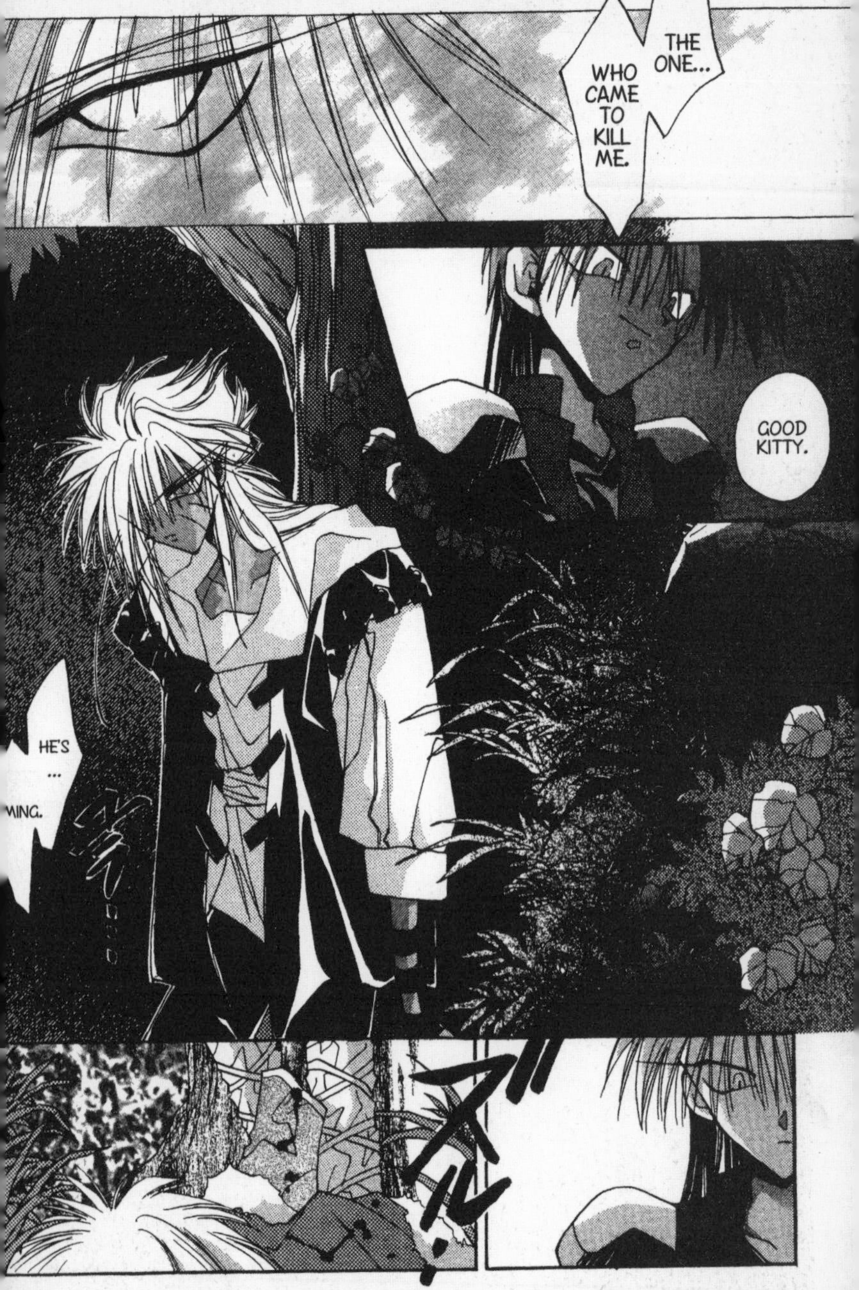
THE ONE...
WHO CAME TO KILL ME.
GOOD KITTY.
HE'S ... MING.

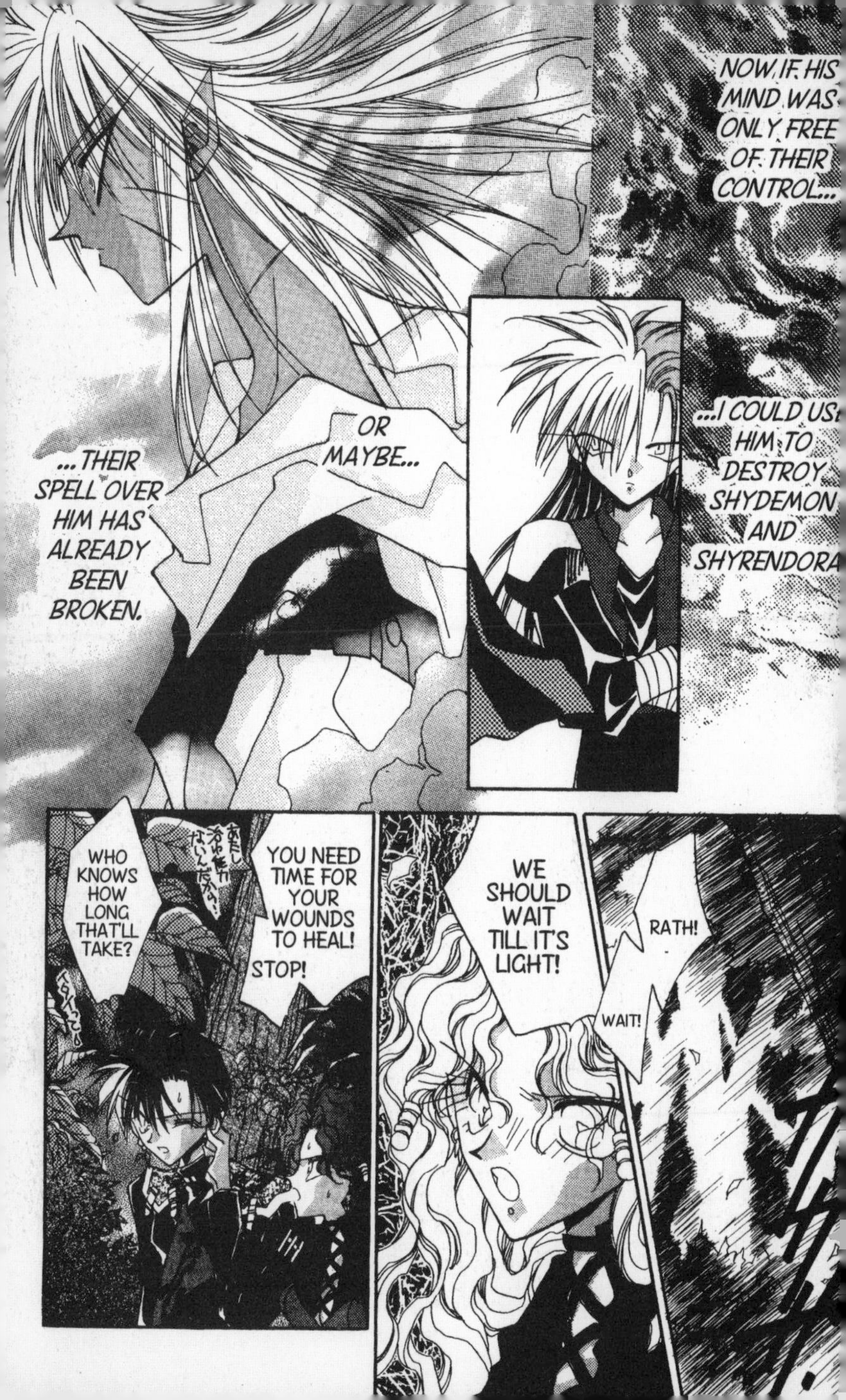
NOW IF HIS MIND WAS ONLY FREE OF THEIR CONTROL...
...I COULD USE HIM TO DESTROY SHYDEMON AND SHYRENDORA
OR MAYBE...
...THEIR SPELL OVER HIM HAS ALREADY BEEN BROKEN.
RATH!
WAIT!
WE SHOULD WAIT TILL IT'S LIGHT!
YOU NEED TIME FOR YOUR WOUNDS TO HEAL!
STOP!
WHO KNOWS HOW LONG THAT'LL TAKE?

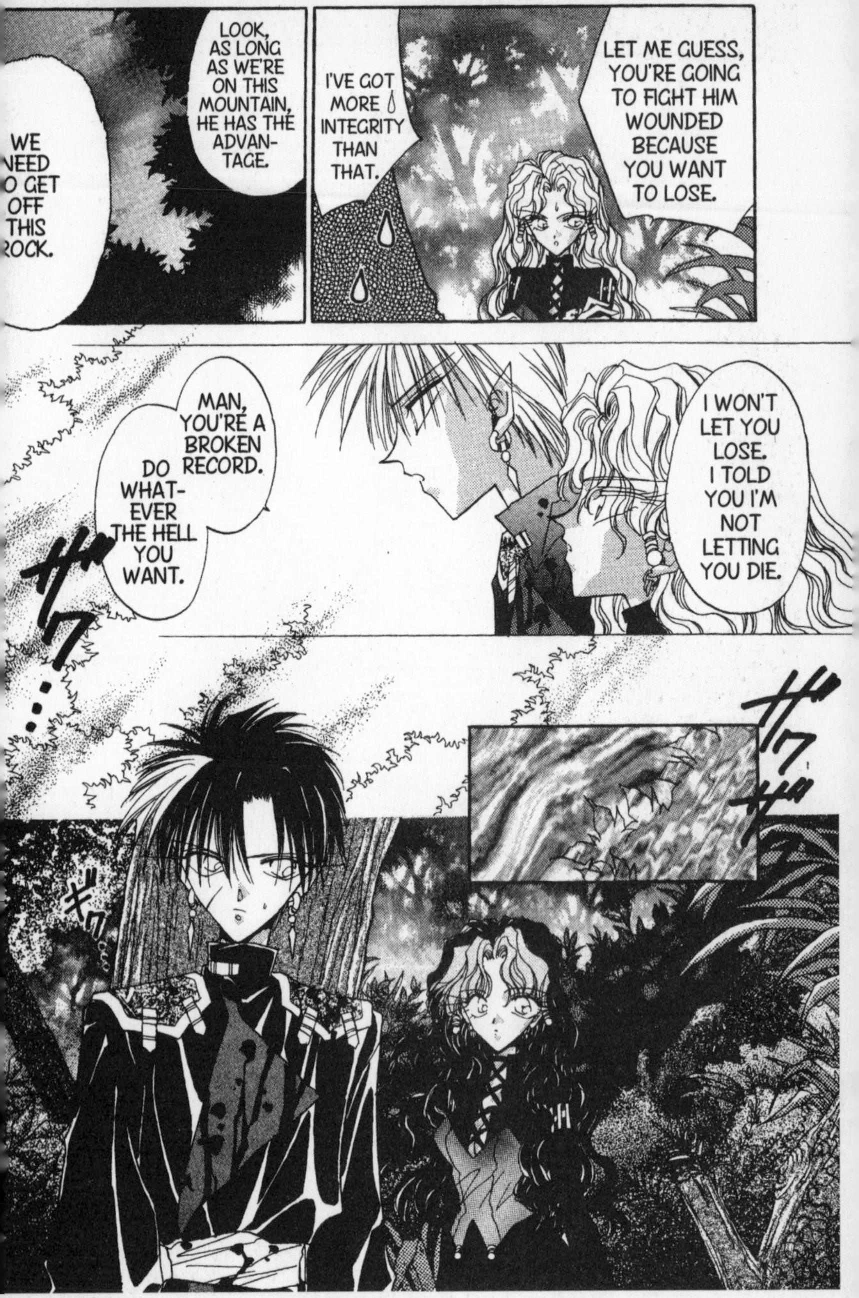
LET ME GUESS, YOU'RE GOING TO FIGHT HIM WOUNDED BECAUSE YOU WANT TO LOSE.
I'VE GOT MORE INTEGRITY THAN THAT.
LOOK, AS LONG AS WE'RE ON THIS MOUNTAIN, HE HAS THE ADVANTAGE.
WE NEED TO GET OFF THIS ROCK.
I WON'T LET YOU LOSE. I TOLD YOU I'M NOT LETTING YOU DIE.
MAN, YOU'RE A BROKEN RECORD.
DO WHATEVER THE HELL YOU WANT.

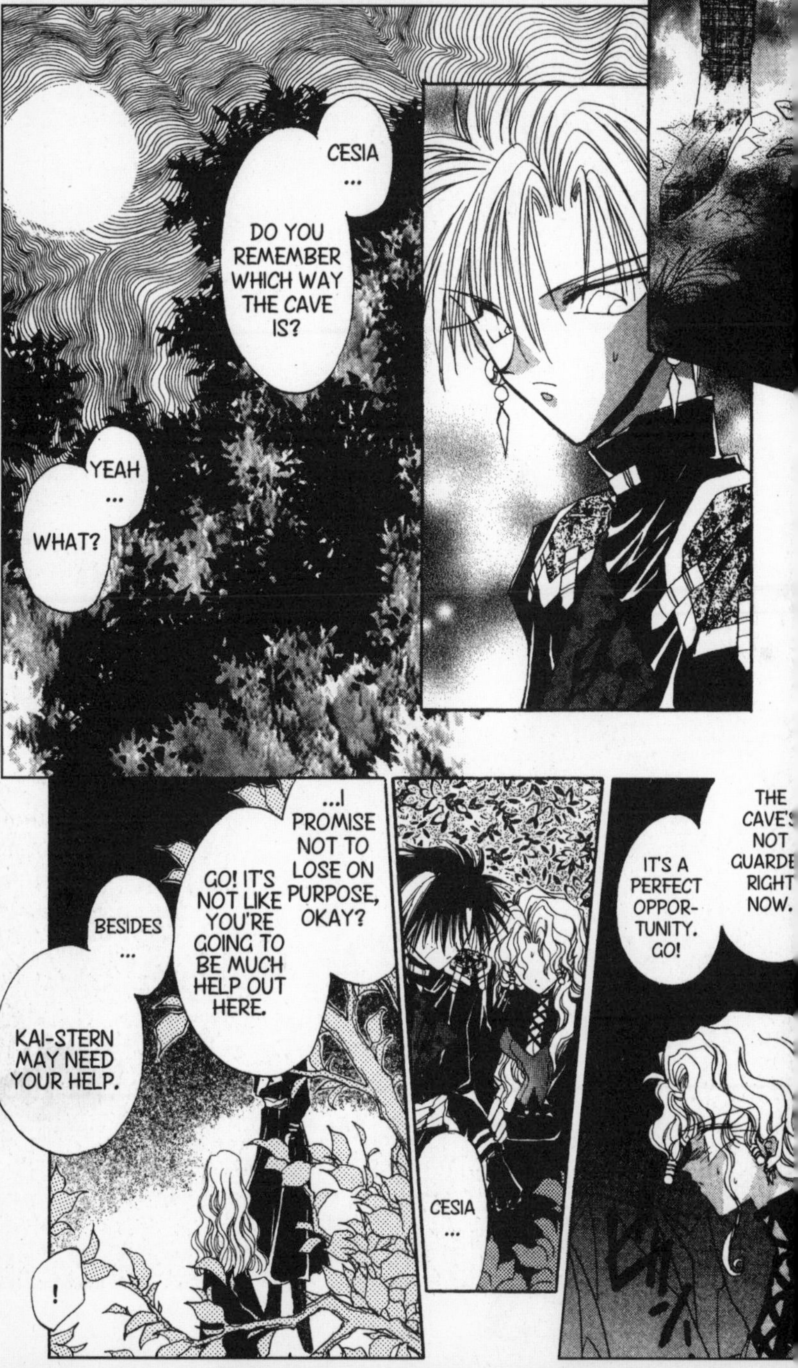

CESIA ... DO YOU REMEMBER WHICH WAY THE CAVE IS?
YEAH ... WHAT?
THE CAVE'S NOT GUARDE RIGHT NOW.
IT'S A PERFECT OPPOR-TUNITY. GO!
CESIA ...
...I PROMISE NOT TO LOSE ON PURPOSE, OKAY?
GO! IT'S NOT LIKE YOU'RE GOING TO BE MUCH HELP OUT HERE.
BESIDES ... KAI-STERN MAY NEED YOUR HELP.
!

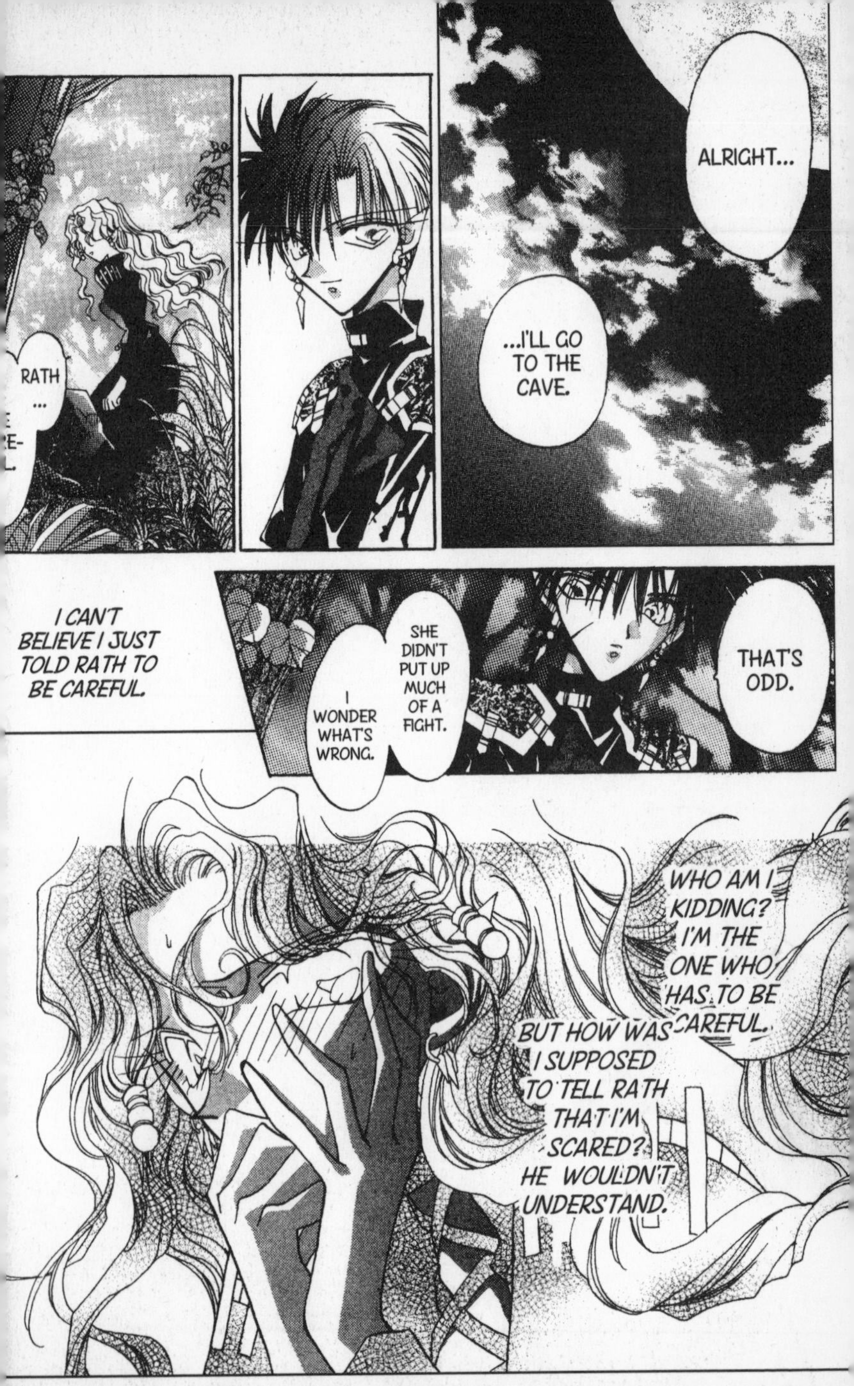
ALRIGHT...
...I'LL GO TO THE CAVE.
RATH ...
THAT'S ODD.
SHE DIDN'T PUT UP MUCH OF A FIGHT.
I WONDER WHAT'S WRONG.
I CAN'T BELIEVE I JUST TOLD RATH TO BE CAREFUL.
WHO AM I KIDDING? I'M THE ONE WHO HAS TO BE CAREFUL.
BUT HOW WAS I SUPPOSED TO TELL RATH THAT I'M SCARED? HE WOULDN'T UNDERSTAND.

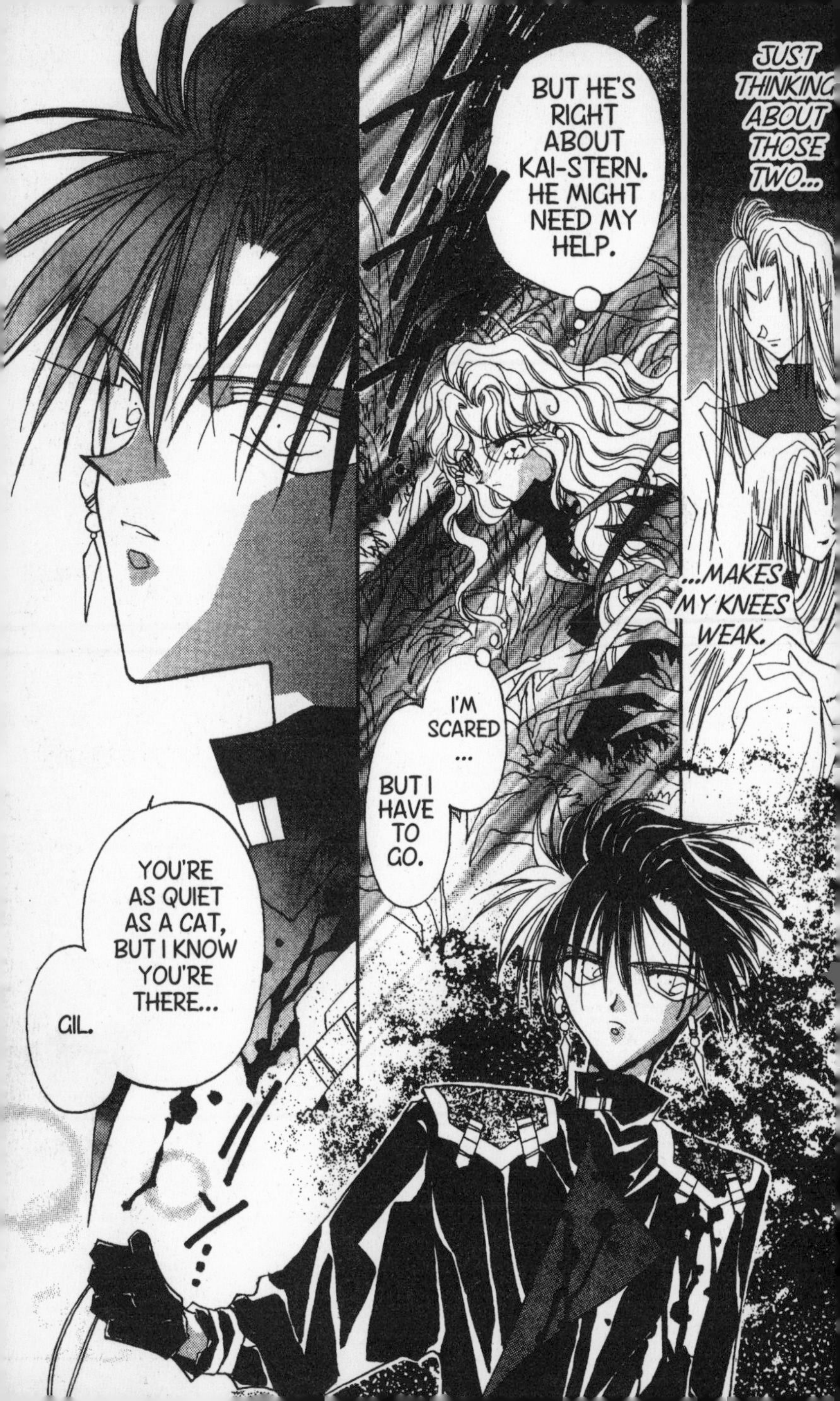
JUST THINKING ABOUT THOSE TWO...
...MAKES MY KNEES WEAK.
BUT HE'S RIGHT ABOUT KAI-STERN. HE MIGHT NEED MY HELP.
I'M SCARED ...
BUT I HAVE TO GO.
YOU'RE AS QUIET AS A CAT, BUT I KNOW YOU'RE THERE...
GIL.

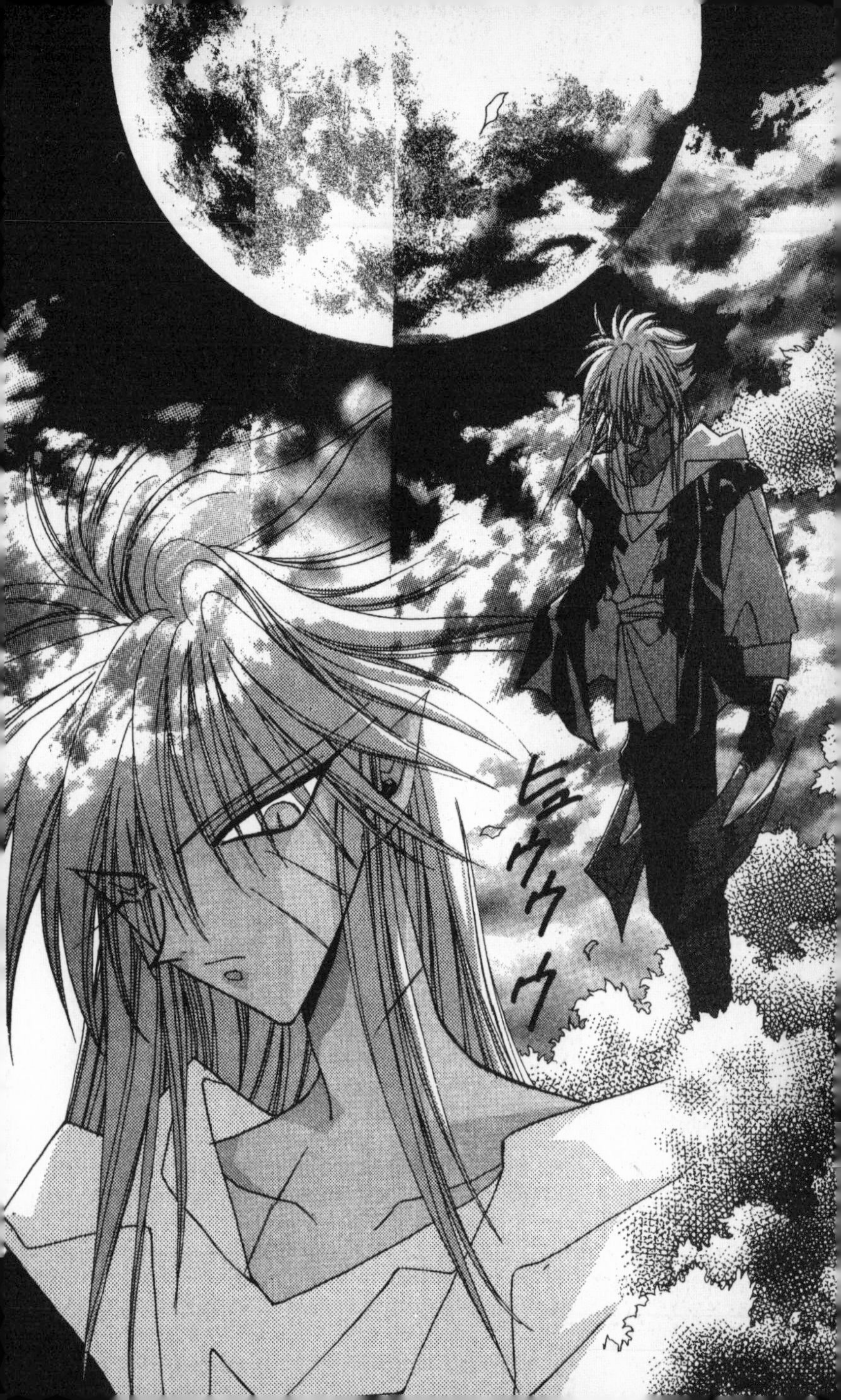
ヒュウウウ

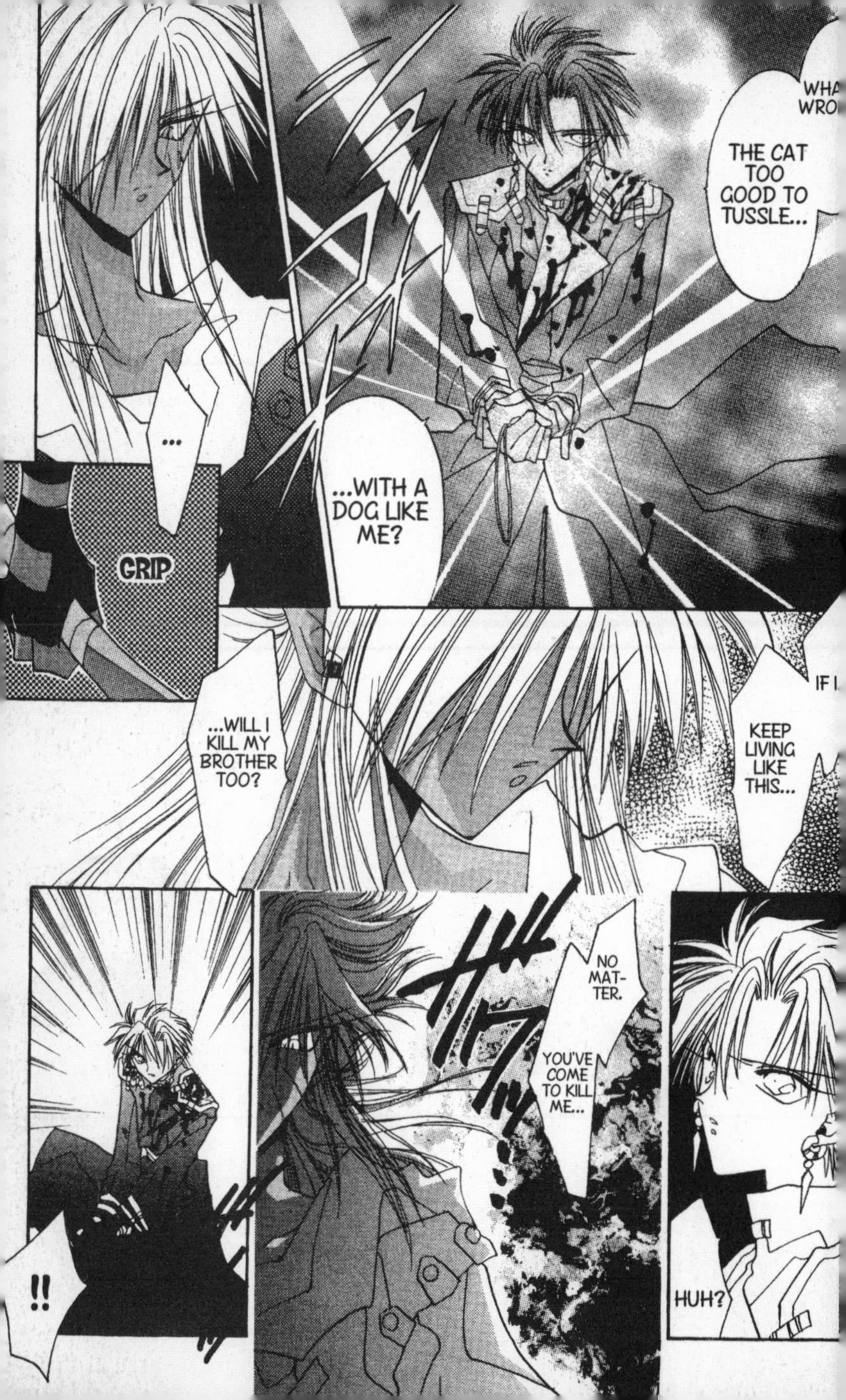

WHA WRO
THE CAT TOO GOOD TO TUSSLE...
...WITH A DOG LIKE ME?
...
GRIP
IF I
KEEP LIVING LIKE THIS...
...WILL I KILL MY BROTHER TOO?
HUH?
NO MATTER.
YOU'VE COME TO KILL ME...
!!

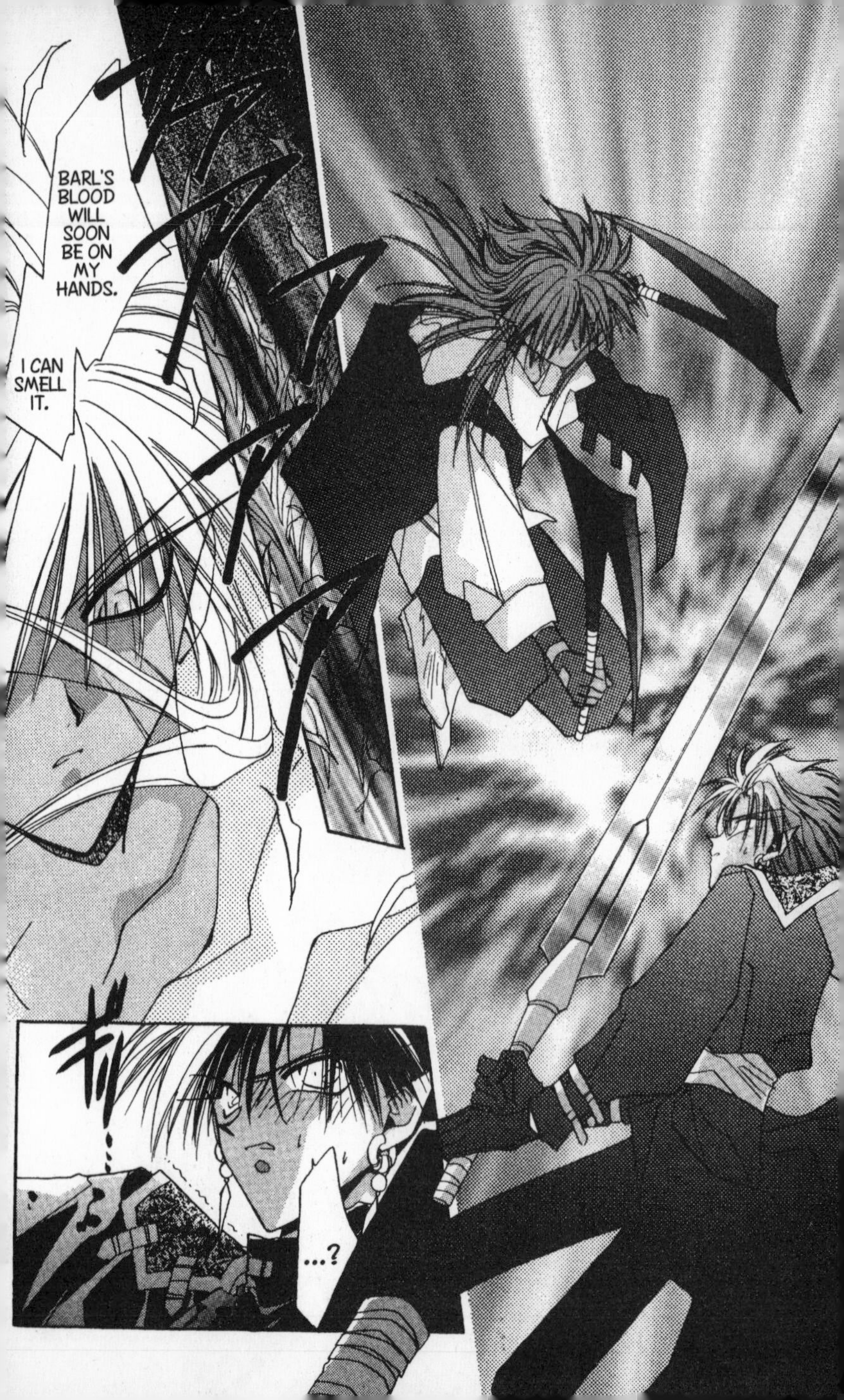
BARL'S BLOOD WILL SOON BE ON MY HANDS.
I CAN SMELL IT.
...?

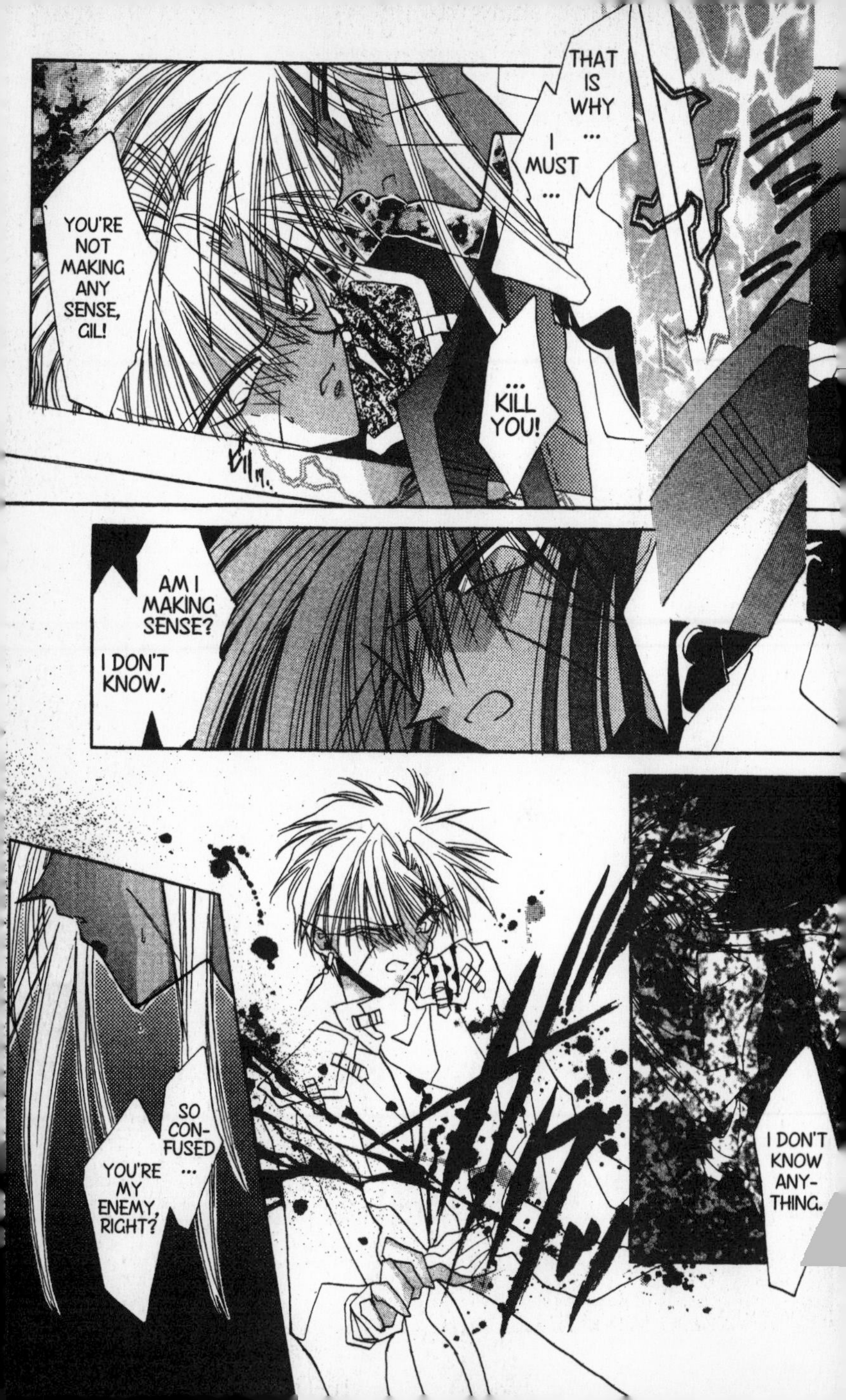
THAT IS WHY ... I MUST ...
... KILL YOU!
YOU'RE NOT MAKING ANY SENSE, GIL!
AM I MAKING SENSE?
I DON'T KNOW.
I DON'T KNOW ANYTHING.
SO CONFUSED ...
YOU'RE MY ENEMY, RIGHT?

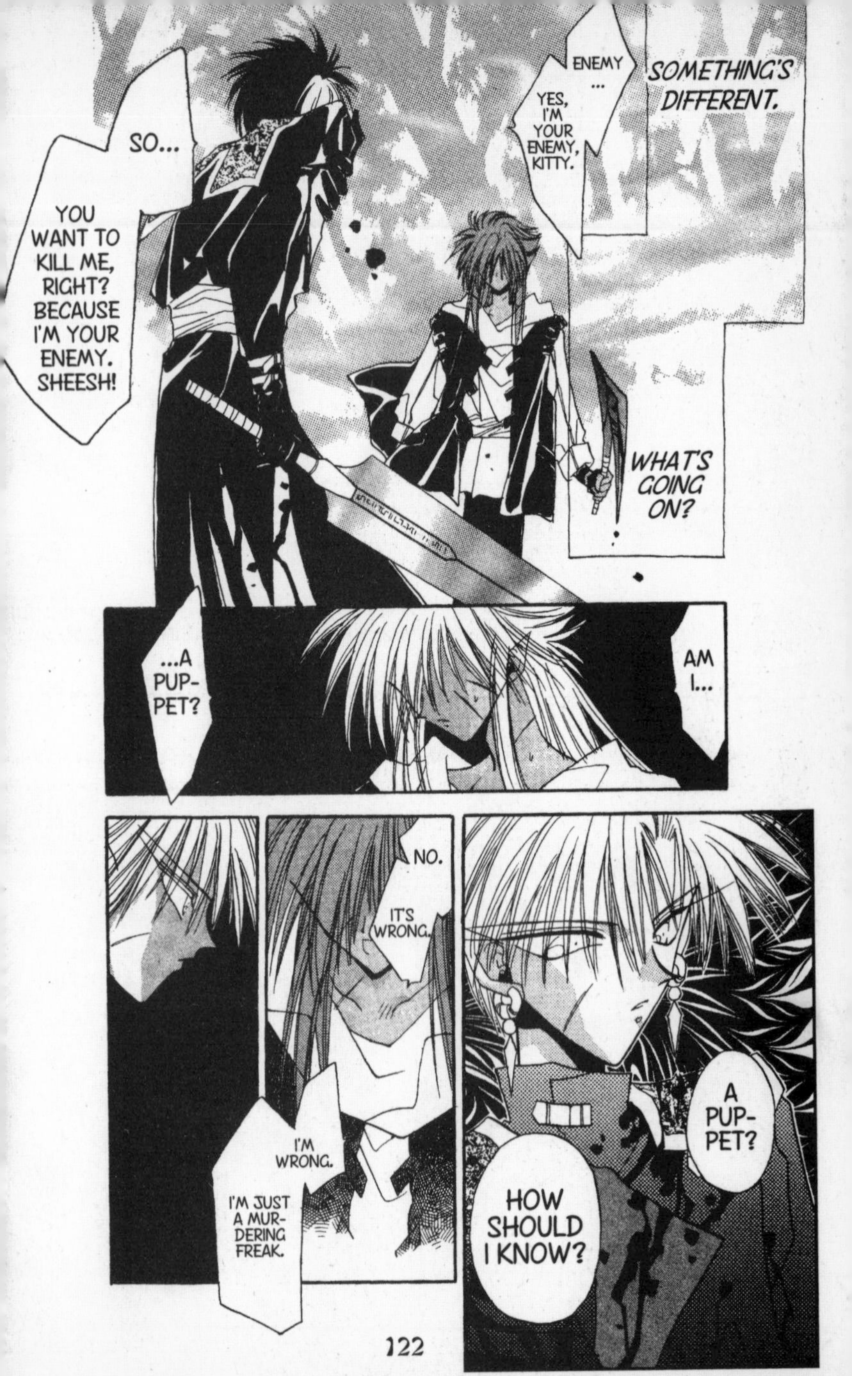
SOMETHING'S DIFFERENT.
ENEMY ...
YES, I'M YOUR ENEMY, KITTY.
SO...
YOU WANT TO KILL ME, RIGHT? BECAUSE I'M YOUR ENEMY. SHEESH!
WHAT'S GOING ON?
AM I...
...A PUP-PET?
A PUP-PET?
HOW SHOULD I KNOW?
NO.
IT'S WRONG.
I'M WRONG.
I'M JUST A MUR-DERING FREAK.

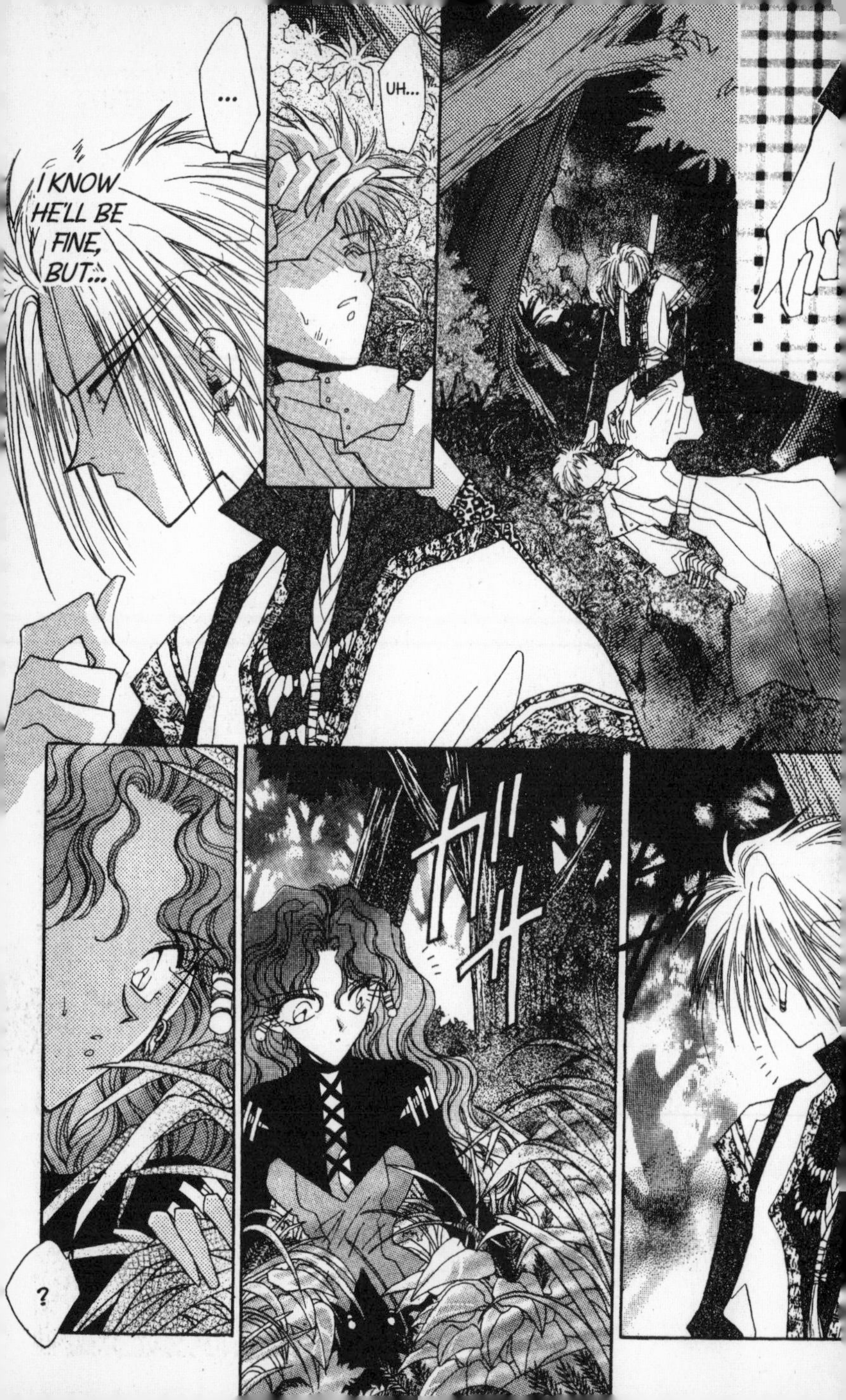
UH...
...
I KNOW HE'LL BE FINE, BUT...
ガサ
?

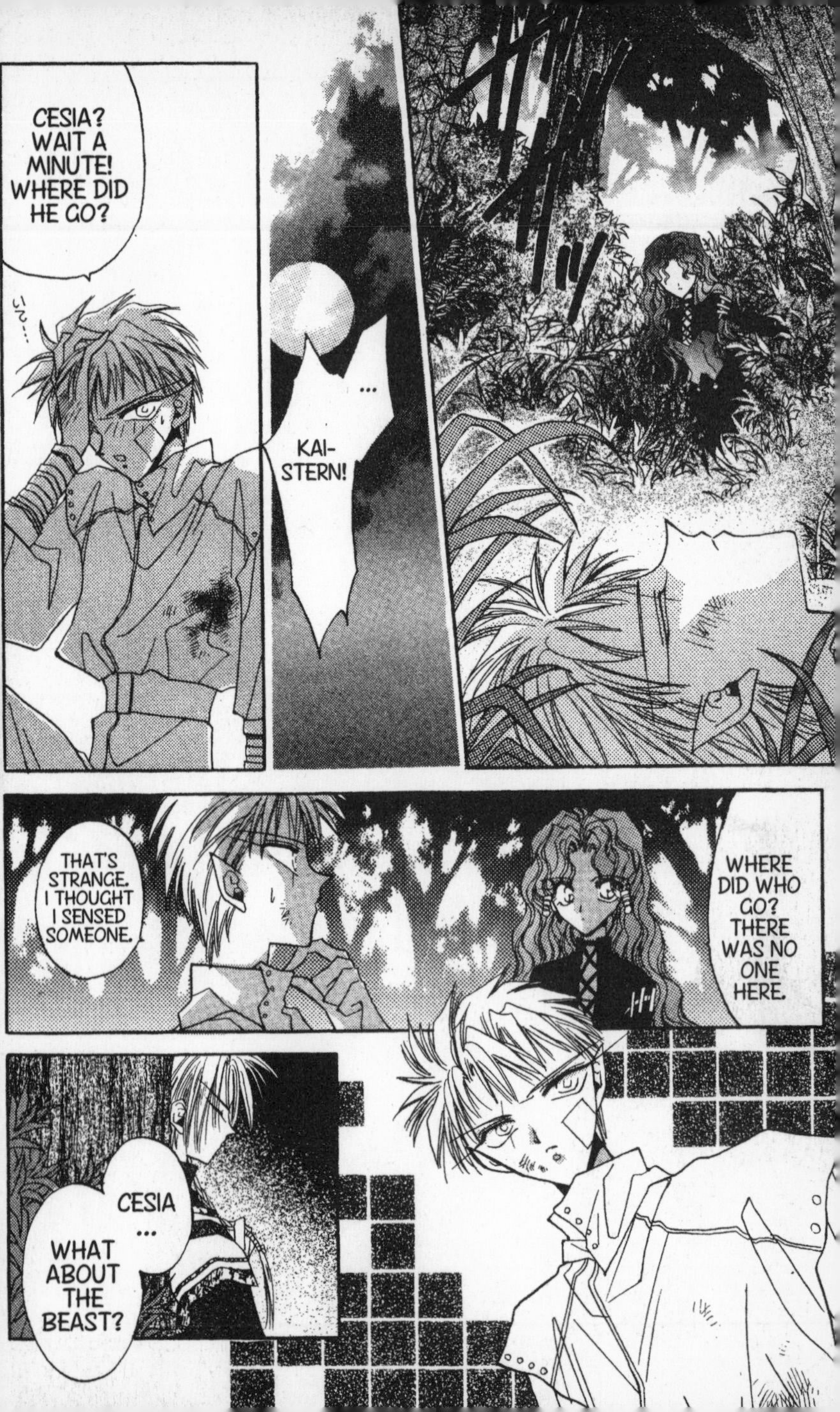
...
KAI-STERN!
CESIA? WAIT A MINUTE! WHERE DID HE GO?
WHERE DID WHO GO? THERE WAS NO ONE HERE.
THAT'S STRANGE. I THOUGHT I SENSED SOMEONE.
CESIA ... WHAT ABOUT THE BEAST?

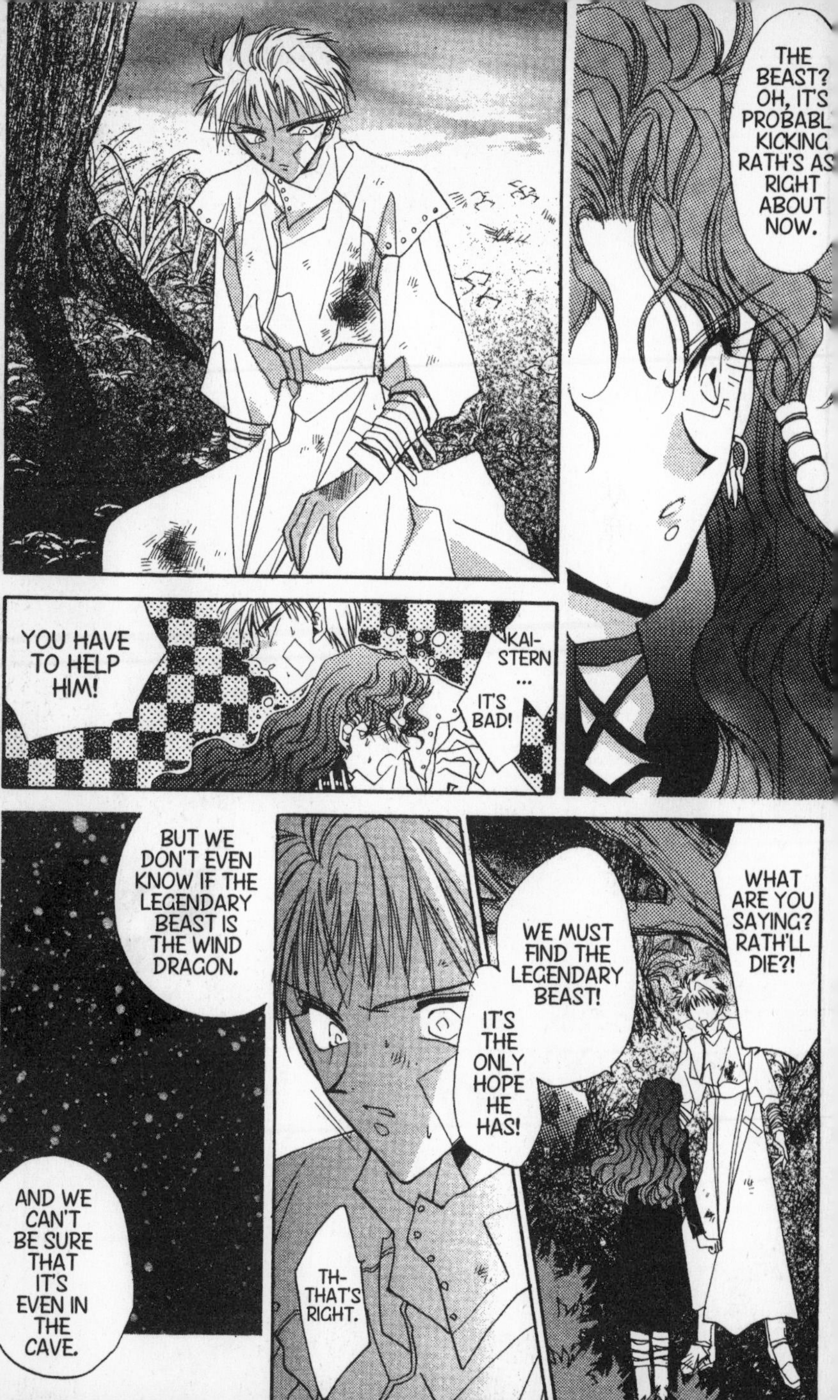
THE BEAST? OH, IT'S PROBABL KICKING RATH'S AS RIGHT ABOUT NOW.
KAI-STERN ...
IT'S BAD!
YOU HAVE TO HELP HIM!
WHAT ARE YOU SAYING? RATH'LL DIE?!
WE MUST FIND THE LEGENDARY BEAST!
IT'S THE ONLY HOPE HE HAS!
BUT WE DON'T EVEN KNOW IF THE LEGENDARY BEAST IS THE WIND DRAGON.
AND WE CAN'T BE SURE THAT IT'S EVEN IN THE CAVE.
TH-THAT'S RIGHT.

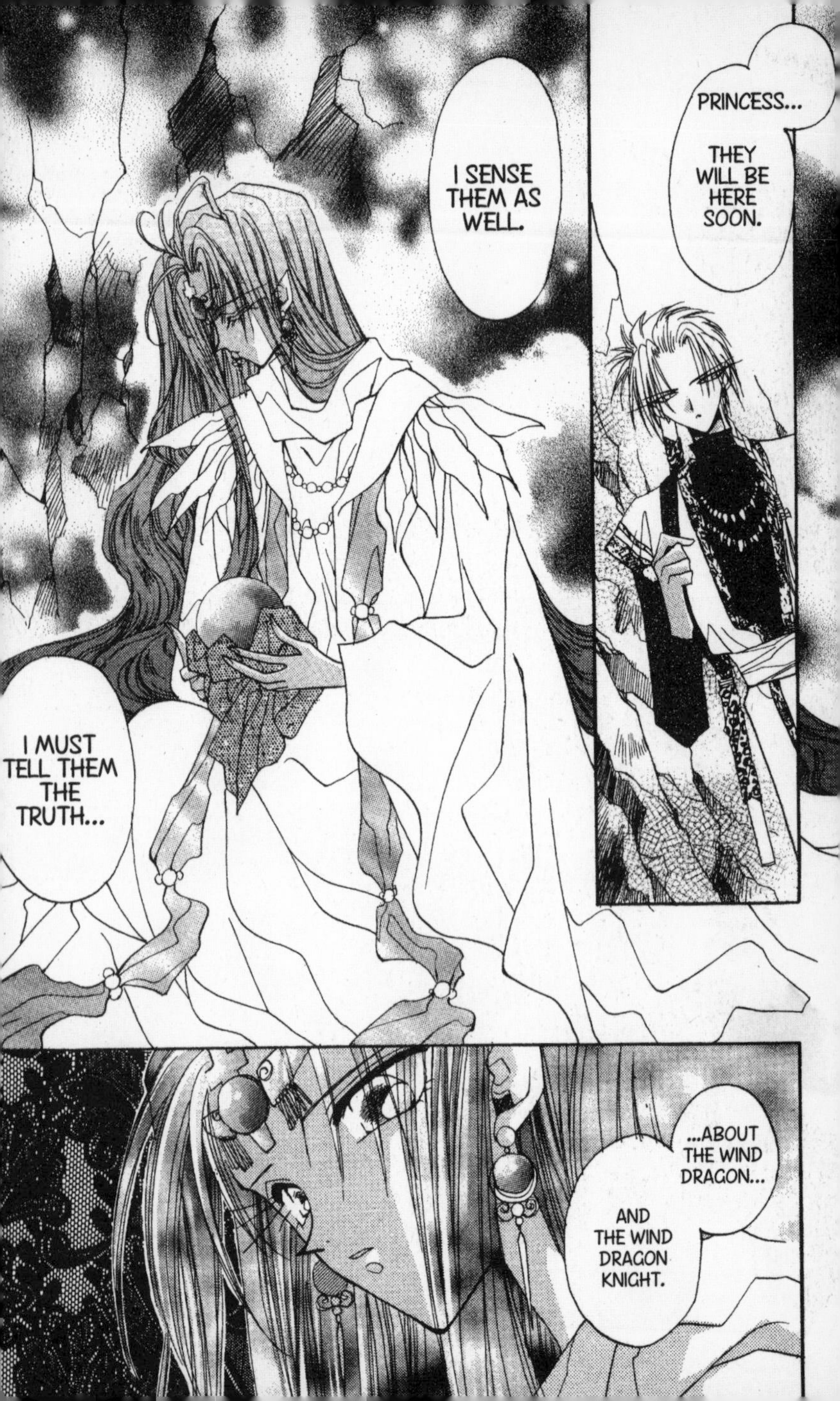
PRINCESS... THEY WILL BE HERE SOON.
I SENSE THEM AS WELL.
I MUST TELL THEM THE TRUTH...
...ABOUT THE WIND DRAGON...
AND THE WIND DRAGON KNIGHT.

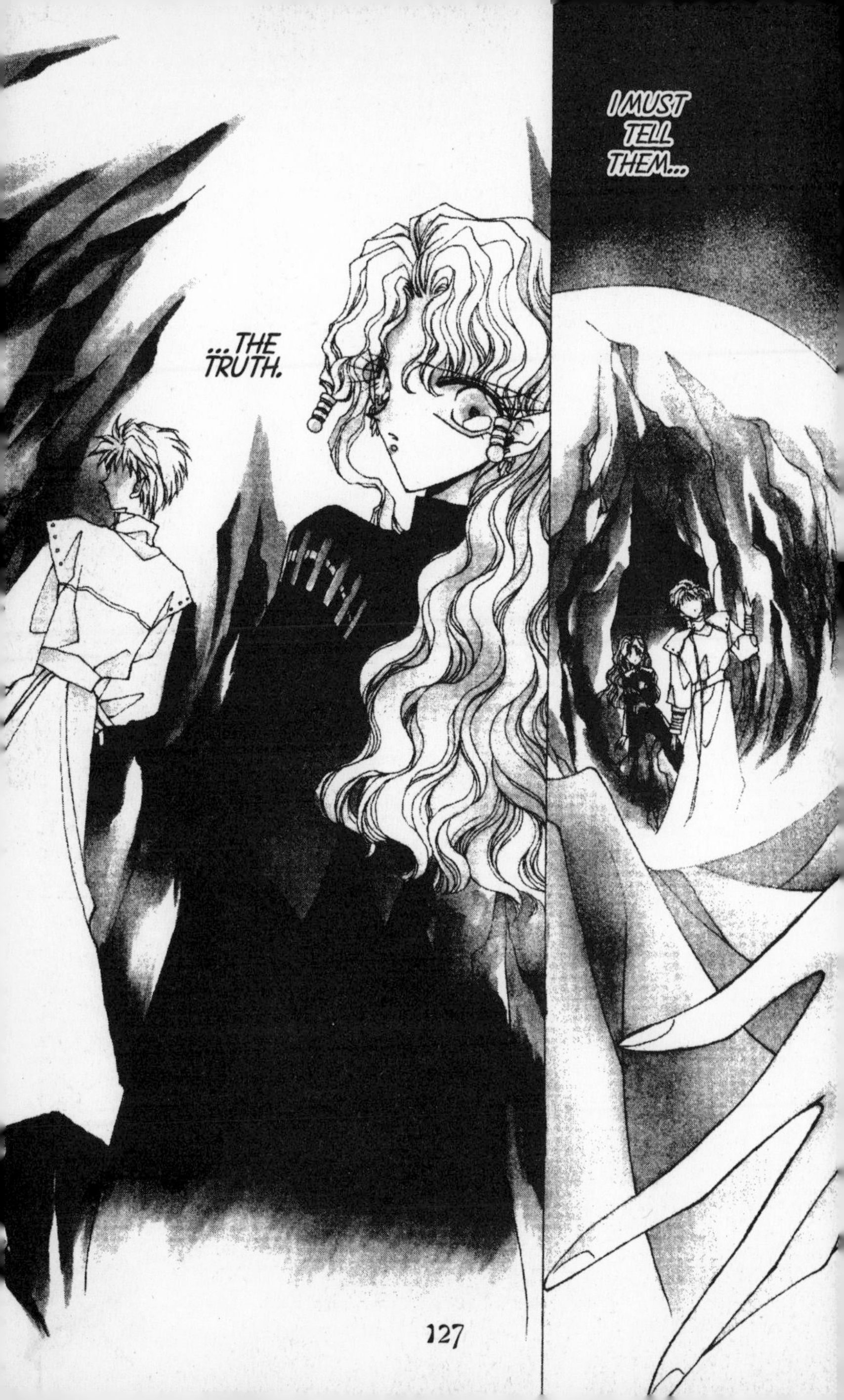
I MUST TELL THEM...
...THE TRUTH.

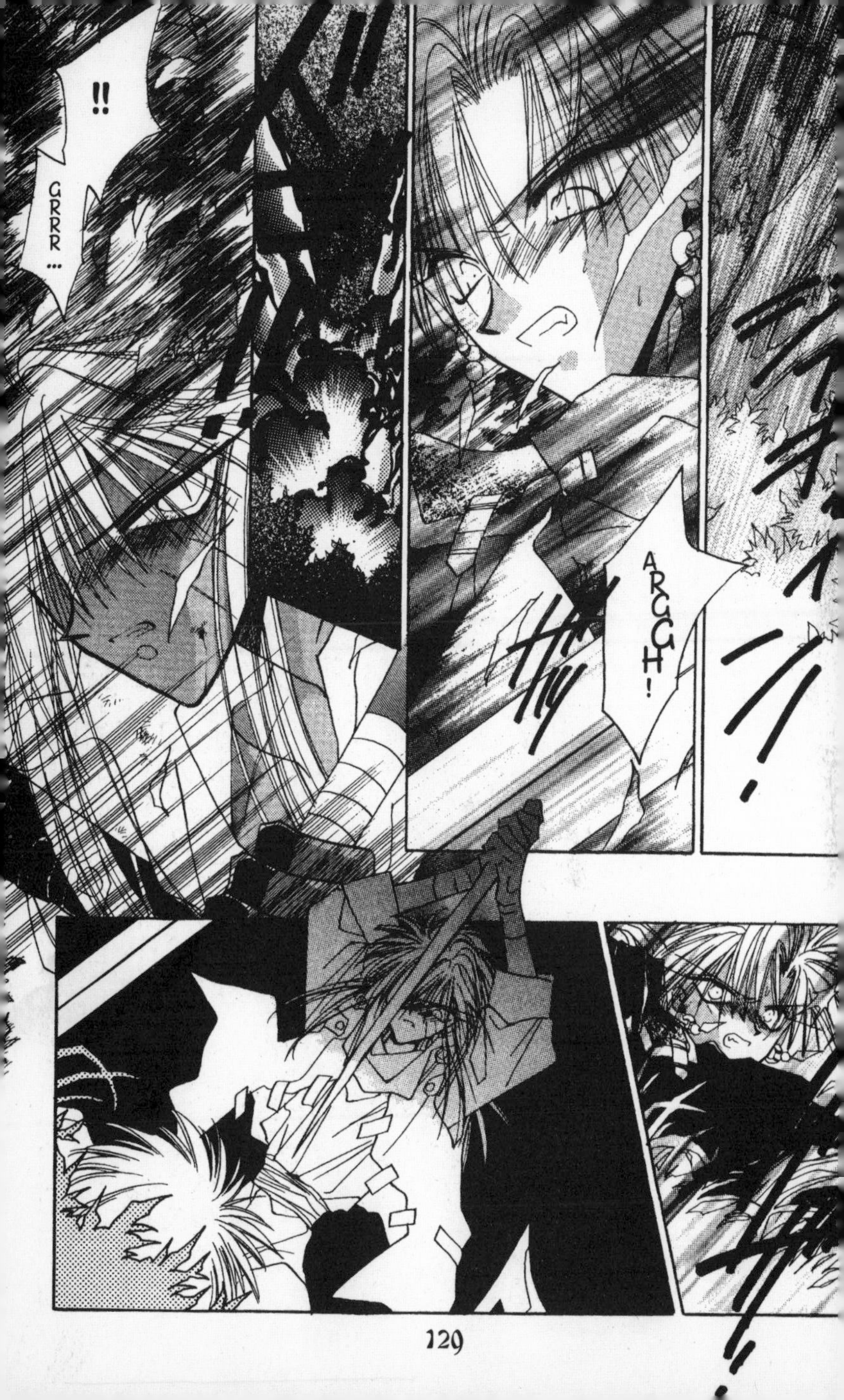
ARGGH!
!!
GRRR...

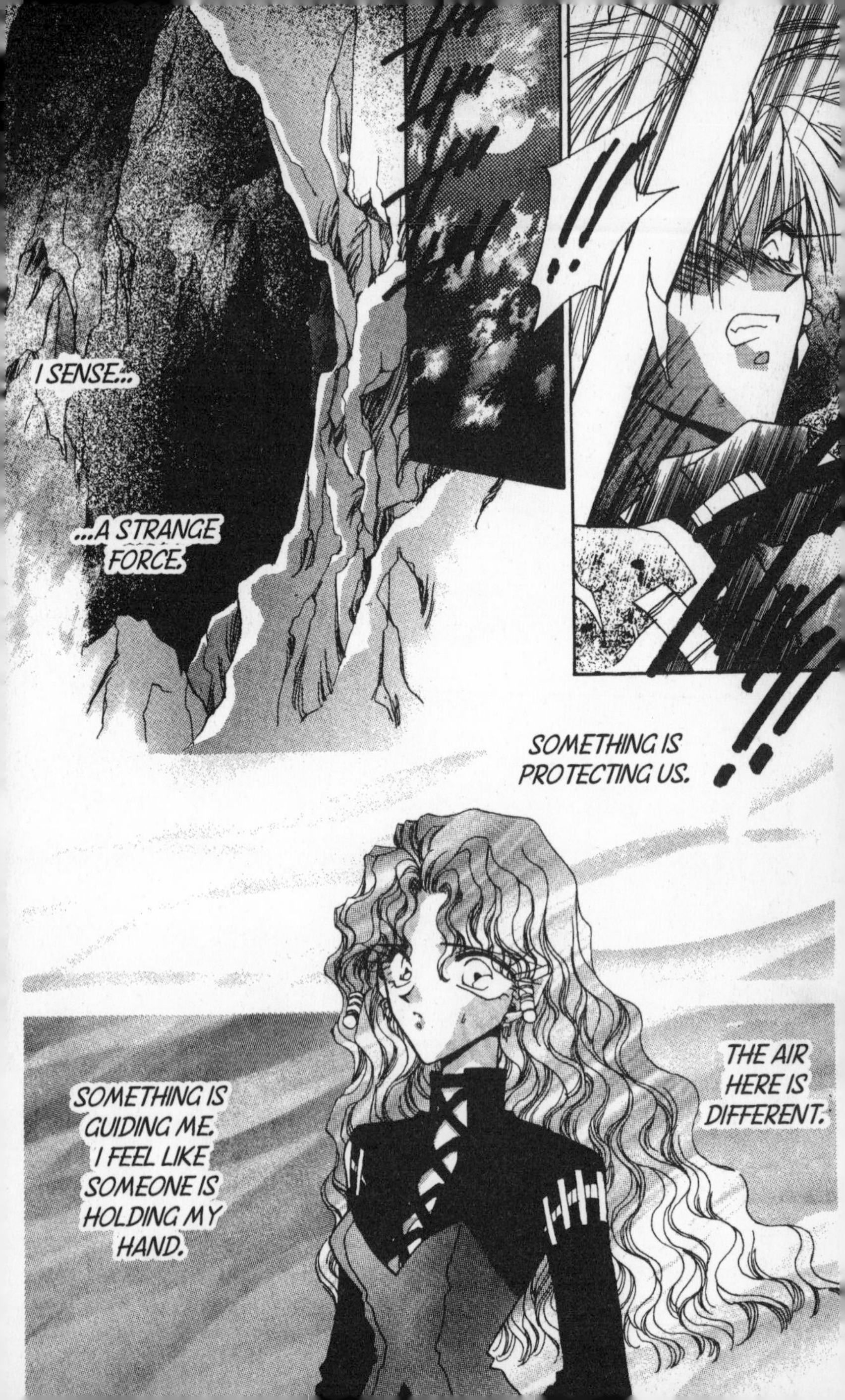
!!
SOMETHING IS PROTECTING US.
!!
I SENSE...
...A STRANGE FORCE.
THE AIR HERE IS DIFFERENT.
SOMETHING IS GUIDING ME. I FEEL LIKE SOMEONE IS HOLDING MY HAND.

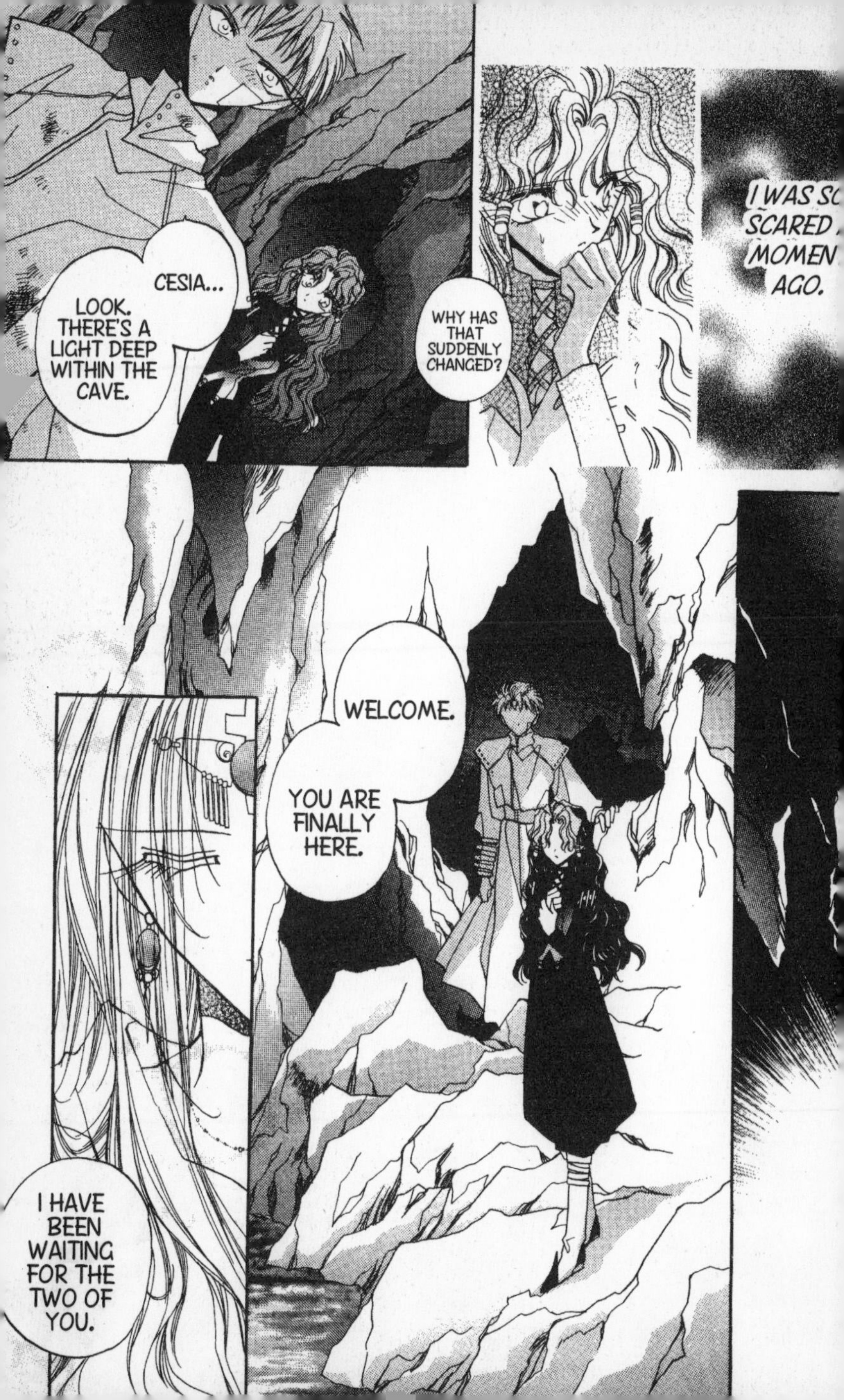
I WAS SC SCARED MOMEN AGO.
WHY HAS THAT SUDDENLY CHANGED?
CESIA...
LOOK. THERE'S A LIGHT DEEP WITHIN THE CAVE.
WELCOME.
YOU ARE FINALLY HERE.
I HAVE BEEN WAITING FOR THE TWO OF YOU.

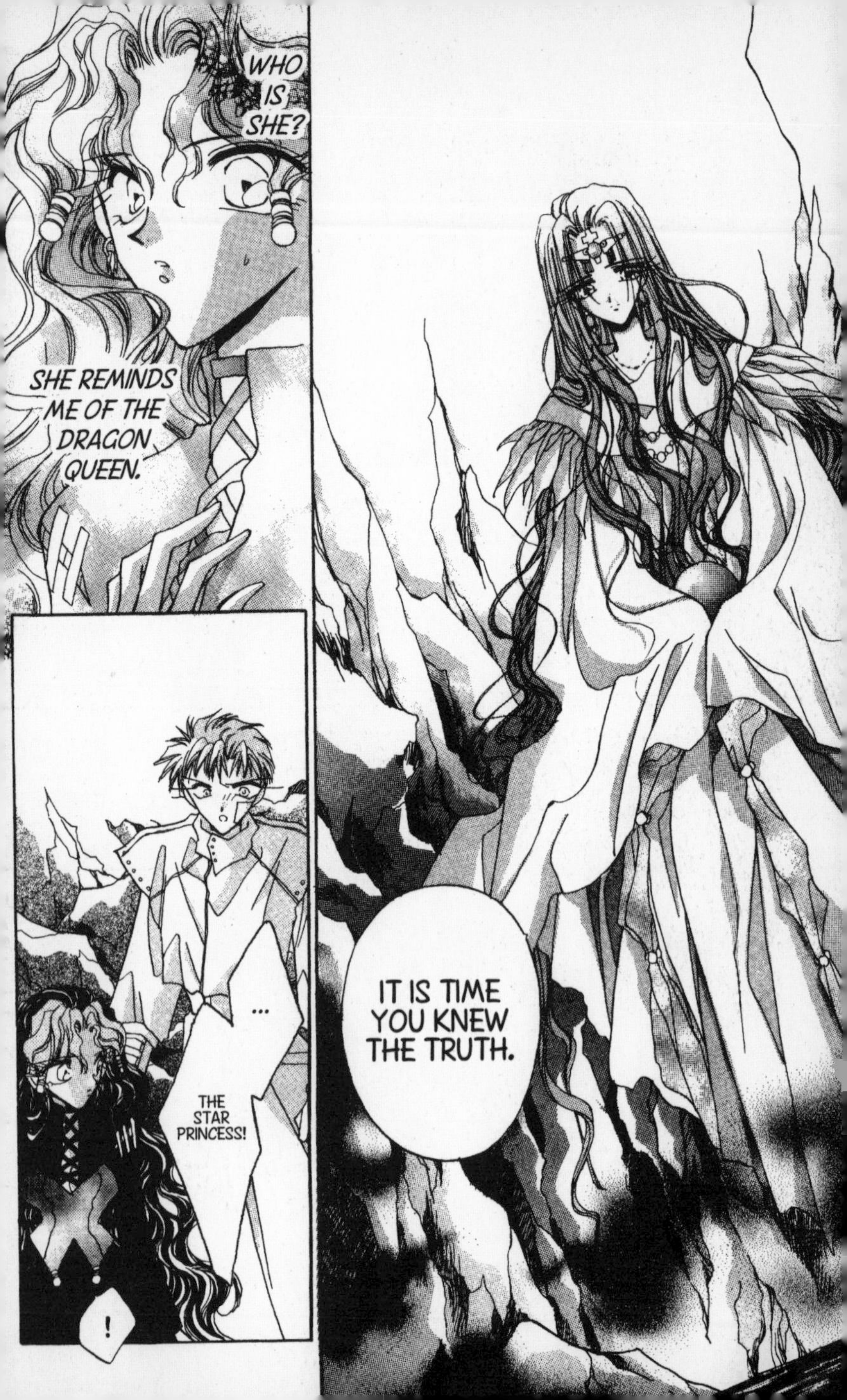
IT IS TIME YOU KNEW THE TRUTH.
WHO IS SHE?
SHE REMINDS ME OF THE DRAGON QUEEN.
...
THE STAR PRINCESS!
!

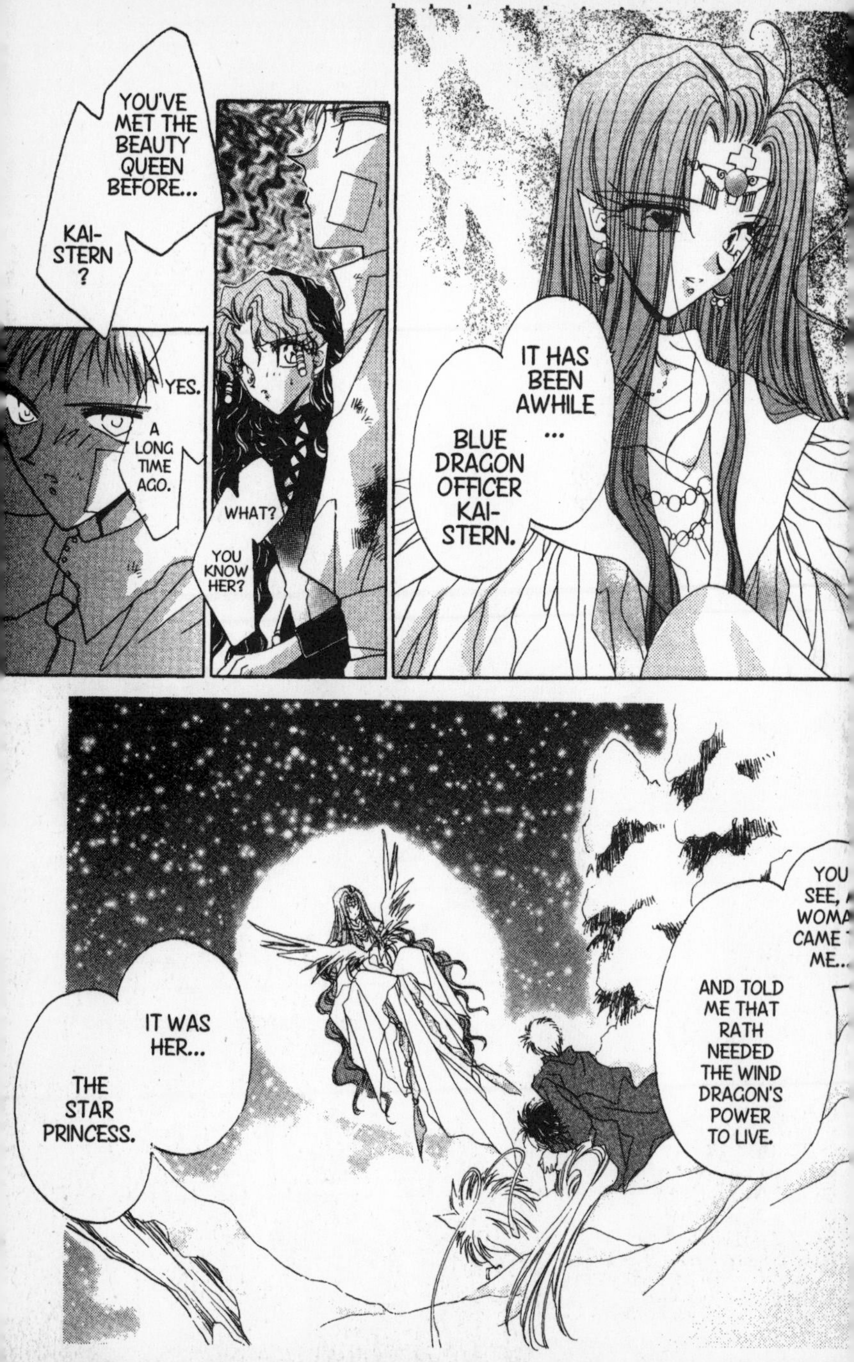
IT HAS BEEN AWHILE ...
BLUE DRAGON OFFICER KAI-STERN.
WHAT?
YOU KNOW HER?
YOU'VE MET THE BEAUTY QUEEN BEFORE...
KAI-STERN?
YES.
A LONG TIME AGO.
YOU SEE, WOMA CAME ME...
AND TOLD ME THAT RATH NEEDED THE WIND DRAGON'S POWER TO LIVE.
IT WAS HER...
THE STAR PRINCESS.

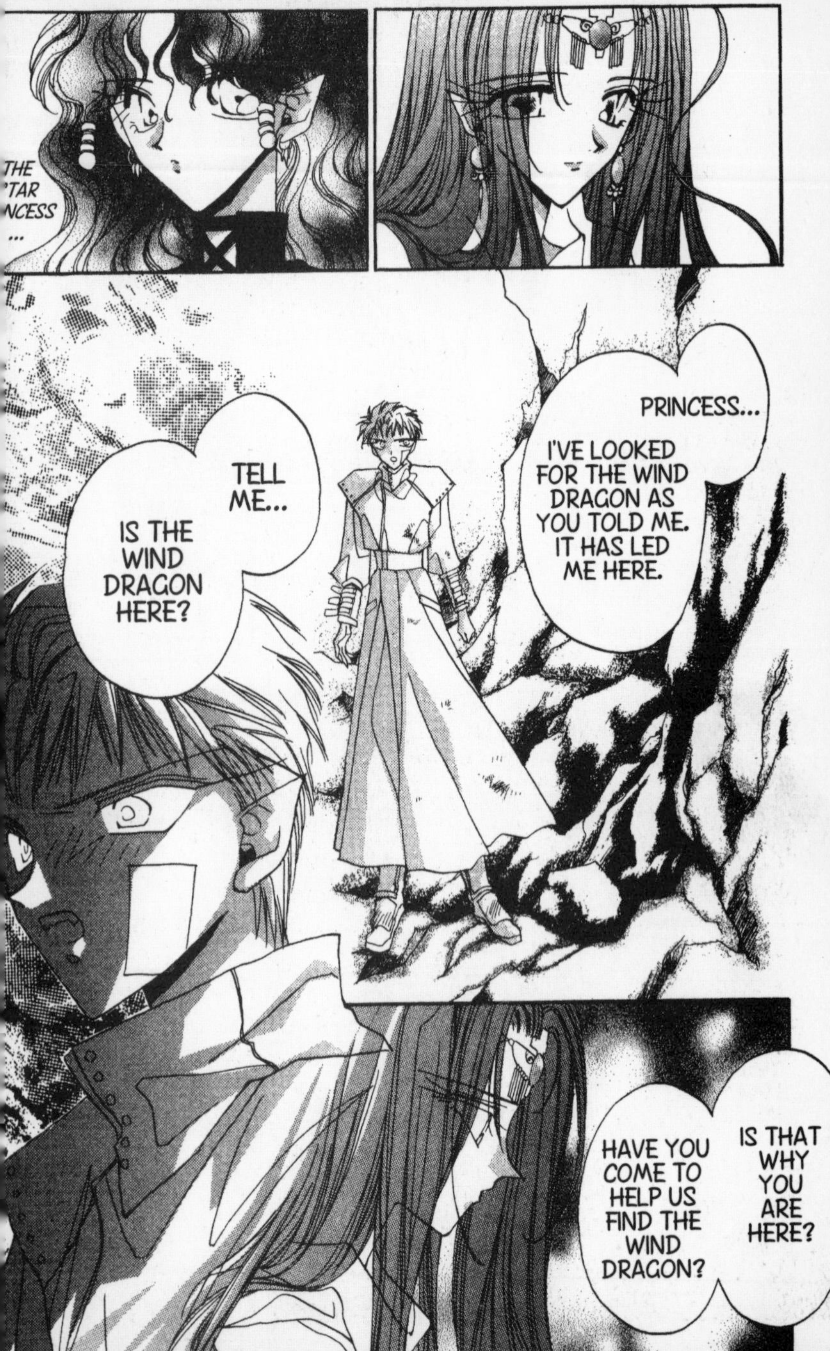
THE TAR NCESS ...
PRINCESS...
I'VE LOOKED FOR THE WIND DRAGON AS YOU TOLD ME. IT HAS LED ME HERE.
TELL ME...
IS THE WIND DRAGON HERE?
IS THAT WHY YOU ARE HERE?
HAVE YOU COME TO HELP US FIND THE WIND DRAGON?

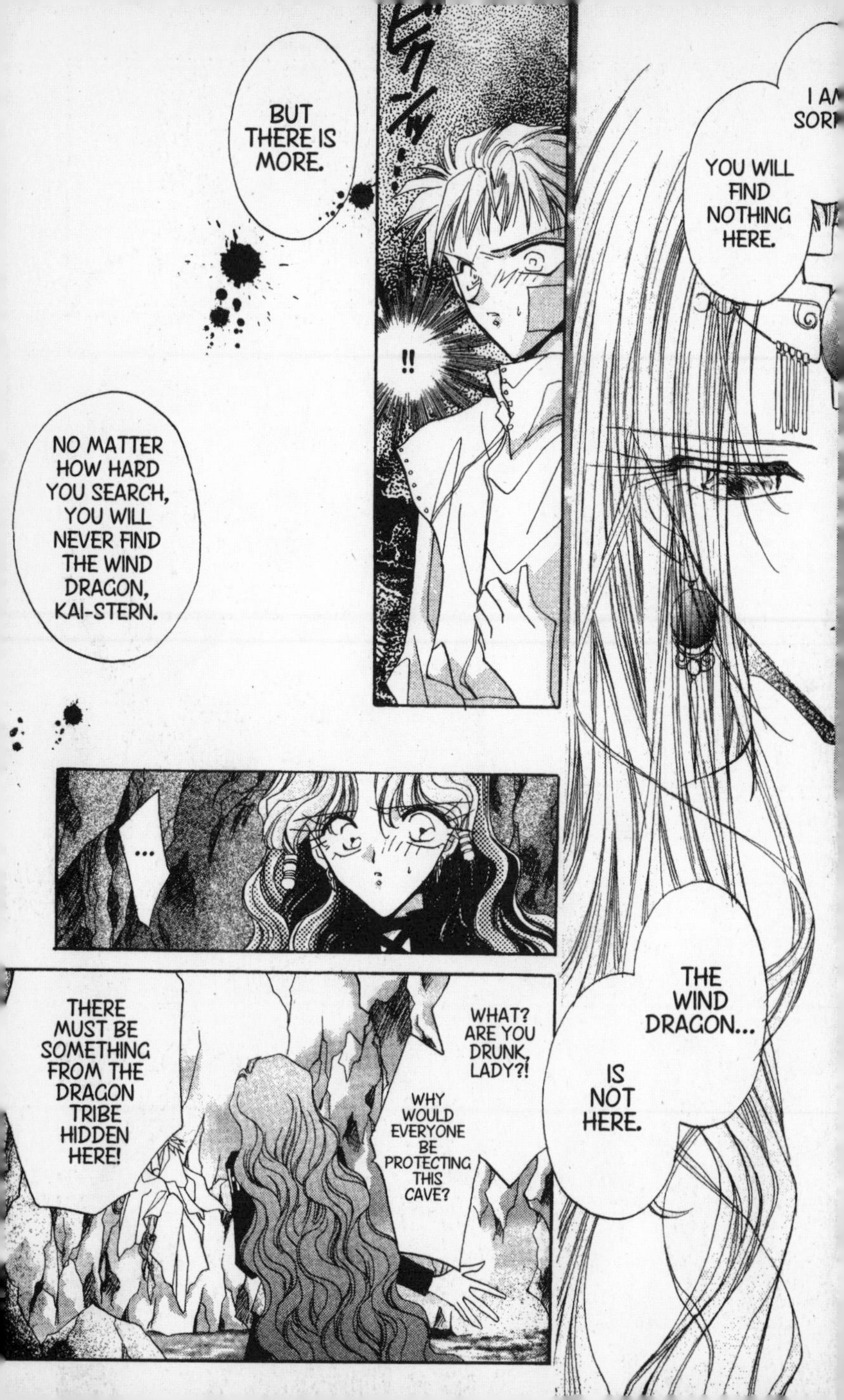
I AM SORR
YOU WILL FIND NOTHING HERE.
THE WIND DRAGON...
IS NOT HERE.
!!
BUT THERE IS MORE.
NO MATTER HOW HARD YOU SEARCH, YOU WILL NEVER FIND THE WIND DRAGON, KAI-STERN.
...
WHAT? ARE YOU DRUNK, LADY?!
WHY WOULD EVERYONE BE PROTECTING THIS CAVE?
THERE MUST BE SOMETHING FROM THE DRAGON TRIBE HIDDEN HERE!

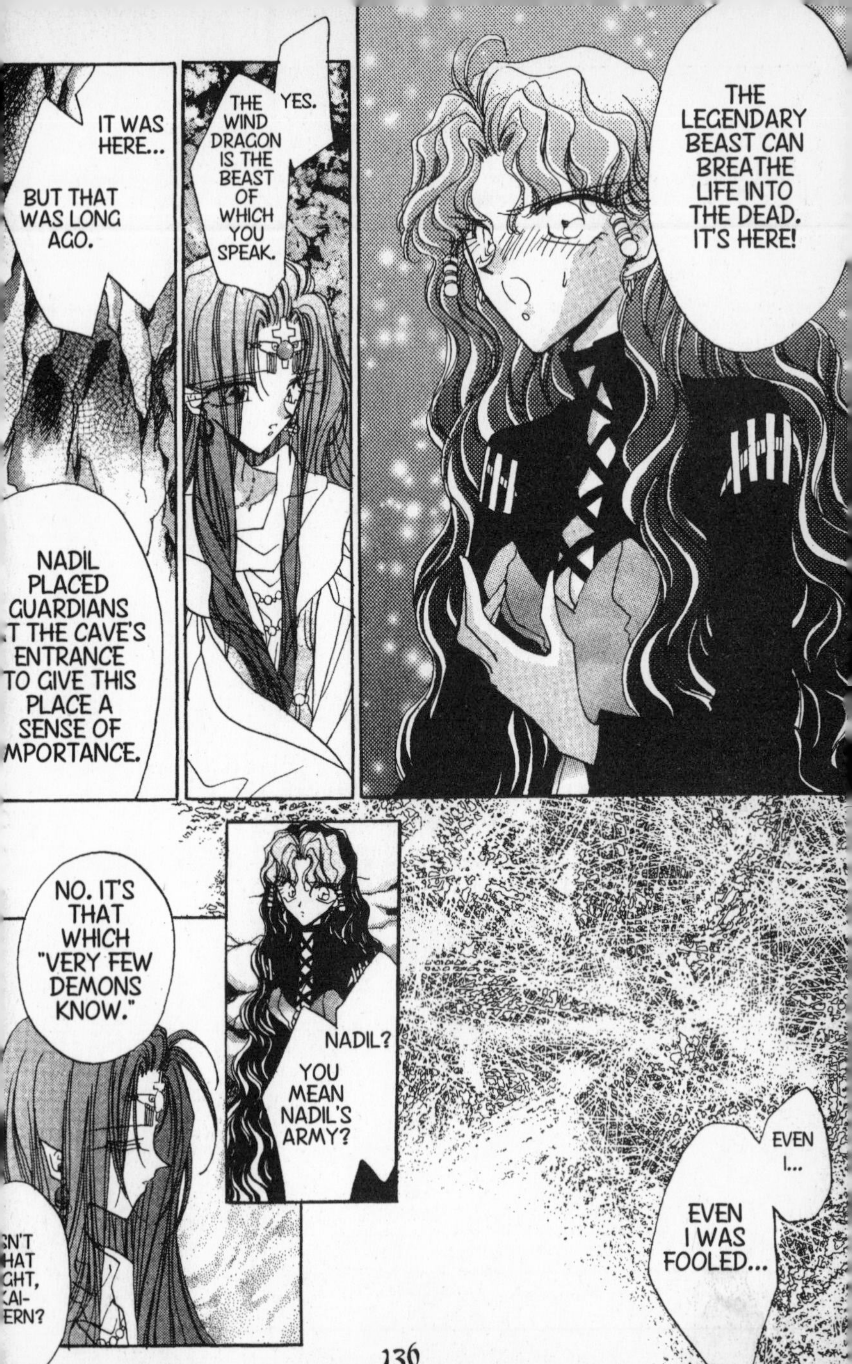
THE LEGENDARY BEAST CAN BREATHE LIFE INTO THE DEAD. IT'S HERE!
YES.
THE WIND DRAGON IS THE BEAST OF WHICH YOU SPEAK.
IT WAS HERE...
BUT THAT WAS LONG AGO.
NADIL PLACED GUARDIANS T THE CAVE'S ENTRANCE TO GIVE THIS PLACE A SENSE OF MPORTANCE.
EVEN I...
EVEN I WAS FOOLED...
NADIL?
YOU MEAN NADIL'S ARMY?
NO. IT'S THAT WHICH "VERY FEW DEMONS KNOW."
N'T HAT GHT, AI- ERN?

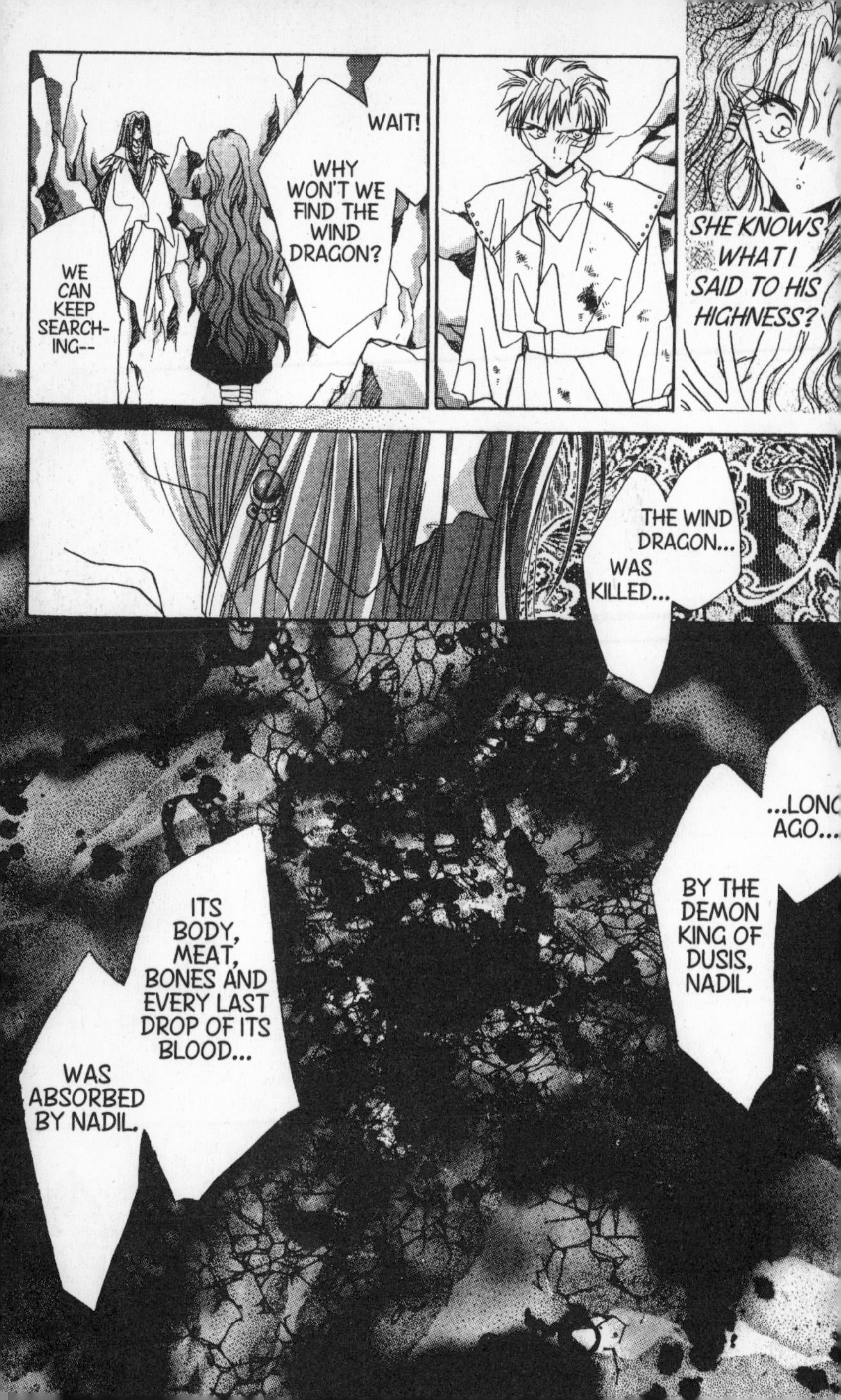
SHE KNOWS WHAT I SAID TO HIS HIGHNESS?
WAIT!
WHY WON'T WE FIND THE WIND DRAGON?
WE CAN KEEP SEARCHING--
THE WIND DRAGON... WAS KILLED...
...LONG AGO...
BY THE DEMON KING OF DUSIS, NADIL.
ITS BODY, MEAT, BONES AND EVERY LAST DROP OF ITS BLOOD...
WAS ABSORBED BY NADIL.

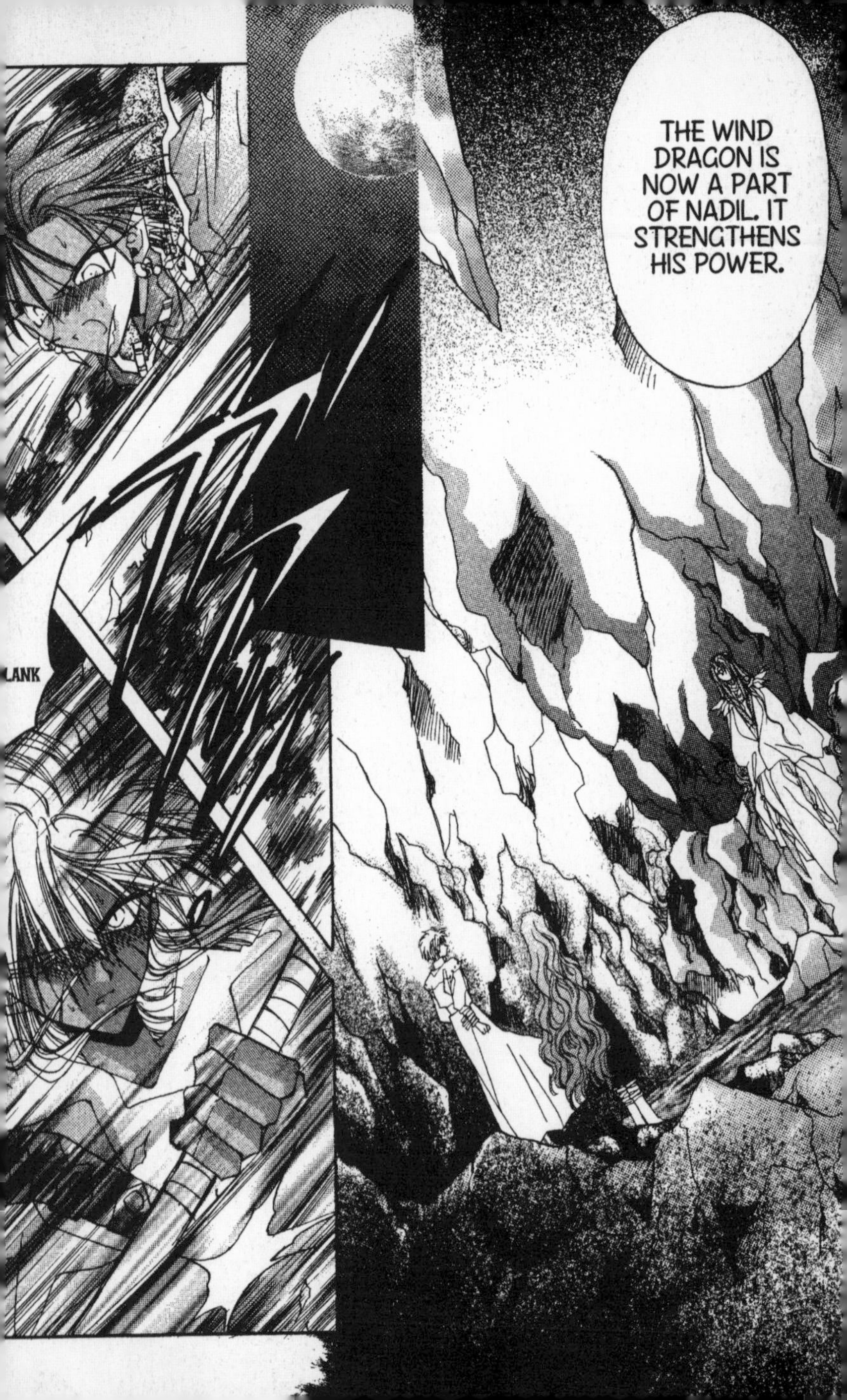
THE WIND DRAGON IS NOW A PART OF NADIL. IT STRENGTHENS HIS POWER.
LANK

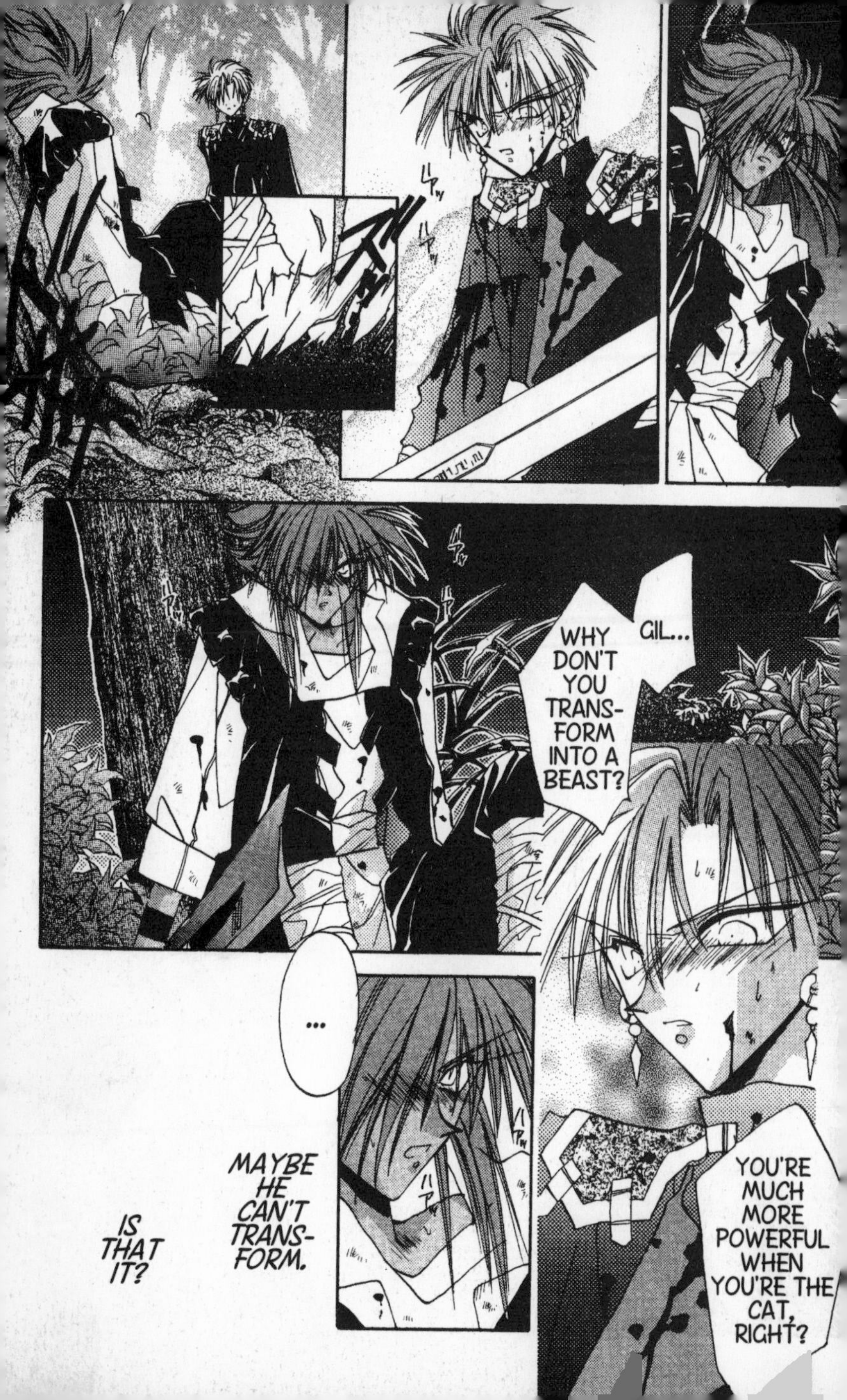
GIL...
WHY DON'T YOU TRANSFORM INTO A BEAST?
YOU'RE MUCH MORE POWERFUL WHEN YOU'RE THE CAT, RIGHT?
...
MAYBE HE CAN'T TRANSFORM.
IS THAT IT?

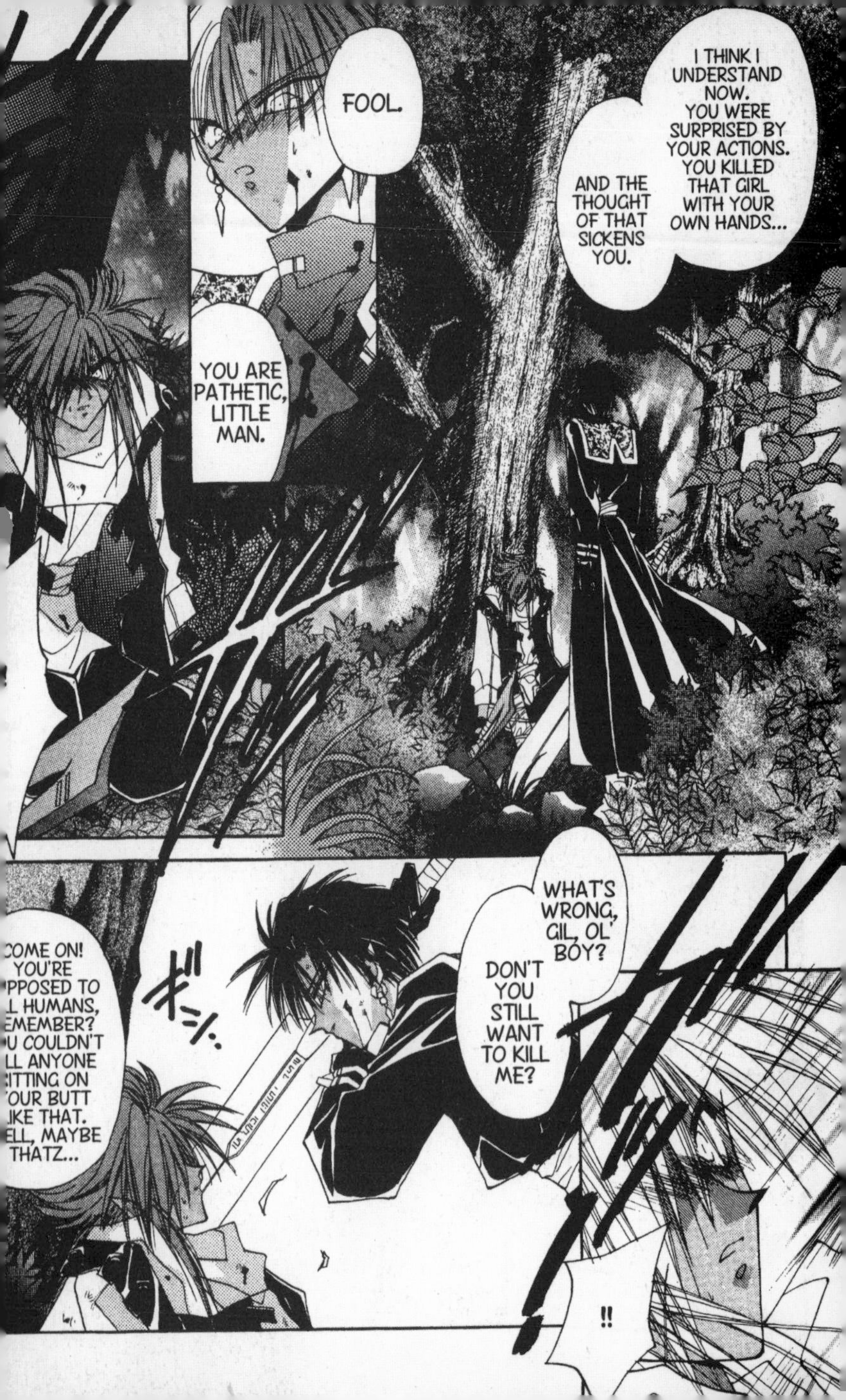
I THINK I UNDERSTAND NOW. YOU WERE SURPRISED BY YOUR ACTIONS. YOU KILLED THAT GIRL WITH YOUR OWN HANDS...
AND THE THOUGHT OF THAT SICKENS YOU.
FOOL.
YOU ARE PATHETIC, LITTLE MAN.
WHAT'S WRONG, GIL, OL' BOY?
DON'T YOU STILL WANT TO KILL ME?
!!
COME ON! YOU'RE PPOSED TO L HUMANS, EMEMBER? U COULDN'T LL ANYONE ITTING ON OUR BUTT IKE THAT. ELL, MAYBE THATZ...

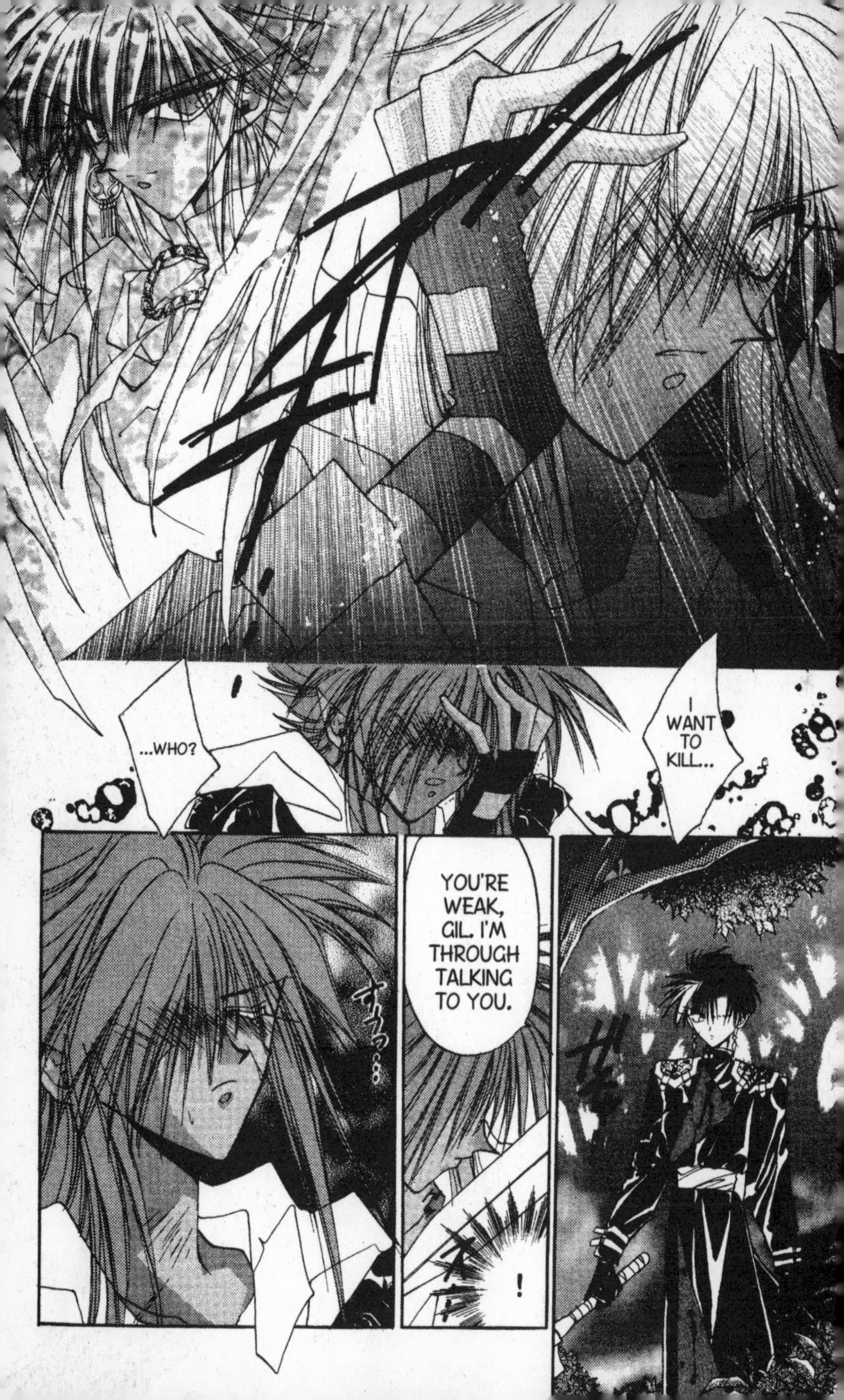
I WANT TO KILL...
...WHO?
YOU'RE WEAK, GIL. I'M THROUGH TALKING TO YOU.
!

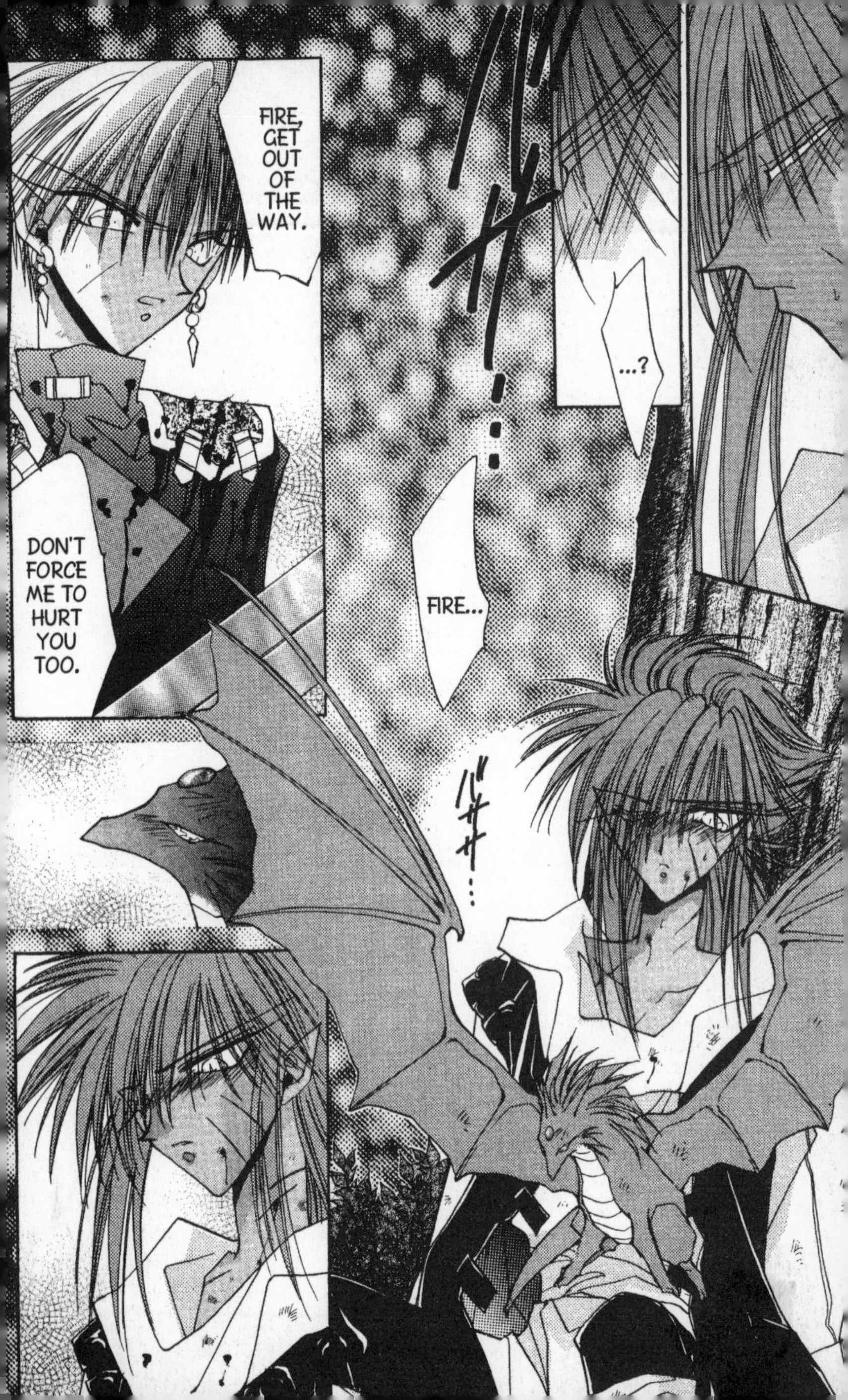

...?
FIRE...
FIRE, GET OUT OF THE WAY.
DON'T FORCE ME TO HURT YOU TOO.
バササ…

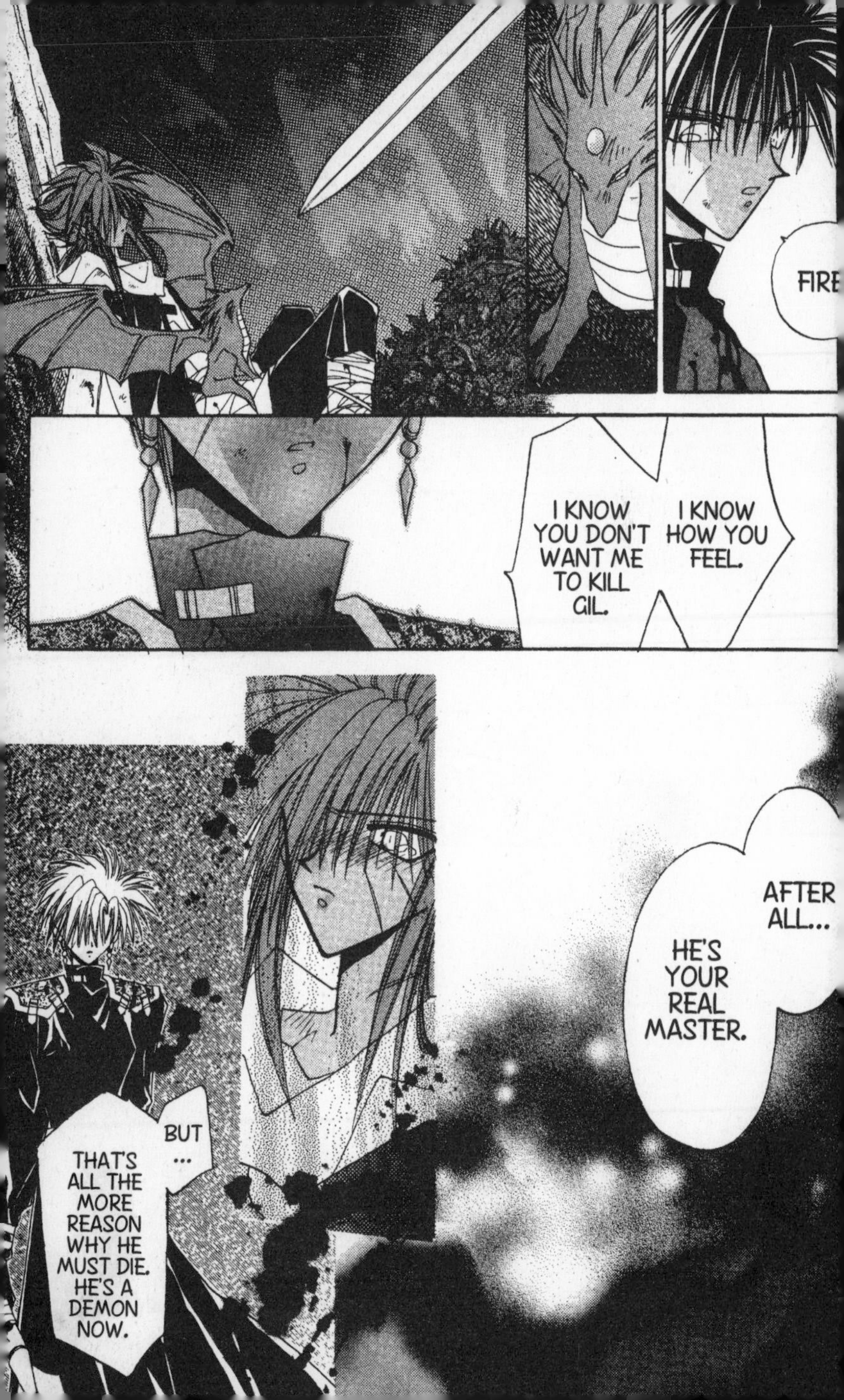
FIRE
I KNOW HOW YOU FEEL.
I KNOW YOU DON'T WANT ME TO KILL GIL.
AFTER ALL...
HE'S YOUR REAL MASTER.
BUT ...
THAT'S ALL THE MORE REASON WHY HE MUST DIE. HE'S A DEMON NOW.

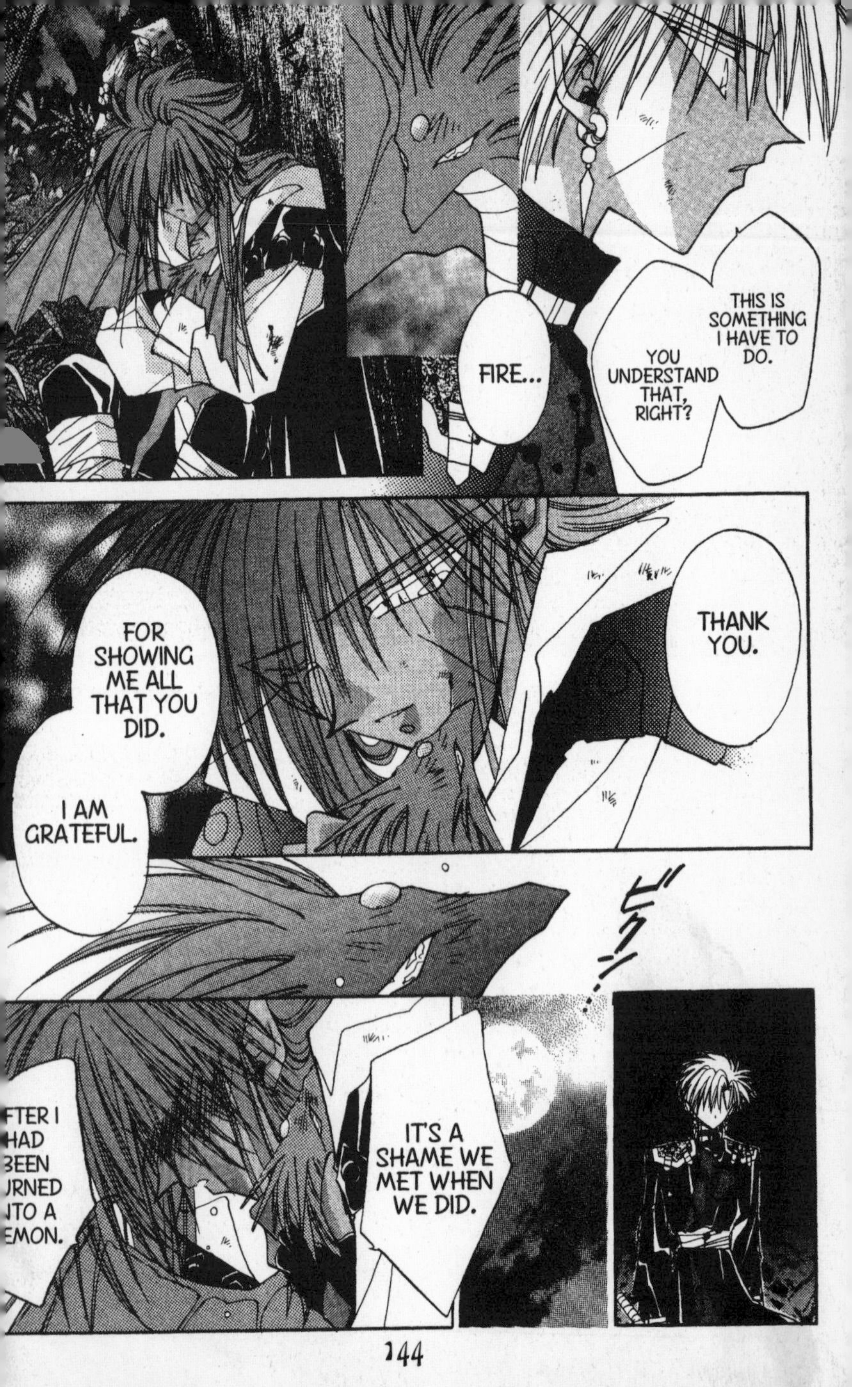
THIS IS SOMETHING I HAVE TO DO.
YOU UNDERSTAND THAT, RIGHT?
FIRE...
THANK YOU.
FOR SHOWING ME ALL THAT YOU DID.
I AM GRATEFUL.
ビクッ
IT'S A SHAME WE MET WHEN WE DID.
FTER I HAD BEEN URNED NTO A EMON.

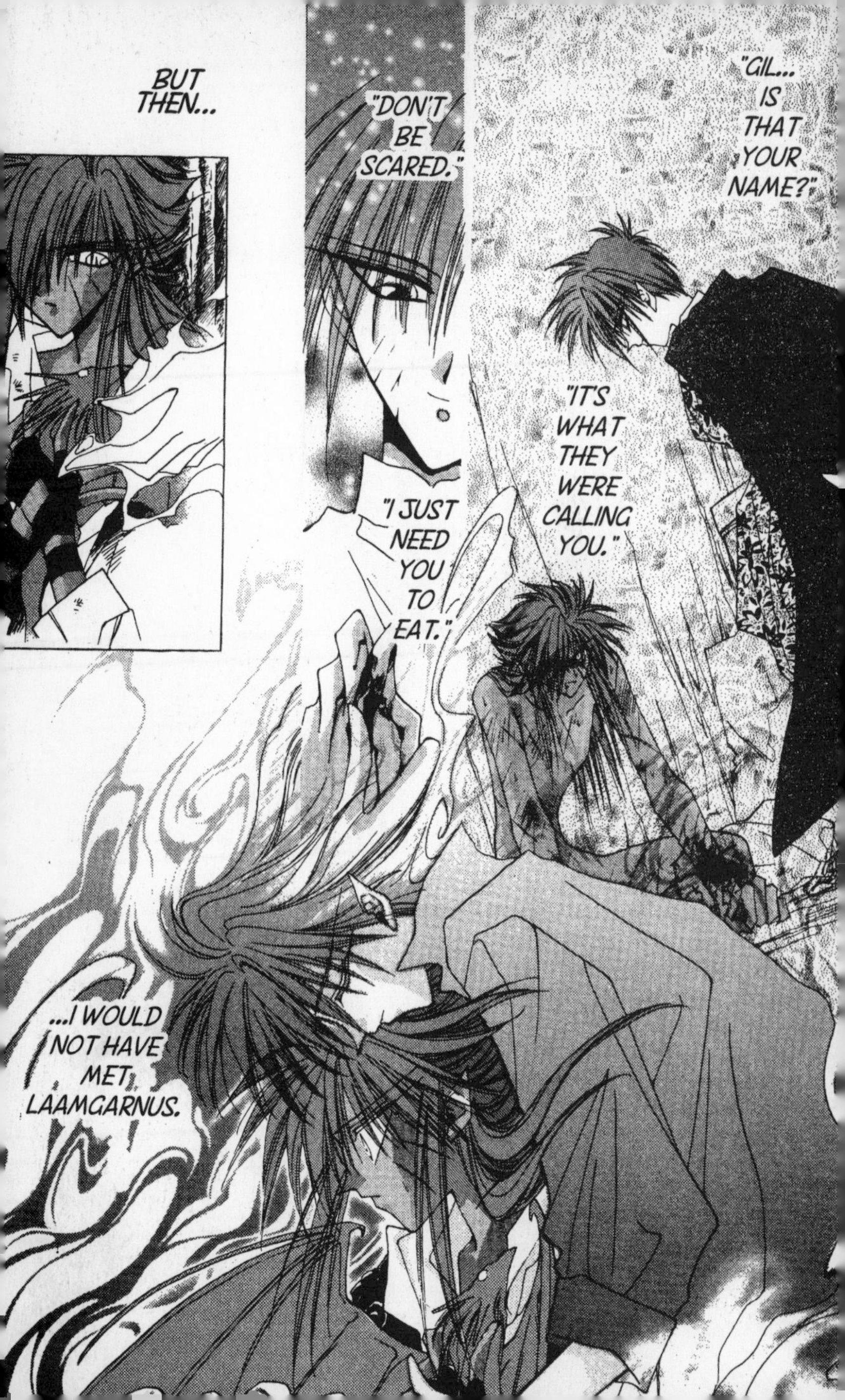
"GIL... IS THAT YOUR NAME?"
"IT'S WHAT THEY WERE CALLING YOU."
"DON'T BE SCARED."
"I JUST NEED YOU TO EAT."
BUT THEN...
...I WOULD NOT HAVE MET LAAMGARNUS.

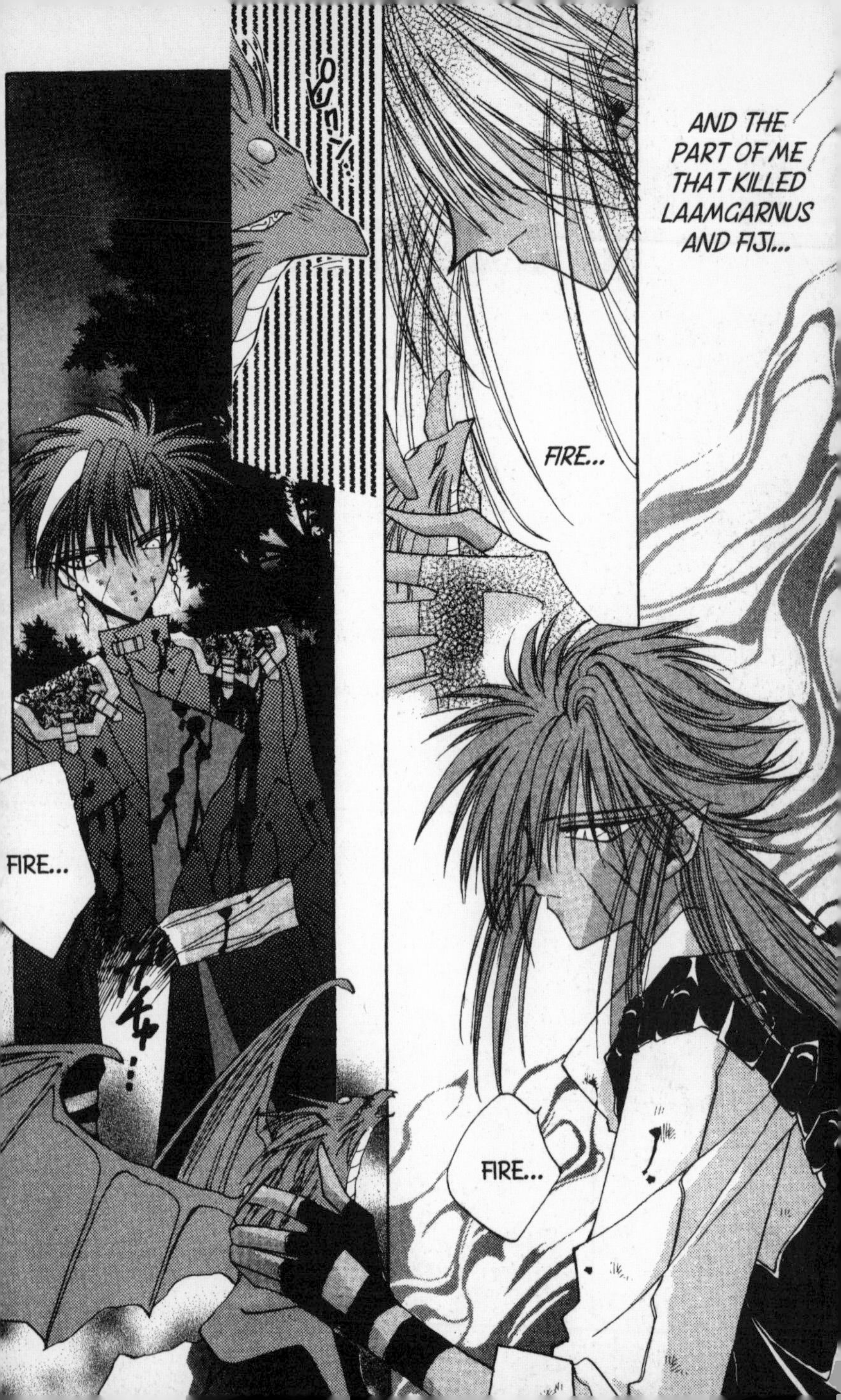
AND THE PART OF ME THAT KILLED LAAMGARNUS AND FIJI...
FIRE...
FIRE...
FIRE...

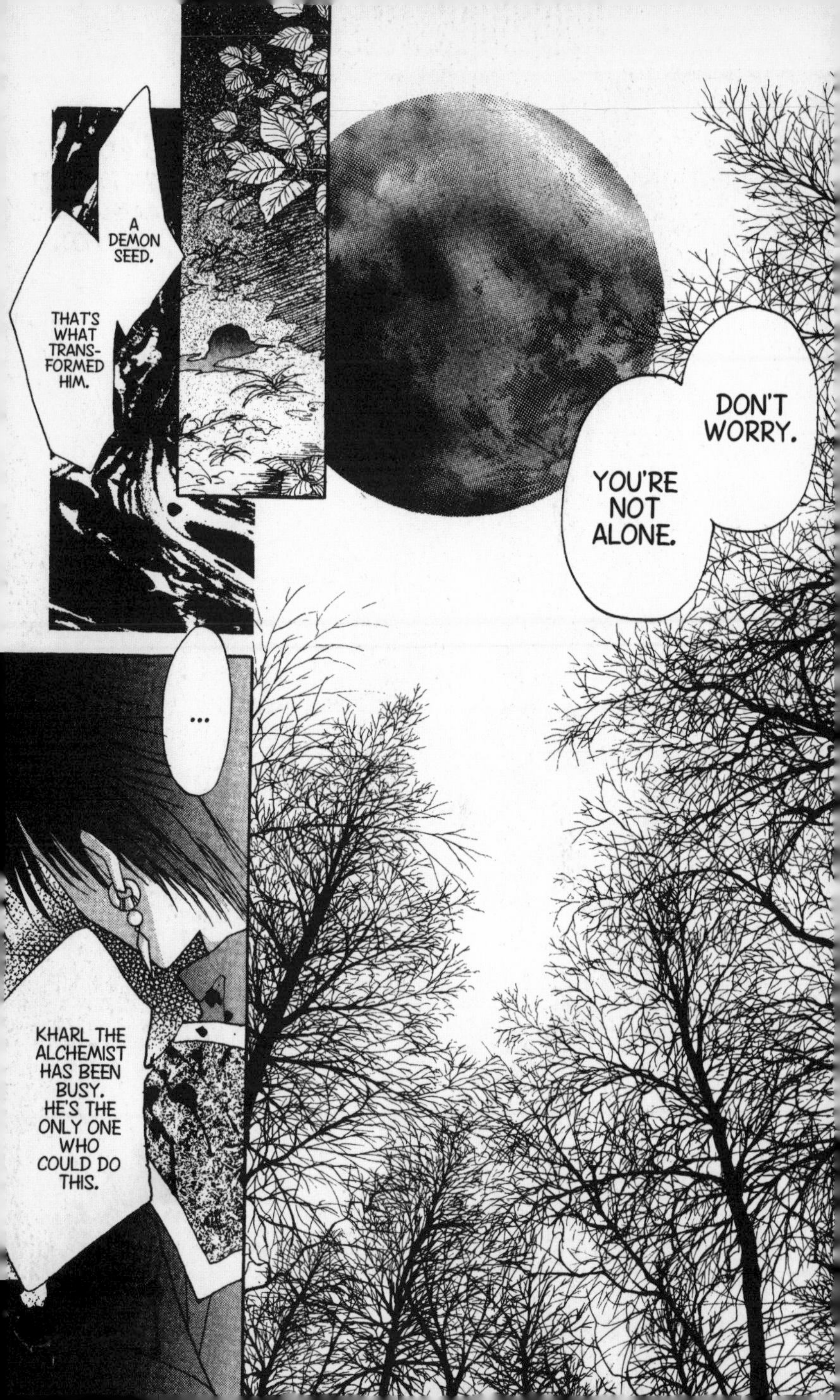
DON'T WORRY.
YOU'RE NOT ALONE.
A DEMON SEED.
THAT'S WHAT TRANSFORMED HIM.
...
KHARL THE ALCHEMIST HAS BEEN BUSY. HE'S THE ONLY ONE WHO COULD DO THIS.

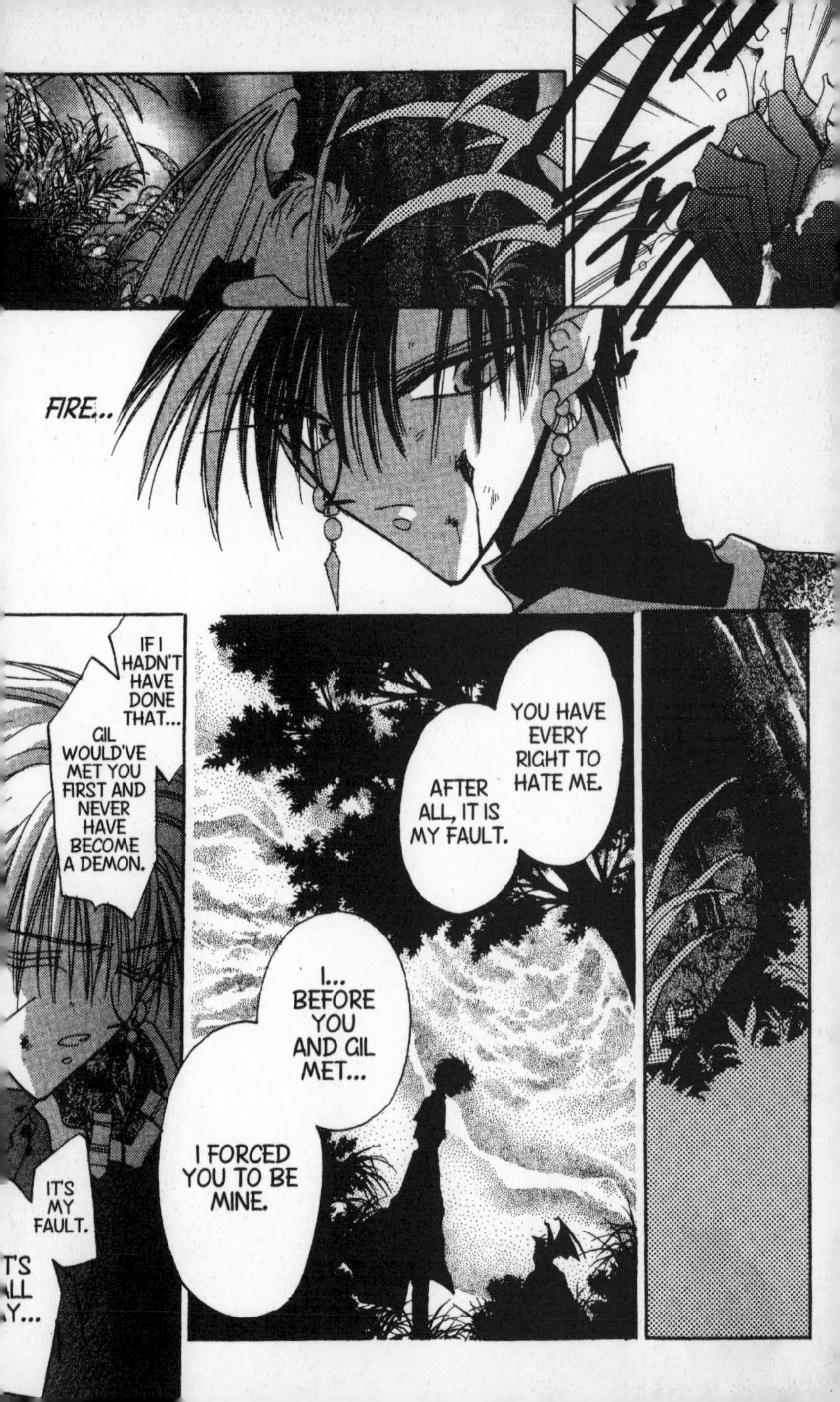
FIRE...
YOU HAVE EVERY RIGHT TO HATE ME.
AFTER ALL, IT IS MY FAULT.
I... BEFORE YOU AND GIL MET...
I FORCED YOU TO BE MINE.
IF I HADN'T HAVE DONE THAT...
GIL WOULD'VE MET YOU FIRST AND NEVER HAVE BECOME A DEMON.
IT'S MY FAULT.

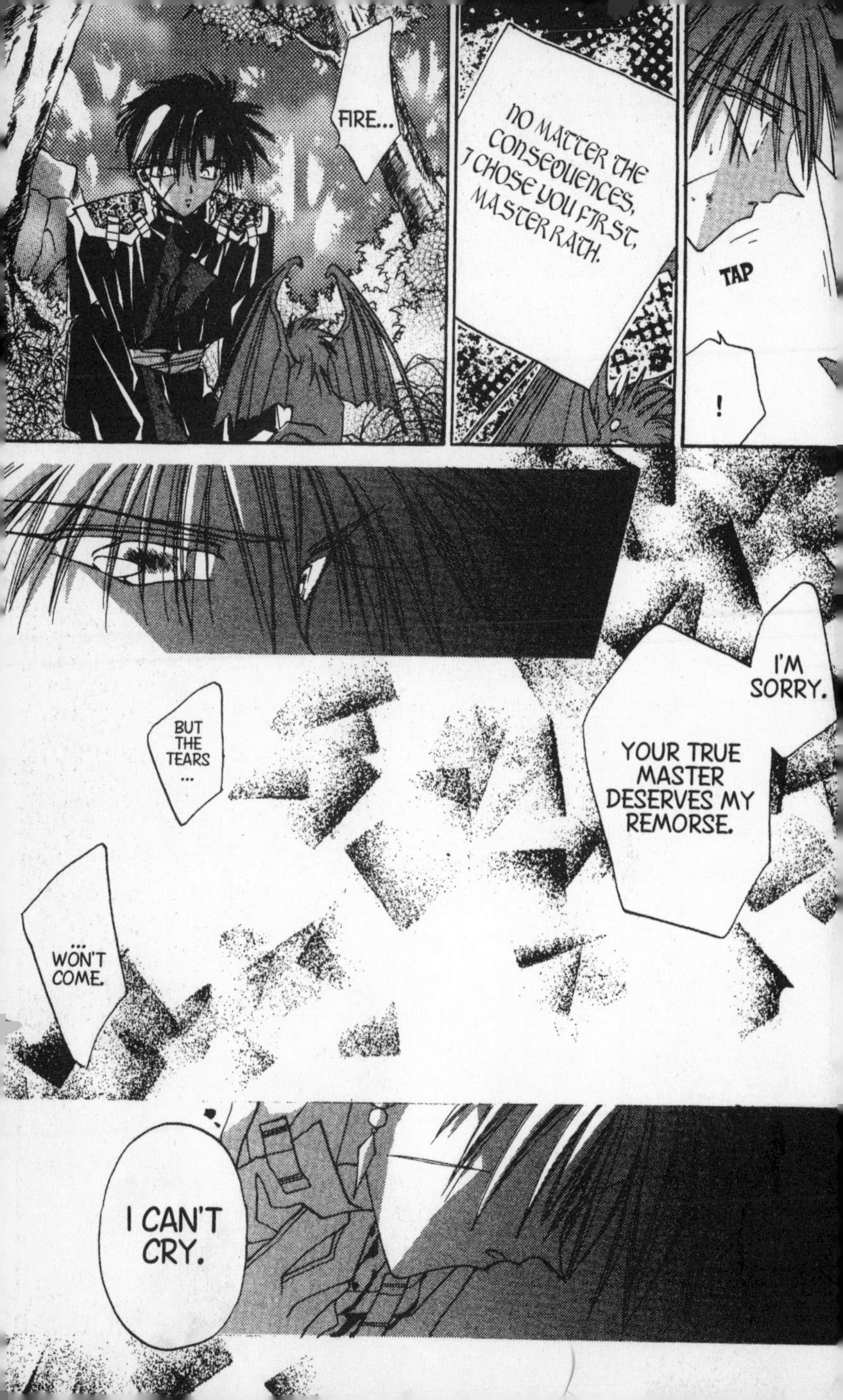
TAP
!
NO MATTER THE CONSEQUENCES, I CHOSE YOU FIRST, MASTER RATH.
FIRE...
I'M SORRY.
YOUR TRUE MASTER DESERVES MY REMORSE.
BUT THE TEARS ...
... WON'T COME.
I CAN'T CRY.

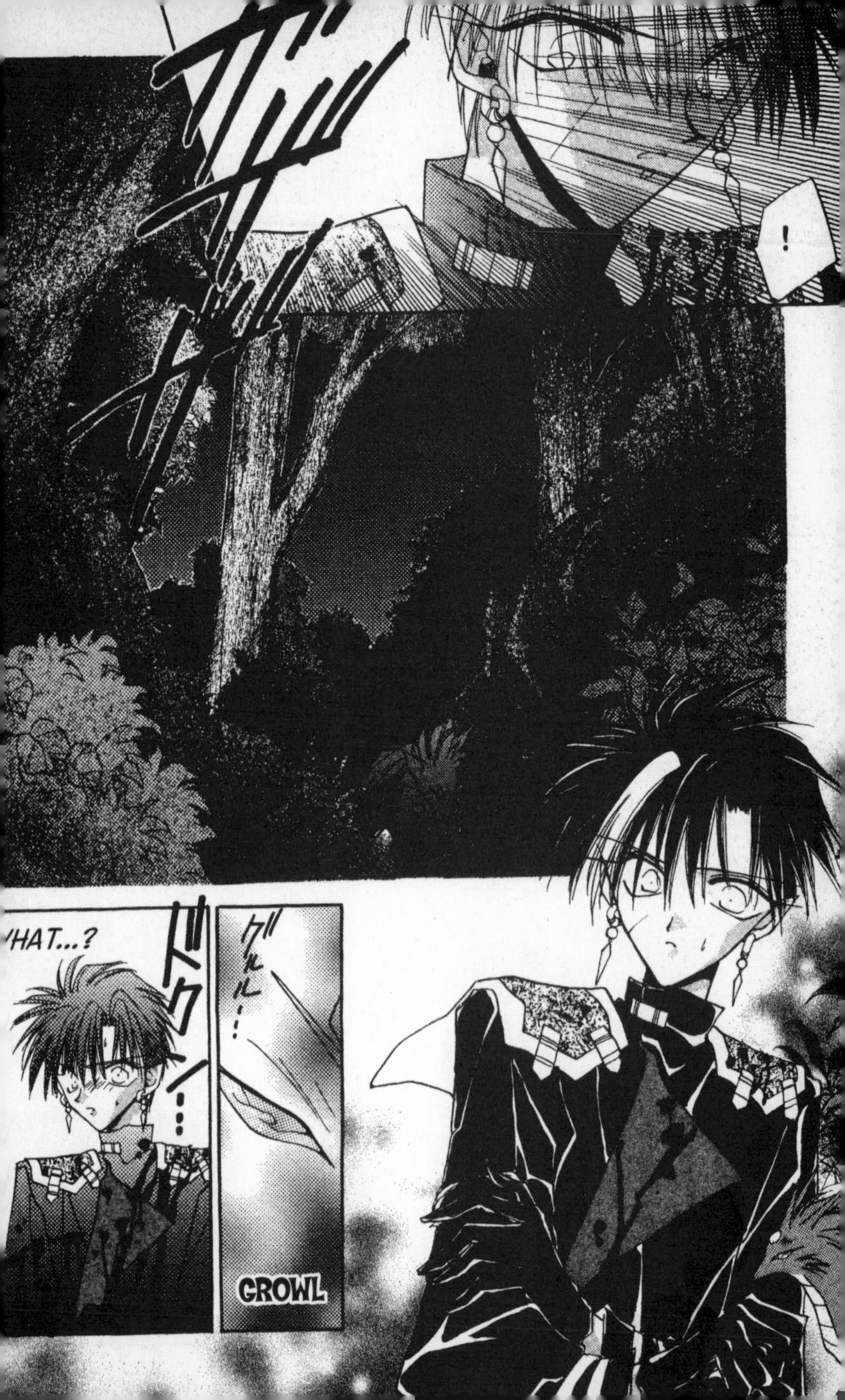
!
GROWL
WHAT...?

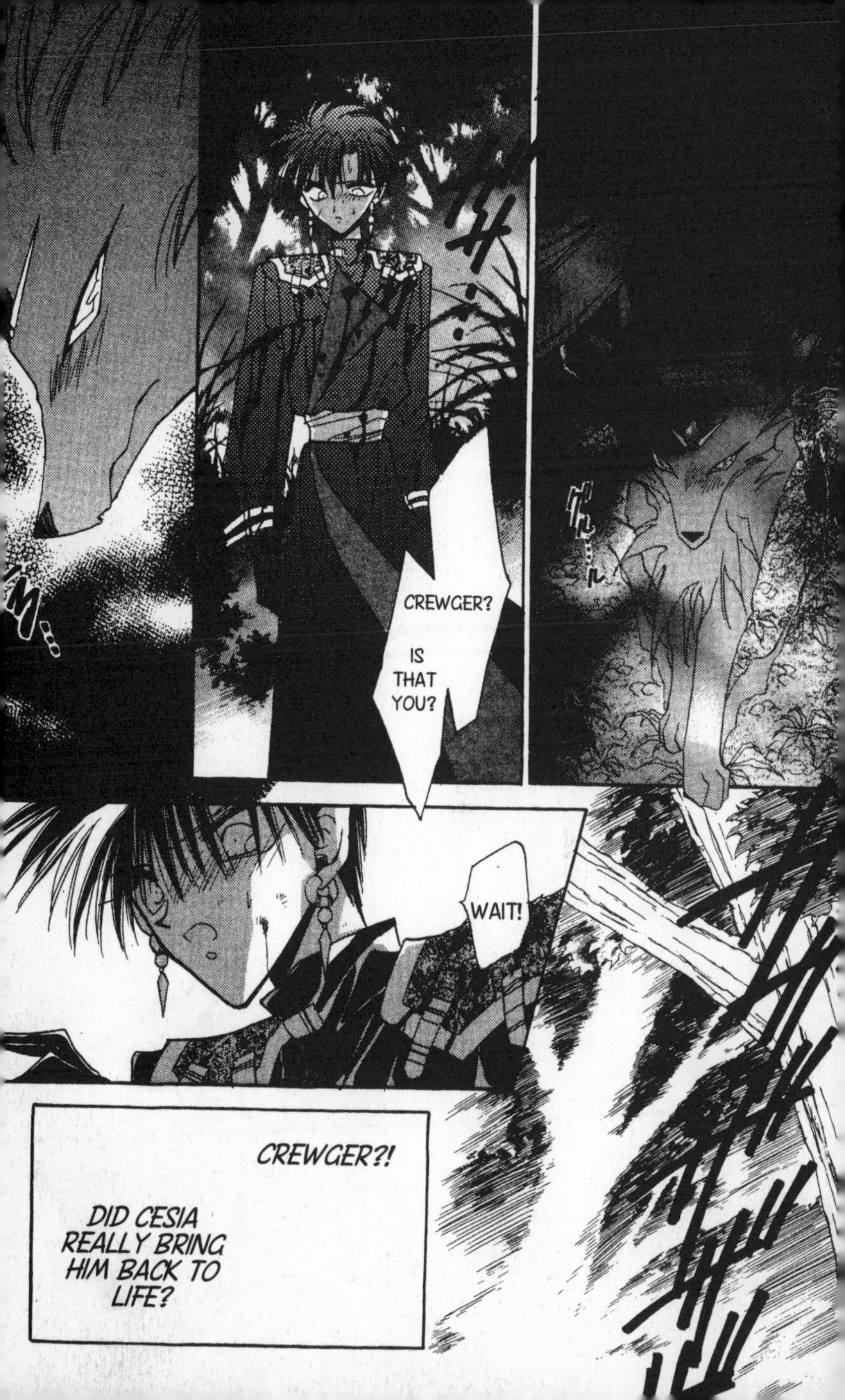
CREWGER? IS THAT YOU?
WAIT!
CREWGER?!
DID CESIA REALLY BRING HIM BACK TO LIFE?

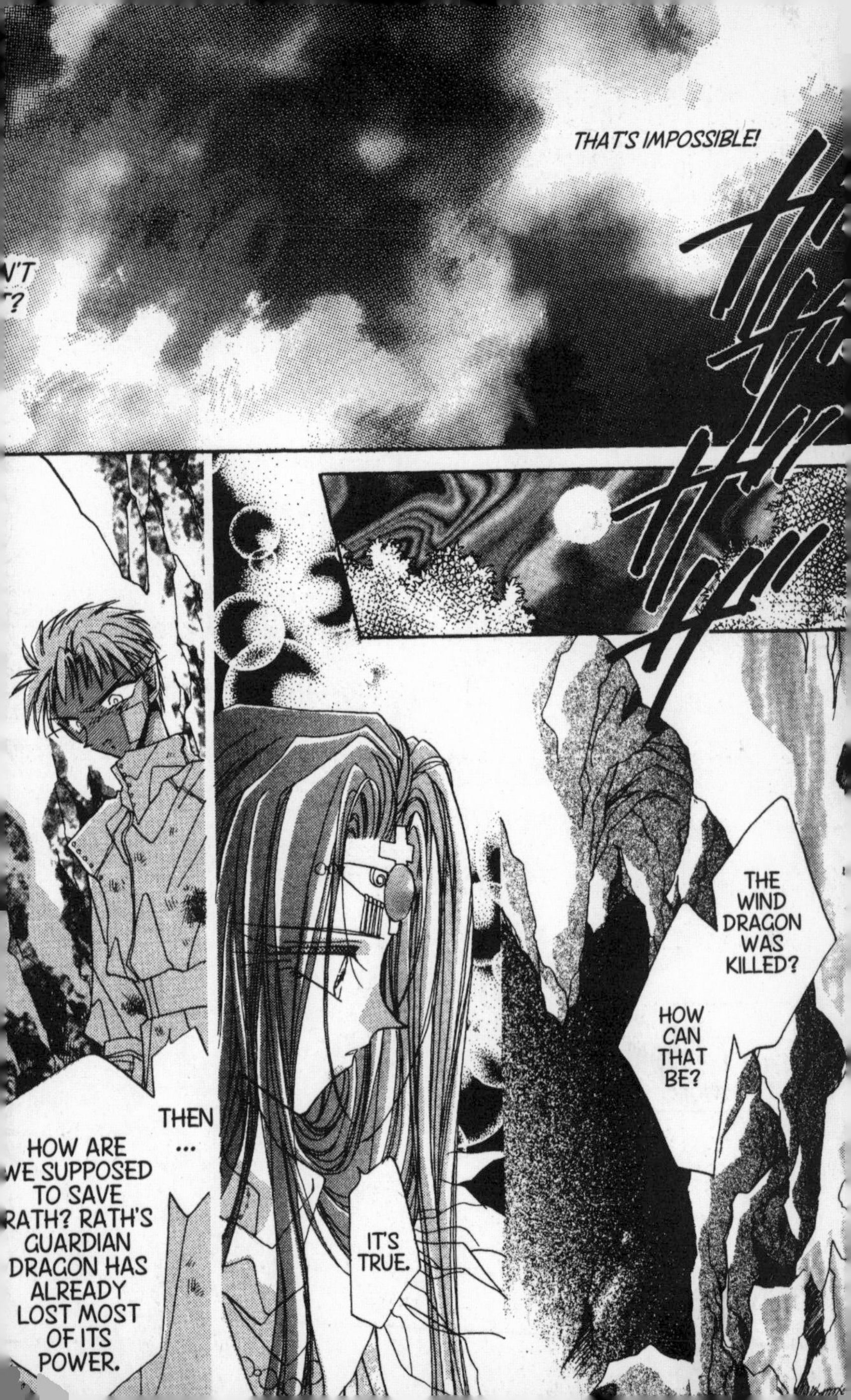
THAT'S IMPOSSIBLE!
THE WIND DRAGON WAS KILLED?
HOW CAN THAT BE?
IT'S TRUE.
THEN ...
HOW ARE WE SUPPOSED TO SAVE RATH? RATH'S GUARDIAN DRAGON HAS ALREADY LOST MOST OF ITS POWER.

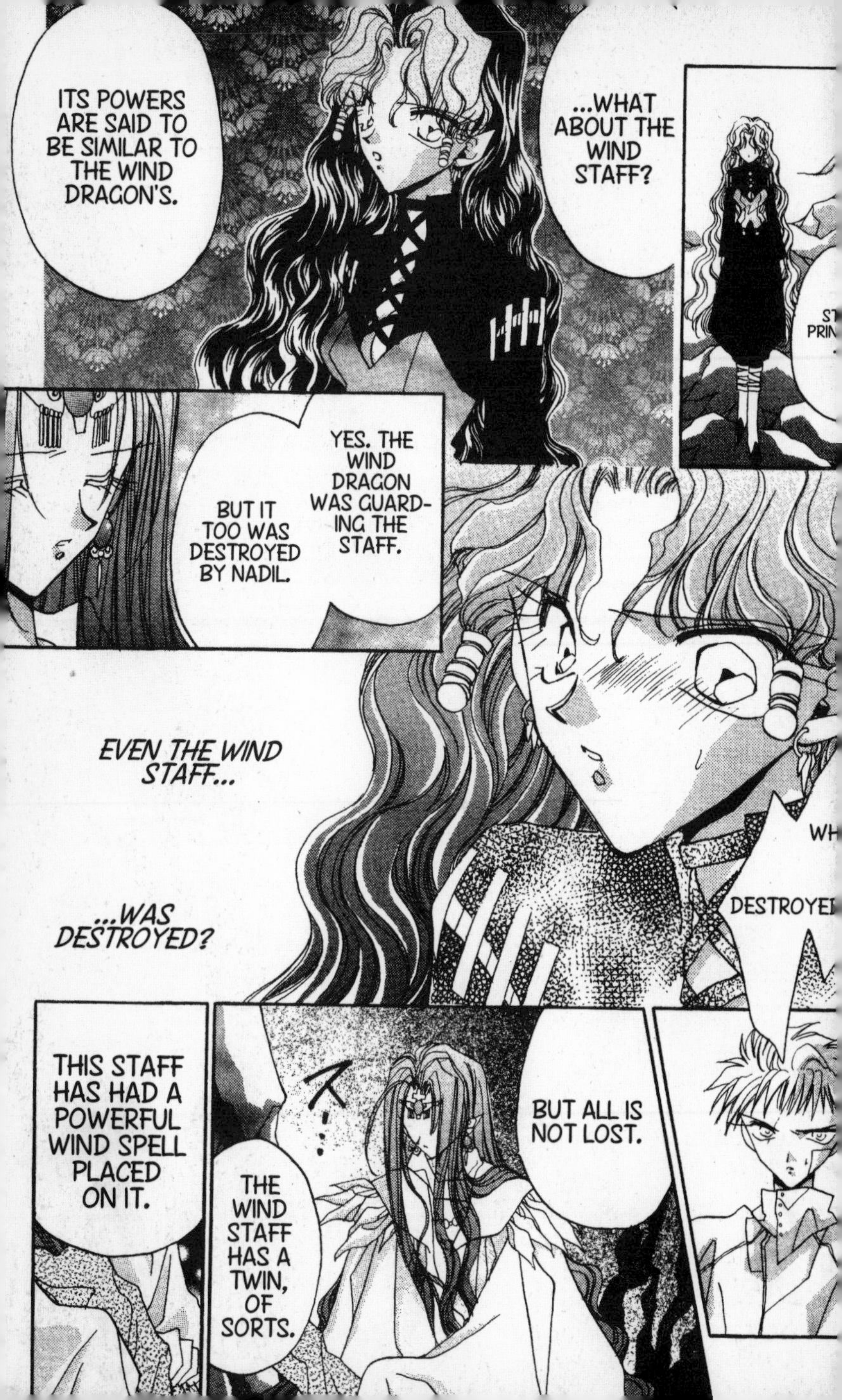

...WHAT ABOUT THE WIND STAFF?
ITS POWERS ARE SAID TO BE SIMILAR TO THE WIND DRAGON'S.
YES. THE WIND DRAGON WAS GUARDING THE STAFF.
BUT IT TOO WAS DESTROYED BY NADIL.
EVEN THE WIND STAFF...
...WAS DESTROYED?
BUT ALL IS NOT LOST.
THE WIND STAFF HAS A TWIN, OF SORTS.
THIS STAFF HAS HAD A POWERFUL WIND SPELL PLACED ON IT.

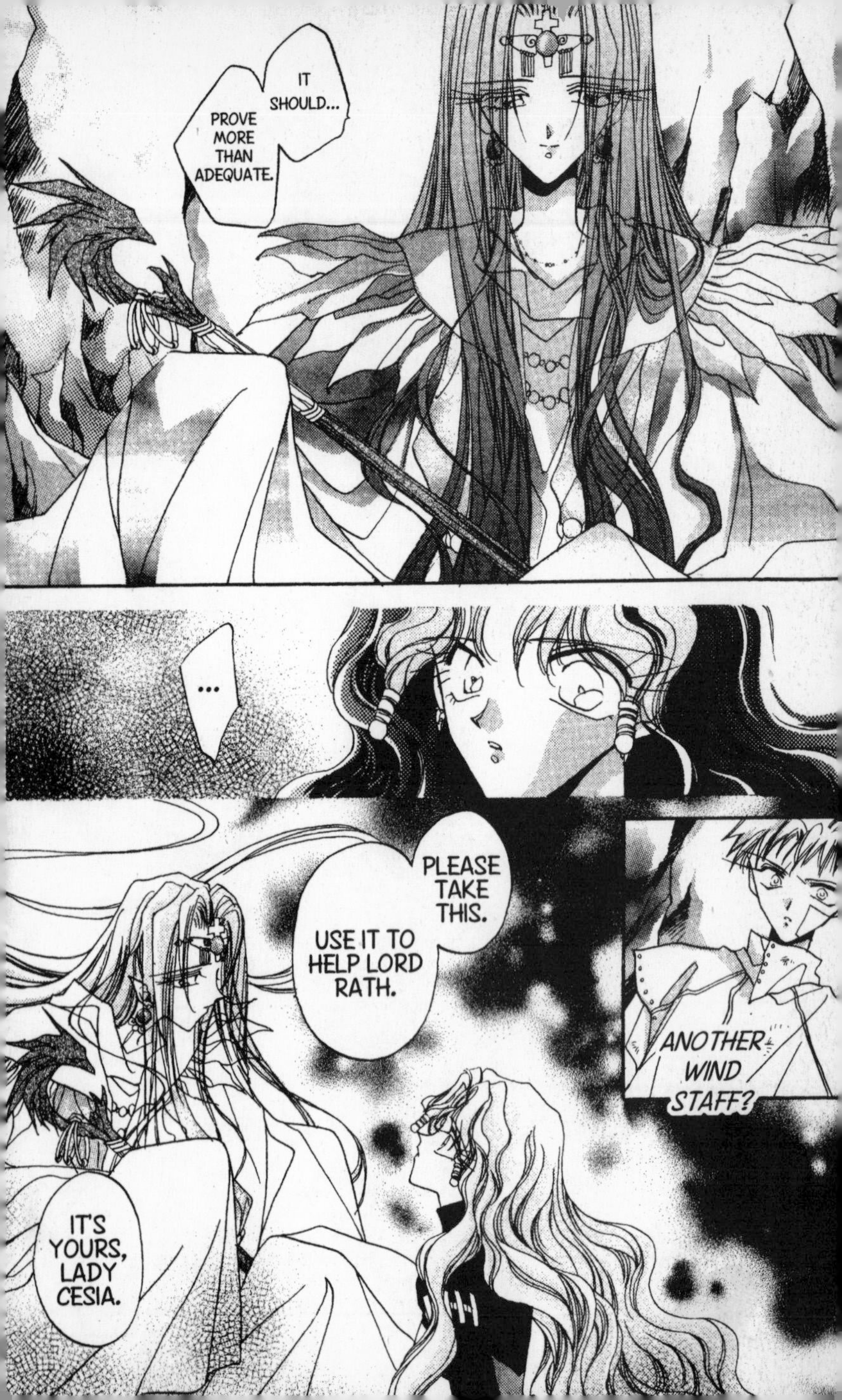
IT SHOULD... PROVE MORE THAN ADEQUATE.
...
ANOTHER WIND STAFF?
PLEASE TAKE THIS.
USE IT TO HELP LORD RATH.
IT'S YOURS, LADY CESIA.

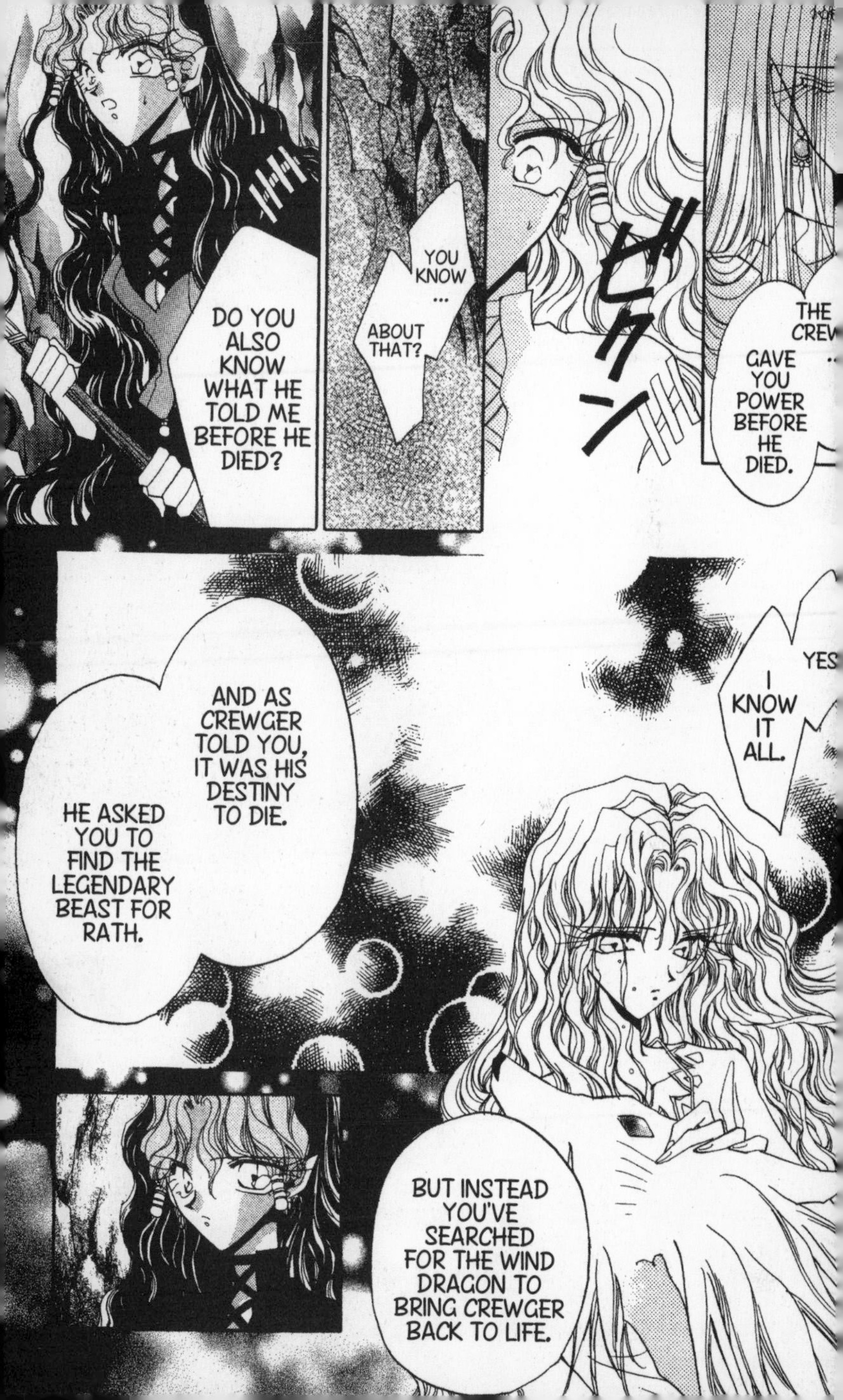

THE CREW ... GAVE YOU POWER BEFORE HE DIED.
ビクン
YOU KNOW ... ABOUT THAT?
DO YOU ALSO KNOW WHAT HE TOLD ME BEFORE HE DIED?
YES I KNOW IT ALL.
AND AS CREWGER TOLD YOU, IT WAS HIS DESTINY TO DIE.
HE ASKED YOU TO FIND THE LEGENDARY BEAST FOR RATH.
BUT INSTEAD YOU'VE SEARCHED FOR THE WIND DRAGON TO BRING CREWGER BACK TO LIFE.

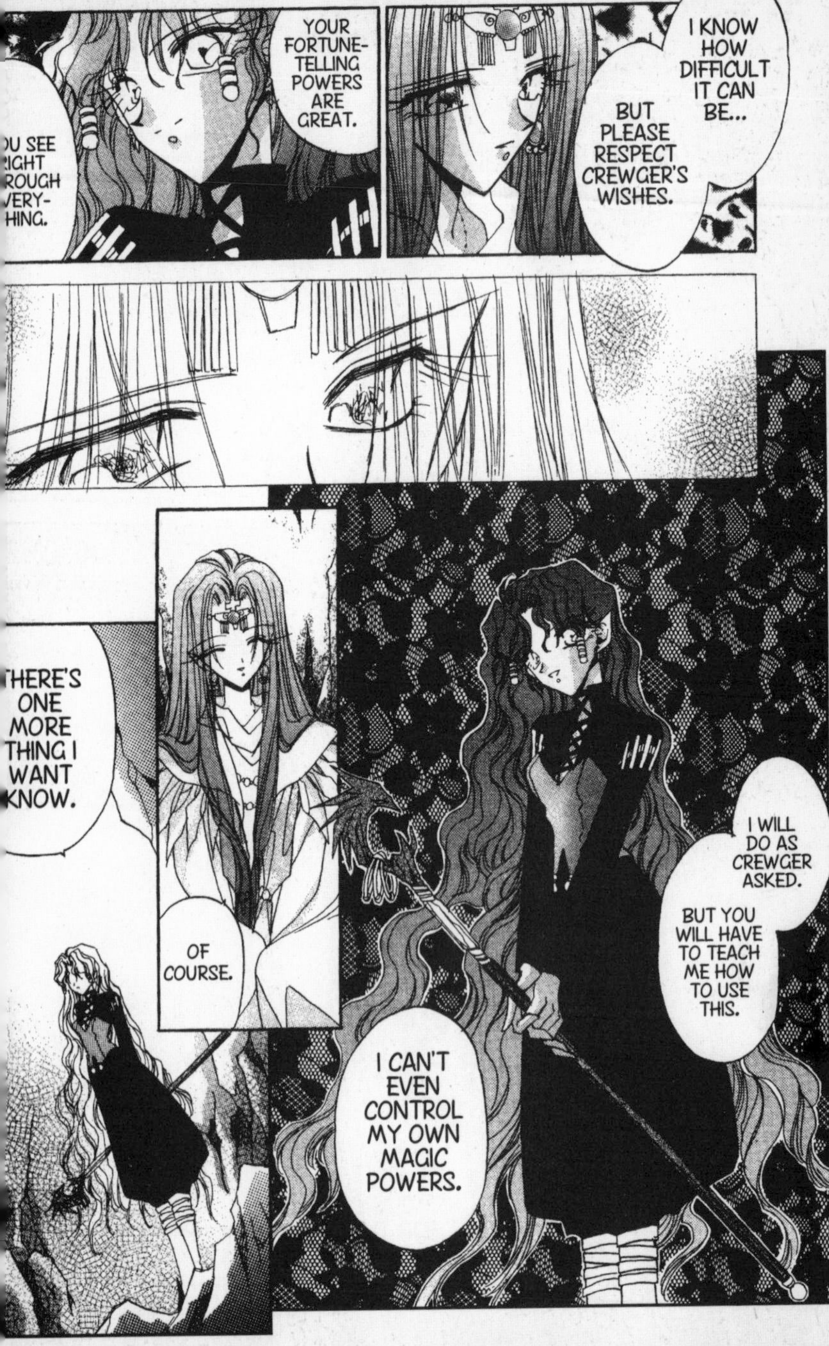
I KNOW HOW DIFFICULT IT CAN BE...
BUT PLEASE RESPECT CREWGER'S WISHES.
YOUR FORTUNE-TELLING POWERS ARE GREAT.
OU SEE RIGHT ROUGH VERY-HING.
I WILL DO AS CREWGER ASKED.
BUT YOU WILL HAVE TO TEACH ME HOW TO USE THIS.
I CAN'T EVEN CONTROL MY OWN MAGIC POWERS.
OF COURSE.
THERE'S ONE MORE THING I WANT KNOW.

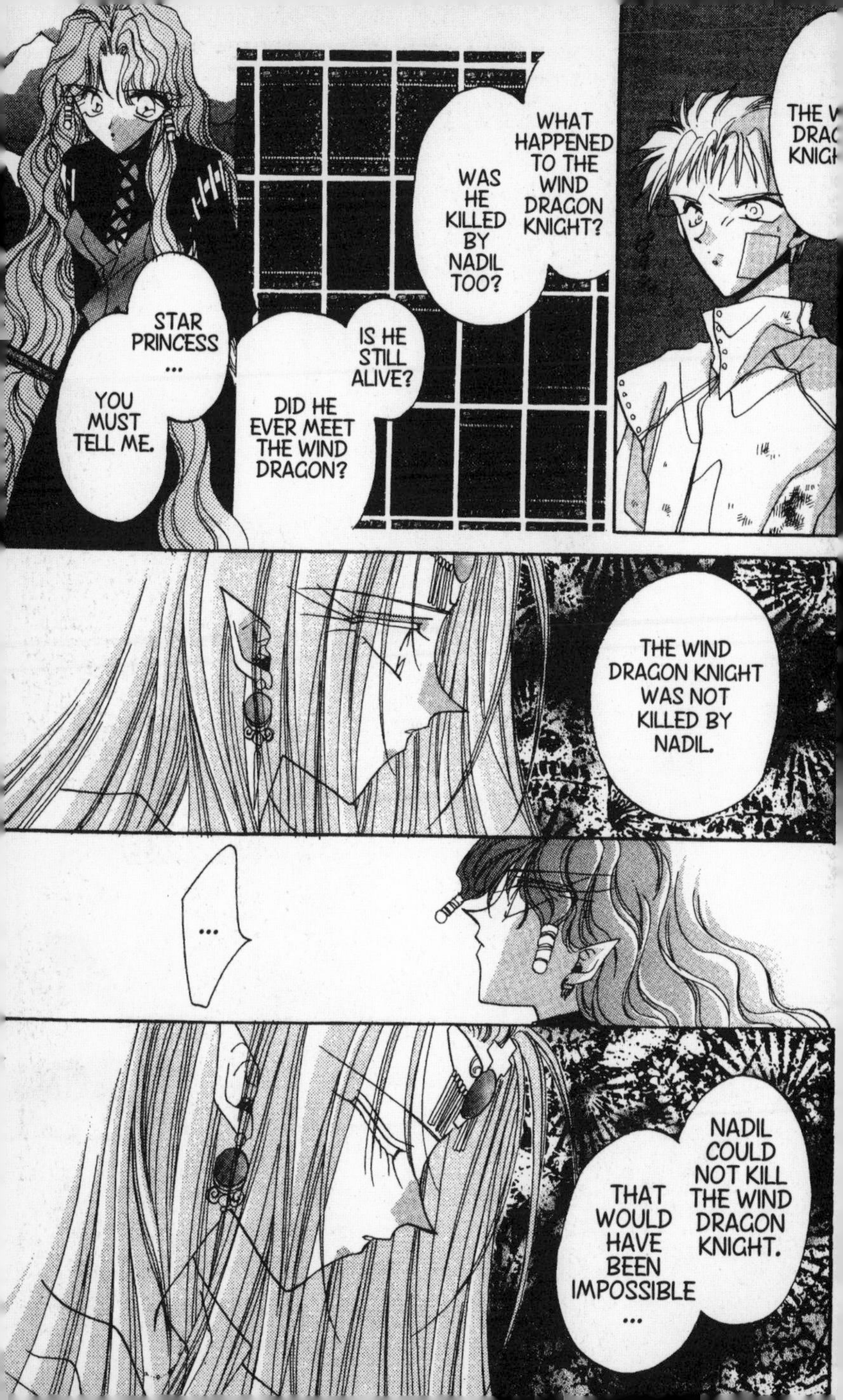
WHAT HAPPENED TO THE WIND DRAGON KNIGHT?
WAS HE KILLED BY NADIL TOO?
IS HE STILL ALIVE?
DID HE EVER MEET THE WIND DRAGON?
STAR PRINCESS ...
YOU MUST TELL ME.
THE WIND DRAGON KNIGHT WAS NOT KILLED BY NADIL.
...
NADIL COULD NOT KILL THE WIND DRAGON KNIGHT.
THAT WOULD HAVE BEEN IMPOSSIBLE ...

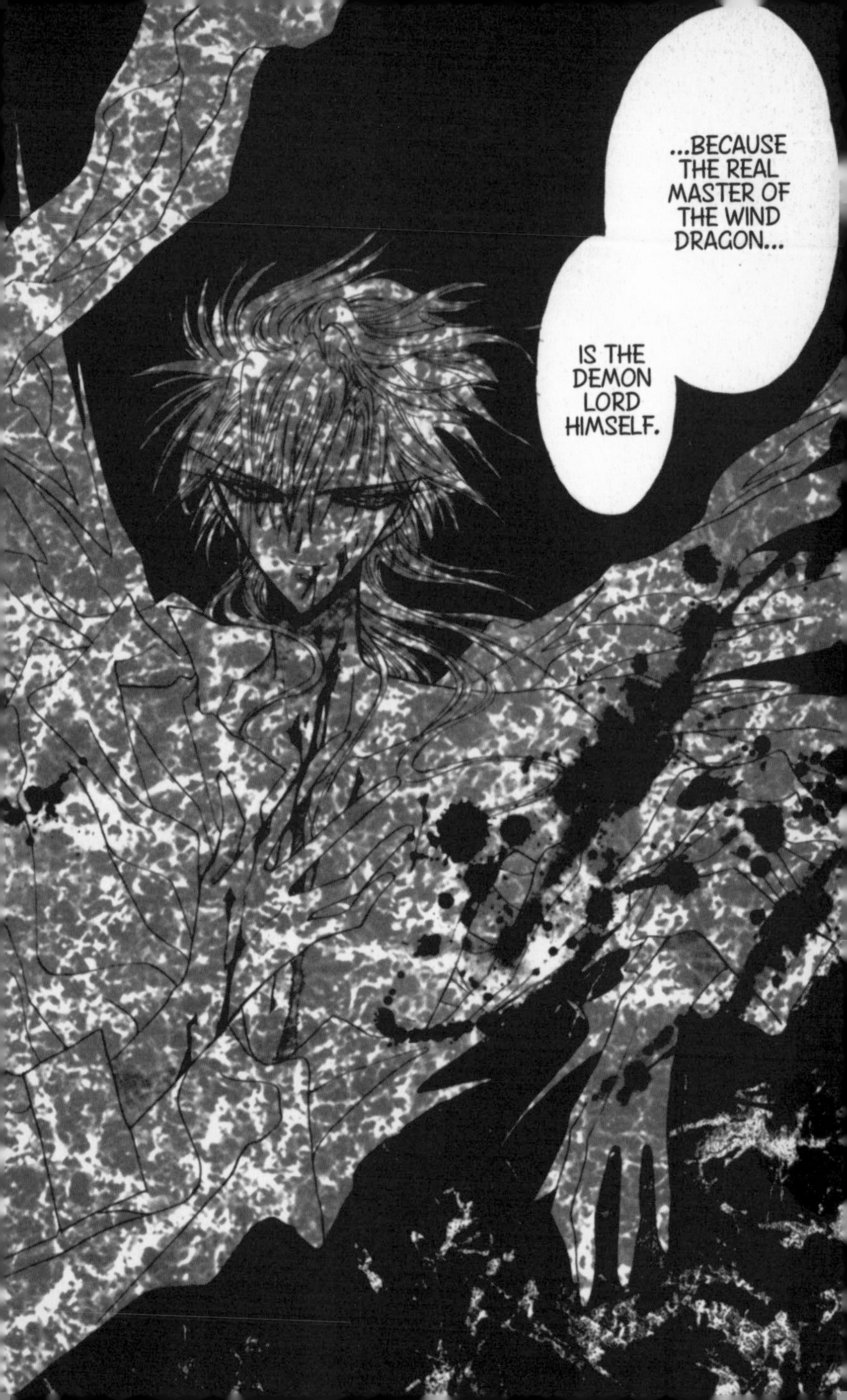
...BECAUSE THE REAL MASTER OF THE WIND DRAGON...
IS THE DEMON LORD HIMSELF.

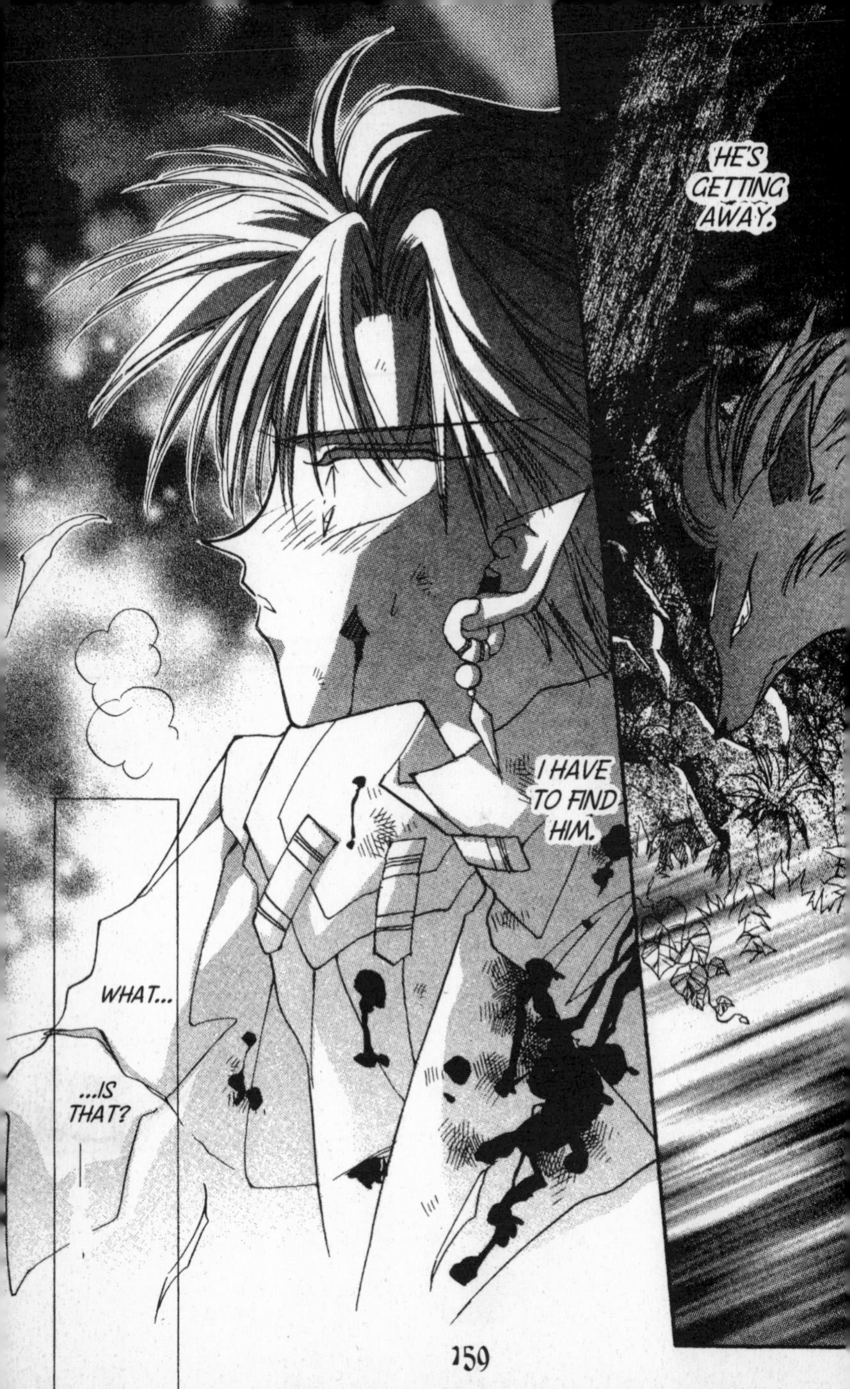
HE'S GETTING AWAY.
I HAVE TO FIND HIM.
WHAT...
...IS THAT?

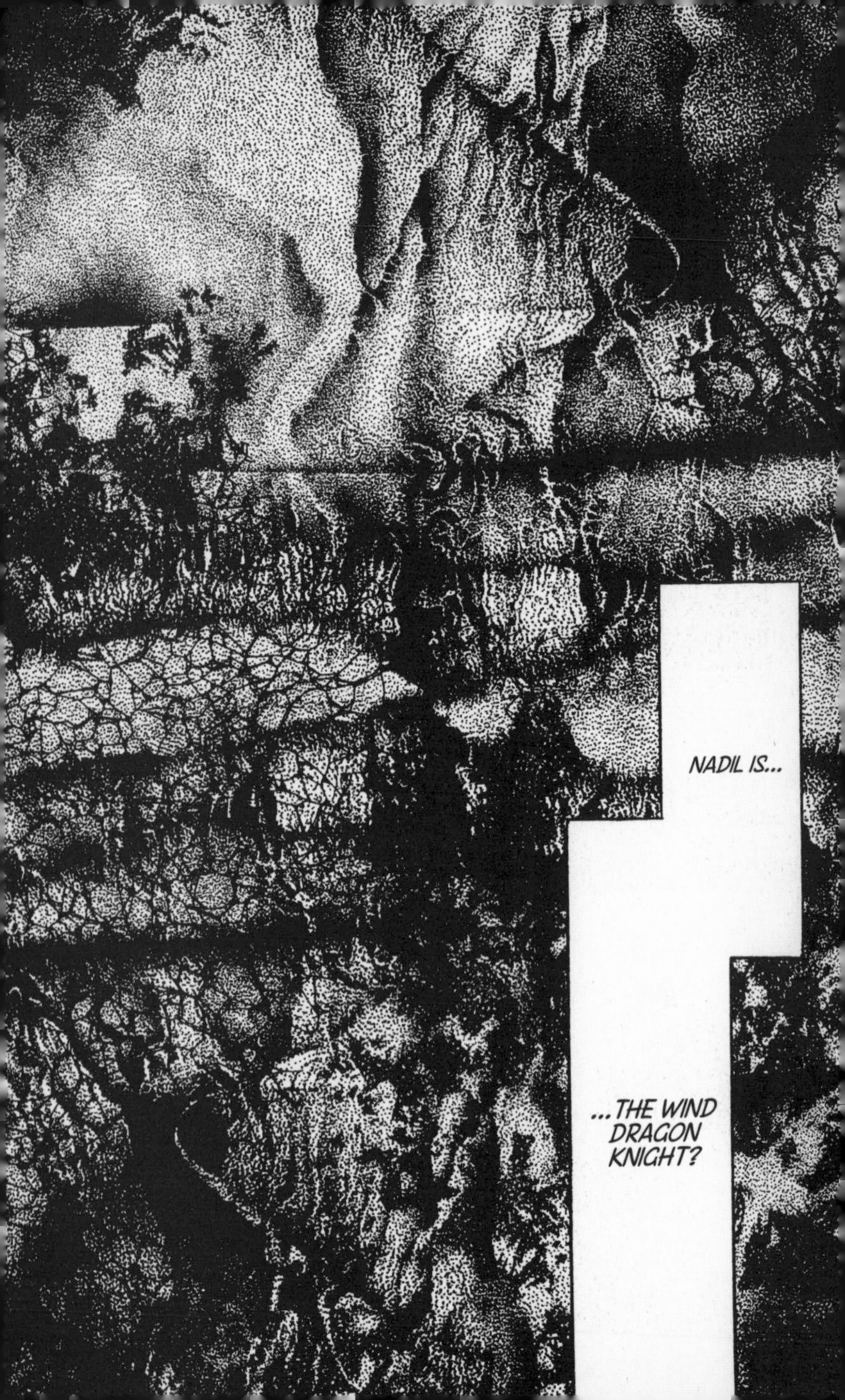
NADIL IS...
...THE WIND DRAGON KNIGHT?

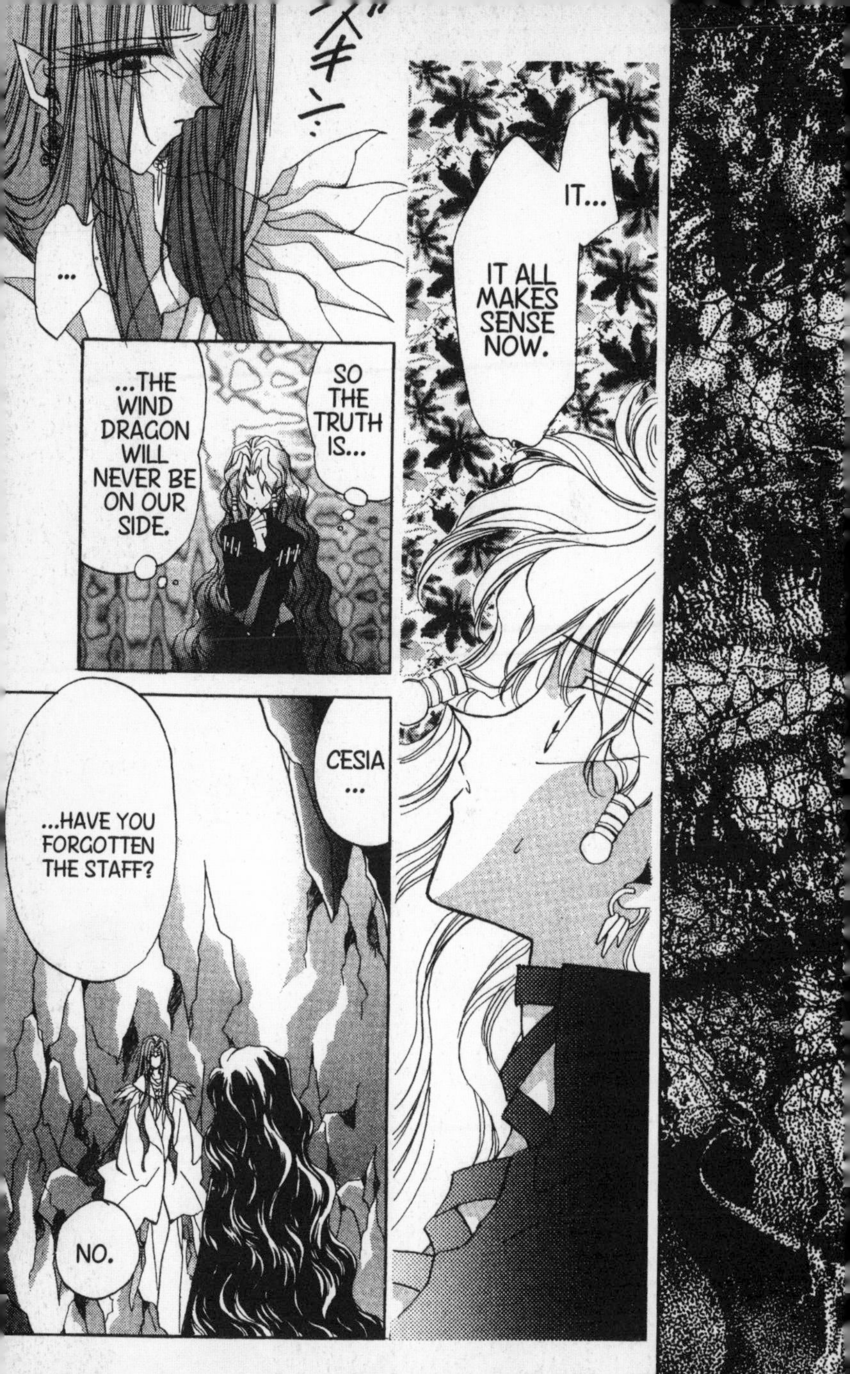
IT...
IT ALL MAKES SENSE NOW.
ズキン…
...
SO THE TRUTH IS...
...THE WIND DRAGON WILL NEVER BE ON OUR SIDE.
CESIA...
...HAVE YOU FORGOTTEN THE STAFF?
NO.

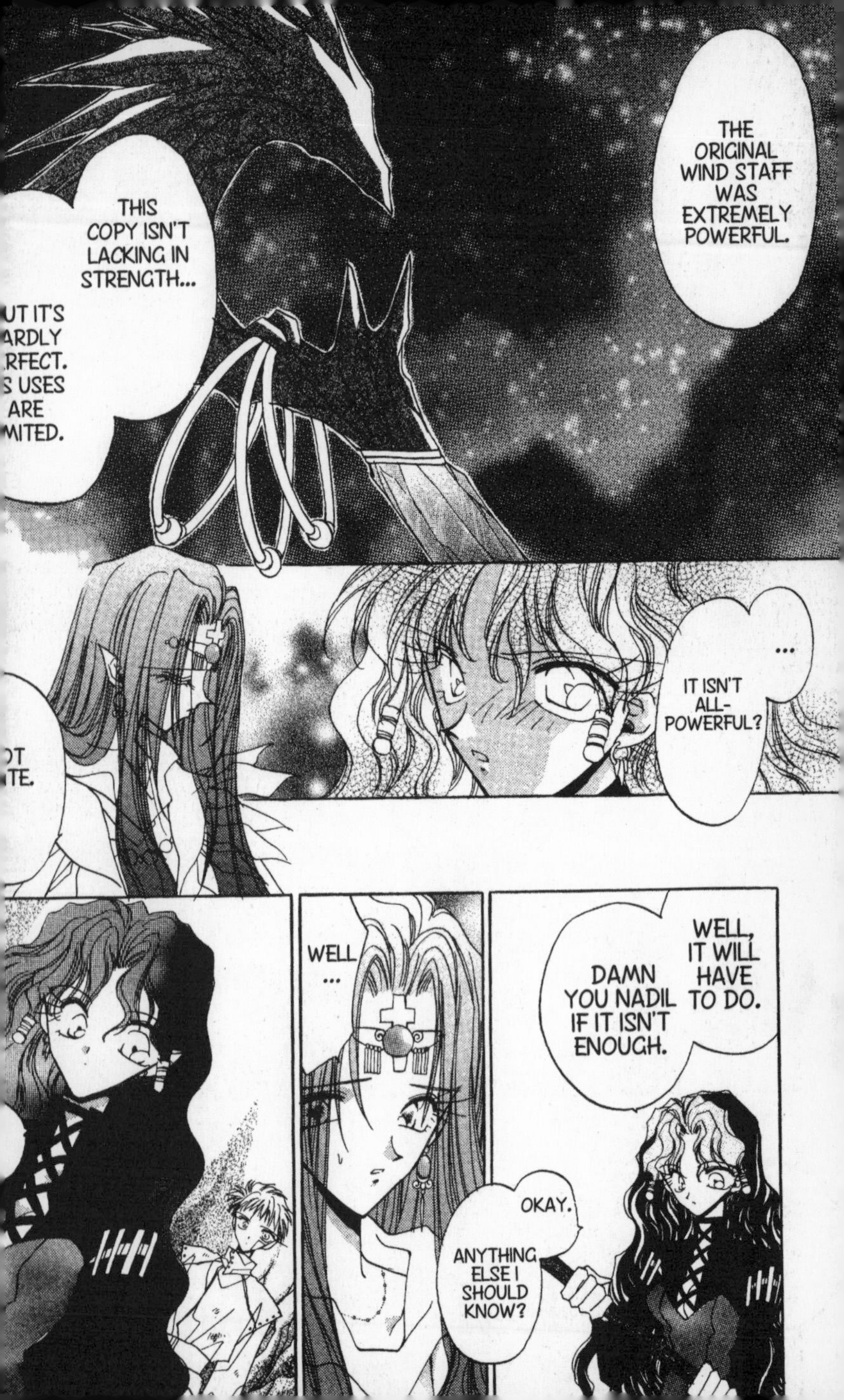
THE ORIGINAL WIND STAFF WAS EXTREMELY POWERFUL.
THIS COPY ISN'T LACKING IN STRENGTH...
UT IT'S ARDLY RFECT. S USES ARE MITED.
... IT ISN'T ALL-POWERFUL?
OT TE.
WELL, IT WILL HAVE TO DO.
DAMN YOU NADIL IF IT ISN'T ENOUGH.
OKAY.
ANYTHING ELSE I SHOULD KNOW?
WELL ...

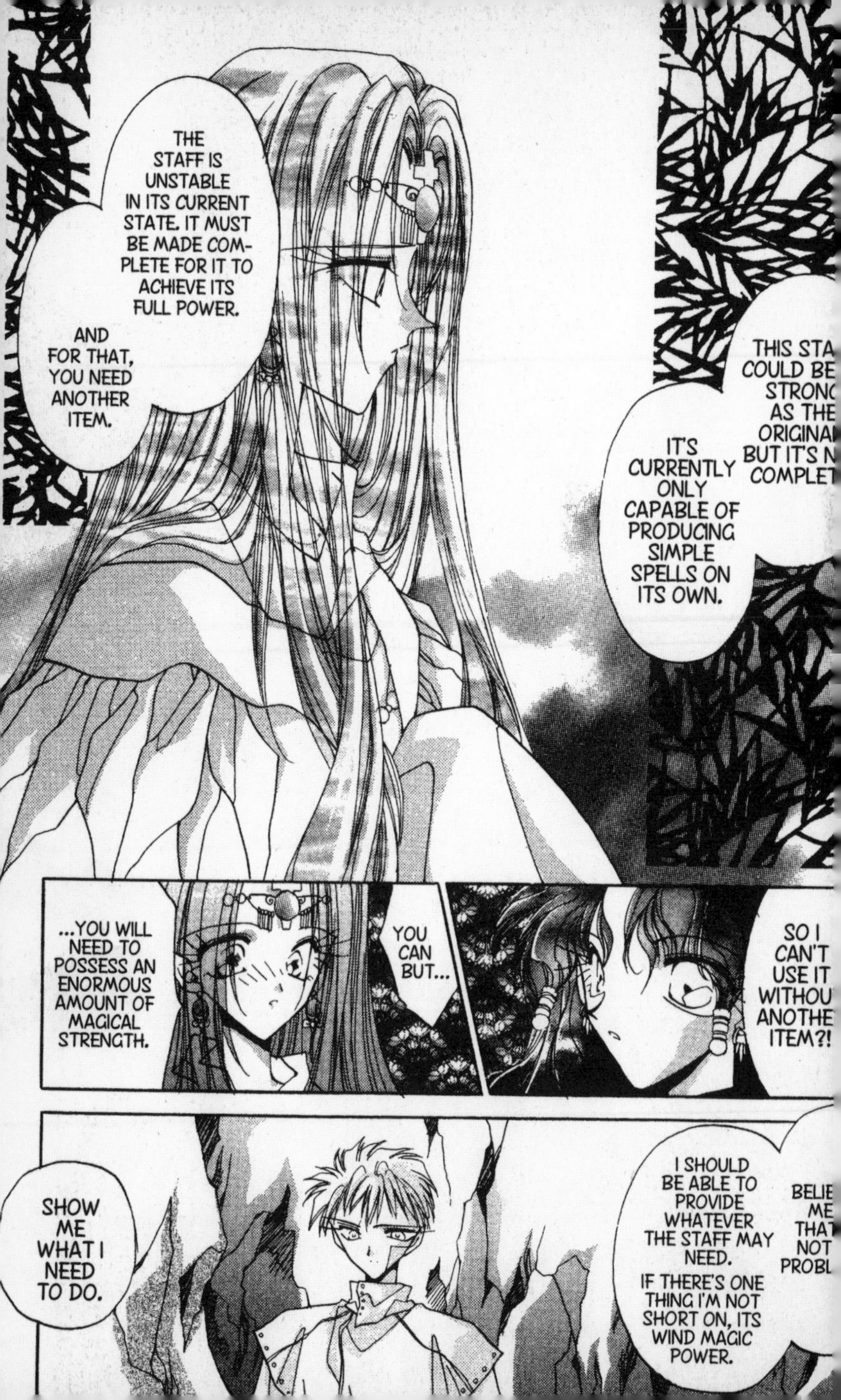
THIS STA COULD BE STRON AS THE ORIGINA BUT IT'S N COMPLET
IT'S CURRENTLY ONLY CAPABLE OF PRODUCING SIMPLE SPELLS ON ITS OWN.
THE STAFF IS UNSTABLE IN ITS CURRENT STATE. IT MUST BE MADE COM-PLETE FOR IT TO ACHIEVE ITS FULL POWER.
AND FOR THAT, YOU NEED ANOTHER ITEM.
SO I CAN'T USE IT WITHOU ANOTHE ITEM?!
YOU CAN BUT...
...YOU WILL NEED TO POSSESS AN ENORMOUS AMOUNT OF MAGICAL STRENGTH.
BELIE ME THAT NOT PROBL
I SHOULD BE ABLE TO PROVIDE WHATEVER THE STAFF MAY NEED.
IF THERE'S ONE THING I'M NOT SHORT ON, ITS WIND MAGIC POWER.
SHOW ME WHAT I NEED TO DO.

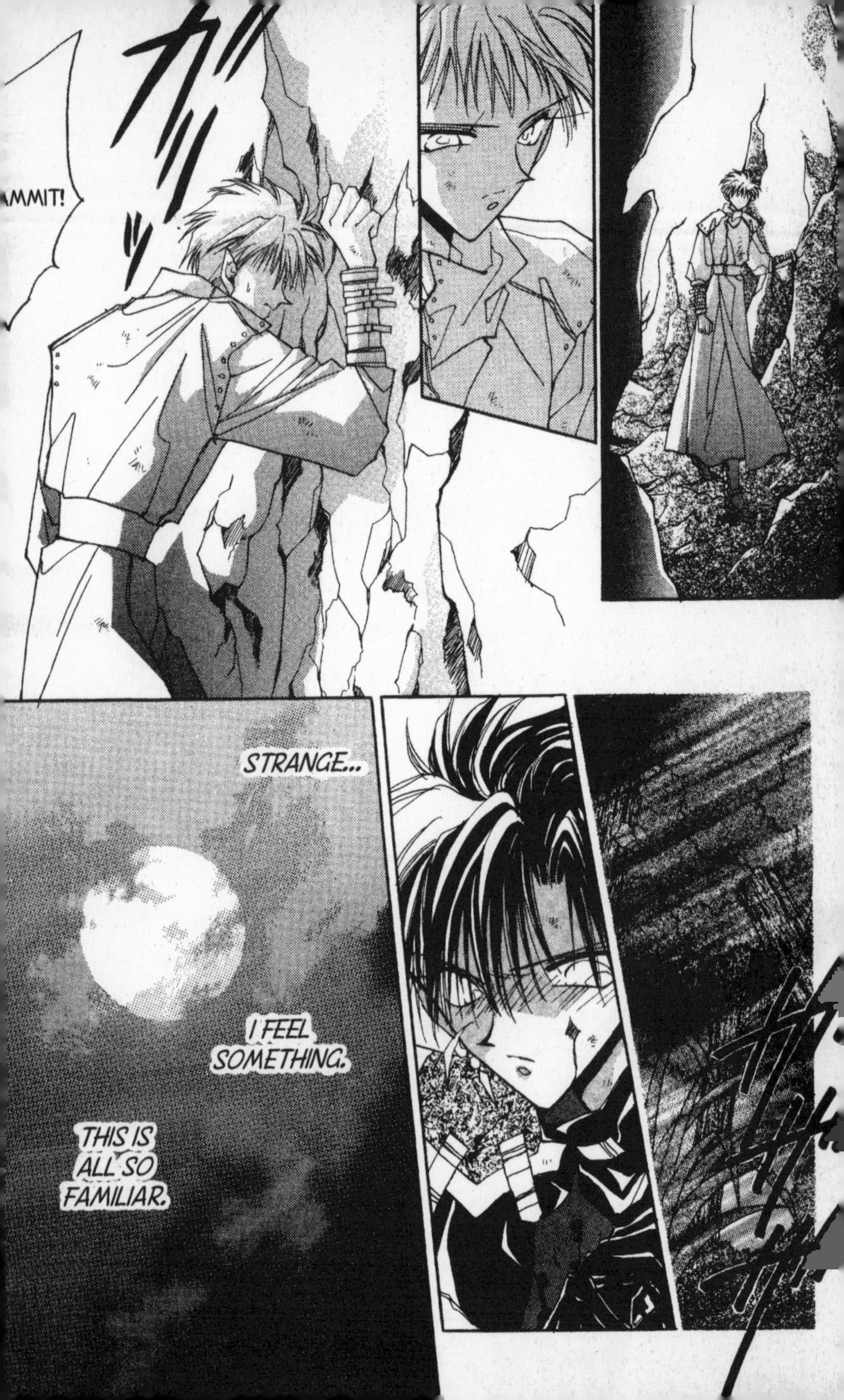
AMMIT!
STRANGE...
I FEEL SOMETHING.
THIS IS ALL SO FAMILIAR.

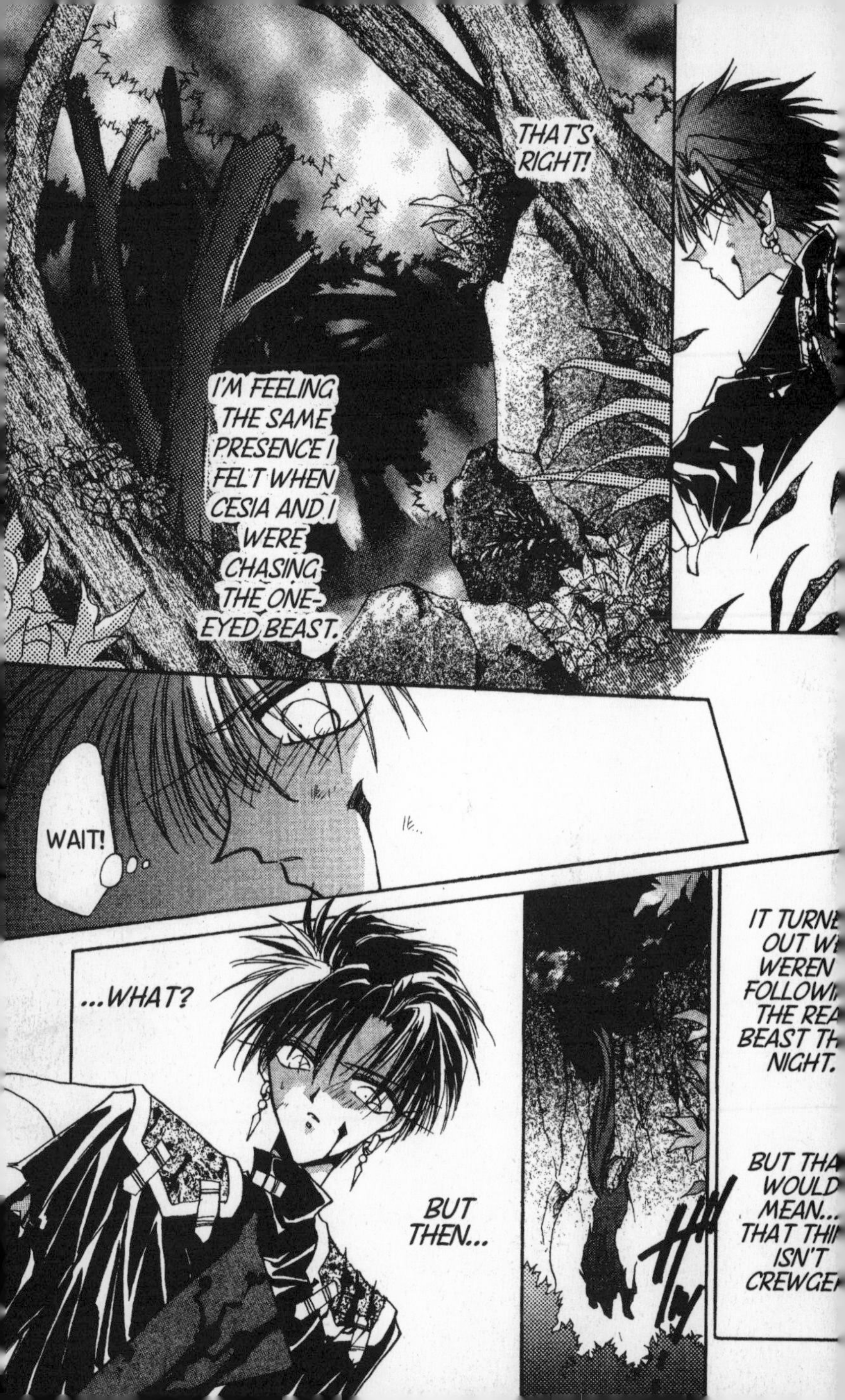
THAT'S RIGHT!
I'M FEELING THE SAME PRESENCE I FELT WHEN CESIA AND I WERE CHASING THE ONE-EYED BEAST.
WAIT!
IT TURNE OUT W WEREN FOLLOWI THE REA BEAST TH NIGHT.
BUT THA WOULD MEAN... THAT THI ISN'T CREWGE
...WHAT?
BUT THEN...

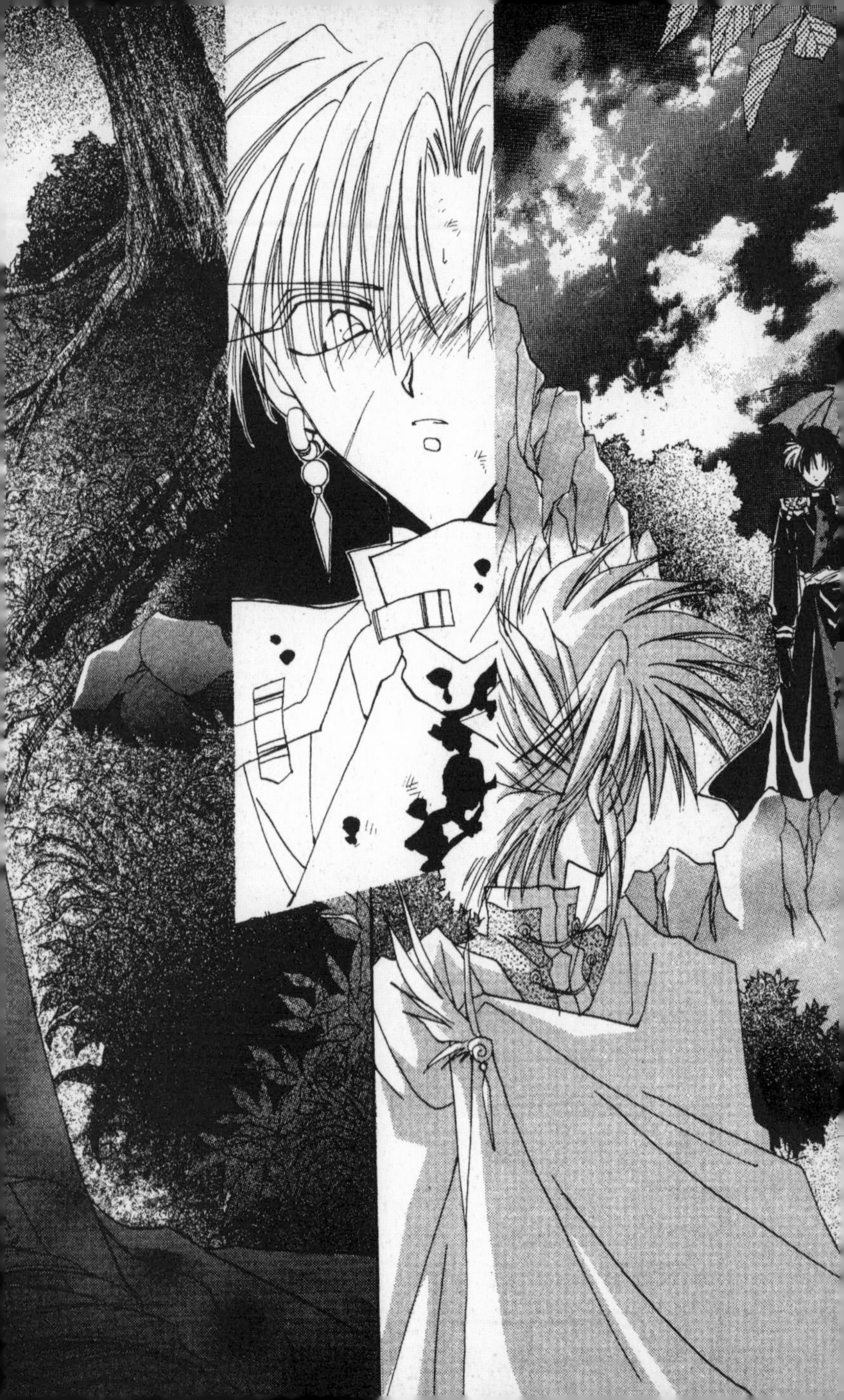

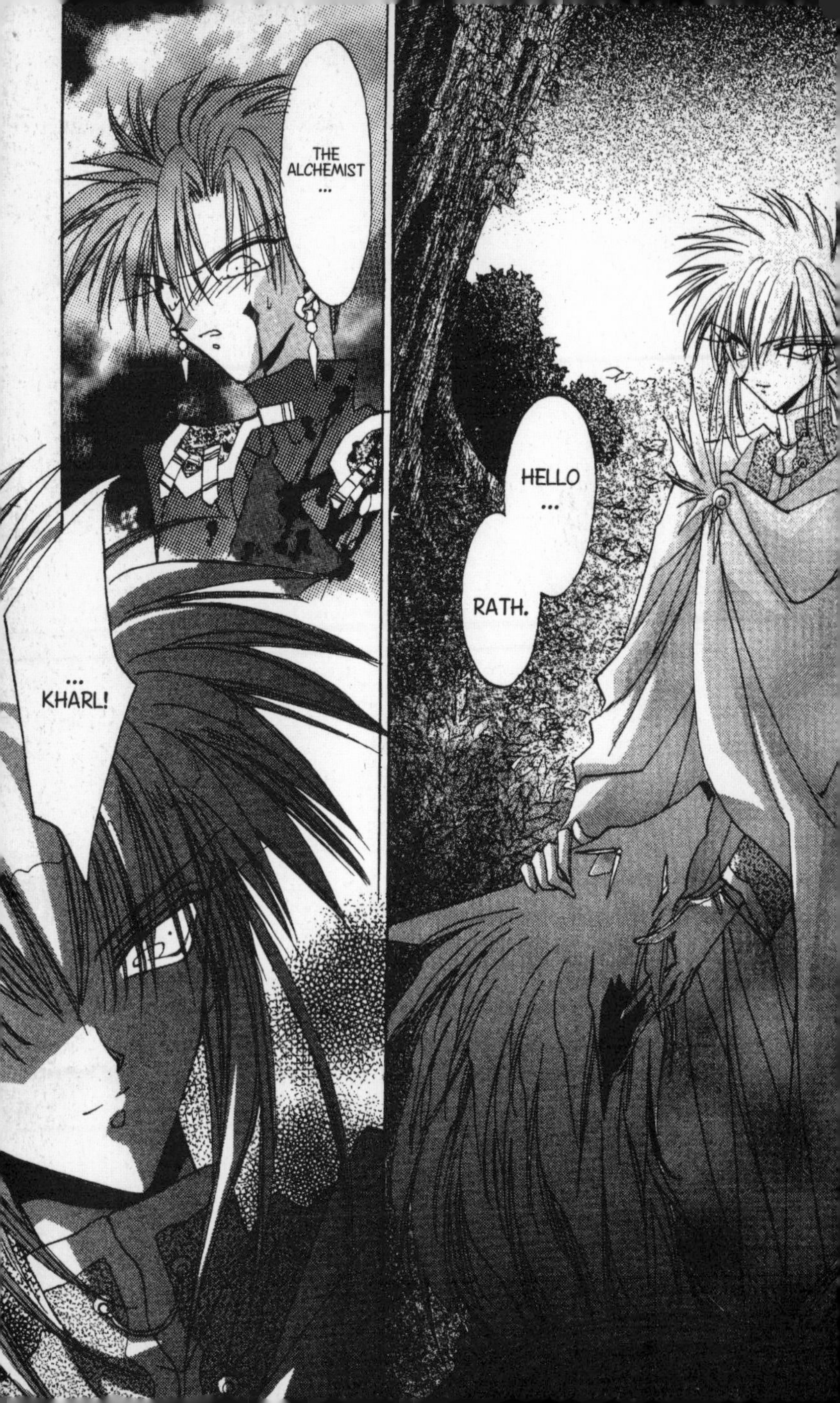
HELLO ...
RATH.
THE ALCHEMIST ...
... KHARL!

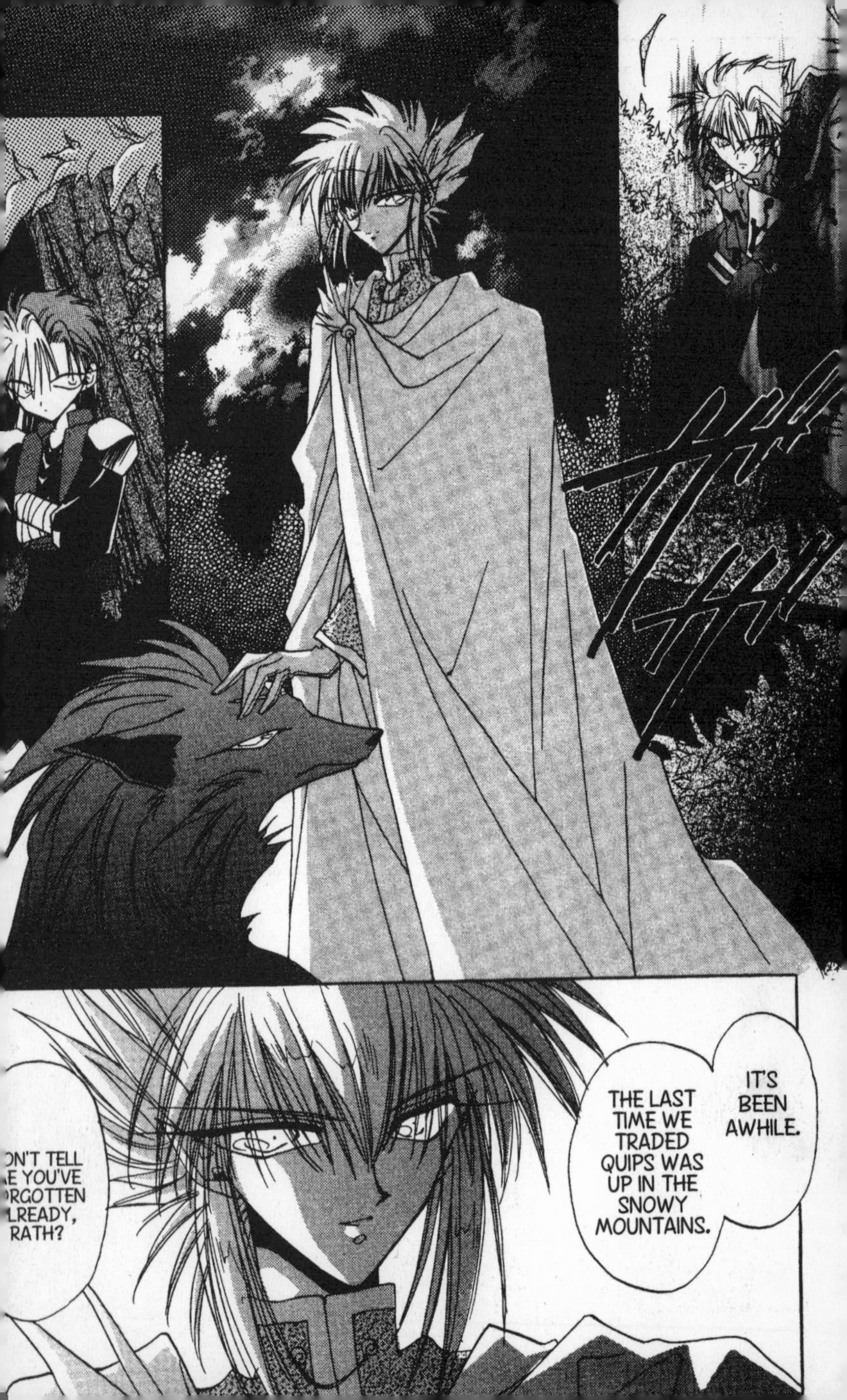
IT'S BEEN AWHILE.
THE LAST TIME WE TRADED QUIPS WAS UP IN THE SNOWY MOUNTAINS.
ON'T TELL E YOU'VE RGOTTEN LREADY, RATH?

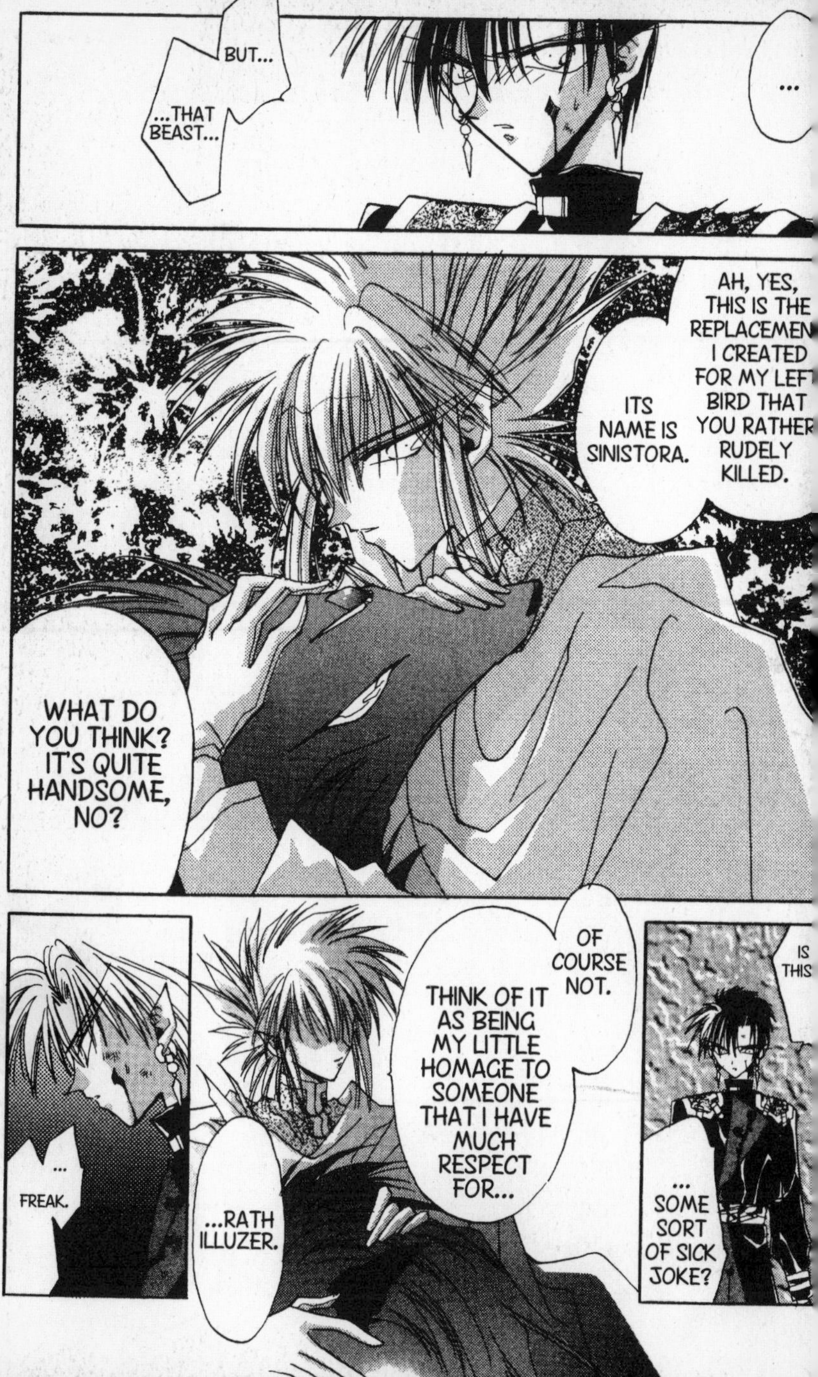
...
BUT...
...THAT BEAST...
AH, YES, THIS IS THE REPLACEMEN I CREATED FOR MY LEFT BIRD THAT YOU RATHER RUDELY KILLED.
ITS NAME IS SINISTORA.
WHAT DO YOU THINK? IT'S QUITE HANDSOME, NO?
IS THIS
... SOME SORT OF SICK JOKE?
OF COURSE NOT.
THINK OF IT AS BEING MY LITTLE HOMAGE TO SOMEONE THAT I HAVE MUCH RESPECT FOR...
...RATH ILLUZER.
...
FREAK.

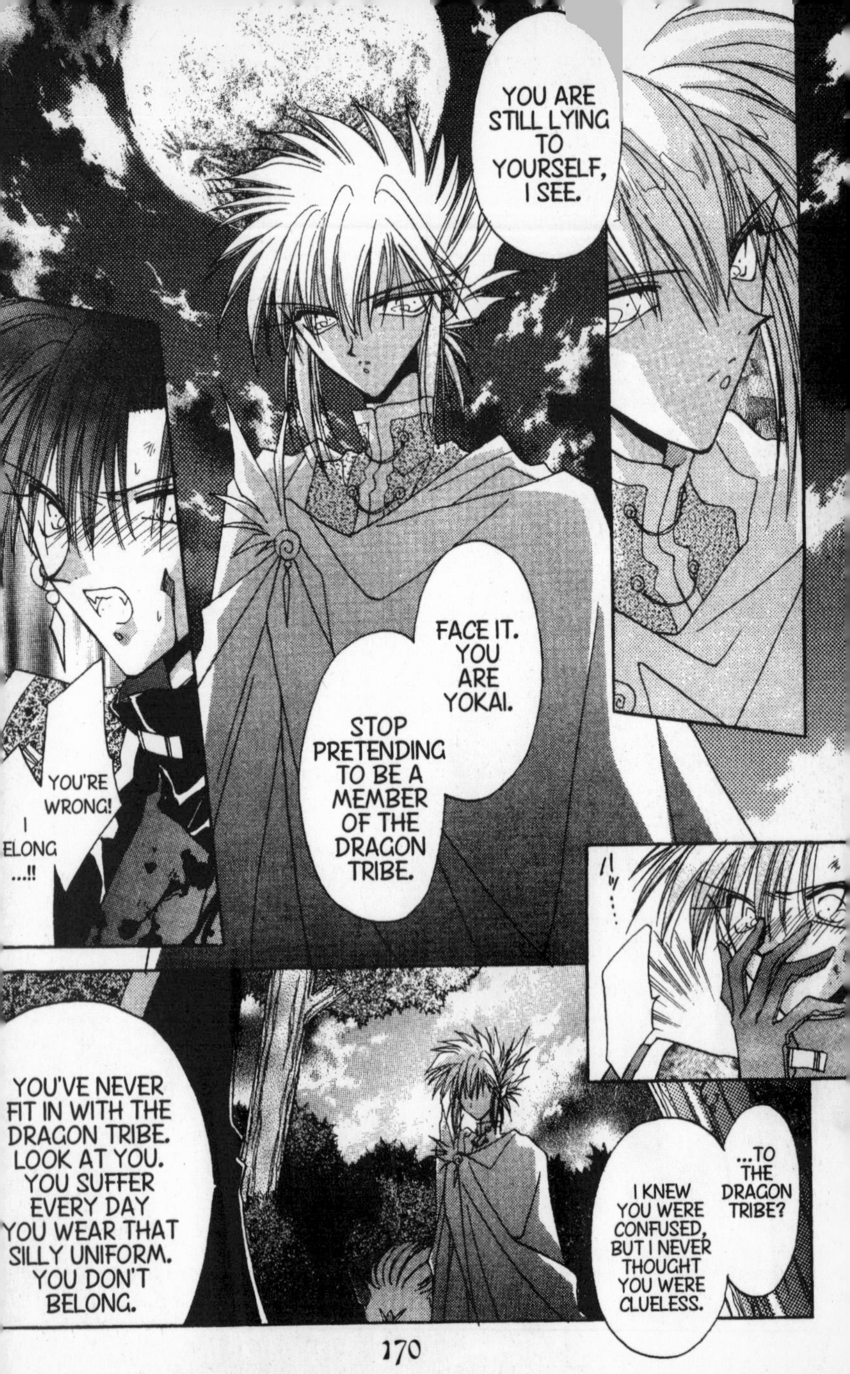
YOU ARE STILL LYING TO YOURSELF, I SEE.
FACE IT. YOU ARE YOKAI.
STOP PRETENDING TO BE A MEMBER OF THE DRAGON TRIBE.
YOU'RE WRONG!
I ELONG ...!!
...TO THE DRAGON TRIBE?
I KNEW YOU WERE CONFUSED, BUT I NEVER THOUGHT YOU WERE CLUELESS.
YOU'VE NEVER FIT IN WITH THE DRAGON TRIBE. LOOK AT YOU. YOU SUFFER EVERY DAY YOU WEAR THAT SILLY UNIFORM. YOU DON'T BELONG.

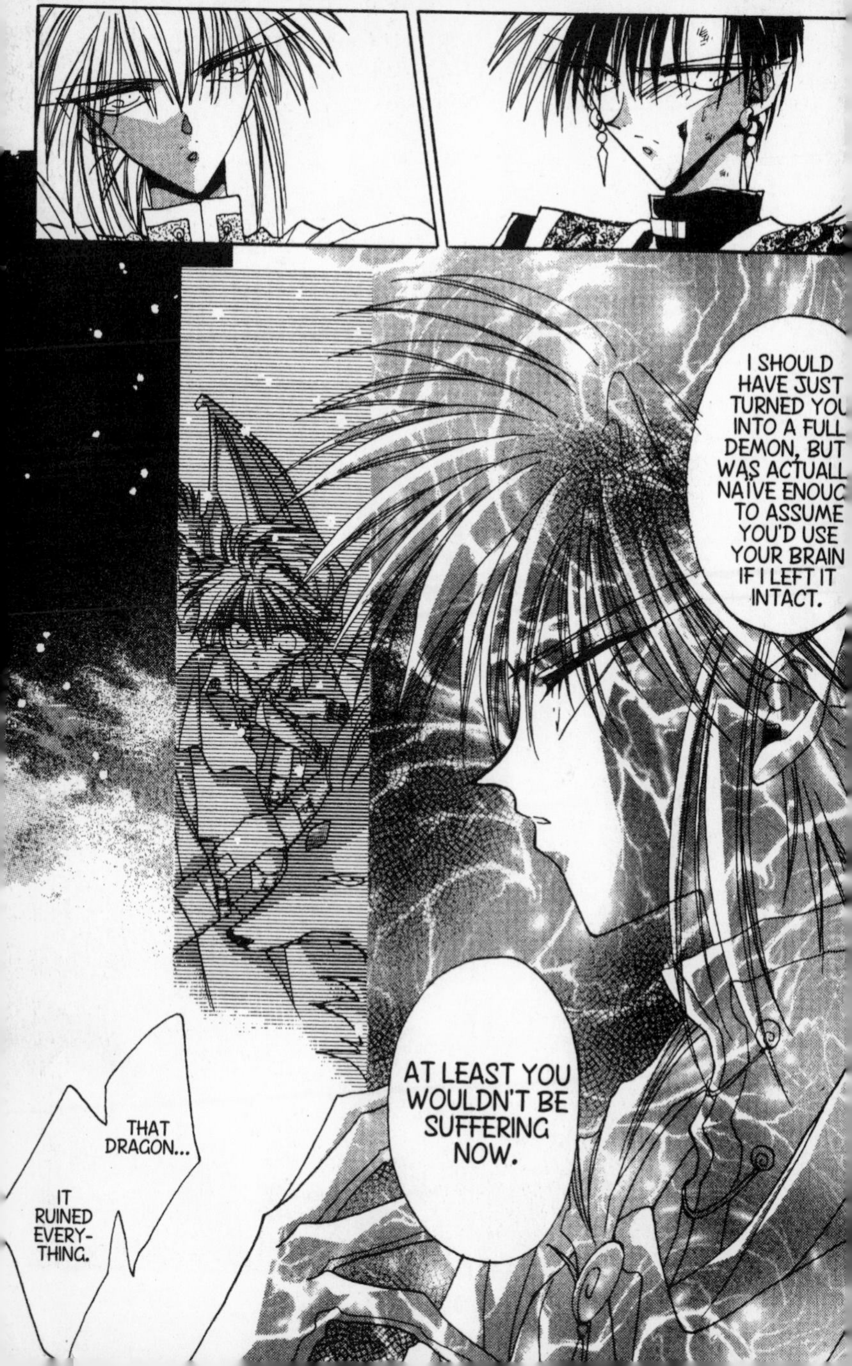
I SHOULD HAVE JUST TURNED YOU INTO A FULL DEMON, BUT WAS ACTUALL NAÏVE ENOUG TO ASSUME YOU'D USE YOUR BRAIN IF I LEFT IT INTACT.
AT LEAST YOU WOULDN'T BE SUFFERING NOW.
THAT DRAGON...
IT RUINED EVERY-THING.

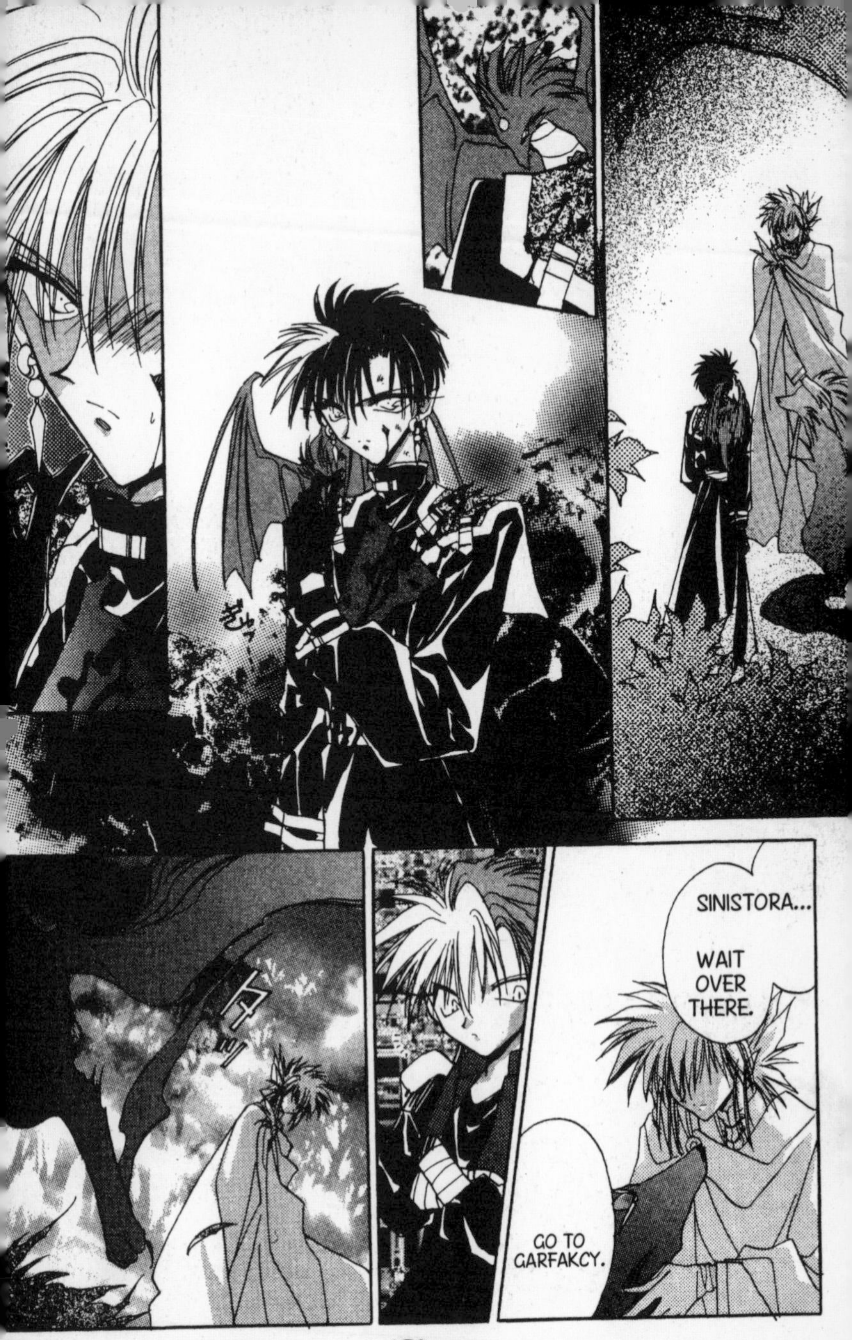
SINISTORA...
WAIT OVER THERE.
GO TO GARFAKCY.

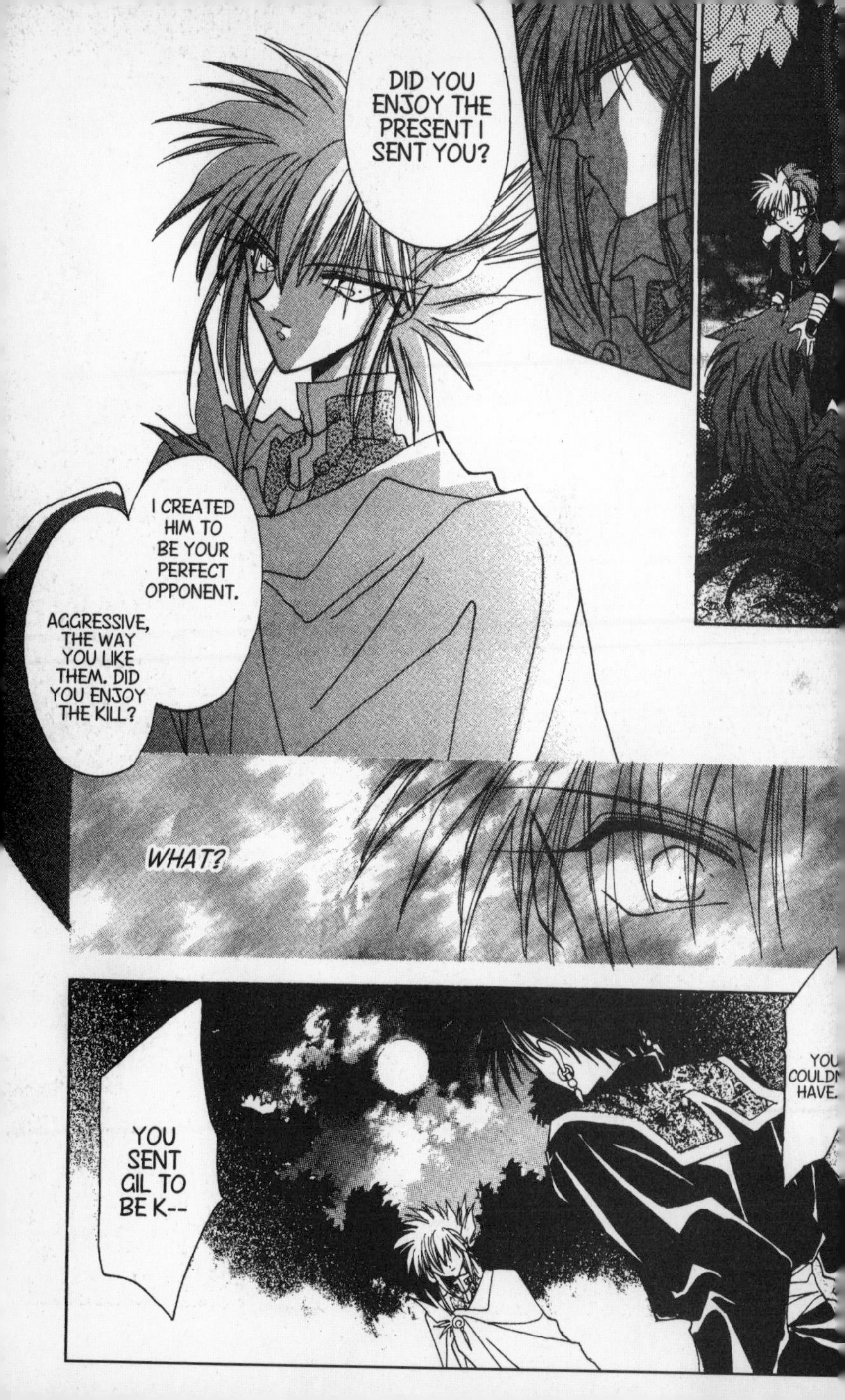
DID YOU ENJOY THE PRESENT I SENT YOU?
I CREATED HIM TO BE YOUR PERFECT OPPONENT.
AGGRESSIVE, THE WAY YOU LIKE THEM. DID YOU ENJOY THE KILL?
WHAT?
YOU SENT GIL TO BE K--

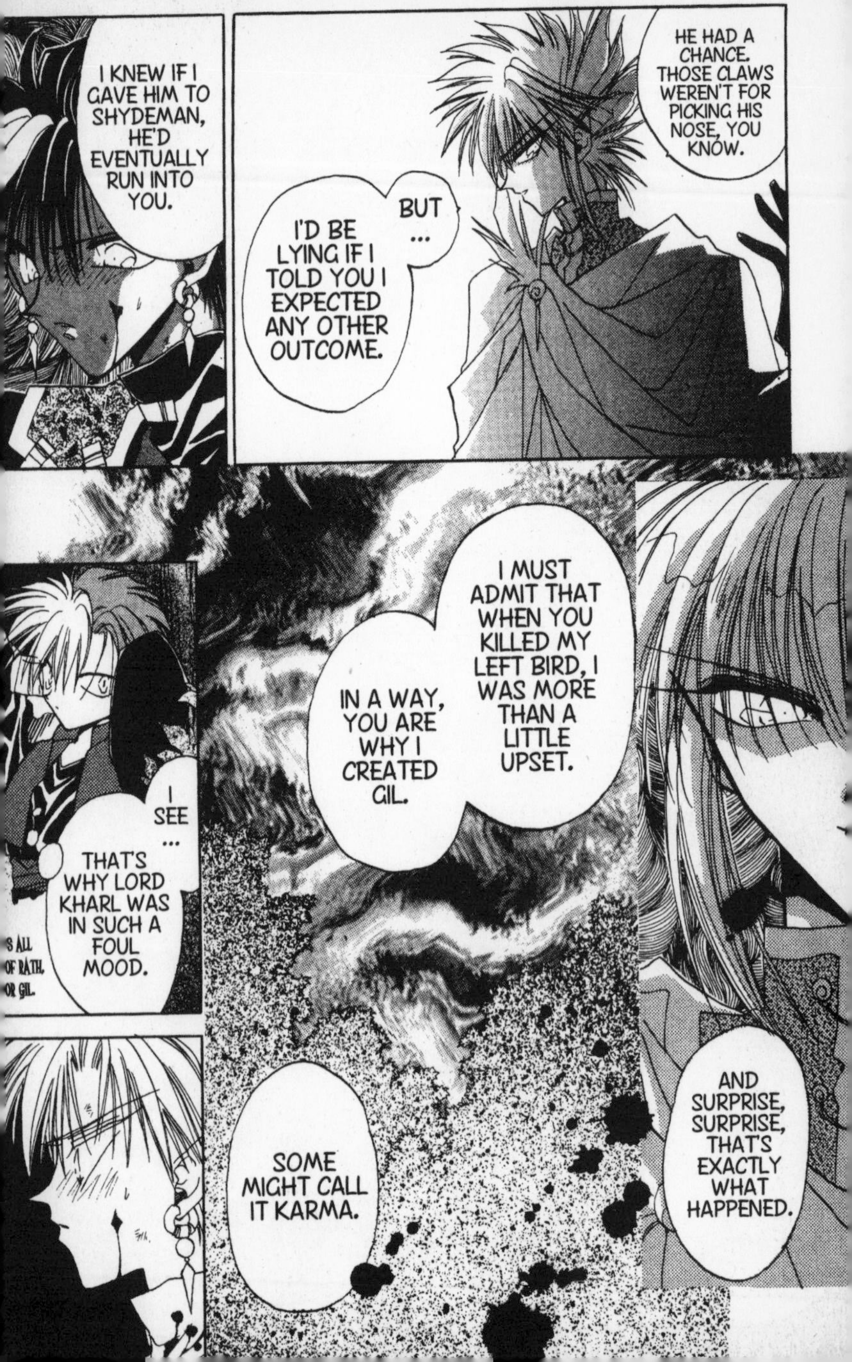
HE HAD A CHANCE. THOSE CLAWS WEREN'T FOR PICKING HIS NOSE, YOU KNOW.
BUT ...
I'D BE LYING IF I TOLD YOU I EXPECTED ANY OTHER OUTCOME.
I KNEW IF I GAVE HIM TO SHYDEMAN, HE'D EVENTUALLY RUN INTO YOU.
I MUST ADMIT THAT WHEN YOU KILLED MY LEFT BIRD, I WAS MORE THAN A LITTLE UPSET.
IN A WAY, YOU ARE WHY I CREATED GIL.
AND SURPRISE, SURPRISE, THAT'S EXACTLY WHAT HAPPENED.
SOME MIGHT CALL IT KARMA.
I SEE ...
THAT'S WHY LORD KHARL WAS IN SUCH A FOUL MOOD.

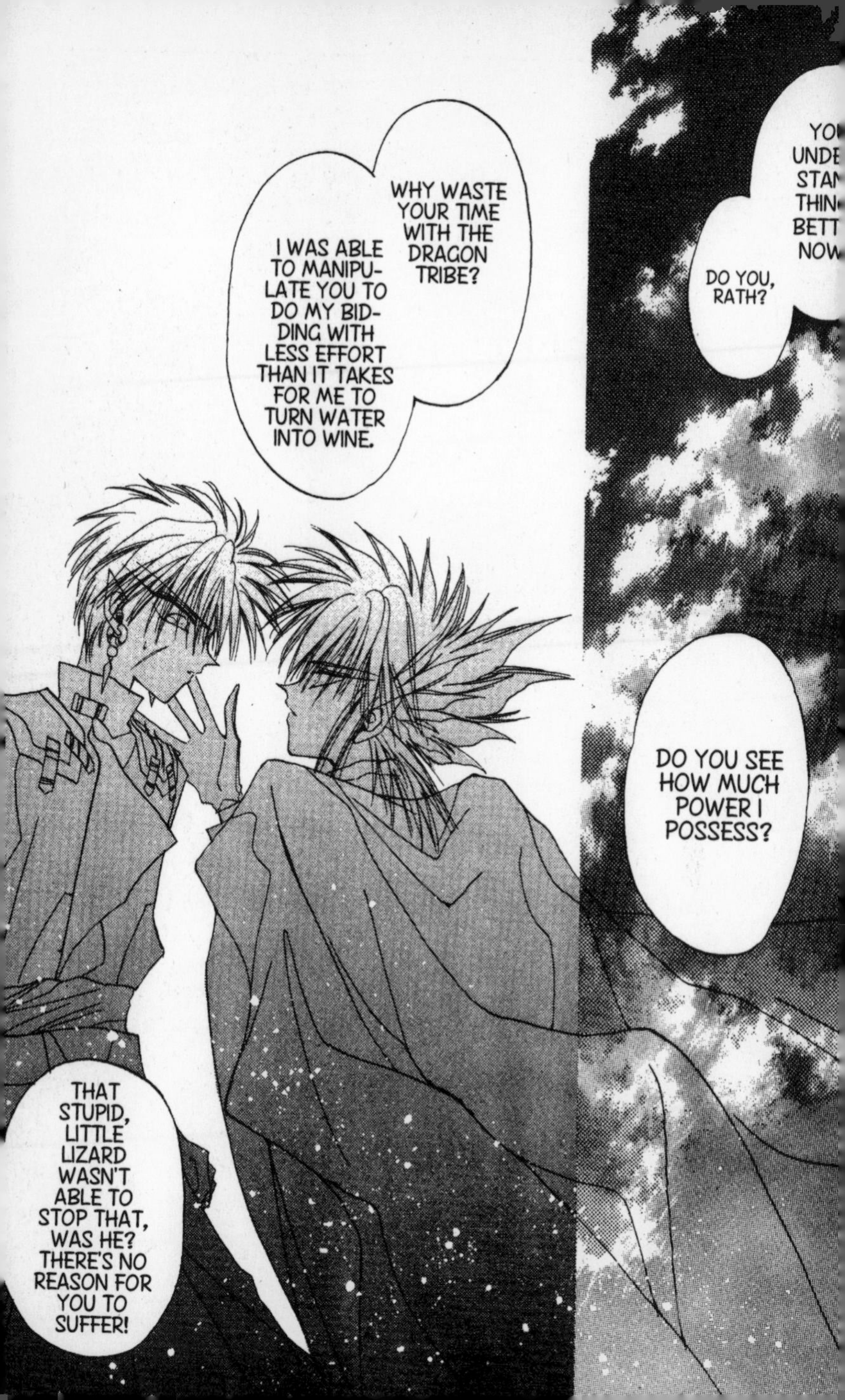
DO YOU, RATH?
DO YOU SEE HOW MUCH POWER I POSSESS?
WHY WASTE YOUR TIME WITH THE DRAGON TRIBE?
I WAS ABLE TO MANIPULATE YOU TO DO MY BIDDING WITH LESS EFFORT THAN IT TAKES FOR ME TO TURN WATER INTO WINE.
THAT STUPID, LITTLE LIZARD WASN'T ABLE TO STOP THAT, WAS HE? THERE'S NO REASON FOR YOU TO SUFFER!

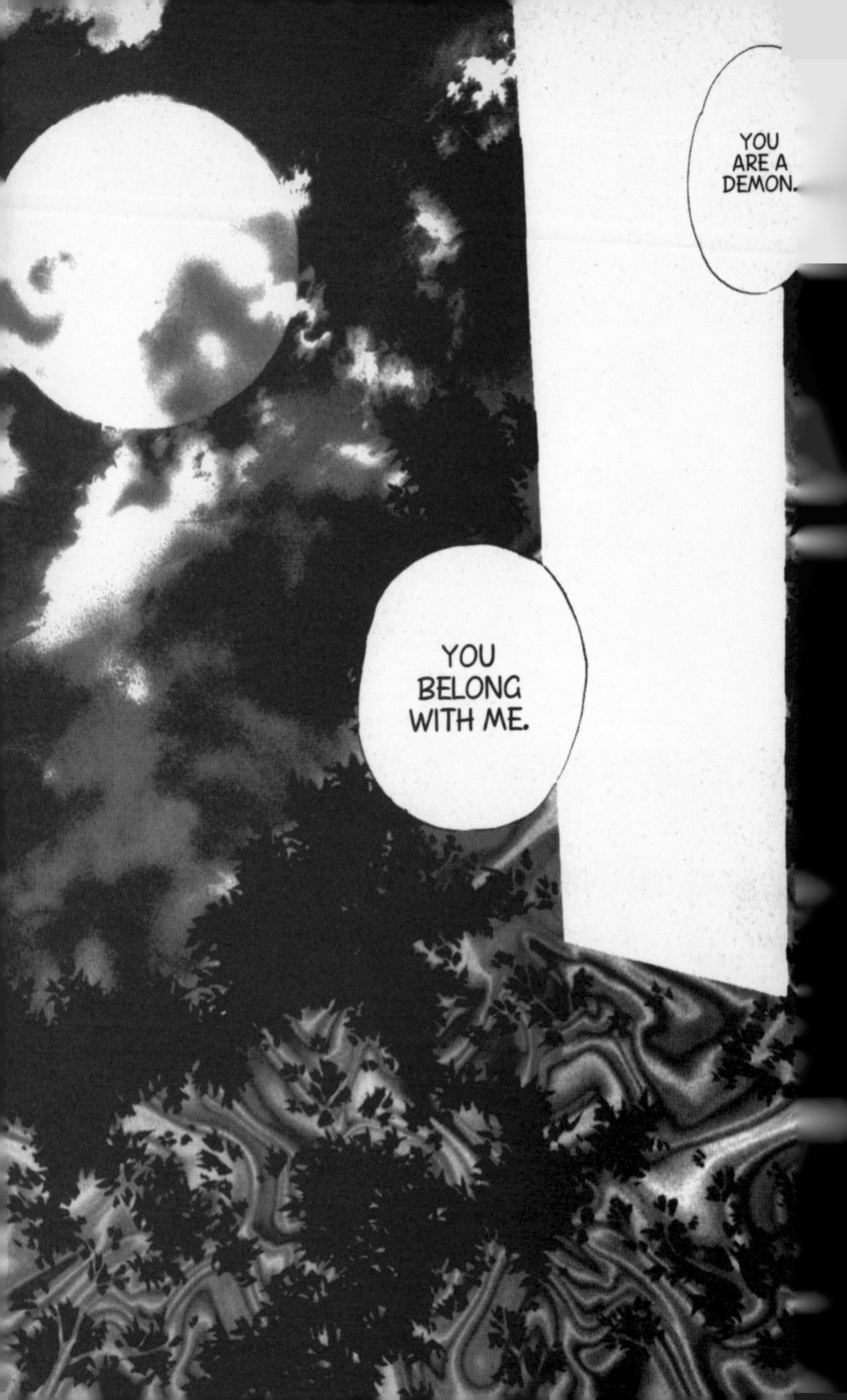
YOU ARE A DEMON.
YOU BELONG WITH ME.

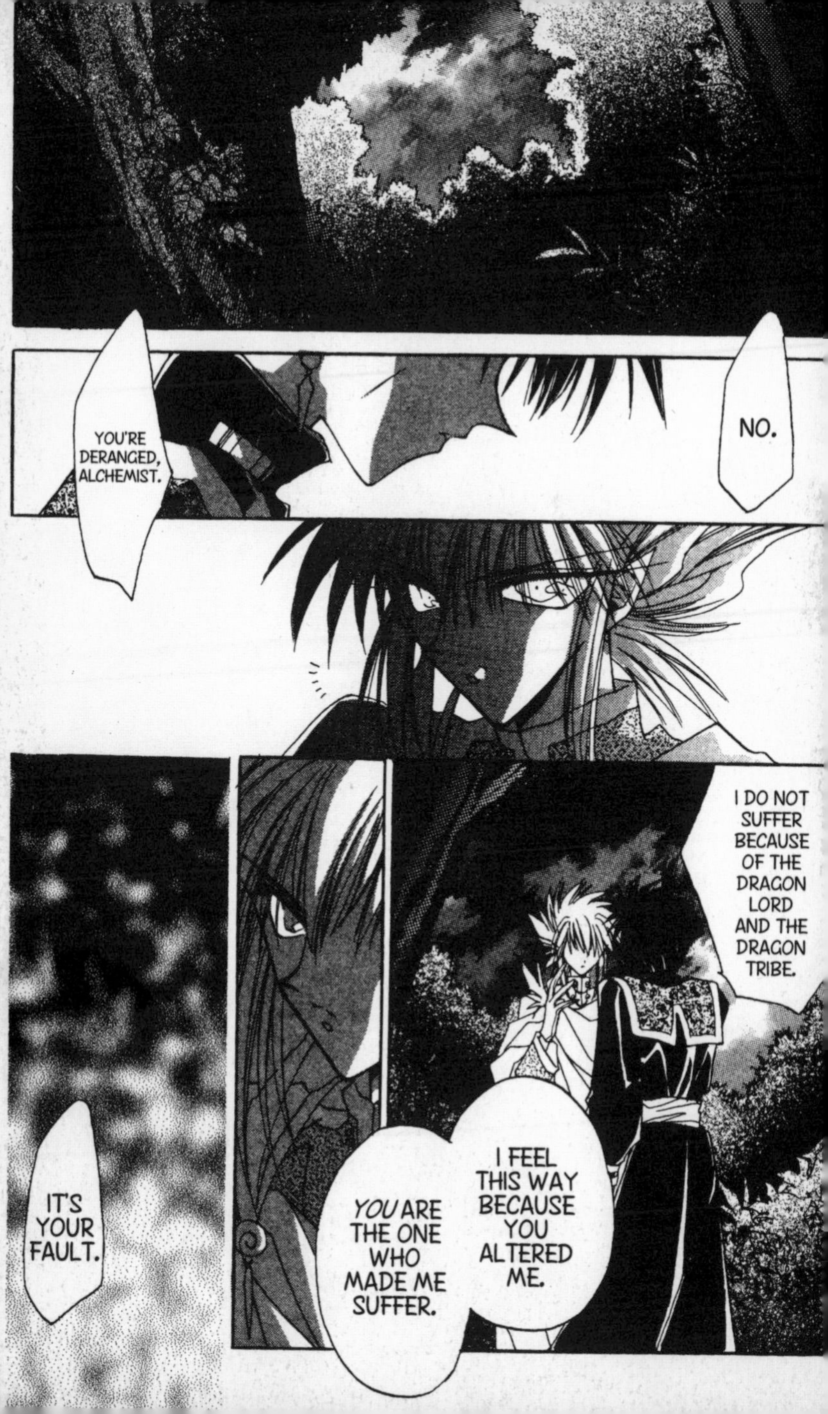
NO.
YOU'RE DERANGED, ALCHEMIST.
I DO NOT SUFFER BECAUSE OF THE DRAGON LORD AND THE DRAGON TRIBE.
I FEEL THIS WAY BECAUSE YOU ALTERED ME.
YOU ARE THE ONE WHO MADE ME SUFFER.
IT'S YOUR FAULT.

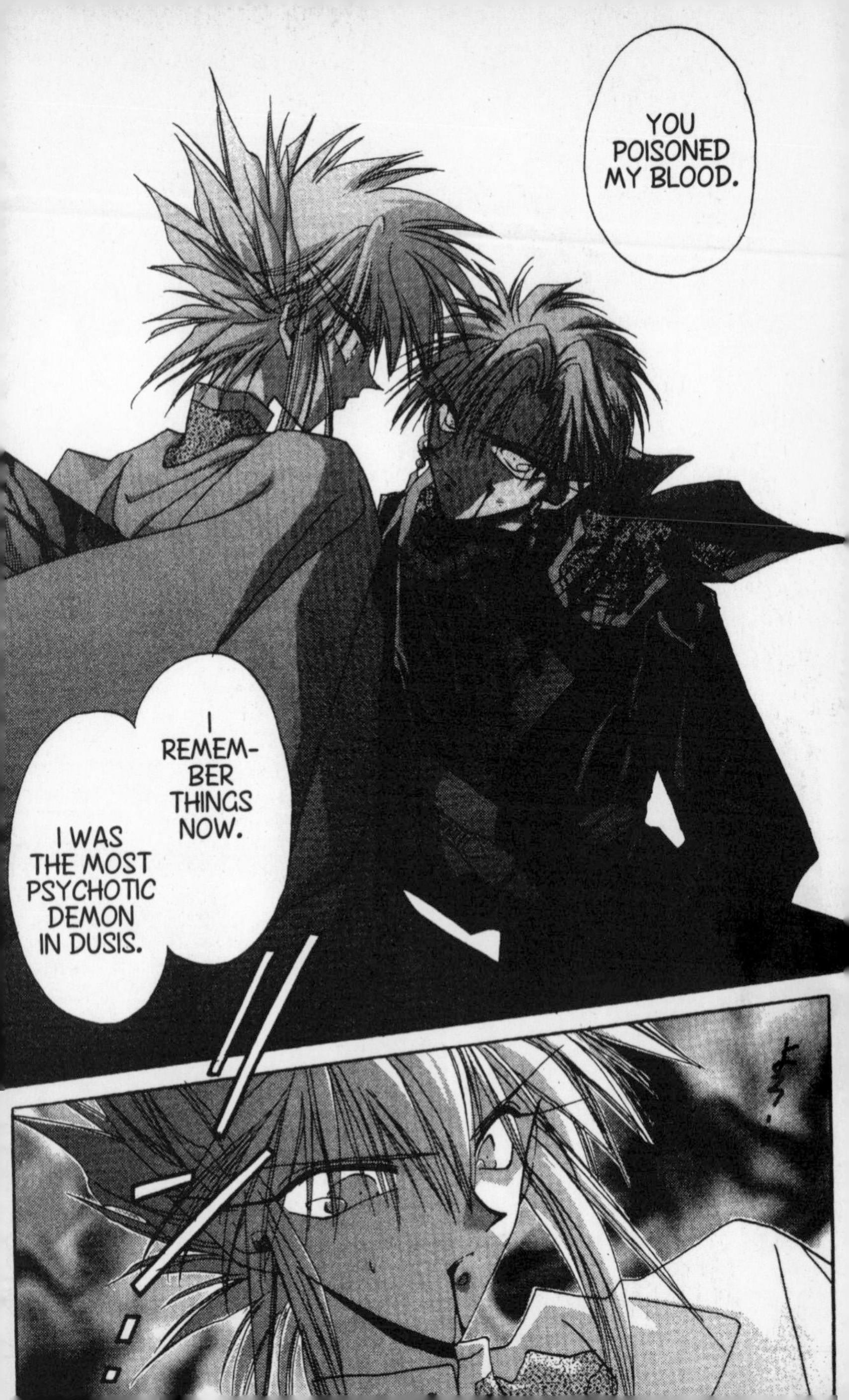
YOU POISONED MY BLOOD.
I REMEMBER THINGS NOW.
I WAS THE MOST PSYCHOTIC DEMON IN DUSIS.

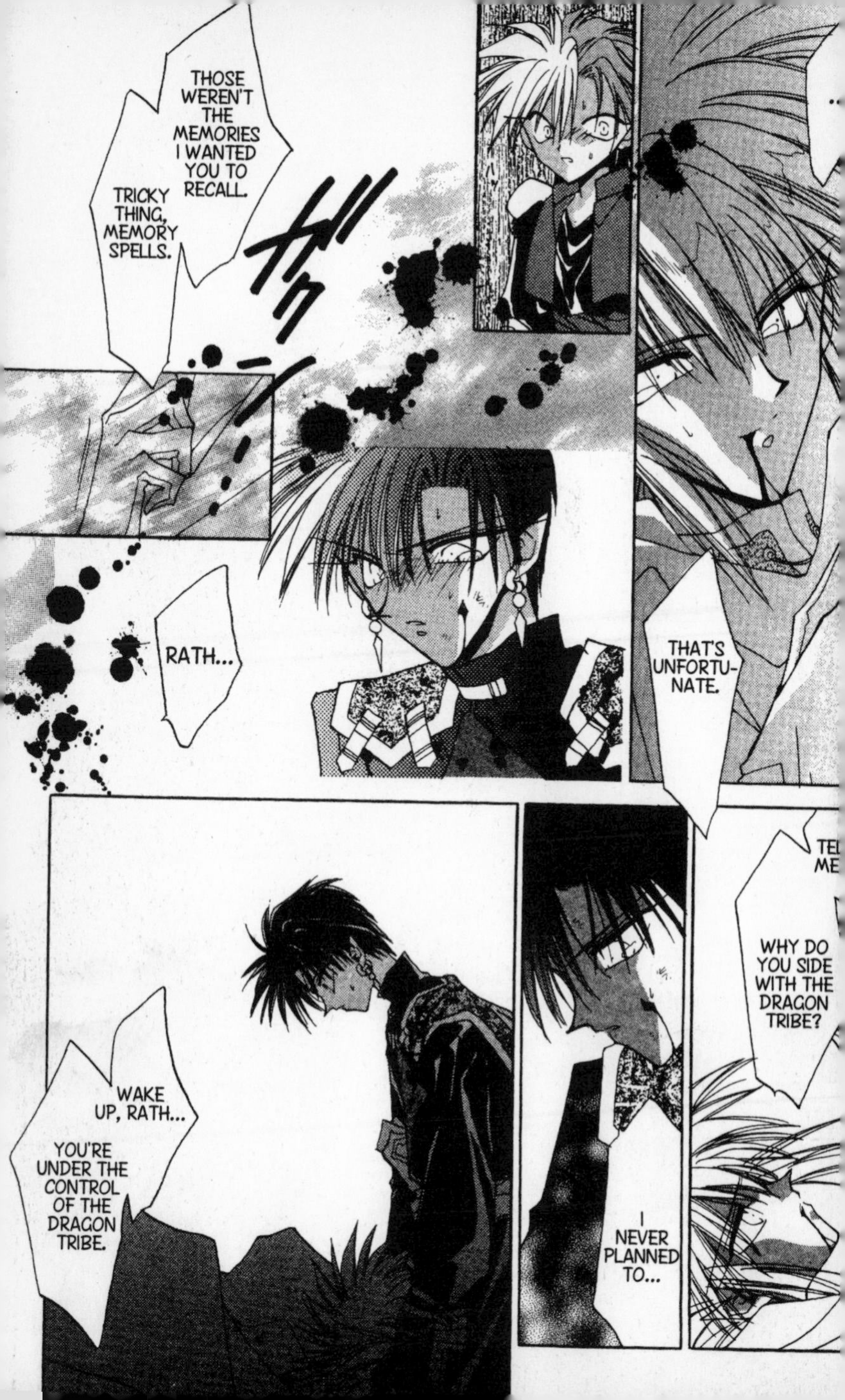
...
THAT'S UNFORTU-NATE.
THOSE WEREN'T THE MEMORIES I WANTED YOU TO RECALL.
TRICKY THING, MEMORY SPELLS.
RATH...
TEL ME
WHY DO YOU SIDE WITH THE DRAGON TRIBE?
I NEVER PLANNED TO...
WAKE UP, RATH...
YOU'RE UNDER THE CONTROL OF THE DRAGON TRIBE.

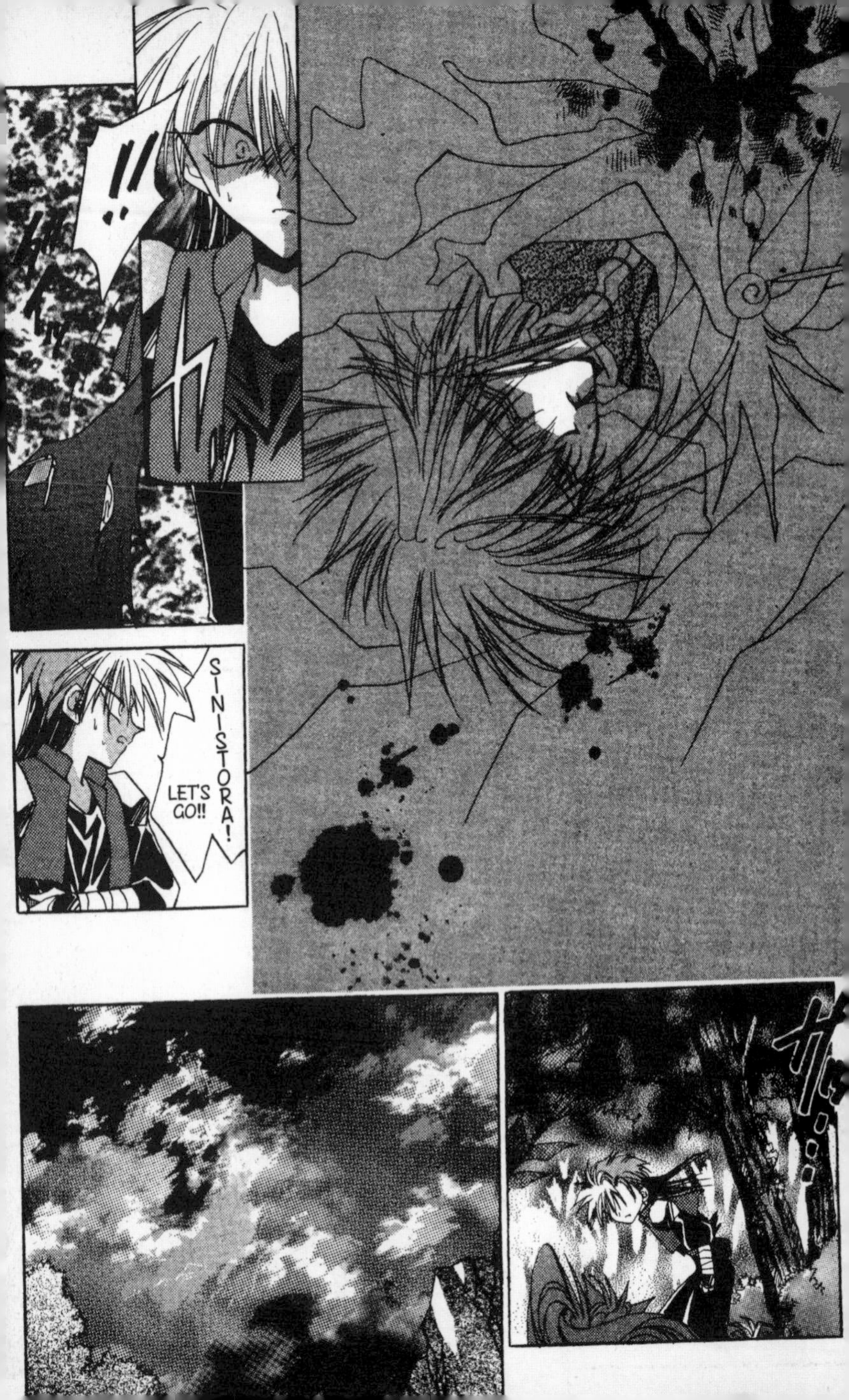
!!
SINISTORA!
LET'S GO!!

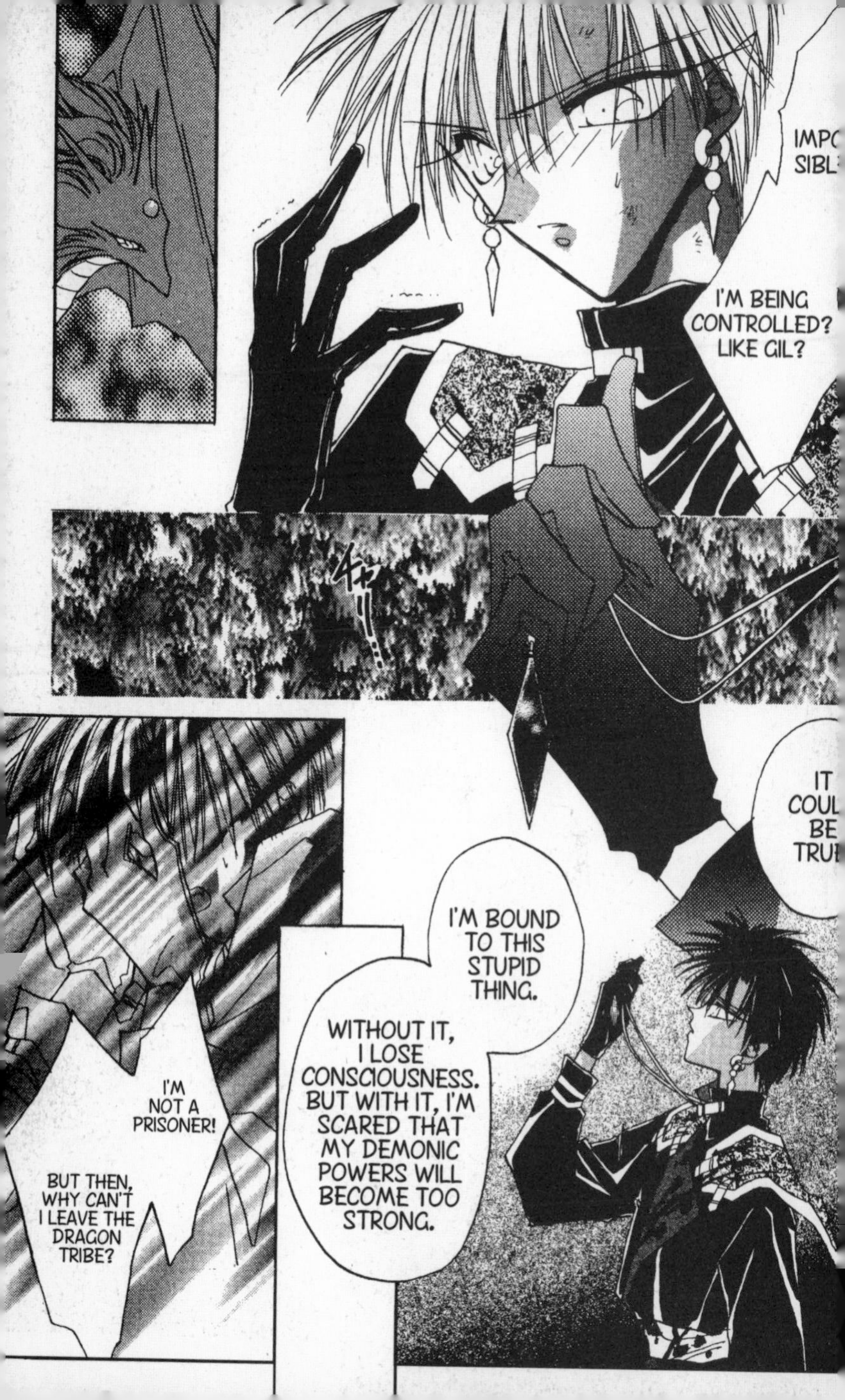
IMPO SIBL
I'M BEING CONTROLLED? LIKE GIL?
IT COUL BE TRU
I'M BOUND TO THIS STUPID THING.
WITHOUT IT, I LOSE CONSCIOUSNESS. BUT WITH IT, I'M SCARED THAT MY DEMONIC POWERS WILL BECOME TOO STRONG.
I'M NOT A PRISONER!
BUT THEN, WHY CAN'T I LEAVE THE DRAGON TRIBE?

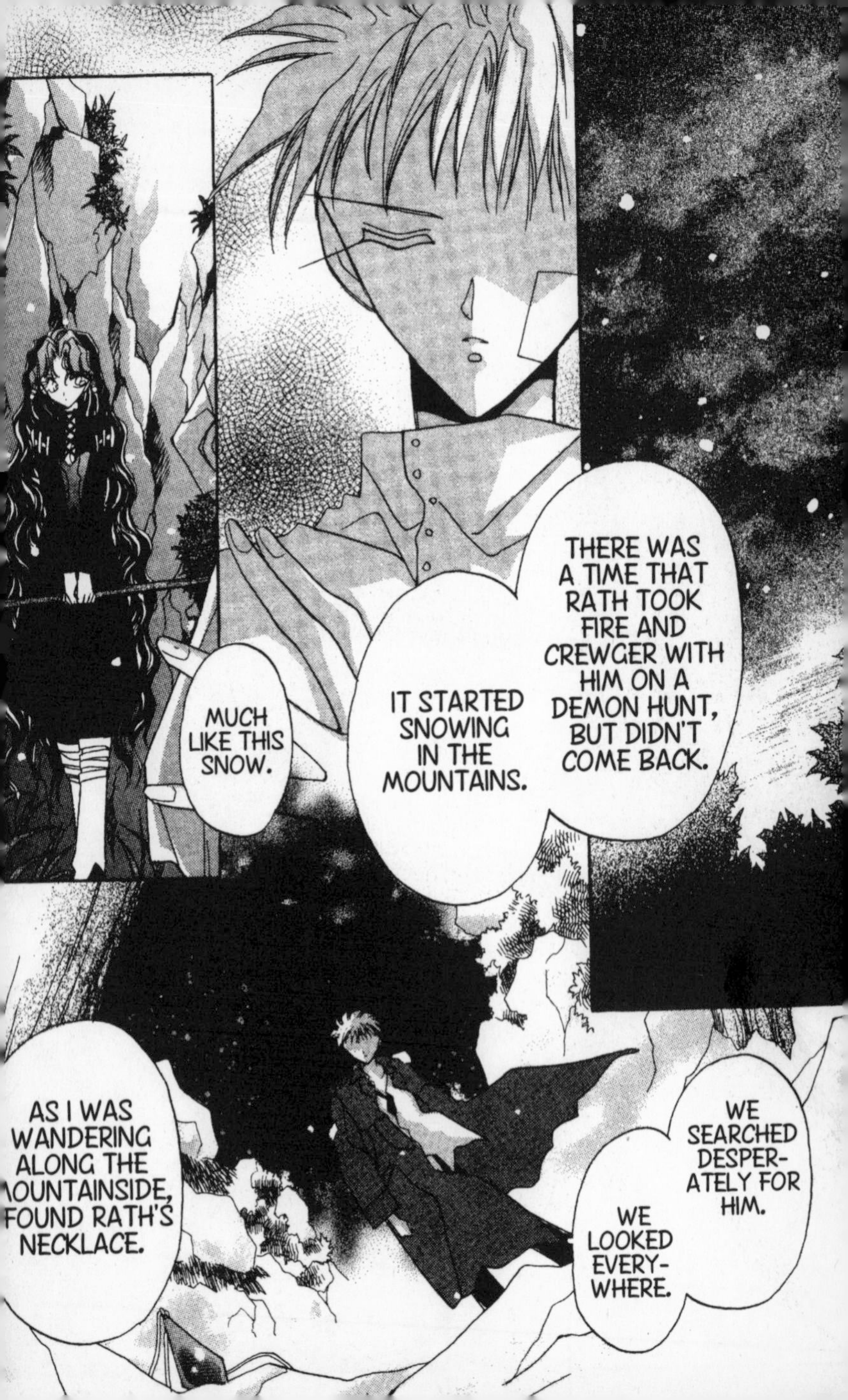
THERE WAS A TIME THAT RATH TOOK FIRE AND CREWGER WITH HIM ON A DEMON HUNT, BUT DIDN'T COME BACK.
IT STARTED SNOWING IN THE MOUNTAINS.
MUCH LIKE THIS SNOW.
WE SEARCHED DESPER- ATELY FOR HIM.
WE LOOKED EVERY- WHERE.
AS I WAS WANDERING ALONG THE OUNTAINSIDE, FOUND RATH'S NECKLACE.

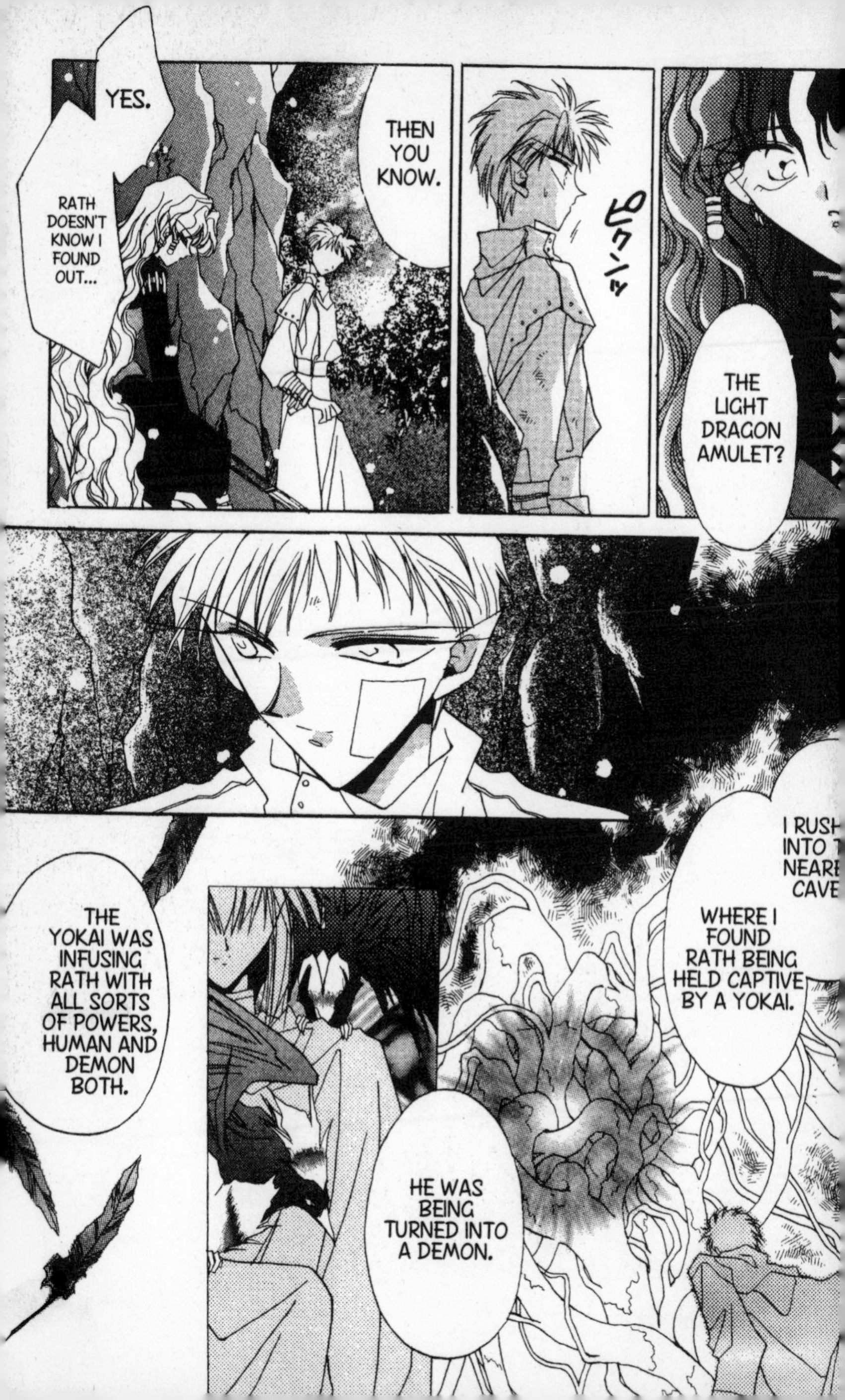
THE LIGHT DRAGON AMULET?
THEN YOU KNOW.
ピクンッ
YES.
RATH DOESN'T KNOW I FOUND OUT...
I RUSH INTO T NEARE CAVE
WHERE I FOUND RATH BEING HELD CAPTIVE BY A YOKAI.
HE WAS BEING TURNED INTO A DEMON.
THE YOKAI WAS INFUSING RATH WITH ALL SORTS OF POWERS, HUMAN AND DEMON BOTH.

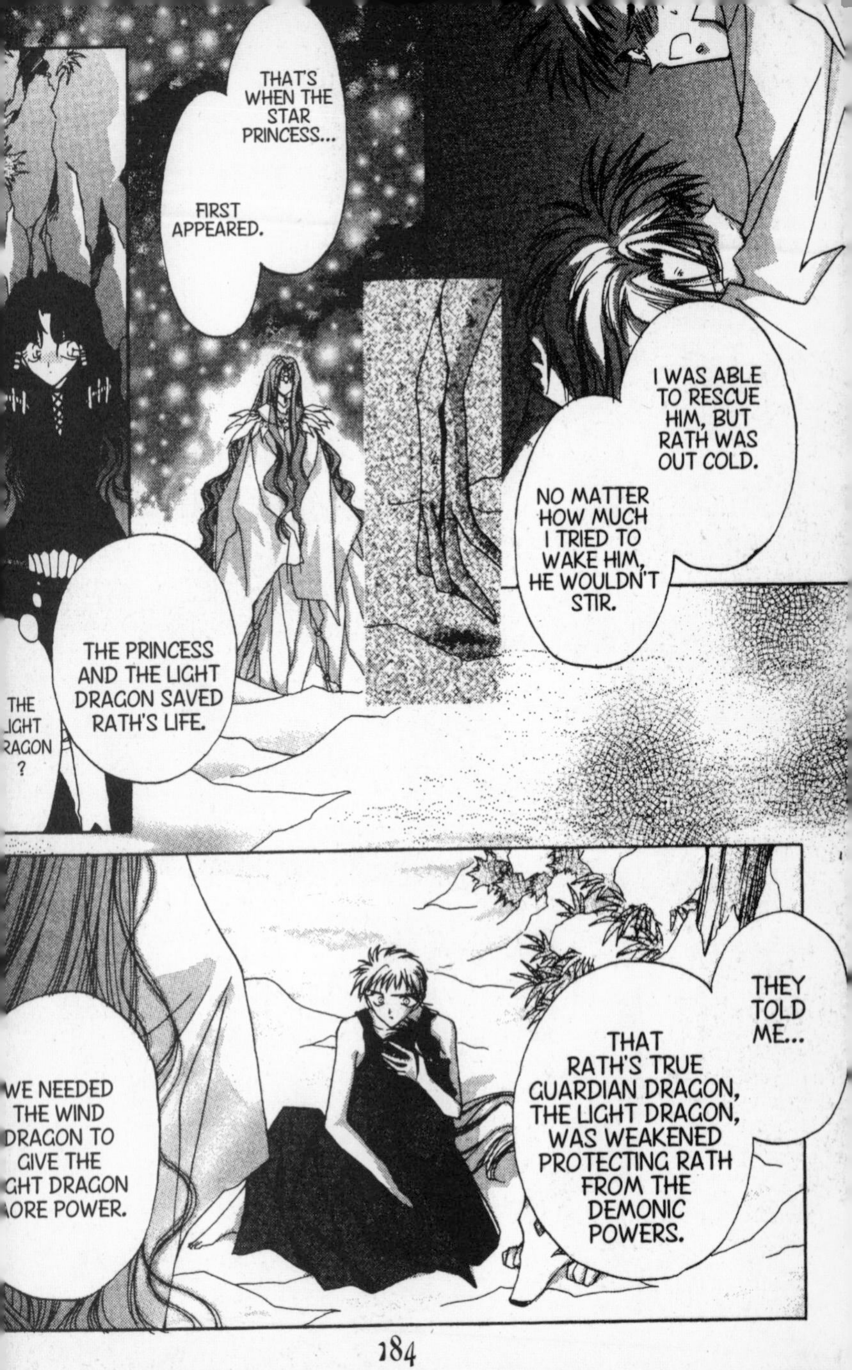

I WAS ABLE TO RESCUE HIM, BUT RATH WAS OUT COLD.
NO MATTER HOW MUCH I TRIED TO WAKE HIM, HE WOULDN'T STIR.
THAT'S WHEN THE STAR PRINCESS...
FIRST APPEARED.
THE PRINCESS AND THE LIGHT DRAGON SAVED RATH'S LIFE.
THE IGHT RAGON ?
THEY TOLD ME...
THAT RATH'S TRUE GUARDIAN DRAGON, THE LIGHT DRAGON, WAS WEAKENED PROTECTING RATH FROM THE DEMONIC POWERS.
WE NEEDED THE WIND DRAGON TO GIVE THE GHT DRAGON ORE POWER.

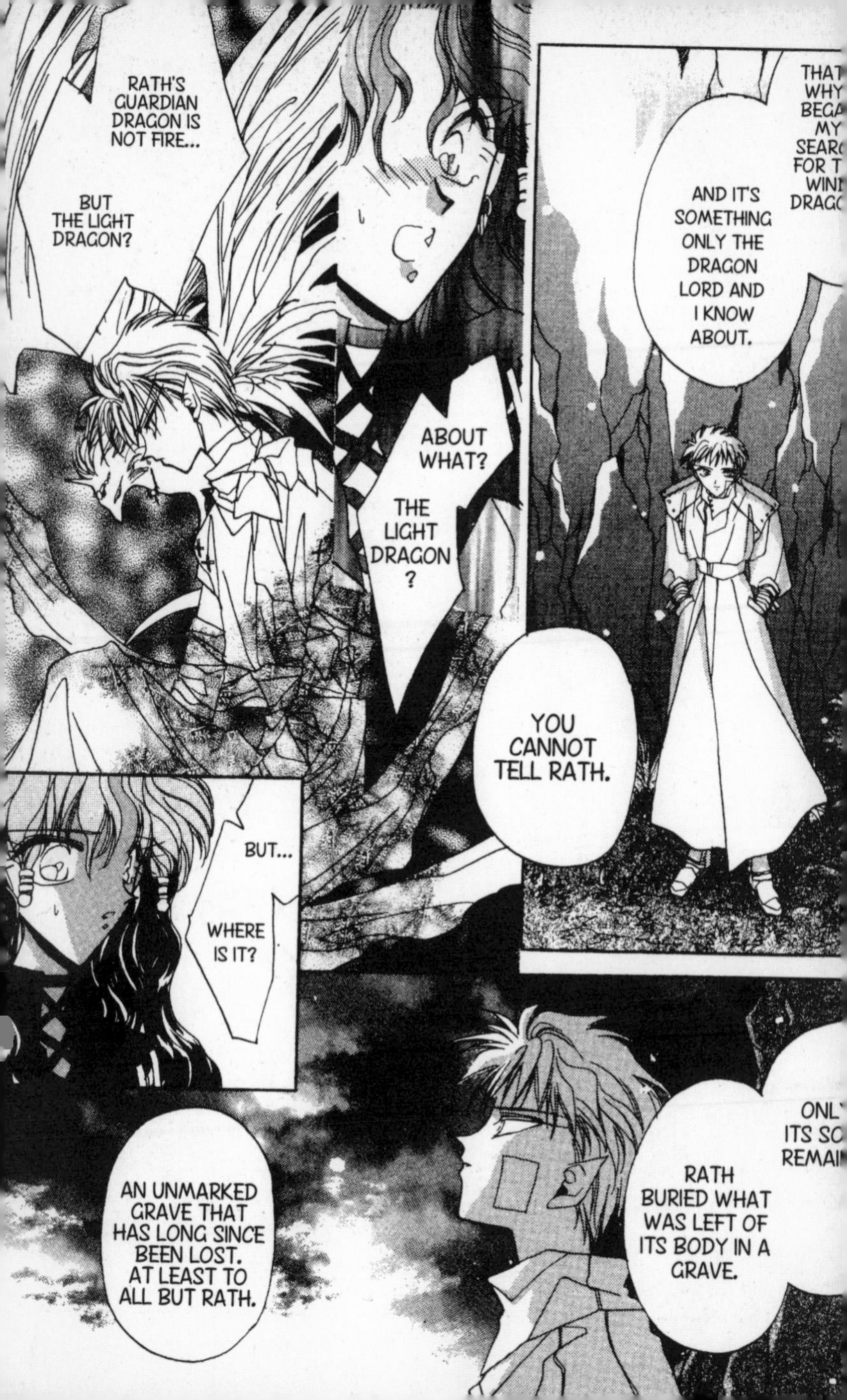
THAT WHY BEGA MY SEAR FOR T WIN DRAG
AND IT'S SOMETHING ONLY THE DRAGON LORD AND I KNOW ABOUT.
YOU CANNOT TELL RATH.
ABOUT WHAT?
THE LIGHT DRAGON ?
RATH'S GUARDIAN DRAGON IS NOT FIRE...
BUT THE LIGHT DRAGON?
BUT...
WHERE IS IT?
ONL ITS SO REMAI
RATH BURIED WHAT WAS LEFT OF ITS BODY IN A GRAVE.
AN UNMARKED GRAVE THAT HAS LONG SINCE BEEN LOST. AT LEAST TO ALL BUT RATH.

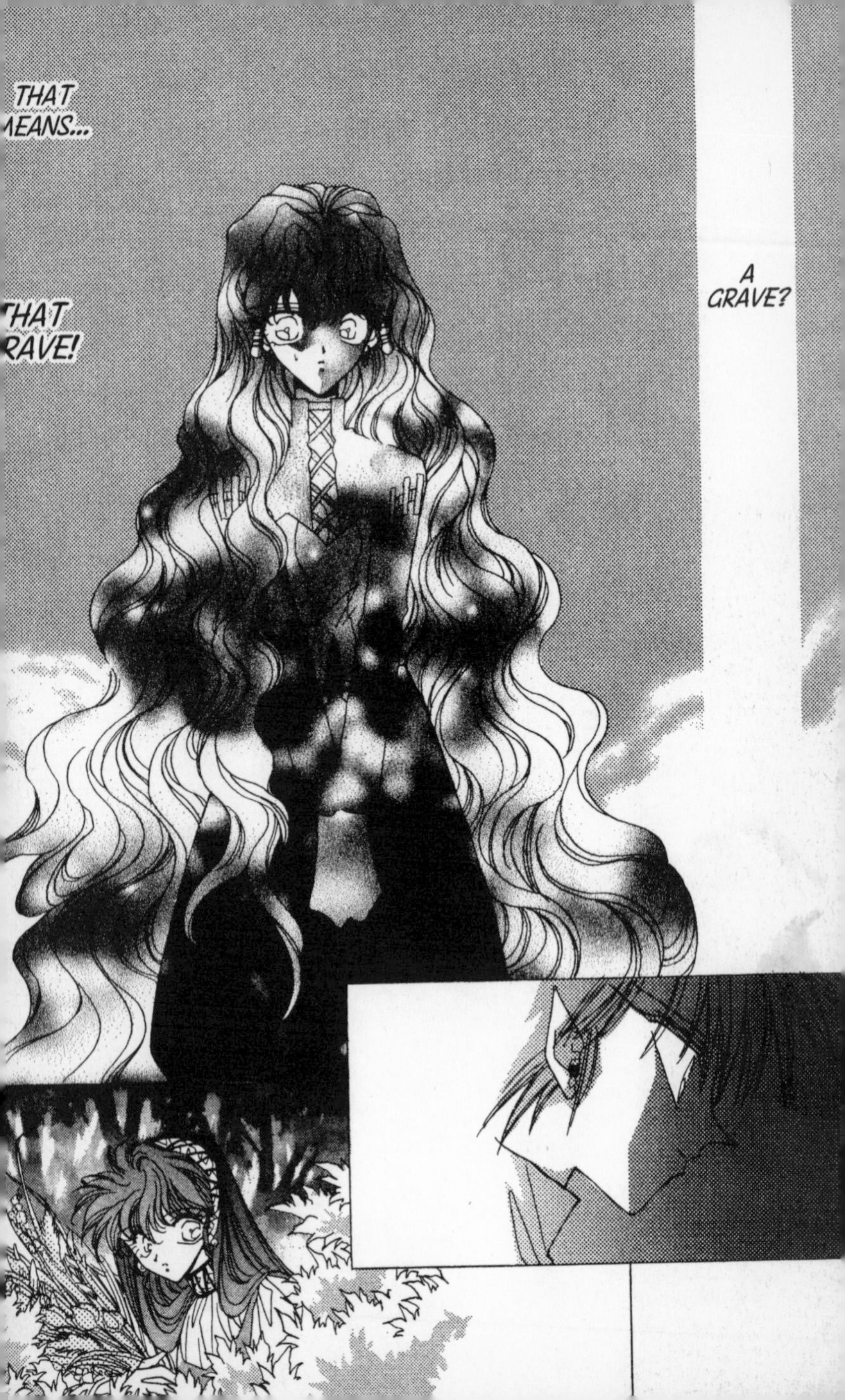
A GRAVE?
THAT
EANS...
THAT
RAVE!

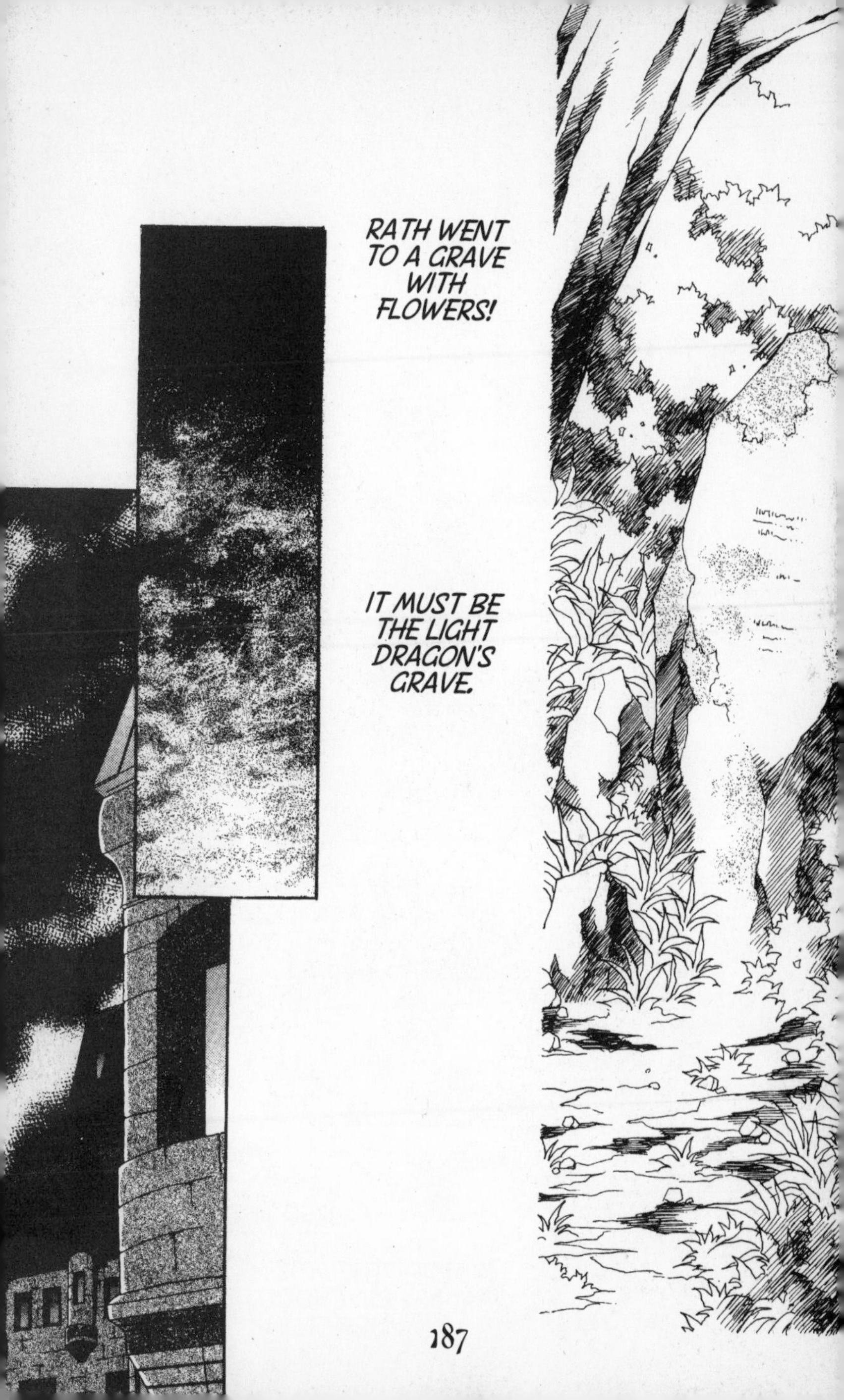
RATH WENT TO A GRAVE WITH FLOWERS!
IT MUST BE THE LIGHT DRAGON'S GRAVE.

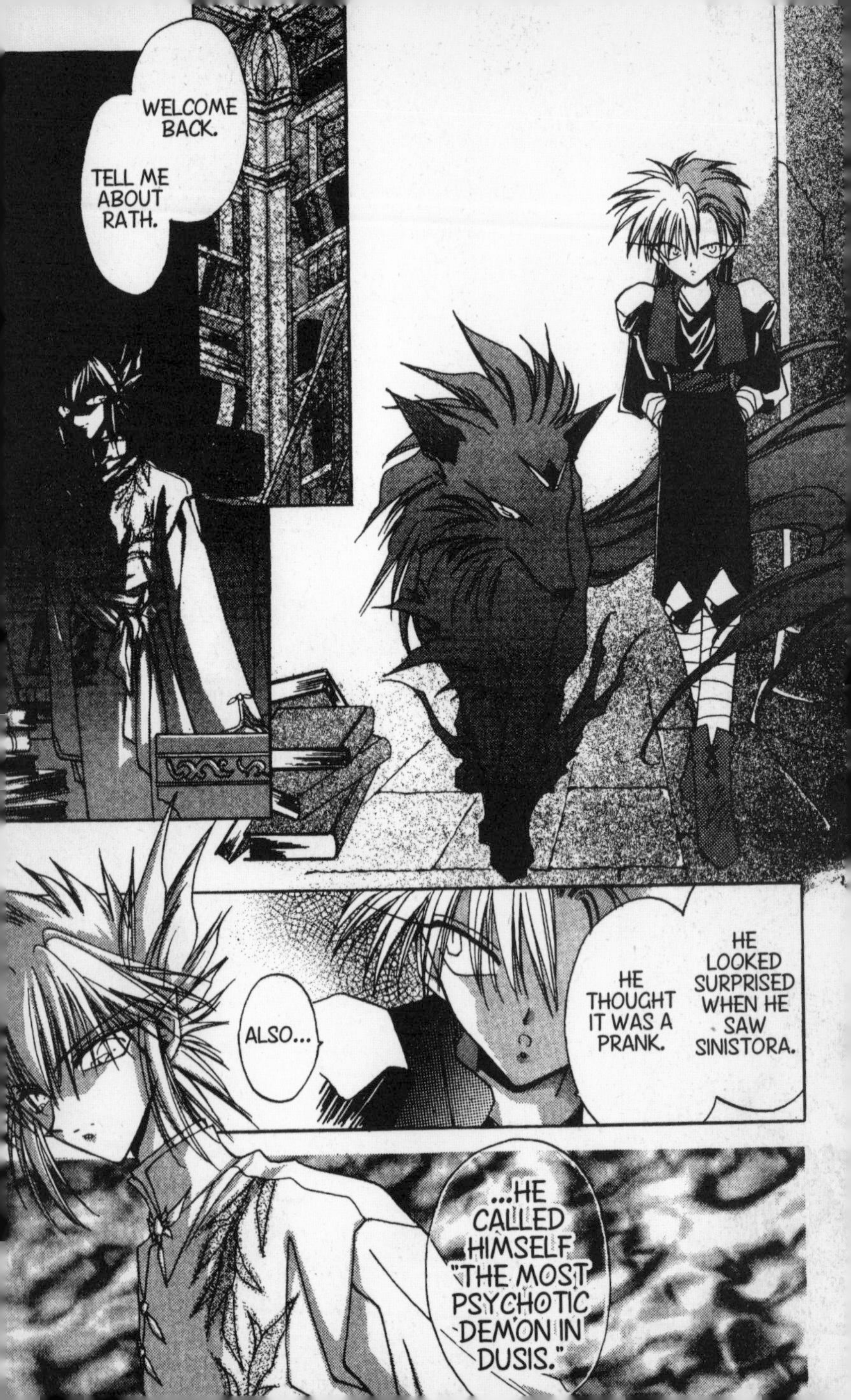
WELCOME BACK.
TELL ME ABOUT RATH.
HE LOOKED SURPRISED WHEN HE SAW SINISTORA.
HE THOUGHT IT WAS A PRANK.
ALSO...
...HE CALLED HIMSELF "THE MOST PSYCHOTIC DEMON IN DUSIS."

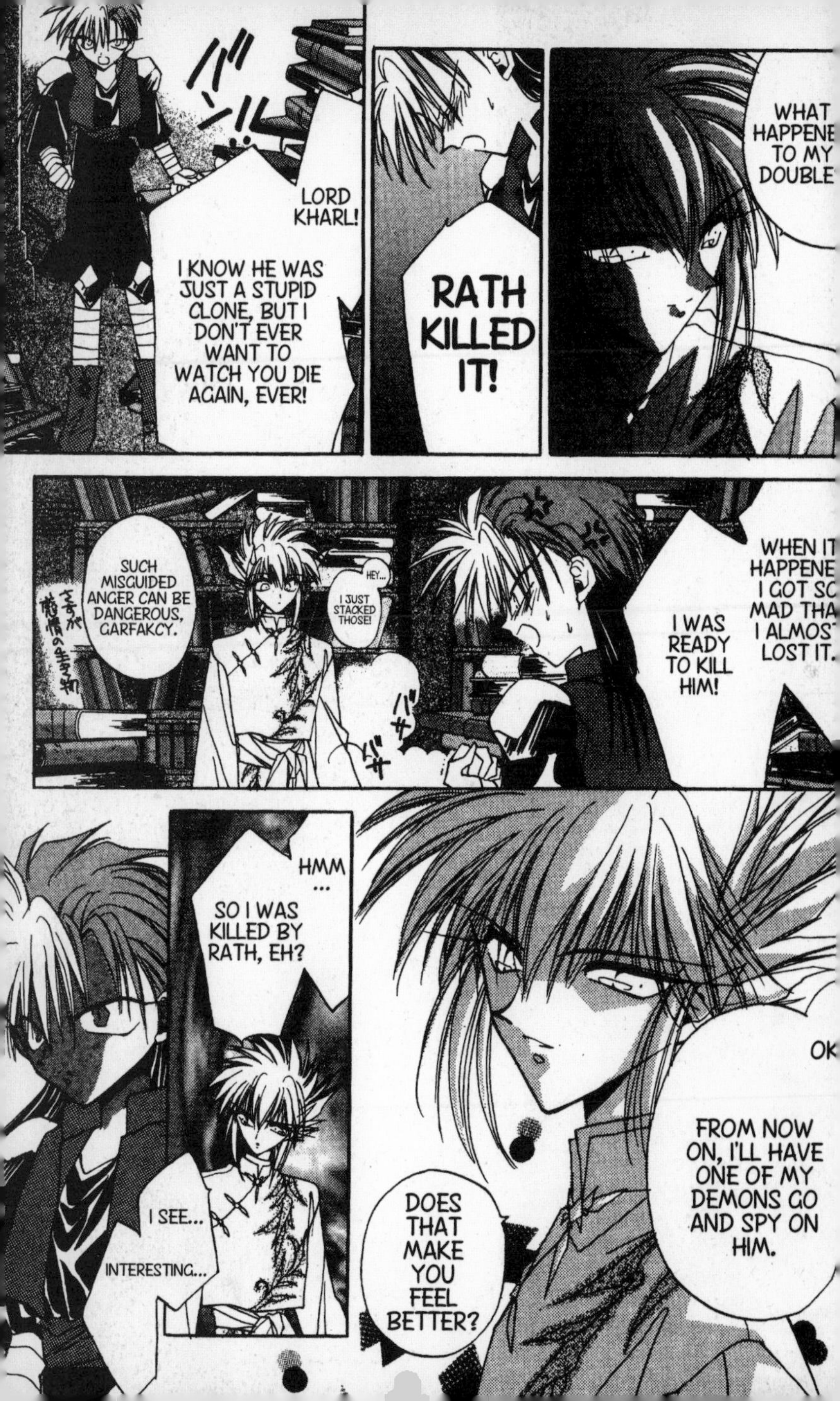
WHAT HAPPENE TO MY DOUBLE
RATH KILLED IT!
バン!!
LORD KHARL!
I KNOW HE WAS JUST A STUPID CLONE, BUT I DON'T EVER WANT TO WATCH YOU DIE AGAIN, EVER!
WHEN IT HAPPENE I GOT SC MAD THA I ALMOST LOST IT.
I WAS READY TO KILL HIM!
HEY... I JUST STACKED THOSE!
バサ バサ
SUCH MISGUIDED ANGER CAN BE DANGEROUS, GARFAKCY.
さすが感情の生き物
OK
FROM NOW ON, I'LL HAVE ONE OF MY DEMONS GO AND SPY ON HIM.
DOES THAT MAKE YOU FEEL BETTER?
HMM ...
SO I WAS KILLED BY RATH, EH?
I SEE...
INTERESTING...

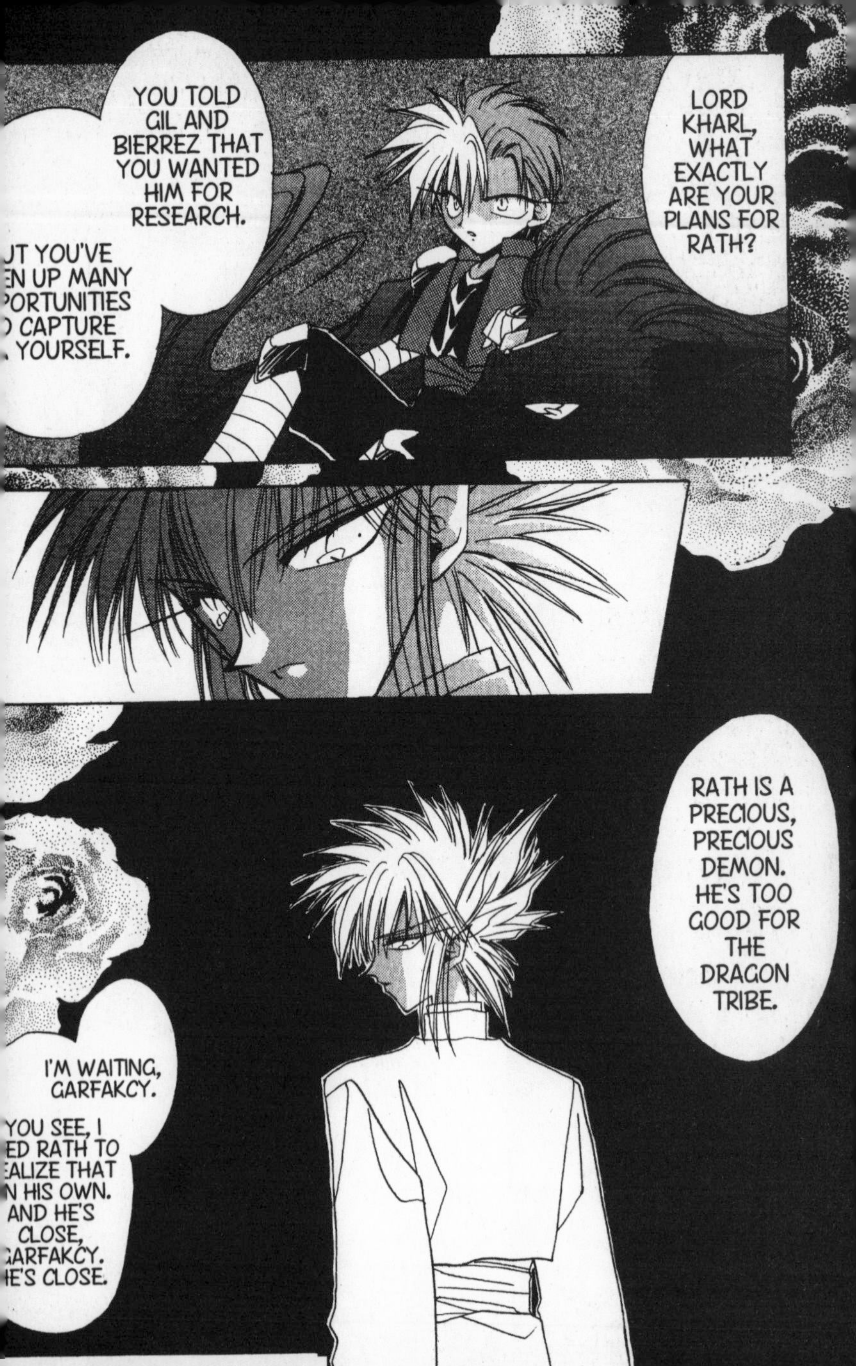
LORD KHARL, WHAT EXACTLY ARE YOUR PLANS FOR RATH?
YOU TOLD GIL AND BIERREZ THAT YOU WANTED HIM FOR RESEARCH.
UT YOU'VE EN UP MANY PORTUNITIES O CAPTURE YOURSELF.
RATH IS A PRECIOUS, PRECIOUS DEMON. HE'S TOO GOOD FOR THE DRAGON TRIBE.
I'M WAITING, GARFAKCY.
YOU SEE, I ED RATH TO EALIZE THAT N HIS OWN. AND HE'S CLOSE, ARFAKCY. HE'S CLOSE.

AGON KNIGHTS 9 THE END

Dragon Knights

10

In Volume 10:

With Gil's blood on his hands and Kharl's words still haunting his mind, Rath returns to the lodge in a foul mood. A mood that fails to improve when he discovers that Shydeman and Shyrendora have kidnapped Cesia. Vowing to find her, Rath's quest leads him to a confrontation with a demon he had hoped to never see again.

Unable to assist the Dragon Knight of Fire, Kai=stern returns to the Dragon Kingdom, hoping that Rath will find his way home. It's not the homecoming he expects. An alarming announce=ment regarding the Dragon Lord's health leads to a frantic search for the wandering Raseleane. But will they find her in time?

Plus, the battle lines have been drawn, now take a look at both sides of the conflict, with two exciting side stories!

Mineko Ohkami

ONE VAMPIRE'S SEARCH FOR
Revenge and Redemption...

REBIRTH

By: Woo

Joined by
an excommunicated
exorcist and a
spiritual investigator,
Deshwitat begins
his bloodquest.
The hunted is
now the hunter.

GET REBIRTH
IN YOUR FAVORITE BOOK & COMIC STORES NOW!

T
TEEN
AGE 13+

www.TOKYOPOP.com

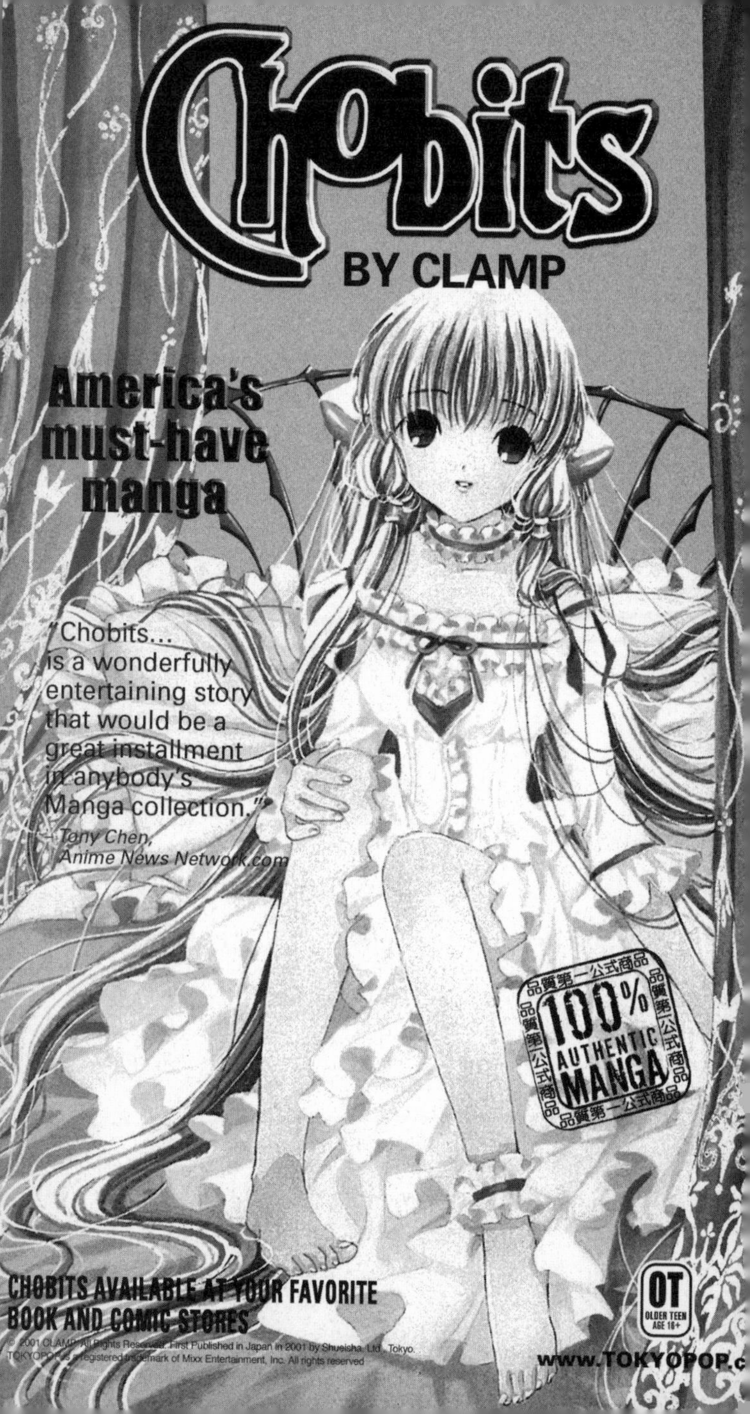
Chobits
BY CLAMP
America's must-have manga
"Chobits... is a wonderfully entertaining story that would be a great installment in anybody's Manga collection."
–Tony Chen, Anime News Network.com
品質第一公式商品 100% AUTHENTIC MANGA
CHOBITS AVAILABLE AT YOUR FAVORITE BOOK AND COMIC STORES
© 2001 CLAMP. All Rights Reserved. First Published in Japan in 2001 by Shueisha, Ltd., Tokyo.
TOKYOPOP is a registered trademark of Mixx Entertainment, Inc. All rights reserved
OT
OLDER TEEN AGE 16+
www.TOKYOPOP.c

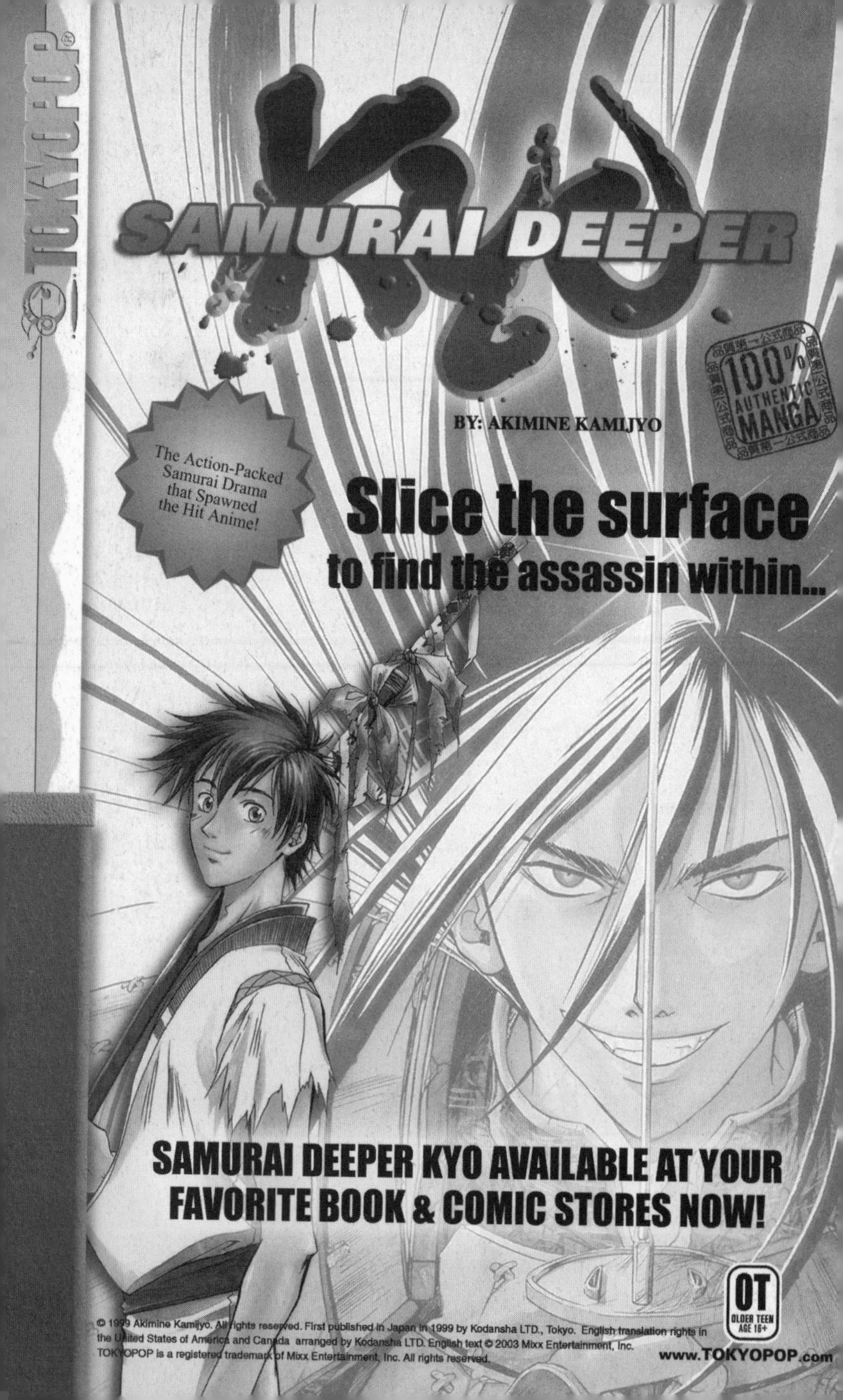

TOKYOPOP
KYO
SAMURAI DEEPER
100% AUTHENTIC MANGA
BY: AKIMINE KAMIJYO
The Action-Packed Samurai Drama that Spawned the Hit Anime!
Slice the surface
to find the assassin within...
SAMURAI DEEPER KYO AVAILABLE AT YOUR FAVORITE BOOK & COMIC STORES NOW!
OT OLDER TEEN AGE 16+
© 1999 Akimine Kamijyo. All rights reserved. First published in Japan in 1999 by Kodansha LTD., Tokyo. English translation rights in the United States of America and Canada arranged by Kodansha LTD. English text © 2003 Mixx Entertainment, Inc. TOKYOPOP is a registered trademark of Mixx Entertainment, Inc. All rights reserved.
www.TOKYOPOP.com

STOP!

This is the back of the book.
You wouldn't want to spoil a great ending!

This book is printed "manga-style," in the authentic Japanese right-to-left format. Since none of the artwork has been flipped or altered, readers get to experience the story just as the creator intended. You've been asking for it, so TOKYOPOP® delivered: authentic, hot-off-the-press, and far more fun!

DIRECTIONS

If this is your first time reading manga-style, here's a quick guide to help you understand how it works.

It's easy… just start in the top right panel and follow the numbers. Have fun, and look for more 100% authentic manga from TOKYOPOP®!

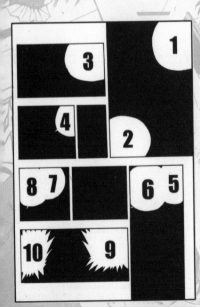